To End the War on Drugs

TO END THE WAR ON DRUGS

A Guide for Politicians, the Press and Public

DEAN BECKER

DTN MEDIA
DrugTruth.Net

ISBN-10:0615969917
ISBN-13:978-0615969916 (DTN Media)

Cover design by Massoud
Interior design by William Dolphin
Published by DTN Media, Houston, Texas
www.DrugTruth.net

TABLE OF CONTENTS

PREFACE

At press time, I am 65 years old. An old hippie at heart, I did thrive in the corporate world when I wanted to. I live a quiet life with my partner, Pam, and our three cats. I have four strong sons, twelve wonderful grand children, and immense hope for their futures.

Reporting the drug war news has enabled me to travel the world. In South America, I chewed coca leaves with a Justice Minister and a prison warden,. On a trip to Mexico, I saw the streets filled with guns and fear. I visited Canada to tour heroin injection clinics and cannabis dispensaries. I have traveled to dozens of cities in the US to report on Senate hearings, medical seminars, and numerous conferences.

I did not have to travel far to meet John Walters when he was our nation's Drug Czar. Walters gave a speech at a Houston Jr. High about gangs and drugs. When it was over, Walters was sitting by himself, packing his briefcase. I had been in touch with his office for weeks trying to arrange an interview. As I approached, him, I smiled, I held out my business card and offered to shake his hand. He looked at me, somewhat like a cow does when looking at a combine. Again I offered my card, and he waved his hand over his head and quickly finished packing. As he stood, four security goons surrounded him as he walked towards the exit. I kept pace with his entourage, offering my card, until Walters mumbled something, and one of the goons stepped in front of me, put his hand in his coat, and said "he doesn't want to talk to you."

This book tells you why.

INCREMENTALISM IS A KILLER

"I think the word 'gradualism' is so often an excuse for escapism and do-nothingism which ends up in stand-stillism."
—Reverend Dr. Martin Luther King Jr

We have been duped! It starts with a small lie that many citizens think does some good for a few. It escalates by bending the Constitution to protect that vulnerable few. It increases when the populace becomes jaded to the mechanism of lies, handing the future of liberty to those who proclaim higher priorities must be given sway over principles. It continues to increase, to grow ponderous, overbearing and inquisitorial. It is what binds us to our terrorist enemies and propels our domestic dilemma of gangs, violence, bigotry, financial overload and societal fragmentation.

It is the drug war.

It's been more than 40 years since President Nixon declared the U.S. War on Drugs in 1971 to "go after the blacks without appearing to do so." It's now more than 50 years since the United Nations declared they would eliminate drugs from planet Earth within five years. Truthfully though, the war on drugs is more than 100 years old. The US began its war on a select few plant products and people in 1909 with the passage of the "Opium Exclusion Act." The opium that whites imbibed as the elixir Laudenum remained legal for another decade, but the Chinese opium smokers went to prison. In 1914, cocaine was made a federal offense when politicians proclaimed that black men high on cocaine would rape white women or, at a minimum, would fail to step off the sidewalk when a white man approached. Then in 1937, because Mexicans were taking our jobs and they just might rape white women while high on marijuana, the feds crafted the Marihuana Tax Act, later declared unconstitutional and replaced by the Controlled Substances regimen in 1970.

So who's going to jail for drugs? It comes as no surprise that the overwhelming majority of those arrested are black, then Latinos, then whites; and it is nearly always the poor. This, despite the fact that rich white people use drugs at least as much as blacks or Hispanics. Over the lifetime of the drug war, more than 45 million non-violent American citizens have been arrested for plant products in their pocket or their home. The US has "invested" well over a trillion of our taxpayer dollars in trying to stop the flow of drugs. At the same time, drug users worldwide have purchased in excess of ten trillion dollars worth of these "controlled" plant products from the only people the government deems apropos: criminals, gangs and terrorists... who rake in $385 billion per year.

By what rationale do we continue to leave the production and sale of drugs in the hands of criminals, gangs, and barbarians? Before the prohibition of these drugs, a gram of pure cocaine could be purchased at the drug store for 25 cents. Today a diluted, in fact, a polluted gram of cocaine can sell for more than $100. Prior to the drug war, a month's supply of heroin could be purchased from Sears Roebuck for a dollar; as a bonus they threw in a syringe.

After 40 years, 50 years, more than 100 years of drug war, it's time to face facts. When I spoke with former President of Mexico Vicente Fox, a man who knows drug war, I asked what positive things have come from the drug war. His response: "Nothing." He provided a succinct summary: "Prohibition doesn't work."

The drug war was the pipe dream of men who have long since died. It has become a quasi-religion, a belief system that has attracted many adherents within law enforcement and the justice system, to speak from ignorance or bigotry. Those who make their bones from this policy, (and yes the cemetery is overflowing) cannot now back down from their prior pronouncements, they dare not jeopardize their reputation, their legacy, by now embracing the truth that drug war is a horrendous mistake.

December 17th, 2014 marks 100 years since the passage of the Harrison Narcotics Act, the beginning of national anti-drug laws. Since that time, more than 45 million US citizens have been arrested and their life's potential tainted if not destroyed by the policy of drug prohibition.

In the early 20th century, corporate heads foresaw gleaming profits in prohibiting the use of certain plants. These men of influence and wealth had the influence to force through laws based on nothing more than rumors circulated through newspapers controlled by these same interests. They claimed that Chinamen on opium were a threat to a decent society, that Mexicans would rape white women after smoking marijuana, that blacks were impenetrable to bullets after using cocaine. The American people were fooled into believing they were saved and that the control and distribution of these herbs and their extracts should be prohibited. This "prohibited" drug commerce, according to the UN, now exceeds four hundred billion dollars per year .

Superstition and ignorance were the original means of creating this drug war.

This drug war began, and continues to this day as an unconstitutional affront to our dignity and our rights as free people. Offered the false hope that professional opinions and supervision over what we should put into our bodies would bring us health and prosperity, the American people succumbed to the pressure to accept the dictates/mandates of the Harrison Act, forgoing our God-given and basic American rights in hopes of a better tomorrow as promised by the greedy pharmaceutical houses, the pontificating politicians, and hard-hearted law enforcement.

Drugs are much more available, purer and cheaper than when President Nixon declared the current version of the drug war. Have we managed to cut down on the violence of the drug war by arresting record numbers of non-violent drug users? Even though we arrested more than 1.5 million non-violent US citizens last year for drugs, the number of users remains just as high, and the violence associated with control of neighborhoods by street gangs continues to escalate.

In 1914, we lost our liberty to choose our own medicines in exchange for supposed security regarding drugs. Today, we are being forced to give up additional, even unknown, liberties in exchange for supposed protection. Our slide into this abyss is facilitated by the fear engendered by 100 years of propaganda that allows the drug war to flourish despite decades of miserable failure.

For nearly 500 years, colonialist powers like England, Spain and later the United States, made it their business to impose their will on lesser countries, to force new religions and morals on all the "heathen cultures" of this earth. In the process, they vilified and demonized the use of such drugs as marijuana, coca and opium which previously had been recognized for their medicinal properties and as sacraments of many religions, many cultures for thousands of years.

Before drug prohibition, drug overdose deaths were practically unheard of. Before the drug war donned the mask of savior, drug use among children was almost non existent. Before we decided to launch an eternal war on "recreational drugs", approximately 1½ % of Americans used heroin or cocaine. Today, after the expenditure of more than one trillion dollars, the wasting of tens of millions of lives destroyed by demonization via our supposed criminal justice system and the moralistic destruction of life's potential... 1½ % of Americans use "hard drugs".

Today, cannabis has been used by more than 100 million Americans as medicine or sacrament or recreation, because it is an obvious fact that cannabis is a much safer intoxicant than other drugs, especially safer than what I consider to be the most dangerous drug of them all, alcohol.

It is time to be brave, lest the chance to restore respect for truth be lost forever to ignorance and greed.

Misunderstanding this eternal war on drugs is not our fault. We have been force fed 100 years of clap trap, balderdash, poppycock and absolute horseshit presented as science, commonsense and reality. Given the current situation, I reluctantly support the incremental drug law changes being promoted, because so few have the courage to say what needs to be said: The drug laws are a scam, a festering collection of lies, innuendo, and fear.

Sometimes people believe what they are forced to believe, for a paycheck, to align with family "moral" standards, because of religious dictates, or simply to be accepted in one fashion or another. Millions more people must embrace what they know to be true.

In the early days of the all-out drug war, users were considered to be subversives, even communists aligned with the Viet Cong, radicals needing a multi-years-long lesson in one of America's many gulags. Over the years, the label has changed, from radical to drug reformer and now to legalizers.

In a couple more years, as this drug war takes its dying breath, I am going to retire, smoke a few bowls, and let "We the People," now fully informed, bring about a proper end to this century of lies.

This book is not just an indictment of cops and prosecutors but also an indictment of the media, religious leaders, scientists, and medical doctors who have chosen to "first do harm" to those they supposedly are to protect. Sadly, also in focus in this regard are many drug reformers who feel compelled to ask for less than they know to be necessary from the ignorant and complicit forces that run the drug war.

What started me on the path to drug reform was a singular website that enlightened me to the fact that like most inhabitants of Planet Earth, I had been duped. The site in question is DrugLibrary.Org, manned by Mr. Cliff Shaffer who I am now proud to call my friend. I was lucky to have a job with a major oil company that in 1997 had a T1 connection, the best internet hookup there was at the time, and printers that could really fly after everybody else went home. Because I am a math whiz and one hell of an auditor, I had lots of time to surf the web, and when I came across Drug Library, I had found my true calling: to end the drug war. Cliff's site has the history, the Congressional records, all the dirty deeds, lies, bigotry, and hatred that crafted this first eternal war.

This work I do does not pay enough to cover my expenses. My costs include travel, production, equipment, supplies, computers, cameras, etc. I want to record for posterity, in every possible way that I can, my understanding and commitment to ending the madness of this eternal war on our fellow man for the use of plant products. These transcripts will someday prove beneficial to future generations, so they will dare not walk down this same path of hopelessness, violence, addiction, criminality, disease, and death.

This book is written for every inhabitant of Planet Earth but most importantly for the President of the United States, all elected officials, and every prosecutor and law enforcement official. The drug war is ending, slow and bloody; we all recognize that fact. The solution now is for politicians to get on the right side of this issue.

President Obama can, with the stroke of his pen, end the federal prosecutions for possession of cannabis or any other prohibited substance. Simply remove cannabis from schedule I of the Controlled Substances Act. We will immediately find that not only was the Schedule I designation for cannabis arbitrary and capricious, we will soon discover that the same can be said for nearly all supposedly

"Controlled Substances."

Legalization is on the horizon. Slowly, after much loss of life, health, and freedom, the drug war is coming to an end. This does not mean the fight is over, it simply means it's okay to come out of your hidey hole and proclaim what you know to be true. What will you tell your kids and grand kids you did about this 100-year fiasco? Remaining silent now will ensure that you will not be remembered as intelligent or courageous. Speak up! The time is now to contact all your elected officials, who have been even more scared than you to speak of what is so obvious and glaring. Be sure to tell your broadcast station managers, newspaper editors, pastors, police chiefs, and school adminintrators that the time of America's war on We the People must be brought to an end forthwith. You now have in this book more than 300 pages of expert opinions to quote, from widely variant fields, when you write, call and visit any and all of your "powers that be." Although the citizens were indeed duped by the press, politicians, doctors and ministers, we will of necessity have to forgive them, if they readjust and redeploy their efforts towards justice and reality.

Decriminalization is somewhat better than all out prohibition of sales, possession, and use. Decrim can mean different things to different people. It varies from telling the cops to make it the lowest law enforcement priority making few if any arrests. Another decrim scenario is to write a ticket, no arrest, pay the fine. There are other variations on decrim, but of those presented thus far, I do not see them as a stepping stone to legalization. I see decrim as a means for prosecutors and law enforcement to continue blustering from their bully pulpit, corrupting the courts and contaminating the community with their knowing lies and terroristic machinations.

Alcohol prohibition of the 1920's and '30's was in fact decrim. You could possess at home and drink to your heart's content and public drunkenness, then as now, was accepted as long as you did not make an ass of yourself. From my perspective, the best we could hope for from decriminalizing drugs is that the violence level in 2014 Chicago might diminish to the level present in Chicago in the 1920's. Have we not evolved? Did we learn nothing from our prior fiasco in controlling the will of our fellow man?

One of the saddest, most amazing facts buried in this drug war is that conscious, intelligent, educated, working, paycheck-earning, government and corporate scientists, and millions of educated and respected doctors, know the full truth of this matter and yet keep their mouths shut. The drug war is a type of mass hysteria that has led us to a decade- long wave of mass psychosis that benefits millions of profiteers and allays the fear and social bigotry of the masses. Until the attack on Pearl Harbor in 1941, America remained a fairly isolationist nation. Following WWII, the US has developed an extreme case of violent PTSD. With our troops, ships, and planes stationed across the globe, US citizens tend to think we are saviors who need lots of weapons to protect the world. This idea of thwarting threats worldwide has led us to several wars where no gain was or ever will be possible, simply to allow the weapons makers to earn enough profit to be able to fund the re-election of the politicians who made the war possible. This circle of political life for the drug war has been cloned and extrapolated for our eternal war of terror.

There is a time and place for incrementalism. Once negotiation has started, compromise may be necessary to create a new paradigm less onerous, less destructive to individuals and to society as a whole. However, in the overall scheme of things, clinging to any aspect of prohibition will ensure more confusion, ignorance, and death.

As of this date in early 2014, the President, his Attorney General, US Congressmen and Senators, governors, prosecutors, priests, and even prison guard unions are starting to call for incremental changes to our drug laws, many using words they have borrowed from the drug reform community. Democrat or Republican, they have all benefited from the drug war. Sadly the hard core drug war addicts who originally stood for ever-lasting, ever-escalating drug war cannot now back down from their stance taken, can never say they were wrong to destroy the lives of millions of Americans by virtue of these drug laws, so they will continue to do everything possible to prevent the opening of the mass graves of drug war inquisition.

After gathering info from Drug Library, MapInc, Drug Policy Alliance and other reform organizations, I began looking for like minded individual's in Houston, Texas and elsewhere with whom to organize for change. In late 2000, in Texas, the pickings were less than slim but I did find the Drug Policy Forum of Texas and their founder Dr. G. Alan Robison. Dr. Al, now retired, was a Professor of Pharmacology at the University of Texas Health Science Center and welcomed my overly enthusiastic embrace of drug reform. I was immediately named as Community Liaison for DPFT and told that there was a Houston Chapter of the National Organization for the Reform of Marijuana Laws.

Not too soon after approaching Houston NORML, I was elected president and set out to educate and motivate pot smokers to work for their own benefit. Using funds from DPFT and working for NORML, I produced music events and speaking engagements to attract and inform Texas voters and motivate them to help end the drug war.

At this same time, I found the Drug Policy Forum on the New York Times website. When I found this site it consisted of rants of other drug reform-oriented individuals along with links to the few drug related stories available on the web. I soon made arrangements with administrators at the New York Times to become liaison for their Drug Policy Forum. With this credential I was able to arrange visits to the forum by Milton Friedman, the Nobel Prize winning economist, along with Doctor Al Robison and dozens of other experts, including police chiefs, cannabis dispensary owners, authors, doctors, and many other notable individuals. In the summer of 2002, I published a booklet: "Drug Truth, Abrahamson to Zeese" which summarized the contents and direction of the NYT Drug Policy Forum.

In late September of 2001, just after the Twin Towers were toppled, the Pacifica Network had a minor revolution and the listeners took back their stations from the corporate toadies. I pitched my idea of a radio show that dealt with nothing but the drug war, a single beat to patrol. The newly elected management thought it might be worthwhile, they would consider the idea. Listening in to our conversation was Ray Hill, KPFT's patriarch, leader of marches on DC for gay rights and anti war demonstrations. Ray also produced and hosted "The Prison Show" which has been on the air for more than two decades reaching out to the hundred thousand plus prisoners locked in Texas penitentiaries.

Ray said maybe it would appeal to his audience, gave me a 3 to 5 minute "Drug War NEWS" right in the middle of his show. Quite an honor considering the usual was wives talking to husbands locked behind bars or little boys telling their mother in jail what they got on their birthday last week.

Needless to say the sky did not fall so they gave me an hour every other Friday at 1:00 AM. This is a time when I could cuss or otherwise be free to air views of the "counter culture". Nobody died, and they gave me a new schedule of every Thursday at midnight. Eventually they moved us into prime time. As of this writing our shows air live on Sundays at 6:30 PM Central in Houston at 90.1 FM and on the web at www.KPFT.org.

As a listener-sponsored station, we are obliged to call upon our listeners with "pledge drives" and our first program Cultural Baggage (CB), set the record for pledge amounts in an hour. Approximately a month after the first CB show was released to the internet, I Googled the shows name and was astounded to learn five other broadcast stations in the US were already carrying our show without asking permission. I soon began a campaign to recruit other radio stations to the Drug Truth Network (DTN). At the peak, around 2009 we had 105 affiliate, broadcast stations in the US, Canada and one in Australia.

October of 2013 marked 12 years of Drug Truth Network which now produces a second radio program "Century of Lies" (since 2004) as well as 7 three minute "4:20 Drug War NEWS" segments (since 2003) which many of our broadcast affiliates in the US and Canada insert into other news or music programs.

In 2003 I had the good fortune to meet Jack Cole then the director of Law Enforcement Against Prohibition, (LEAP). We were attending a Drug Policy Alliance conference in New Jersey. Jack and four law enforcement associates had recently created LEAP to enable law enforcement and criminal justice officials to join an organization dedicated to ending the drug war. Because of my experience as a police officer in the Air Force I was allowed to join as an official "Speaker" for LEAP. After joining forces with my "band of brothers" I have presented for LEAP to Rotary clubs, Elks, Lions, College classes and one High

School class. Since I am a minister I have also been invited to share the gospel that "Prohibition is Evil" from the pulpit of at least eight Houston area churches.

My latest foray into spreading the good news that the drug war need not last forever involves "Unvarnished Truth" our weekly, one-hour television program. Originally airing only on HMSTV, the Houston access channel, our show is now broadcast on a few independent stations. As with all our programming at college, independent and pirate stations, all we ask of new affiliates is basic contact info and the day and time the programs air.

Likely some readers of this book work at or know someone who works at a local, independent radio or TV station where Drug Truth programs might be broadcast. There is no charge, no cumbersome paper work. All I seek is the day and time of the broadcasts. Please contact dean@drugtruth.net

"Opening up a can of worms... and going fishing for truth" is an extract from one of the PSA's used on my radio shows. We shall open that can of worms in this book as well.

In the beginning, after my first few radio shows back in 2001, I was paranoid, wondering if the cops or the cartels might be upset with my broadcasts and kick in the door. I must report that in 12 years of producing radio and TV, in writing and speaking about the horrors we inflict on ourselves via the policy of drug prohibition I have never received even one threat from anybody at all. Therefore, if you have concerns about speaking what you know to be true, take heart.

Given the overwhelming evidence, there is no other explanation other than the drug war is a sham, scam, flim-flam hoax of Biblical proportion. Forces at every level of government in the US and nearly so worldwide are in league for profits and power derived from the continuance of the war on drugs. The horrors we inflict on ourselves via this policy are enormous, outrageous and obvious as hell. Who will be the hero, what politician will dare to speak the truth, reveal the whole truth, that drug war is akin to treason?

America is waging an eternal war wherein our efforts directly empower the enemies we seek to destroy. Our mandate to the world ensures planet wide corruption via the hundreds of billions of dollars that flow each year into the hands of barbarians. Shall we forever entice criminals to overthrow civilized nations via profits easily generated by defying laws against possession of a select few plant products?

We must work to disprove the postulation of former head of the CIA William Colby who stated: "The Latin American drug cartels have stretched their tentacles much deeper into our lives than most people believe. It's possible they are calling the shots at all levels of government." Given that US banks have been convicted of laundering hundreds of billions of dollars for the cartels with nobody arrested and considering the escalating number of instances of governmental and organizational corruption entwined with drug war, the concept is not inconceivable.

In August of 2013, US Attorney Eric Holder made statements that seemed bold to many pundits and way too little, too late by others, including me. Holder recognized the drug war as racist, corrupt and too often off track. He did however, promise a new perspective and diminishing prison terms in the future.

In early 2014, Senator Harry Reid, President Obama, Governor Chris Christi and my own Governor Rick Perry admitted that it was time to reexamine our nations drug laws. This modern perspective flies in the face of decades of hypocritical and propagandist rhetoric these politicians made over the years.

In 1914 with the passage of the Harrison Narcotics Act, in 1937 with the Marijuana Tax Act and again in 1970 with the passage of Nixon's ludicrously named Controlled Substance Act our nation chose to become one of control and domination over the habits of our fellow man. We now dictate this policy to the whole world. As a result of this decades old folly, deadly cartels are profiting and rising up around the globe. Millions of bloody criminals owe a huge debt of gratitude to the US drug warriors for the 400 billion dollars per year they harvest for growing forbidden flowers, shrubs and weeds. The dictators of all this madness are our own elected officials, clinging to lies, fearful of speaking the truth. They made their bones through this policy and feel they cannot now back down from their prior pronouncements.

This book is dedicated to all those whose lives have been diminished or destroyed by the ignorance, cowardice, greed and lies of drug war addicts.

JUDGE NOT

"Drug Prohibition is the biggest failed policy in the history of our country, second only to slavery."
—Superior Court Judge James P. Gray

When "the land of the free" leads the world in incarceration rates, what does that say about us? When we are perfectly willing to let white collar criminals go with a fine, like we did with the traffickers of Purdue Pharma's Oxycontin, that killed thousands of users and addicted thousands more, what does that say about us?

Fraud of any kind is given a wink and a knowing smile. Those charged with greed, corruption, bribery, most any kind of corporate or government malfeasance, are given ample time to prepare before trial, are given every leeway the criminal justice system can mete out to allow balance and time to seek out evidence to benefit the accused. Ask the Enron millionaires or the ones at WorldCom. That's not how we've filled our prisons.

The US Congress back in the 1980's expanded their crusade against drug traffickers, crafting mandatory-minimum laws to stop the flow of drugs. Their original focus was on cartels and gangsters, those who provided millions of units of drugs, thousands of kilograms, boat loads, plane loads or truckloads of drugs. The congressmen in the Midwest realized that they were unlikely if ever to have such large amounts of drugs in their state, no way to look tough, so the barrier just kept getting lower and lower.

So the states all followed suit, legislators became Chinese acrobats jumping through hoops to ratchet up the drug laws around this nation. No need for a knock, a warrant, evidence, corroboration, or a chance to confront witnesses. Those accused of drug crimes became unconditionally exterminable, untrustworthy, cast off from society. More than 45 million Americans accused of choosing non-Fortune 500 intoxicants have thus been cast off, exiled from the mainstream, forever unable to exist as full citizens of this nation.

My hometown of Houston has for decades been a primary hub for drug distribution to the rest of North America. At the same time, Houston has been functioning as the "gulag filling station" of Texas. Each year we arrest tens of thousands of young people and send thousands of them to years long prison sentences for the crime of having more than a miniscule amount of forbidden plant products. Our district attorneys all beat their chest and proclaim the city to be saved.

We must hold all elected officials to be responsible for our drug policy in every public venue. We must bring forward the subject of drug prohibition, to challenge the logic which allows them to stand eternally with millions of criminals worldwide. Why do they leave in place a policy which entices our children to lives of crime, degrades our neighborhoods and cities, ensures corruption so vast and deep that its simple pervasiveness has made us numb to the situation. We now have so little regard for the consequence of choosing to represent blind ignorance over truth, justice and reality itself.

Hell exists today, right now, for two million mostly young black and brown citizens of this nation behind bars, the largest portion there because of this eternal war on drugs. Most obvious and glaring is the misery inflicted on minority communities via this new Jim Crow mechanism of drug law enforcement which takes 14% of America's population, the black population, and creates 58% of our prison population. This is called success in the drug war.

MICHELLE ALEXANDER

Michelle Alexander is a distinguished law professor and author of *The New Jim Crow: Mass Incarceration in the Age of Color Blindness*, a book so powerful that its publication in 2010 awakened politicians and pundits alike to the nature and abject failure of drug prohibition Since its first publication, it has been featured on MSNBC, NPR, *Bill Moyers Journal*, Tavis Smiley, C-SPAN, and *Washington Journal,* among others, and in 2011 won the NAACP Image Award for best nonfiction.

DB: In your book, your write: "Like 'Jim Crow' and slavery, mass incarceration operates as a tightly controlled system of laws, policies, customs and institutions that operate collectively to ensure the subordinate status of a group defined largely by race." This should be an eye opener for a lot of people. I wish every politician in America had a chance to read it. There are so many ways that this Drug War impacts on our society, including making us the world's leading jailer. Tell us about the escalation of the prison building era and how this came about.

MICHELLE ALEXANDER: Within a relatively short period of time, we went from a prison population of 300,000 to now, nearly 2,500,000 in basically just a few decades. Our prison population quintupled. Not doubled or tripled—quintupled! This exponential increase in the size of our prison system was not due to crime rates, as is so often believed and is told to us frequently by politicians and media pundits. Rather than crime rates, the explosion of our prison population has been due, largely to the Drug War, a war that has been waged largely in poor communities of color, even though studies have now shown, for decades, that people of color are no more likely to use or sell illegal drugs than whites. People of all races and ethnicities use and sell legal and illegal drugs in the United States.

It has been primarily and overwhelmingly poor people of color in the United States who have been stopped, searched, arrested and incarcerated for drug offenses. Once you're branded a drug felon, you're relegated to a permanent second-class status. Once labeled a felon, you may be denied the right to vote, automatically excluded from juries, legally discriminated against in employment, housing, access to education and public benefits. So many of the old forms of discrimination that we supposedly left behind during the "Jim Crow" era are suddenly legal again, once you've been branded a felon. It's the Drug War primarily, that is responsible for the return of millions of African Americans to a permanent second-class status, analogous in many ways to "Jim Crow".

DB: The thing that strikes me is that we have walked away from The Bill of Rights now that the Supreme Court and other courts have determined there is a Drug War exception to the Constitution, which allows all of this to unfold.

MICHELLE ALEXANDER: I devote a whole chapter in the book to the shredding of the Fourth Amendment in the Drug War. Once upon a time, it used to be the case that law enforcement officials had to have reasonable suspicion of criminal activity and a reasonable belief that someone was actually dangerous before they could stop them or frisk them on the street, on the sidewalk or stop and search their car. Today, thanks to a series of decisions by the US Supreme Court, as long as police can "get" consent from an individual, they can stop and search them for any reason or no reason at all. Giving the police license to fan out into neighborhoods and stop and search just about anyone, anywhere. Consent is a very easy thing to obtain. If a law enforcement officer approaches you with his hand on his gun and says, "May I search your bag? Will you put your hands up in the air and turn around so I may search you?" and you comply, that's interpreted as consent.

But of course, it's precisely that kind of discriminatory and arbitrary police action that led the framers of the Constitution to adopt the Fourth Amendment prohibiting unreasonable searches and seizures. Today, law enforcement feels free to stop and search just about anyone, anywhere they please and they know very well that almost no one will refuse consent to a search especially in poor communities of color where people have been trained and disciplined that resisting police authority can lead to violence.

DB: I want to read a portion of a page here: "With no means to pay off their debts back in the 'Jim Crow' days, prisoners were sold as forced labor to lumber camps to brick yards, railroads, etc. Death rates were shockingly high, for the contractors had no interest in the health or well being of their laborers." We have a very similar situation that has developed in America now where prisoners work for pennies on the dollar, earning great profits for prison guards unions and others that are in effect "contractors" here.

MICHELLE ALEXANDER: Many people have no conception of how extraordinarily difficult it is for people once they are released from prison to "reintegrate" into mainstream society. Not only may they be denied the right to vote and not only are they ineligible for jury service for the rest of their lives and if they've been branded a felon but employment discrimination is perfectly legal against them. Every time they've got that employment application, you got to check that box, "Have you ever been convicted of a felony?" It doesn't matter if that felony happened last week or thirty-five years ago, for the rest of your life you have to check that box, knowing full well that the odds are that application is going in the trash once that box has been checked.

Housing discrimination is perfectly legal against those branded felons. Public housing is off limits to people released from prison for a minimum of five years and regulations encourage public housing agencies to discriminate against formerly incarcerated people for the rest of their lives. Even food stamps are off limits to people who have been convicted of drug felonies. People with HIV/AIDS and pregnant woman, aren't even entitled to food stamps for the rest of their lives, no matter how sick or hungry they may be. The kicker here is that people released from prison are often saddled with thousands of dollars in fees, fines, court costs and accumulated back child support. You know, in some states, a growing number of states you're expected to pay back the cost of your imprisonment once you're released. Up to 100% of your wages can be garnished to pay back all of these fees, fines and accumulated back child support.

Back in the days of convict leasing, there was a system where African Americans were arrested for minor offenses, like loitering. They were arrested, imprisoned and then leased back to plantations where they were forced to work for little or no pay. Today, we have a similar system where African Americans are arrested for extremely minor nonviolent, drug related offenses. Arrested en mass and sent to prison where they are often forced to work for little or no pay for either private companies or their imprisonment itself. It enriches prison guard unions and private prison companies and then once they're released, if they're lucky enough to get a job, 100% of their wages can be garnished, resulting in what? Them unable to survive, to make it in a legal economy, and they are returned right back to prison. In fact about 70% of people released from prison return within three years and a majority of those who return, do so in a matter of months because the challenges associated with mere survival after being branded a felon are so immense.

DB: It used to be America was the Land of Second Chances, that a person could always start again, perhaps, prosper, but it has been stacked against the potential of making that second chance for those convicted of drug crimes. That black market is always out there, enticing people to come back to work for them, is it not?

MICHELLE ALEXANDER: Yes, absolutely, you know that's the thing. Many people say, "Well, people who commit drug offenses, particularly those who sell drugs, well they're making a choice to violate the law and so they deserve whatever they get." First of all, most of us, most people in the United States, have violated the law at some point in their lives. Most of us have broken the law by experimenting with illegal drugs at some point in our lives or by speeding on the freeway, which certainly posses more risk to human life and potential harm than smoking marijuana in the privacy of one's home. All of us have broken the law, all of us have made mistakes but it's poor folks of color, primarily, who are asked to basically forfeit their lives for youthful mistakes or indiscretions, mistakes of judgment that result in relatively minor, non-violent drug offenses. It's youth of color in inner city schools that have their school swept for drugs and have drug sniffing dogs brought to sniff all their schools' lockers. They are stopped and frisked while waiting for the school buses. This Drug War has resulted in branding young people before they even have the opportunity to reach a voting age as criminals and felons for engaging in precisely the same kind of illegal drug activity that is largely ignored on college campuses and in middle class white communities.

Back during the "Jim Crow" era, literacy tests and poll taxes operated to keep African Americans away from the polls. On their face, they appeared race neutral. They said nothing about race, but the laws were enforced in such a racially discriminatory manner that they operated to create a caste system. The same is true with drug laws in the United States today. On their face, they appear race neutral, but the way they're enforced is so grossly discriminatory. In fact, in some states, African Americans have constituted 80-90% of all drug offenders sent to prison, even though we know that people of color aren't any more likely to violate our nation's drug laws.

DB: Isn't there one of the states where your chances of going to prison is about fifty times more likely because of these drug laws?

MICHELLE ALEXANDER: Yes, absolutely. In the Chicago area, nearly 80% of working age African American men have criminal records and are thus subject to legalized discrimination for the rest of their lives. These men, this group is part of a growing racial "under caste" not class but "caste," a group of people defined largely by race that are relegated to a permanent second-class status by law and custom. You know that's why I say we have not ended racial castes in America; we've merely redesigned it through facially race neutral drug laws that are enforced in a racially discriminatory manner and through a whole host of laws that deny basic civil and human rights to people branded felons. We've managed to effectively to create a caste system even in the age of Obama. That's the great irony.

People say, "How can there be a racial caste system today when we've just elected Barack Obama, our nation's first African American President?" but the reality is that every caste system in the United States has had Black Exceptionalism. During slavery, there were some black slave owners. During "Jim Crow" there were some black lawyers, some black doctors and some black success stories. There are far more black success stories today, yet the reality is that there are actually more African Americans under correctional control today, in prison or jail, on probation or parole than were enslaved. If we're going to talk about the sheer scale of this system and not just those who have escaped it and proven to be exceptions to the rule, it is destroying and devastating more lives of African Americans today then slavery did at its peak.

DB: I learned from the Sentencing Project that under the most racist regime in modern history, South Africa's Apartheid Law, 851 black men were imprisoned per 100,000 population. In 2008, under the United States Drug Prohibition Law, we imprison 2,770 Hispanic men per 100,000 and 6,664 black men per 100,000. That's seven or eight times more than did South Africa under Apartheid.

MICHELLE ALEXANDER: Yes, we are incarcerating African Americans at a higher rate than South Africa did in the heart of Apartheid. We have higher incarceration rates than any other country in the world, including the most repressive regimes in the world. The excuse that's often given, of course, is violent crime and particularly violent drug-related crime. Well, nothing could be further from the truth. The Drug War has never been aimed primarily at rooting out violent offenders or drug kingpins. Federal funding flows to those state and federal law enforcement agencies that boost dramatically the volume, the sheer number of drug arrests. They're not rewarded for bringing down the drug kingpins or the most violent offenders. Law enforcement agencies have a financial incentive to round up as many people as possible and cast the net as widely as possible in poor communities of color, where these stop and frisk tactics are feasible. They can't get away with that kind of stuff in middle class white communities or on college campuses.

Many people think that the Drug War was announced in reaction to the emergence of crack cocaine in inner city communities, but it's just not true. President Ronald Reagan officially declared the current Drug War in 1982, a few years before crack first hit the streets in Los Angeles and later spread to communities of color across America. The Drug War was declared in response to racial politics, not drug crime. It was part of the effort of conservative whites, particularly in the South, to appeal to the racial resentment and the racial anxiety of poor and working class Whites particularly in the South who were anxious about, quite understandably, anxious about desegregation, busing, affirmative action and many of the gains of the civil rights movement. Pollsters and political strategists found that they could appeal to those voters and get them to defect from the Democratic Party and join the Republication Party by using racially coded "get tough" appeals on issues of crime and welfare.

DB: The Southern Strategy.

MICHELLE ALEXANDER: Absolutely, the Southern Strategy. H.R. Halderman, President Richard Nixon's former Chief of Staff, said explicitly, "The whole problem is really the Blacks. The key is to divide the system that recognizes this, while not appearing to." Well, they certainly succeeded. With the Drug War, they were able to effectively recreate a caste system that locks millions of African Americans in a status not unlike the one they thought they left behind.

DB: Speaking of Presidents, the last three Presidents are known to have used drugs yet the Drug War continues.

MICHELLE ALEXANDER: You would think, given the drug use of President Clinton and President Obama, their own criminal history really, that they would have a more forgiving and understanding attitude toward those who are cycling in and out of prisons for relatively minor drug crimes. The perception many people have is that most people who are in prison doing time for drug offenses are doing time for serious drug crimes. Not the case! In 2005, for example, 4 out of 5 drug arrests were for simple possession; only 1 out of 5 were for sales. Most people in state prison for drug offenses in the United States have no history of violence or significant selling activity.

In the 1990's, the Clinton era, the Drug War escalated far beyond what the Republicans even dreamed possible. In the 1990's, nearly 80% of the increase in drug arrests was for marijuana possession, a drug less harmful than alcohol or tobacco and equally, if not more prevalent, in middle class white communities and on college campuses as it is in the Hood.

DB: Why does not the black community focus more on this problem and work to help bring it to an end?

MICHELLE ALEXANDER: Well, it's a good question. I wrote the book in large part because I was so alarmed by the failure of the civil rights community to prioritize the War of Drugs and the mass incarceration of poor people of color in the United States. You would think that given the sheer scale of the Drug War and of mass incarceration and its impact in the black community, that it would be the number one priority of every civil rights organization in the country.

The African American political leadership should be outspoken, calling for an end to the Drug War, but instead there's been a relative quiet. Happily, the NAACP in recent years, under new leadership, has become more vocal and aggressive and calling for an end to mass incarceration, but there has been an eerie quiet.

I think there are many reasons for it, not at least of which is the fact that one of the primary strategies that racial justice advocates have used for centuries, since the days of slavery, has been to try to identify with those African Americans who defy racial stereotypes and try to attract public attention to them. You know, people like Rosa Parks. Try to identify with those individuals who defy prevailing racial stereotypes and hold them up as examples of why the prevailing caste system, the prevailing system of discrimination is unfair and unjust and should be eradicated but today, where the prevailing system of control criminalizes the black community, that strategy of distancing yourself from kind of the "worst" elements of your community and trying to shine a light on those who are the most noble within the community doesn't work so well.

So there's been a reflexive tendency in the African American community to try not to draw public attention to those within the community who have gotten into trouble or who might look bad. So the plight of those cycling in and out of the criminal justice system unfortunately hasn't been a top priority, but issues like Affirmative Action have topped the list. Efforts like struggling to get African American students into the best high schools and colleges have been a higher priority. As civil rights organizations have agonized over Affirmative Action, millions, millions of people of color have been rounded up, branded felons and relegated to a permanent second-class status.

JEFF BLACKBURN

In 2000, more than 40 black people were arrested in one night in the town of Tulia, Texas. Defendants were handed sentences of 60, 75 and 90 years for sales of minor amounts of cocaine to an undercover officer Tom Coleman. Attorney Jeff Blackburn represented several of the Tulia drug sting defendants and joined other civil rights attorneys to investigate the soon to be discredited agent Tom Coleman, leading to the eventual prison release and pardons for all the convicted Tulia defendants. After his work in Tulia, Blackburn founded the West Texas Innocence Project at the Texas Tech University School of Law in Lubbock, where he continues to assist people wrongfully imprisoned in Texas. He also has a private law practice in Amarillo, where he lives. This interview is from the Oct 15, 2008.

JEFF BLACKBURN: I've done a lot of cases against the government dealing with their insane and misguided drug war. I'm the lawyer that did the Tulia case and in the wake of the Tulia case founded an outfit called the Innocence Project of Texas, which is still doing a lot of work all around the state. But another part of my job has always been to deal with the consequences of marijuana prohibition and the insanity of the drug war as we know it. Consequently we've been working along with other lawyers, especially members of the NORML legal committee, to always find chinks in the armor and ways to use the legal system not only to win for the client but also, more important I think, to strike a blow against this failed policy.

So lately we've been doing that, and I was very fortunate to have gotten a verdict in my hometown of Amarillo, Texas, not known as a real bastion of liberal thinking, that I think will have some good consequences and some far reaching ones for other folks. We got a not guilty based on an old legal doctrine called necessity on behalf of a guy, 53 years old, who was smoking marijuana in order to deal with his symptoms caused by HIV. As far as we know, it was the first medical necessity defense that had been successful in Texas. It may be first now but I doubt that it will be an only. I foresee a period opening up where more and more lawyers will aggressively fight these cases using the right facts. We're going to be able to win. And reason we're going to be able to win is real simple. It's ultimately political. Because what these cases do, when you're dealing with somebody that's sick and has done their best to deal with their own health problems and has had to resort to smoking because it is a proved great remedy for all kinds of health problems, when you have a person like that and they run up against the government, most people, average people, are going to say 'Hey, give the guy a break. Let him do that.' The government shouldn't be controlling every aspect of that. People are tired enough, not only of big government, but also the rule of pharmaceutical companies, to be wise enough to give people the right to control their own healthcare. And so in this very narrow way I think that we can see a lot more of these victories if lawyers will aggressively push them and if they have the right facts.

DB: Polls find 60, 70, 80, 85 percent of people approve of medical marijuana. It is the politicians who are still lingering in the early part of the last century, right?

JEFF BLACKBURN: Absolutely. I mean the people are way, way ahead in their thinking of the authority structure right now. You know, one thing that this trial illustrated to me, and it's nothing new, but it's still kind of nauseating when you see it played out all over again, is the absolute rigidity and dogmatic inflexibility of the authorities. My client, Tim Stevens, was arrested for three grams of marijuana. Under an eighth of an ounce; that's right, ten bucks worth of weed. When the cops put him in the car he explained to them that he was an HIV patient, that he was sick, that that's why he had gone to buy it, and of course what the cops on the scene told him was 'So? You should have gone to a doctor instead of doing this. That's not an excuse.' They could have even written him a ticket for that because we now can do that under Texas law but in many jurisdictions, certainly my home town included, they don't do that because they're addicted. On the one hand they fill up the jails with people accused of petty crimes and on the other hand they complain that the jails are overcrowded and they need yet more money to build bigger jails.

DB: Very symptomatic of many States across this nation. I saw where the U.S. Attorney in Tuscon is refusing to arrest people with less than 500 pounds coming across the border. It's very hypocritical, this man with three grams brought to trial.

JEFF BLACKBURN: But I think in jurisdictions all over the country where you've got law enforcement running amok and where you've got them believing that the surefire way to political popularity is to go after every single drug case like it's the end all of law enforcement, you see this kind of thing. They're hopelessly addicted to imprisonment. They're hopelessly addicted to bloated budgets. They're hopelessly addicted to looking good by getting numbers. You know, that's what the drug war has really become, it's about numbers for these guys, it's a racket. It's about money and numbers. The Tulia fiasco, Hearne, the Sheetrock scandal in Dallas, these were all caused by law enforcement's implacable desire to get more numbers, which gets them more money, which gets them bigger grants, which gets them fancier cars and so forth.

DB: Tell us about the Innocence Project of Texas.

JEFF BLACKBURN: A lot of our work right now is dealing with people who've been in prison 25, 26, 27 years. We've been heavily involved in that work, but I've never wanted to limit the work of our Innocence Project just to those kinds of cases--the flashy cases that people see in the media and that gain instant publicity for a day or two. What we're trying to do is to create a permanent institutional counterweight to the government through our project that can eventually begin to address the number of people that are undoubtedly innocent, falsely convicted of low level drugs crimes, which I think accounts for a huge percentage of people in the Texas Department of Corrections.

I think that there are all kinds of crimes that go without notice because they don't have that flashy DNA evidence to get them out and what we're campaigning, what we're working for on a daily basis, is to open people's minds to the fact that there are hundreds, in fact thousands, of people in TDC that don't belong there. I think the average person is willing to call a halt to this kind of government over-expansion and over-reaching. People are tired of it and I think that verdict in Amarillo, on our little marijuana case, is solid proof of that and it's one proof that we see amongst many out there of the gap that exists now between the authorities on the one hand and the way real, ordinary people think on the other.

DB: Yeah, and Jeff, we saw a major awakening not just for Texas but for the nation on the heels of the situation in Tulia. And for those who don't know or can't remember, give us a brief summation of what went on there.

JEFF BLACKBURN: Tulia was a common place throughout Texas when we had regional drug task forces, where small counties in order to get money would stage a major arrest, you know, arresting in the case of Tulia, one tenth of the entire Black population, nearly all the breadwinners in the population, for supposed drug deliveries. All the cases were made by one cop. This was common throughout Texas for years, for many years. In Tulia the difference was that this one cop was so bad that we were able to expose him successfully, not without five years worth of effort, and also not without many people going to prison on nothing but his word that they had delivered drugs to him. As we discovered, once we finally got access to test the drugs, once we finally got transcripts to show that he was a perjurer, we were able to bring him down.

But what people need to realize is that the amount of effort that you have to put into, into--you know, it takes ten minutes to convict somebody in this State and ten years to get them out. It's, the effort that has to be made is completely out of proportion to the minimal effort the State has to make on shoddy evidence, cruddy witnesses, and virtually no truth at all, to put people in. Until you rectify that imbalance and begin to make institutional changes, we're going to continue to see more Tulias. I'm convinced there are dozens of them out there that so far have gone unnoticed because some band of lawyers hadn't been able to get together and do something about.

We know if we get involved and pass incremental laws, laws that don't seem great and certainly not exactly what we wanted, but still nonetheless make a difference, like we did in the wake of Tulia. A difference does happen. We know that after we passed the law in the wake of Tulia that required undercover snitches to be corroborated, 631 criminal cases were dismissed within three months. So we at least saved those people from clearly bogus cases, uncorroborated cases, from being convicted.

That was an incremental law; it wasn't what we wanted; it was about a quarter loaf, because what we wanted was a law that would have required cops to be corroborated. But what we got was that incremental reform. Well, it made a difference.

So progress is being made through fighting and through conflict. I'm hopeful that the verdict that we got will carry a message into the legislature in Texas and that folks will begin to question the wisdom of, at least, having this prohibition on the medical use of marijuana. One thing that I learned in the course of this case from dealing with doctors, researchers and people that are in the know on such matters is that marijuana is a very, very valid medical remedy.

The information is out there and we presented that all to the jury, we found a way to get that in through evidence, and it impressed them too. I mean, people are ready to be open on things and let me tell you something, I can pretty safely bet that not one person on our jury was a weed smoker. These are pretty square, regular people, but they were also open-minded regular people, and they were conscientious, just like you're going to find with most folks that actually get on a jury. They want to be open-minded, they want to be conscientious, and I think they're ready to reject the government on these issues. These people can continue to cling to a system that doesn't work, to an approach that nobody believes in anymore, but eventually it can give way and that's where my sense of optimism really lies.

CLAY CONRAD

Clay Conrad is an attorney at the Houston firm of Looney & Conrad, P.C. whose specialty is the history and development of the jury system. He is the author of *Jury Nullification:Tthe Evolution of a Doctrine*, the latest edition of which has been published by the Cato Institute."

DB: Jury nullification has a huge history. It was abused in many cases in prior times during slavery, racial bias in the old south in particular. There is a positive side to it. Tell us the potential for jury nullification.

CLAY CONRAD: First, let me talk about the abuse that you speak of because I think the stories of its abuse are grossly exaggerated. The jury has power. It has discretion and like any other discretion that can be abused. Just like the discretion of police officers, of judges, of prosecutors can be abused.

The jury is a deliberative body. You take 12 people, hopefully from different sections of the community, and they all have to agree to come to a decision. If you have a fairly selected jury, the chances of racial bias or bigotry carrying the day are pretty small.

The other thing is those cases in the deep south that you refer to—the lynching and civil rights murder cases—very often involved prosecutors who didn't want a conviction, police officers who didn't want a conviction, judges who didn't want a conviction, and then after there was an acquittal, they all blamed the jury, for the outcome, and the jury broke up and they never were in a position to respond. When I looked into individual cases I found, for instance, in the Medgar Evers murders there were police officers who testified that they saw Byron Dillenbeck with the killer something like 200 miles away at the time when Meager Evers was getting himself killed. You can't turn around and blame the jury after they've had that kind of testimony come into court.

In another case, the prosecutor advised the jury that the evidence wasn't very strong and didn't merit a conviction. That was a case out of Pennsylvania. In another case, I found the coroner testified that the victim died in a traffic accident and that the lead pellets in his face were just dislodged dental fillings. Now they don't use lead in dental fillings, but that's what the coroner testified to.

So we have all of these cases, and then the jury gets blamed for the outcome, which was the only possible outcome under the law. Have there been cases where the jury has misbehaved? Certainly. Juries aren't perfect, just like any other human institution isn't perfect, but I think they're less likely to have done bigotry than prosecutors, judges, or police officers. They're probably the most responsible actors in the system.

Now the second question is, "What does jury nullification have to offer us today?" I know that your focus is the War on Drugs. Juries have a long history in alcohol cases of refusing to convict. In the Prohibition era as many as 60% of cases ended in acquittal. That's particularly important because under prohibition manufacturing, distributing, and selling was all that was illegal. Possessing and consuming alcohol was perfectly legal under Prohibition. So you're not talking about the users. You are talking about the dealers. You are talking about the manufacturers. 60% of the time the juries refused to convict.

If we had a 60% acquittal rate in marijuana possession cases, it would be almost impossible to maintain the War on Drugs. If we had a 60% acquittal rate in all drug cases, this nation's drug policies would be changed by this time next year. Juries are the most powerful actors in the criminal justice system. If they say not guilty, the case is over, and it doesn't matter what any of the officials in the system say.

DB: You mentioned during alcohol prohibition perhaps 60% of those accused were acquitted by some type of jury nullification. I want to bring that to the modern era where some 90 something percent of drug cases are plea bargains. They never even go to trial. The jury never hears the evidence. Were we to take these to trial, perhaps we could again generate a number of acquittals through jury nullification. Your thought, Mr. Clay Conrad?

CLAY CONRAD: As a lawyer, the first thing you are going to look at is what is the acquittal rate that you're getting through these cases right now. If juries started to acquit at an inordinate rate in marijuana possession cases, more cases would go to trial. As more cases went to trial, the desire of the state to prosecute those cases would go down. So we would see a change in policy almost immediately if juries started refusing to convict in those cases.

Right now juries are not saying no. They are not standing up and objecting to these prosecutions. It really only takes one juror to hang the trial, to get a hung jury, so it doesn't take unanimity among the public in order for juries to make a difference. If we start seeing stubborn jurors refusing to convict in drug prosecutions, we will see cases having to be retried over and over again, which ties up the court, takes an enormous amount of resources. You will see a change in policy.

Juries have control over the system. They are the safety valve. Legal change is very slow as a rule. The laws change slowly, painfully slowly. Social change is faster. Society can change positions pretty quickly. Right now, something like 58% of society thinks marijuana should just be legal. We're not seeing that out of D.C. We're not seeing that out of the state legislatures. Even in Texas, we're seeing a majority in favor of legalizing marijuana. Nationwide, the numbers are over 80% that medical marijuana should be legal, and we've only got one-third of the states that have legalized medical marijuana.

So legal change is not keeping up with social change. Juries can make the difference. Juries are sort of the safety valve. When social change has occurred and legal change is lagging behind the juries can let the steam off. They can say we're not going to send more people to prison. We're not going to ruin more lives enforcing laws that don't protect society, don't make us any safer, and really just victimize the people who get caught in the cross-hairs. Juries have that authority.

DB: I don't know if you are aware of this or if you recall but I believe it was Jeff Blackburn up somewhere in Odessa, Tulia, somewhere who was able to get a jury to nullify a marijuana arrest up there with the thought that the gentleman needed it for medical reasons. It can happen even in Texas, right?

CLAY CONRAD: It does happen. We see it occasionally. A lot of times juries find some evidence particularly unconvincing because they just find it so unpalatable. You never really know in any individual case whether they committed jury nullification. That was one of the real challenges in writing this book.

You can look at a lot of cases, and you know if there's a 60% acquittal rate that prosecutors are not getting that sloppy and that there's some nullification going on. Any individual case, it can be very hard to say whether the jury was unpersuaded or whether they just said no because the law was misapplied or unjust. It's kind of a challenge, but you do know that in a good portion of cases (some researchers have put it at 4%, some at 15%) but in a good portion of cases juries do decide to nullify the law because they find thats it's either unjust or unjustly applied.

If you factor in mistrials the numbers are probably higher—cases where the jury just couldn't reach a decision, where they couldn't all agree. There's probably even a larger number of those that involves someone who just said, "I just cannot convict in this case." It could be a drug case. It could be a 17-year-old with an underage girlfriend. A case of a battered wife killing or injuring her abusive husband in his sleep. There are just so many different scenarios that come to mind that even a good law could be misapplied, and, of course, a bad law can never be properly applied.

DB: My limited exposure to actual courtrooms kind of stifles my opinion here, but I've seen it too often on TV where the district attorney tries to eliminate anybody who thinks that the law might be wrong, and they actually set traps to try to keep them off the jury panel, right?

CLAY CONRAD: Certainly both sides try to keep off people that they know are going to vote against them. One of the biggest lies in the legal practice is that we all go up in front of the jury when a jury is being selected and say, "We all want a fair and impartial jury." Well, that's not true. The prosecutor wants the jury that's going to convict. The defense attorney wants a jury that's going to acquit. The judge wants a jury that's going to come back in time after lunch. But, we all want a jury that's going to vote our way.

Let's say that you are facing jury selection, and you know about this doctrine. There's two routes you can take. One is you can stand up, and you can tell everyone who's sitting in the room about it. That will really irritate the judge and will ensure that you will not get on the jury. They might dismiss the whole panel because they feel you've tainted the panel by letting them know about this "forbidden doctrine." Or you can keep your mouth shut, just answer the specific questions that have been asked of you, and then there's a pretty good chance you might get on the jury and really be able to piss the judge off.

DB: That brings to mind that we are starting to see surreptitious jury nullification in states like Colorado, California where the knowledgeable folks about marijuana or other drugs allow themselves to be chosen to make a difference. Each one of us has that potential, do we not?

CLAY CONRAD: Certainly. I think that one of the most ludicrous things in American education is the kids go to school and they're taught all about the role of the president, all about the role of congress, all about the role of the courts but they are not taught anything about the role of the jurors. They are not taught the history of the jury system. They are not taught the purpose of the jury system. They are not taught how the jury system operates.

Very few of those kids are going to grow up to be the president, senator, congressman or judge. A lot of them are going to grow up to be jurors but they are not prepared for it. We see that fewer and fewer cases go to jury trial, fewer and fewer people show up when they get a jury summons. Most of them just ignore it. Fewer and fewer people are interested in serving as a juror.

It's very predictable. If you don't understand why something is important you are not going to value it. We haven't taught kids this most American institution and why they should value it, so now we have generations of people who think that jury duty is a nuisance and that the jury themselves can't be trusted to make a logical decision or a rational decision, so when you argue that the jury should have the ability to say no to unjust or misapplied laws, they look at you as though you are crazy because they've been taught that jurors are idiots, and the jury system is a nuisance. That's not what the founders thought. That's not what the history is and it's an institution that we need to resurrect to society so that the "people" can once again say, "These are our courts. These are our laws. We're the last ones who make the decisions."

JUDGE JOHN DELANEY

Judge John Delaney is a retired state district court judge who continues to adjudicate in Texas. He is a graduate of Princeton University and the University of Texas School of Law and a former Navy officer. John had his "light-bulb moment" in the Bryan Rotary Club in 2008 when he attended a Drug Policy Forum of Texas presentation by fellow Houston native Jerry Epstein. From Cultural Baggage / August 28, 2011.

DB: Here in Texas we're running out of money, we're firing teachers, we're shutting libraries, we're doing all kinds of things but we're not focusing on the fact that the expenditures involving most of these drug busts is a waste of our resources. Your response.

JUDGE DELANEY: Yes. We spend too much money chasing people for low-level crimes that involve possession of marijuana and even other drugs. We should be focusing our efforts on other criminal activities that impacts humans more directly and this is a hard concept for people to get their arms around but the argument really is all about harm reduction.

Where is the least harm created? Nobody in their right mind advocates the world getting stoned on drugs on a regular basis. I'm not in favor of drug abuse either. Don't use, don't intend to. Do drink coffee so I guess I use caffeine. But, the question is not whether drugs are bad or good. The question is are we creating greater harm by trying to combat drug abuse through the use of criminal law.

And the resounding answer is we are.

We've created a black market because a certain percentage of people (always has been, always will be) who want to use mind altering substances. When we make those substances criminal, that drives up the cost for them on the black market which causes criminal activity. So now drugs are still out there they just happen to be regulated by criminals instead of by government.

DB: Judge Delany, five years back there was a situation here in the Houston area where a bunch of cocaine users went to pick up their weekend supply of cocaine from their distributors. Took it home, did their usual dose and did not wake up the next morning. 14 young people. Turns out the cocaine they bought was not cocaine at all—it was 85% heroin. Another example of the failure of controlling these drugs, right?

JUDGE DELANEY: Drive drugs underground and you put their production, distribution and sales in the hands of the criminals who don't care how old you are, only that you've got the money. Don't have a license to lose like a liquor store does and, yeah, they're likely to peddle anything that they happen to have on hand. They don't analyze it. So it's not surprising that we get people overdosing and dying. It's part of the insanity.

Let me jump in here, I've got to make an apology / disclaimer. I'm state judge that still sits. I'm subject to prudent judicial ethics and I'm subject to being sanctioned for misbehavior as a judge and I promise you that I took the oath to enforce laws and I still do that every day. My feeling about the laws being wrong-headed doesn't mean I don't have the stomach and will to enforce them. So I needed to make that disclaimer. I'm allowed to speak out about needed changes to the laws and legal system and that's what I'm doing. I'm exercising my right to do that.

DB: The federal mandatory-minimums have been handcuffing judges. That no matter what the situation, no matter how it came about, judges were forced to sentence these people to prison for long terms. Many of the judges started objecting though they did sentence them, as you say—doing their duty, but I wanted to ask you, as a working judge, is there ever any back room discussions about how stupid these laws are?

JUDGE DELANEY: Well, I don't deal in the federal system. I deal in the state system. We don't have near as many of those restrictions on us. Every once in a while the legislature will nip around at the margins and try to get tough on drugs again but that trend has kind of diminished in the state of Texas.

The federal system still has it and, of course when you have mandatory-minimums what you really have is the discretion about how to sanction a drug dealer, user, possessor that shifts into the hands of the prosecutor. Prosecutors now decide what kind of charge they're going to lay on the guy to fit within the punishment range that they think is accurate instead of letting the judge have discretion.

It's a wrong-headed system. There's no question about it.

At some point, people ask me when I talk to a rotary club or lions club like I did a couple weeks ago, "What can I, as an individual, do to make a difference?" These people are not people who use drugs, they just have relatives dying from overdoses and are upset. I say, "Well, you can make a noise. You can make the noise repeatedly. One noise is not good. It doesn't help a lot. We need to have a consistent noise-making effort made." You can write every congressman that you can think of. Now the only ones that will listen to you are the ones that represent you. People in other districts don't care about you. But if you vote for them, you're in their congressional district—they will listen to that. That does not mean they will change their mind overnight but Rome wasn't built in a day. You can bite at their ankles repeatedly and lend your voice to the effort.

This is a movement that has got wind in its sail. Just 10 days ago a Chicago jury in a federal trial awarded a young man named Russell and his family over 300,000 dollars in money damages for the loss of his dog. His 9-year-old Labrador Retriever, named Lady, came walking into the room, wagging her tail, when the police broke into young Russell's apartment while executing a drug warrant. As the police sadly often do, they shot the dog to death. That was in 2009. That case finally came before a jury and incredibly, with a resounding shout, they said that dog is worth 300,000 dollars. They were so outraged by the police conduct. So the sentiments out there. It's just a matter of tweaking the power brokers to make them toe the line behind the people.

We know what happened during alcohol prohibition. We know how that all changed. As soon as we decriminalized alcohol…and I know…I know for a fact that we're not alone in this idea. Every time I talk to a rotary club, a lions club, I ask them three questions to start out. "Have we won the War on Drugs?" That's the first question. No hands. Second question, "Do you think the Drug War is working?" No hands. Third question, the hardest one, "Do you think if we keep doing the same thing we're doing in the Drug War for say the next two years, we will have begun to have won the Drug War? Will the tide change?" Again, no hands.

So the most conservative members of our community have already made up their mind that this drug war is senseless and needs to be changed somehow. What they're not convinced about exactly is how to go about changing. So, again, they say, "What shall I do?" And I say, "Write your congressman. Write your state legislature."

Here's an interesting anecdote. I was at the National Convention for State Legislatures in San Antonio a week ago manning a booth along with another member of Law Enforcement Against Prohibition and these state legislatures kept coming by and looking at our display and engaging us in some talk. One very interesting woman from a western state said, "You know, if the medical marijuana people and the legalize and control people would quit fighting with each other, I might be able to get something done." I said, "Explain that." She said, "The medical people want to keep it and control it…doctors and like that. And the legalize and regulate say 'let anybody have it under state regulations.' They're in conflict with each other. I can't invest my political capitol if the proponents of drug liberalization won't get on the same page."

JAMES GIERACH

James is a former Assistant State's Attorney of Cook County, municipal attorney, Village prosecutor, and general practitioner. A former candidate for Cook County State's Attorney and Illinois governor, raising drug policy and prison issues. One newspaper called him, "Illinois' premier conscientious objector to the war on drugs." Cultural Baggage, April 15, 2012.

DB: Right now we have a former prosecutor based in Chicago, Illinois, Mr. James Gierach. Quick quote from him, "The War on Drugs puts more drugs everywhere and is at the heart of American crisis." Much is happening in the drug war in recent days. You were an attendee to the UN Convention on Drugs this spring, correct?

JAMES GIERARCH: Yes, the Commission on Narcotic Drugs met last month in March in Vienna. I and several other LEAP members and speakers were there.

DB: There was discussion on the sidelines…much discussion about the need for change, correct?

JAMES GIERARCH: Well, individually the delegates from these almost 200 nations who are members of the three prohibition treaties that the United Nations has passed with the aid of its member states and they put prohibition in place. The delegates who came to the 55th session of the Commission in Vienna were basically sent with marching orders to support prohibition even though all of the reports that came from the secretariat regarding drug use were negative. Drug use is up. Drug trafficking is up. Therefore what do we do? More of the same.

The United States introduced a resolution to celebrate the Hague Opium Treaty, the first international prohibition treaty against opium, which was passed in 1912. This was the 100-year anniversar,y so the United States introduces a resolution that says, "We should reaffirm the prohibition treaties," three of which are in place, and nail, really, all the countries of the world to the cross of drug prohibition.

DB: President Obama had something to say at the Summit of the Americas in Cartagena, Colombia, this is U.S. President Barrack Obama.

PRESIDENT OBAMA: I think it is entirely legitimate to have a conversation about whether the laws in place are ones that are doing more harm than good in certain places. I, personally, and my administration's position is that legalization is not the answer. That, in fact, if you think about how it would end up operating, the capacity of a large-scale drug trade to dominate certain countries if they were allowed to operate legally without any constraint could be just as corrupting if not more corrupting than the status quo. Nevertheless, I'm a big believer in looking at the evidence, having a debate. I think ultimately what we're going to find is that the way to solve this problem in the United States is by dealing with demand in a more effective way, but it's also going to be strengthening institutions at home.

DB: James, what did you think of the President's remarks?

JAMES GIERARCH: The President is obviously dead wrong. Prohibition is the most effective way to put more drugs everywhere. In February I was in Mexico City and Antonio Mazzitelli was the representative of the United Nations. We were there at a drug policy conference. Mazzitelli gets up and says, "We can't legalize drugs because it would make the problems of health around the world worse." I was the speaker who followed him and I turned to him and I said, "Well, how is it that this policy, this Al Capone, UN-policy paradigm that we have in place now (prohibition) it has resulted in 50,000 murders here in Mexico since Calderon took over in 2006. How is that good for the public health?!" And then I said to him, "While we're here, we've got 38 speakers from around the world, and you're saying we're worried about the health, this drug policy just resulted in the seizure of 15 tons of meth while we're here giving this speech. How is that good for public health?!"

President Barrack Obama just refused to take up the subject of legalization saying it's not his policy, it's not the U.S. government's policy and the fact is that's the policy that's turning American cities into jungles. Where you can have safe streets or drug prohibition and we keep choosing prohibition.

DB: Yeah, James, I picked up from him that he said it's time to have a legitimate conversation but he's worried about certain places where, you know, the large drug trade would dominate countries. And the fact of the matter is if it were legal, nobody's going to dominate because we'd grow it in our backyard if we want to. The price would drop to a penny on the dollar. It has no basis in reality, does it?

JAMES GIERARCH: Al Capone was in favor of the prohibition of liquor because the prohibition was the foundation of his business. Today the drug cartels are in favor of prohibition because it's the foundation of their business. Yesterday when President Obama made his statement that he was opposed to drug legalization, control and regulation of substances he was siding with the drug cartels. He was siding with the street gangs. He was siding with the murder cases, with the overdoses, with the bullet holes, with the addict crime, with the building of American prisons.

Public enemy #1 in America and the world is the War on Drugs, and we have a President who, thus far, has said he supports prohibition. Inexcusable. And these Latin American leaders are putting Obama's feet to the fire, as they should be, and the American people should be putting Obama's feet to the fire because he is leading our country right into the mouth of the dragon of "public enemy #1" which is the War on Drugs, prohibition.

He's making war on people who need medical marijuana in the marijuana states where the people themselves in this country have voted in favor of it and have declared that it's medicine. He has sicked the DEA, the Internal Revenue Service and federal agents on Oaksterdam and these other sites in California, Washington, Oregon and the western states of our country. It's outrageous and it's inexcusable for a president who cares, purportedly, about the public health, safety and welfare.

DB: James, also President Obama says that he wants to deal with demand. He's talking about American demand.

JAMES GIERARCH: This business about reducing demand is a bunch of poppycock. We have the President of the United States who with the Secret Service goes down to the Summit of the Americas in Cartagena, Colombia, and while they're down there, because of the temptation of women, because of the natural attraction of men to women, these agents get in trouble. So now how are we going to reduce the demand of the agents for female company? Outlaw female company, I suppose. We can outlaw drugs, but you can't eliminate something that's inborn with man. You can encourage him to do the right thing, but prohibition then puts the price so elevated that it tempts people to go into the business and to do these things they certainly would not be doing on the scale that they are in this War on Drugs.

DB: Well, you know, the *Guardian* newspaper had an article today taking about Colombia calls for a global task drugs task force. Let me read a bit from it. Quoting the President, "Why is Colombia leading this? Because we learned the hard way and we have the moral authority in the 1980s. We failed to face reality and as a result our society was taken to the brink and almost destroyed by violence and cartels. We do not want other places in Central America or Africa to go through the pain we went through. They and all of us have to act fast because the many-headed monster grows very fast and destroys very fast." Very profound words, aren't they?!

JAMES GIERARCH: Well, they are. This War on Drugs is number 1 the most effective way to put more drugs everywhere. Number two it's the heart of whatever crisis you want to name in America or in the world, virtually. The problem of guns, gangs, crimes, prisons, taxes, deficits, AIDS, health care, trade imbalance, corruption, no money for schools, job programs, the funding of terrorism, the corruption of the kids, the corruption of the police…and why has this war been in place so long when it's failed so mightily as the people of the world overwhelmingly conclude?

The answer is the "good guys" and the "bad guys" are both on the same side of the line of scrimmage—both in favor of drug war. Both because they're riding the drug war gravy train though in different ways. Prohibition puts money into the cartels' pockets. If you legalize any substance and you make the substance available in a regulated way it takes money out of the cartels' pockets. On the other side of the coin you've got Clinton who says we have to hire 100,000 more policemen because we've got so much crime and violence. Well, we did—why? Because of prohibition. Then we build prisons to the point where it's the fastest growing housing in the United States in the 1990s. Where the United States—the "Land of the Free"—is now the prison capital of the world with the highest rate of incarceration than any country in the world.

We take black people and put them in jail and hire white people to run the prisons and it's a racist, just absolutely indefensible policy.

JUDGE JAMES GRAY

Judge James Gray, a former Superior Court Judge in Orange County, California, was the Libertarian Vice Presidential candidate in 2012. He is the author of *Why Our Drug Laws Have Failed And What We Can Do About It: A Judicial Indictment of the War on Drugs*. His experience as a former federal prosecutor, defense attorney and trial judge convinced him that our nation's program of drug prohibition was not simply a failure, but a hopeless failure. Cultural Baggage / May 26, 2013.

DB: Judge, there is starting to be an avalanche of information, of politicians and publications and people willing to say what needs said.

JAMES GRAY: You know that I wrote a book called *Why Our Drug Laws Have Failed,* and whenever I endorse it, I always write, "It's OK to discuss drug policy." If we were just to allow ourselves as a society to discuss this area honestly, truthfully, fully, we would have changed away from drug prohibition years and decades ago. So, yes, we are now allowing ourselves to discuss it, and now we're changing. These laws, initiatives in Colorado and Washington are going to be noteworthy, historic. We can now see that proverbial "light at the end of the tunnel" in view.

We are going to see that just because they do allow the recreational legal use of marijuana that that does not turn us into a bunch of drug zombies, like they've also learned in Portugal. We're going to get along very well—thank you very much—take away a whole bunch of revenue from really bad people like Mexican drug cartels and juvenile youth gangs and other thugs and really convert that money like we do with alcohol to paying our fire fighters, paying our teachers, fixing our roads.

The end is in sight and it's long since time for that to have occurred. Thanks, again, in no small measure to those like you who help get this word out.

DB: Thank you so much. To kind of underscore what I was saying a minute ago, this is yesterday's *New York Times* opinion piece by Attorney Paul Zukerberg. He was discussing the number of arrests in Washington, D.C. This is just an extract: In 1995, police in the District arrested about 1,850 people for having pot. By 2011, the number had skyrocketed to more than 6,000. It's still rising.

JAMES GRAY: You can extend that. I see this on the bench. I was a trial court judge in California for 25 years, and the tougher we get with regard to non-violent drug offenses, literally the softer we get with regard to the prosecution of things like robbery, rape, and murder because we only have so many resources to pursue criminal justice issues. The tougher we get there, the softer we get on the prosecution on crimes that really do affect us.

In addition, the biggest safety measure we could pursue for our police would be to repeal drug prohibition. It was dangerous for Elliot Ness and those folks to attack Al Capone and the rest, and once we repealed alcohol prohibition, that problem went away. Their lives were so much safer.

If you were arrested and convicted for even a marijuana offense, the rest of your life you will probably lose your eligibility for federal educational benefits, probably for federal housing benefits. You can be convicted of rape and not lose those benefits, so it's just crazy.

So many folks believe that this is done for a racist reason. We all know that it does not take a sociologist to go through any jail or prison in our country and see the people of color are vastly overrepresented. I don't think it was intended to be that way, but it certainly has brought that result. I believe the most patriotic thing I can do for the country I love is help us repeal drug prohibition.

DB: You talk about the focus of the dollars and effort and the one that grates me so much is that if a person is busted with a bag of weed, cocaine, or any kind of "illegal drug," that bag is almost instantly analyzed and set up so they can bring that person to trial and work them through the process, whereas we have tens of thousands of rape kits around this country that sit on a shelf without the dollars, without the emphasis, without the work to get them done.

JAMES GRAY: Even in states like California where we basically made under an ounce of marijuana for an adult be a citation with the maximum penalty of $100 fine, nevertheless we still have to process those marijuana seeds or whatever in order to determine that they're actually marijuana or whatever, so, again, the rape kits are not analyzed, and the marijuana and other drug violations are using our chemists all the time.

It just goes on and on. We've lost more of our civil liberties because of the War on Drugs than anything in the history of our country. Are we in better shape today because we lost those civil liberties? No, but it just continues to go forward.

Then you can ask the people in Mexico how many they've lost. You know better than I, 60,000 people in the last five years have died a violent death in Mexico not having anything to do whatsoever with drugs. It's all drug money that has caused those deaths and the corruption.

It just goes on and on in so many different areas. I say in front of rotary clubs and other groups, "You tell me any area of society, and I will show you how it is made worse because of our policy of drug prohibition. You can talk environment, education, health care—I don't care what you talk about, I will show to your satisfaction how this area is made worse because of this terribly failed and hopeless policy of drug prohibition that we have pursued basically since 1913."

DB: I read the *Houston Chronicle* a lot—home town paper. I see of late we've had several murders of people that were either growing pot or had a stash of pot in their house. The write up always says it was a drug-related shooting. The fact of the matter is somebody wasn't so high on marijuana that they killed this man. No, sir, this was a prohibition-related shooting.

JAMES GRAY: Precisely., I was in the Navy in Guam—a Navy JAG attorney in the early 1970s, and when I was there, they had headlines in the local paper showing that the first homicide since the second world war had occurred, and they were so concerned, "How could this happen on our wonderful island?!" and the rest of that. It turned out it was drug prohibition-related. It was drug money-related. By the time I left about two or something years later, we were having something like every month or two another homicide that was drug-related. It's the money. It's the just the drug money that is doing this.

You can look at high school kids; they are not selling Jim Beam bourbon to each other in their high school campuses, but they're selling methamphetamines, marijuana all the time because of the money. You do not see Mexican drug cartels raising illegal vineyards in our national forests in competition with Robert Mondavi. They could, but there's no money in it. It's the illegality that brings these things forward.

I tell a lot of high school/college students that prohibition is never as good as regulation and control. Prohibition simply doesn't work because as soon as you prohibit some of these substances you give up all of your controls completely to the bad guys. Quality control—huge issue—the bath tub gin problem went away when we repealed alcohol prohibition. Place of sale, pricing, age restriction—all of those are completely abandoned to the bad guys such that, Dean, the term "controlled substances" is the biggest oxymoron of our lives today because, once again, once you prohibit something you give up all of your controls to the illegal drug gangs and juvenile street gangs and the Mexican drug cartels. We couldn't design a worse policy if we tried.

DB: Exactly right. Judge, let me take a guess…when the violence started in the Philippines was it? '69/'70 was that about it?

JAMES GRAY: Yeah, it was in Guam and about early 1972.

DB: That's when it all started shifting here. I'm old enough to remember when you could legally…well, not legally but you could smoke pot near a cop in Houston, and they didn't care. It was when the "Nixononians" took hold.

JAMES GRAY: That was about 1971, Dean. Just around this same period of time. I'm just finishing writing a column for a local legal newspaper, and in that I say that in California, where I'm from, throughout our history until the year 1980 we had built 13 state prisons. Now we have 33.

So in that 33 years, we have built an additional 20 state prisons. It's enormously expensive. The United States leads the world in the incarceration of our people both by sheer numbers as well as per capita. Here, I assure you that "We're number one!" does not make me proud. So many of those are non-violent drug offenders, and a lot more of those are caused because of drug money.

It's just unbelievable the corruption, the violence we get involved with with drug money. Like you were saying earlier if I were growing marijuana or any other illegal deal or I were selling cocaine on the street corner and somebody were to rob me, I'm not going to call the police. I can't do that because it's illegal, so I start carrying guns to protect myself just like with alcohol prohibition.

Now if Coors has a distribution problem with Budweiser they don't take guns to the streets. They come to judges like me, and they adjudicate it peacefully. It's all connected.

I tell people and I mean it that drug prohibition is the biggest failed policy in the history of our country—second only to slavery. The closer you get to seeing it (as you know, my friend) it is when we finally repeal prohibition I guarantee that everybody within three or four years will link arms and look back and be aghast at how we could have perpetuated such a failed system for so long.

JUDGE MARIA LUCIA KARAM

Even in the earliest days of her career in criminal justice, as a public defender working in Rio de Janeiro in 1979, Maria Lucia Karam was interested in helping those whose criminality was a product not of malice but of being subject to adverse circumstances, with designs on doing what she could to break the vicious cycles in which many of the least fortunate in society get caught. By 1982 Maria had already become a judge, feeling that from the bench she would have more leverage to help her fellow Brazilians. She worked in the criminal courts for eight years, where she routinely cleared defendants of drug-possession charges on the grounds that laws criminalizing behavior that does not affect the rights and freedoms of others are unconstitutional. Century of Lies / August 15, 2010.

DB: The Drug War seems to have its focal point seems to move from Colombia to Mexico to Afghanistan to the United States, and just a month or so ago in Jamaica there was more than a hundred dead in a shoot out, but Rio has its problems as well. Do you want to tell us about the situation in Rio de Janeiro?

MARIA LUCIA KARAM: Over here, it is not as different as Mexico. Even if Mexico now is growing violent especially because of the last four years of intensification of the war on drugs there. In Brazil, you also have the serious consequences of this violence produced by prohibition. In Rio de Janeiro, for instance, we have an average of 3,000 deaths caused by murders through the years. In 2008, for instance, there were 2,757 murders, all in the city of Besame. One in every five of these murders were summary executions during police operations against drug dealers in the slums.

DB: The police would just kind of go out and find these drug dealers and take them out? Is that what you're saying?

MARIA LUCIA KARAM: Yes. Definitely, in Rio de Janeiro the drug dealers have their marginal lives and their territories. There's the slums, and the police go there in operations to combat them, to battle them. Many times they just kill them. There are summary executions. This is a war. It's not surprising. In a war, you have the drug prohibition brought to the criminal justice system, the idea of a war. Then the criminal became the enemy. The enemy is supposed to be eliminated. So, that's why the police in Rio is stimulated to kill.

DB: Now, here in the US, we don't have that many murders but we do have situations where the police kick in the door. They throw in a flash grenade. They point guns at the children. They shoot the dogs. They terrorize the home and on occasion, they do kill one of the children or the mother and father because of the heightened atmosphere. That they go in all excited thinking they are doing something important, when usually it's not that much drugs and it's not as dangerous a situation. The police have the upper hand and sometimes it's out of control.

MARIA LUCIA KARAM: Yes, the kings are out of control and it became a stimulation to act illegally. People, most people are proud of this violence and excess that the police make. This is also very bad for the police officers themselves. In Brazil, and I have also heard about that in Mexico, many people are more afraid of the police than of the drug dealers. The police should be respected, but people don't respect the police because the police don't respect people, especially in poor neighborhoods.

DB: A recent multi-decade review by the International Centre for Science in Drug Policy found that, when police crack down on drug users and dealers, the result is almost always an increase in violence

MARIA LUCIA KARAM: We can see that very clear, especially from the current situation in Mexico because at the end of 2006, President Calderón finally recognizes the failure of his strategies. But in late 2006, he lauded the special war against drugs there in Mexico. He sent the army, not only the police but the army. He sent more than 40,000 soldiers to battle with the cartels and after that, after four years offenses, more than 28,000 people were killed in Mexico. And it's for nothing. Because the the drug supply, the drug business goes on in Mexico. When there is an advance or a reduction in someplace, they just move to other places. This is also happening in Latin America where Colombia reduces their production but Peru increases their production. It's a business. It's life. There will be a demand and a supply

DISTRICT ATTORNEY PAT LYCOS

Patricia Lycos is the former District Attorney of Harris County, Texas (Houston) who held office one term and was replaced in 2012 by a zealous Republican who soon died and then this new DA's even more zealous wife was given the job. In Houston, the party never ends. Lycos took office when the former DA, Chuck

Rosenthal, resigned in response to a scandal involving his own drug addiction as well as racial and sexist messages and jokes found on his computers. Little wonder that Houston is still the "Gulag Filling Station of planet Earth." Cultural Baggage / January 22, 2012.

DB: Judge Lykos, do you think the application of the drug laws are applied fairly in our community?

PAT LYKOS: I think we have to work much more intelligently in combating the illicit drugs. What's happening now is that you have these transnational criminal organizations and they are extremely sophisticated. We're not approaching it by attacking their business model. We are not disrupting their command of control. We're not dismantling their supply routes and their retail outlets. I believe that the war has not been prosecuted correctly.

DB: Do you feel that over the last 5 or 10 years we've made any difference with the law enforcement, the criminal justice system—any real accomplishments in ending or correcting the Drug War?

PAT LYKOS: I think it's had some reduction, but I think it's been a misallocation of resources. I've implemented my trace policy and that is, for us to prosecute someone for possession, the minimum amount they must possess is 1/100th of a gram. That's 1/100th of a packet of say "Sweet n Low." That's the minimum amount that can be tested twice. That's a due process issue.

As a result of what we're doing, police officers no longer are taking two and three hours off the streets to book someone, charge them with the offense of possession. They are out there patrolling and preventing crime. What I want the officers to do is arrest the drug dealer and the person who supplied the drug dealer and the person who supplied him and work their way all the way up the chain and seize that bulk cash that's going south.

DB: Taking under consideration your stance in the regards to the less than 1/100th and the thought that it frees up law enforcement time that they're not spent booking and perhaps going to trial and all of these things...

PAT LYKOS: Well it's two things. One, it's justice because if it can't be tested twice it's not fair. The defense would not have an option. Secondly, it does free the officer up.

DB: Right. So they can attend to more violent crime or crimes of another nature. I wanted to extrapolate or think upon that that the same scenario could be found within writing tickets for less than four ounces of marijuana as the legislature and the Governor signed a law to do. That would free up the police to go after more dangerous criminals amongst us.

PAT LYKOS: We cannot implement that here in Harris County. Harris County, first of all, is the third largest county in the United States. Houston, of course, is the fourth largest city but we have 34 municipalities.

If some municipalities decide to write tickets and others don't, can you just see the mess that that would create and the disparity that there would be in enforcement? And if you cross the street you can get a ticket and if you're on the other side of the street, you get arrested. If the legislature wanted to do something, then they could change the law and make it universal.

DB: I'm wondering if there isn't a kind of awareness of many of these politicians that we put in office of that need for change but there seems to be a great deal of fear of touching that third rail.

PAT LYKOS: I think there certainly is posturing by some. I do think that the legislature is making a good faith effort to recognize all the dynamics involved. I can tell you that I'm the new chair of HIDTA. (See Furce, Stan) Our whole focus is going after the really bad guys and girls—the one's who are smuggling not just drugs but can be involved in human smuggling, extortion, kidnapping, assassinations and so forth. That's who we're going to focus on.

DB: HIDTA is High Intensity Drug Trafficking Area Group. And it involves kind of an association between various law enforcement, the DEA, and others, correct?

PAT LYKOS: Federal, state, and local law enforcement agencies, yes.

DB: I want to take out those high echelon guys just like you. Truthfully, those are the barbarians. They are the ultra-criminals living on this planet.

PAT LYKOS: The barbarism is just unbelievable when you see what they engage in—the torture and the mutilation of individuals and so forth. It's indescribable. It is such evil that the mind can't comprehend it. Also these people are financing terrorism. They're financing Al Qaeda. They're narco-terrorist. They are taking over entire governments. Do you know what the murder rate in Honduras is now? It's 82 per 100,000 because it's a corridor for smuggling. And there's 8 million people in that country. Los Angeles County, which has 10 million people, their murder rate is 7 per 100,000. It shows you the evil and the tragedy that results from the illicit drug trade.

DB: Do you feel we need to at least reexamine this policy and perhaps make some changes to our drug laws?

PAT LYKOS: I think we need to reexamine our strategy but, Dean, let me pose a question to you, alright? You know what pharmaceutical diversion is.

DB: Oh yes.

PAT LYKOS: OK. These are legal drugs and yet people are going in there and physicians, pharmacists and others and diverting these drugs and selling them in the underground. I mean we are the hub for the transshipment of pharmaceuticals, OK? We even have a name called the Houston Cocktail which is Vicodin, Soma and Xanax. Legalization is not the answer. Why do people want to poison themselves? Isn't life itself a high?!

DB: I would agree that it's driving itself off the cliff—this situation. I agree with you 100% but I don't think that more people in jail is going to be the solution. More education, more treatment but the fact of the matter is that despite

100 years or 40 years since Nixon declared the Drug War—drugs are cheaper, they're purer, they're more freely available to our children than ever before. So therefore I don't feel that prohibition is the answer.

PAT LYKOS: Well, what's happening now in Los Angeles County is the cartels are moving in on so-called legal purveyors of marijuana. I agree with you that we need certainly more treatment and certainly more education, more public service announcements. The way I was reared it just isn't done. That's all. Period. No matter how much you're tempted, we do not do that. So if we could impose more social control that way…those are the strongest anyway.

DB: The Drug Czar and his minions go around the country talking about the need for more treatment, more education but the fact of the matter is the Drug War rolls on—still arresting 1.6 million basically young people and basically of color for minor amounts of drugs. Your response.

PAT LYKOS: Well that's one of the benefits of my trace policy. Believe it or not that's a state jail felony. A first time burglar of a motor vehicle is a misdemeanor offense so these people who have a trace (not a useable amount—less than 1/100th of a gram) were being prosecuted for a state jail felony. I agree with you that that is inequitable but, again, because it's a due process and a fairness issue—I have to have an amount that's useable. Substance abuse, and that includes alcohol, is involved in 50—80% of the child welfare caseload. As a society we have to do something about that.

DB: The fact of the matter is 5 out of 6 of those abusive situations deal with alcohol and not hard drugs.

PAT LYKOS: How do you propose to distribute drugs? If you could wave a magic wand and legalize—what would you legalize?

DB: For the hard drugs go through a doctor. The doctor would educate you on how to use them properly. How not to kill yourself and get some sort of maybe a stamp on your driver's license that says you're authorized. As far as marijuana or the softer drugs—adults only and anybody selling drugs to our kids—lock them up.

PAT LYKOS: Who's going to produce these drugs, and who's going to sell the drugs?

DB: I would prefer Merck and Pfizer make them and so far as marijuana just the good name of the grower.

PAT LYKOS: But you see the problem we have with pharmaceutical diversion, and these are legal drugs. Can you imagine what legalization would do?!

EUGENE OSCAPELLA

Eugene Oscapella is a Canadian attorney who specializes in research about legislative, trade, and social policy developments in Canada. For more than a quarter century he has produced research and policy advice on issues including privacy, human rights, drug policy, medical-legal subjects, defense, intelligence, national security and criminal justice matters. Century of Lies June 7, 2009.

EUGENE OSCAPELLA: I've worked for over twenty years on Drug Policy Reform issues. I teach drug policy at the Department of Criminology at the University of Ottawa here, as well and I've been pressing for a long time for a move away from using the Criminal Justice System to deal with drugs, to treat it more as a health and a social issue.

DB: Canada is trying to follow, it seems like, in the footsteps of the US 'Draconian' drug war. Are they going to get there?

EUGENE OSCAPELLA: Well, It's a very scary time right now. Because a bill was introduced in Canada's Parliament a few months ago that was going to introduce mandatory minimum penalties, just at a time when the Rockefeller Drug Laws are being abandoned or greatly changed and moving away from mandatory minimum penalties, in many American jurisdictions. The Canadian government is moving towards mandatory minimum penalties for drug offences here, and in Canada the legal system's a little bit different. Our drug law's are all federal, so we have one federal drug law. So, if the federal government introduces mandatory minimum penalties, it applies right across the country. So there's no escaping it. We're just very afraid that we're going to go in that direction. We've watched in the United States how badly mandatory minimum penalties have failed, and yet, for some reason, Canada wants to do the same thing, and the one political party that could put a stop to this, is sort of cowering in the corner, afraid of arousing any public angst about it. They're so concerned about getting re-elected that they don't want to do anything that could receive any sort of criticism.

DB:That's kind of the way it works everywhere though.

EUGENE OSCAPELLA: Yes, yes. Politician's cower in the corner. They're supposed to lead, not cower. But, unfortunately, they cower more often than they lead sometimes.

DB: Canada's backsliding into our abyss. That's scary.

EUGENE OSCAPELLA: Yeah. Well, we seem to make the same mistakes, only we do them about five years later so, there's just a bit of a time lag and so, that's the scary thing right now. There's a chance that some of these laws will be declared unconstitutional, but only a chance. That's the problem.

DB: A week or two ago I had David Rosenbloom, the new head of CASA— the Council on Alcoholism and Substance Abuse and I tried to ask him if they ever considered 'the cut'; the contaminates that are put into these 'street' recreational drugs. The Levamisole—which is a de-wormer for animals—that is used in about one third of the cocaine here in the US, and it actually destroys a persons immune system. I asked him, 'Did they ever take into consideration the contaminates that are put into these so-called recreational drugs?' and he said, "Oh, it doesn't matter either way. They're both bad for you."

EUGENE OSCAPELLA: I think I would disagree very, very strongly with him. Some of your listeners will remember, I think it was the 1970's, the US government was helping to spray Paraquat on Mexican cannabis fields and that ended up causing tremendous harm to people who bought the cannabis. Because, of course, the people who were selling it didn't care and Paraquat is a very dangerous substance when it's ingested.

The contaminates that are associated with these drugs are terrible. Look at all the quality control's we have on other normal consumer products in society. We have them, because we know the dangers of getting adulterated products. Why is there no concern about adulterated drugs?

Essentially what it is, that to me, is an attitude that says that, 'Look, they're drug users. We don't really care what happens to them,' and there's this mythology around the notion that the drug itself is so terrible. In fact it's quite often, as you point out, the contaminates that cause much of the harm and, of course, you don't know the potency of the dosage you're getting in a situation like that. So, the total absence of quality control is extremely dangerous.

DB:A word I use about that stance taken to drug users is that, they're unconditionally exterminable,...

EUGENE OSCAPELLA: Yes.

DB:...because well, if he died in a ditch, he's better off than using.

EUGENE OSCAPELLA: They're expendable people. They don't figure as members of society. That is the attitude of too many people who look at drug users and that's an attitude that we've been trying to change for decades now. Because these people are human beings and some of them have problems with drug dependencies, there's no doubt about that. It's pretty hard to find a human being who doesn't have a problem of some kind and I think we need to exercise the same sort of compassion about people who have drug problems as we do for compassion as we do for people who have other sorts of problems in their lives. But that's part of the fear mongering that goes along with attempts to stop the legitimate, sort of medicinal uses of some substances too.

DB: I often hope or just wish that we could bring your Parliamentarians to Houston and let them see what the world's leading jailer looks like. Let them take a look though our jails. Let them visit our prisons. Let them go to the nearby states where we house the rest of our prisoners because we don't have enough prison beds to hold them all, and let them look at the reason's why. It's for minor amounts of marijuana and microscopic amounts of hard drugs.

Our moral 'benchmark' is broken. Just this past week, it was discovered by the Federal Government that our jails are unconstitutional. Depriving people of their rights, medical attention and all of these things, because we can't keep up because we have so many thousands of people in jail and in prison, for basically nothing; for minor amounts of drugs. I only wish they can come down here and see what they're envisioning.

EUGENE OSCAPELLA: I wish they could too, because we've been watching this for years, from Canada and I'm watching us go in the same direction. Unfortunately, some politicians, they're so ideologically 'hide bound' by their thinking that nothing is going to change the way they think. I think some of them, when they realize what's going on, if they could see that, it might help. But there are others who it doesn't matter.

These guys have a 'bent' on punishment. It's almost what I would consider an authoritarian instinct, to punish; to control other people and the fact that people suffer because of it, is irrelevant to them. I hate to have to say this, because that's not the sort of leaders I want in my country. That's not the sort of democratic representatives I want, but some of these people with this very, very, I call it the weak conservative 'bent' here meaning conservative in the sense of controlling, in the way that we would use it in this country. They frighten me, because I don't think they can be persuaded by the facts

JUDGE ELEANOR SCHOCKETT

Another favorite LEAP speaker on the Drug Truth Network was Judge Elanoer Schockett who passed from this earth in 2008.   This was recorded just weeks before her passing. Cultural Baggage, January 16, 2008.

ELEANOR SCHOCKETT: If you want to get rid of cases you plea bargain. But that doesn't mean that people are going to get justice. Forget it. There is no such thing as justice. I'm sorry that I ever used the term. You tell somebody "if you want to get out of jail, sign this piece of paper." If you don't want to get out of jail right now, if you're sure you're innocent and you want to plead innocent, well you can stay here another six months or a year before we'll get around to trying you. Now, is something wrong with that folks? I think there is.

Are you a better or more efficient judge because you coerce people in taking pleas? I've actually tried to talk people out a plea, and I would say to them "this plea is a trap." They know you can't make probation. They probably also know that they're not going to be able to convict you. Because they don't have time to convict you, they don't have the money to bring the policeman in, whatever, they just want you out of their way. And they don't have to worry, because you will plea, and you'll violate your probation because most of the time you're homeless, and you can't live up to the criteria, and the probationary requirements generally are so ridiculous that nobody can survive them.

You have to use triage in the justice, don't call it justice, in the judicial system just the way you do in a hospital. There are only so many patients you're going to be able to take into an emergency room. You have to take the most important. And they're not willing to take the most important.

They are looking for statistics, they want to see how many cases they can get off the books and off the streets in a hurry. The policemen want to make a lot of arrests because it helps their statistics with the legislature. The prosecutor wants to make the policemen look good. And this is the way they do it.

It was when I was in criminal court that I saw how bad it was. And I related it back, things had only gotten worse. They hadn't gotten better. The statistics have gotten worse. It was cheaper to get drugs, more people were getting killed on the street. What have we been doing in all these fifty years? What was the benefit? I couldn't see it.

I used to say there were people in my own motions calendar, I am going to, my new life's work is going to be drug reform. I can't stand this anymore. We need to do something to help people, not to hurt them. And I'm seeing the politics, the dirty under side of all of this.

So, that's how you found me here today. Because, fortunately for me, when I retired from the bench I went online to try to find an organization. And I couldn't find one that was for me because I don't use, I don't drink, I don't have friends or relatives or family that are in prison because of the unfair laws. None of these applied to me.

But then the president of one of the Florida organizations put me in touch with Jack Cole, and that was a marriage made in heaven. He invited me up to the DPA conference in New Jersey at the time, and we've been working together ever since. And this is what we need to do. My patience with stupidity has run very thin. I'm tired of people pretending that they're being tough on crime, they don't need to be tough on crime, they need to be smart on crime. You don't have wars internally. So don't tell me this is a war on drugs, because it's a war on people. Its not a war on drugs. And why? They don't really even know.

I've talked to an awful lot of prison officials, and what every single one of them tells me is that you cannot take drugs out of a maximum security prison. And I ask you, if you can't take it out of a maximum security prison, how are you going to take it out of a grammar school or a high school? You're not.

TONY SERRA

Tony Serra is a renown San Francisco attorney and civil rights activist who was the subject of the 1989 movie *True Believer*. Century of Lies April 13, 2007.

DB: Tony Serra is a very busy fellow. He just got out of the federal pen for the second time. If you will, Tony, for our listeners out there who don't know about your career tell about your time as an attorney.

TONY SERRA: I'm the "last of the Mohicans" and that means that I started in the mid-60s in San Francisco. I'm local to San Francisco. I went to both UC Berkeley for law school and undergraduate to Stanford. I started in the era of mass protests, demonstrations firstly centered around the Vietnam War and then became more expansive. I represent all the so-called radical groups in the 60s. That's when I first started. I always, in retrospect, say that was the golden age in the practice of criminal defense because the Constitution was alive and well. The judges were anxious, really, to suppress evidence if there was a bad search. Jurors were anxious to acquit if there was reasonable doubt. Law enforcement at that time hadn't the swollen strength and the aggressiveness that they have presently. The Constitution was strong so it was a wonderful way to start.

I represented Black Panthers and White Panthers. I represented SLA. I represented leaders of a number of prison groups. I represented the World Liberation Front. I later represented the Hells Angels and their large RICO prosecution. I did very well. I was a back-to-back trial specialist. and I certainly won more than I lost. I kind of achieved a name for myself as a radical lawyer. I've been now practicing for 44 years. I've continued to try to have as many politically orientated cases as I can. I still do back-to-back jury trials.

I have become in the last 20 years a medical marijuana activist. I started prior to the passage of so-called Prop 215 in California. which was the medical marijuana allowance. I've gone on circuit and talked about medical marijuana. Gone on circuit and talked about the diminishment of constitutional rights throughout the country and the burgeoning strength of the prosecution and the burgeoning strength of law enforcement.

I'm anti-government informant which I think has polluted the integrity of the judicial system. I'm, on occasion, what they call an "anti-lawyer lawyer." I'm a person who has been a tax resister for 44 years. I just recently did 10 months in Lompoc prison—the camp facility which is very benign. These are only misdemeanor convictions—not moral turpitude—so, although I get suspended for a short period of time, I'm fully licensed and restored to my status quo ante which is that I vigorously pursue justice through the justice system.,

When I got out, I carried with me the image of the prison industry which, from my perspective and the perspective of the inmates, is very oppressive and very exploitative. People in camps are deemed to be non-violent (federal camps I'm talking about) and deemed to be non-escapists and, therefore, really should be allowed home. There's no parole in the federal system now but still they should be allowed out. Instead they're placed in the camps where they are forced to work for prison industries and many times exposed to toxic elements, industrial type accidents. They are weary. They work hard. They are dirty at the end of the day. Their clothes, you know, are soiled.

I saw that and then I saw, through research, that in the prison industry—UNI-CORE as it is called—there is about 80 different types of work that are performed, different factories, different service industries...like down in Lompoc camp there is a dairy industry and a cable factory, and they are forced to work there. That's why these camps exist.

It's a form of in-sourcing because they pay pennies. They pay anywhere from 5 cents an hour to about a buck sixty-five. I got 19 cents an hour, and they are making millions—profiteering off of the slave labor, involuntary servitude (from my perspective) that they enforce on the inmates in these camps.

For instance, in 2005 they report approximately $165 million gross—that's national. There's about 65 different industries, private, that contract with the Bureau of Prisons, and they exist in the camps throughout the country. So they reported $165 million gross and they claim $65 million net. From my perspective, part of the component of this large profiteering is the low amount of money that they pay the inmates.

So as soon as I got out, I brought as plaintiff not as a lawyer but as a plaintiff, as an ex-inmate at a camp facility, I brought a class action against the Bureau of Prisons and prison industries to force them to pay the inmate laborers a minimum wage. Minimum wage, as you know, is for the most part 5 dollars and I think a quarter per hour. Out here in California, it's much higher. In San Francisco, it's much higher and probably varies from state to state, but nonetheless it's still peanuts, but they still will make their millions. This would be a great benefit to the inmates who are forced into this involuntary servitude because they would have money to send home. They would have pride. They would have self-respect. They could support their children. They could save a little bit so it would ease the transition when they are ultimately discharged.

It wouldn't hurt one bit to dignify the working class. But understand the prison industries and Bureau of Prisons have no interest, no incentive, to seek rehabilitation, to seek job training, to seek education. They pride themself in some sadistic way in the statistic that 60 to 70% of these federal inmates will be recidivistic. It's almost like they encourage recidivism by not training, by not giving them self-respect, by not encouraging work ethic by payment.

Prisoners have such a small degree of due process afforded to them. I anticipate it will be thrown out. They are fearful that if we ever get to a jury, we would really make an impact because juries would sympathize with the human plight, and, if not, they would see that these forms of monopolistic Bureau of Prisons industrial activity deprive the working class and the unions of contracts of work and money, so the middle class and upper-lower class suffer as a consequence.

From many perspectives it's a good thing, and a jury would reward us, but I have a hunch it will be dismissed, and we'll be up on appeal. We want to illuminate this condition. It's becoming more and more present. As we inhibit the ability to have migrant workers from Mexico, many states are trying to use inmate labor. Some will pay minimum wage, and others won't. I'm talking about some get 2 cents an hour working in state facilities.

It is a dirty little secret that the prison industries and the Bureau of Prisons and some of the states seek to hide that they are profiteering, they are capitalizing, they are exploiting prison labor.

The announced objective of the federal system...they presently statistically claim they use 17% of the prison population in prison industries and they want to use 25%. After they get 25%, they'll want to use 50%. Then they will convert ultimately the inmate population into slave labor category and make millions.

There's no real reason not to, and the far cry from the right is, "They're prisoners. This is part of the punishment. What do you expect?"

But that's not the law. The law is, the punishment is what is meted out by the judge. The punishment is being incarcerated. The punishment is being exiled. The punishment is isolation and deprivation of social contact with friends and loved ones and family. You're not put into prison so that the prison guards punish you. That, you know, is something that no sophisticated, no civilized country has ever done in present time. We're kind of carrying that torch outside of prison but in order to reform prison.

It's sad, but the prison inmates are not in a position really to militate against this inequity because should they do that they would be thrown back into the hard concrete and steel facility, so they kind of take it. They universally disdain it. They don't want to work for nothing, and they don't want to bare the prospect of injury and toxic whatever damage to their system, but it's better than being in the hard jail, the hard prison behind bars, and so they have to kind of just accept it as victims, oppressed victims at every level have to.

It is something that you can only bring from the outside, so it's kind of one of the things I'm proud of bringing from my very easy prison experience. I'm old now. I'm 72, so I didn't have to do hard labor, but I watered the grounds and attended the plants and the flowers and the trees. It was kind of relaxing in a way. Lompoc camp is very esthetic. There's woods, trees and fields and meadows that surround it, so it was a benign experience for me, but I went to the verge. I looked in. It's like looking in at the first circle of "Dante's Inferno" and you can see how bad it gets as it proceeds into the more darker regions of prison.

Lots of reform is necessary. I wrote an article for the California State Bar that they solicited about prison reform—things like no parole, no conjugal furloughs, and medical services being wholly inadequate, the law library kind of like being a sick joke, the camp being infested with informants, the brutality and sadism of the administrators and the guards. All of these kinds of things I gave protest to.

I often remark that being in prison for me was like a doctor being locked up in a hospital because they use my people, and I respect their plight, and I respect their being psychologically damaged forever. Their sentences, in general at the federal level, are what they call draconian—young people going in for 10, 15, 20 years, drug offenses being the most flagrant of these long sentences. People's lives taken from them, people being kicked out of the gene pool and left to be withered and warehoused in prison conditions.

It's, as I said before, kind of like a dirty little secret that our prisons domestically kind of metaphorically are the same as what we have been doing and what they have been uncovering in terms of what we did in Iraq. America is going along. Prisons are part of the wrong that ended the strengths of the Constitution.

So there is a lot out there. I tell young lawyers nowadays, "My God, in the sixties there were all these clauses, and you could be idealistic and proud of your work, and it becomes a calling, and it has political and even spiritual overtures to it." Even now—this is true now more than ever—we need young, idealistic lawyers to go out there and fight the oppressive government, to fight the evils of the prison system, to fight for mental integrity, to fight against racism and sexism. There is a lot of good, idealistic work for young lawyers. I'm about at an age where I'm going to pass the baton in about 10 years so I'm hopeful. I see in San Francisco a lot of them. We see in the urban areas of San Francisco and New York City and Los Angeles and Miami. I've encountered them more in the urban than in the rural areas. I think there's still a lot of hope that the pendulum will swing back.

DB: You mentioned about the slave wages, basically pennies an hour, if I dare say my experience talking to people at the Harris County Jail what little monies they have they use to buy a jar of peanut butter or something to that effect.

TONY SERRA: Exactly the same. They are not paid enough to save or to send home money and really to dignify their labor, so it's all expended in the commissary, and the commissary is another device for the prisons to make money. You don't get anything cheap in the goddamn commissary. Just what you said, people supplement their diet so you can get some good things, and peanut butter is one that is purchased a lot. There's vitamins you can buy in the federal system.

Too often the inmates crave the things they miss most in their imagination, and so they'll buy sweets like candies and cookies and stuff like that, so it's kind of like taking your pennies to buy necessities and the indulgences are a peanut butter or can of sardines along with sweets, so they get back every goddamn cent that they give out. They give out pennies, and they take out pennies, and the money goes directly into the commissary. You never see a dollar.

DB: And the same holds true with, at least here in Houston, with the the phone companies charging inordinate amount for a phone call.

TONY SERRA: You're right. They rip off the inmates left and right. We have to put money on the telephone account so you have money sent in. It goes to your commissary account, and then it can be funneled over to the telephone account but it's a huge expense. You're cut off, so they only give you calls (at least at Lompoc camp) that are 15 minutes in duration, and then they cut you off and you can't call immediately thereafter. There's a wait period. I guess that's one way of monitoring the expense.

I do agree with you that probably it's the prison putting the surcharge on what the telephone companies charge, so probably they're making money on it. What is even worse and sicker than that is every single phone call that goes out of the facility at Lompoc camp is recorded and the administration has immediate access to it. A lot of times they'll bring inmates in and they'll say, "You were swearing over the phone." Or "You were treating you wife poorly." They'll castigate them after listening to the conversation, so you just have that feeling that big brother is everywhere, and there's utterly no privacy.

We don't expect Fourth Amendment in prison, but we expect to be treated humanely. It's just not true. They go through your lockers periodically in your absence, and they look in all the mail that comes in and all the mail that goes out. You are not treated with any civility. You are not a human being. You are an automaton to them. Your life is programmed.

The routine and the conformity are the attributes of prison life, and that ultimately destroys the best part of people—your emotions, your softer feelings, your feelings for love, your feelings for empathy with common people is all destroyed because you have to be hard and brittle on the outside to resist the tedium of the conformity. Then, with time, the inside goes also, and you see long-termers who have lost an awful lot of their humanism and emotional life. They have few words and few feelings for esthetics or love or things like literature and poetry. It's very sad. It's a dehumanizing procedure with draconian sentences. The feds aren't dealing with homicides very often—1 out of 10,000 is a homicide—so there's no reason why any federal crime should not have just a top of 10 years for everyone. They're putting these people in for 20s and 30s and 40s and I'm talking literal—20, 30, 40 years. Some of these sentences are for dope cases and these large conspiracies that they concoct out of dope cases. It's just ridiculous.

You know how large a percent of minorities are there. They prey on minorities. A lot of crimes are crimes that arise out of privation and deprivation, economic stresses. They take these people as a consequence when they were just really struggling to survive. These large sentences are just not fair, and no civilized country should have them.

DB: You were talking about the need for these young attorneys to embrace the need for standing up for the truth, for embracing the Constitution, for helping to re-instill that spirit in America but the voters out there need to step up, need to quash this fear which is disseminated by the government everywhere you look. They need to stand up and make their difference as well. Do they not?

TONY SERRA: I'm a jury trial specialist so what I see that has eroded since 9/11 is that the jurors are completely pro-law enforcement and pro-prosecution because they are in a state of fear and trembling. They are in a state where they believe they are in imminent peril. They think terrorists lurk everywhere. The police state, the "KGB-ing" of America, is predicated on manipulating their fears.

They're voting things in like death penalty, things like three strikes. They're voting things in like no parole. It's all based on the fear factor that the government manipulates and exasperates. It's the sad demise of our Constitutional rights because the citizenry will give up the Constitutional rights, "Well, I don't have drugs in my house so therefore the Fourth Amendment exclusionary rule shouldn't really be actionalized."

Well, you find out when your 4th Amendment goes or your 1st Amendment goes or your 5th Amendment goes, and mind you they are evaporating right in our faces—you never get them back. That is, what is taken is never given back. It only goes harsher.

You ought to see some of these white collar criminals in the camp that I've seen—business people who enjoyed material wealth and prosperity and, in their minds, because of technicalities that should have been civil they find themselves in prison, felons doing 5 or 6 years. They are so enlightened. They become politicized. They never knew their government was corrupt. They never knew their government was oppressive. They never could believe that law officers would lie. They never believed that the informant system lacks credibility and the white collar persons' establishment in prison becomes the most vociferous voice for reform.

That's the way totalitarianism works. First you attack a class that is vulnerable. The inmate class is a victim class in our culture, and you can attack that with impunity. Then it spreads from there to criminal prosecutions. It spreads from criminal prosecutions to what used to be civil matters, and ultimately your relative, your child, your loved one will be incarcerated.

In this country, the statistics show one out of five is going to be incarcerated—the hugest amount of prisoners in any civilized country, so it's not a good thing, and the citizenry has to wake up. The ordinary person who is not touched by criminal law and is beholden to law enforcement has to take another look at what they are doing by their silence.

There was a time in this country that wherever there was inequity and reform was needed, there would be a rush from all strata to try to change it, to better it. Moral rights for more people, more distribution of wealth—these were creeds that I grew up on. Now it's just the opposite. The rich are getting richer, and the poor are getting poorer. The middle class is shrinking. Constitutional rights are evaporating. The government is so strong; the Executive has never been stronger in the history of our country. The judicial process has been swallowed up by the legislative process. There's an awful lot of change needed. Without the citizens being enlightened, nothing is going to change—it will only get worse.

LAW ENFORCEMENT AGAINST PROHIBITION

"Kicking in the door, kicking in the door. We shall bring
salvation, kicking in the door."
—DTN bumper (to the tune of "Bringing in the Sheaves")

I am a former policeman. I worked for the US government guarding nuclear weapons. I strapped on a gun, pinned on the badge, and swore to uphold the US Constitution. I'm still trying to uphold the Constitution. So, just what is Law Enforcement Against Prohibition? We are current and former police officers, police chiefs, wardens, prosecutors, judges, a few senators, members of the European parliament, and many high-echelon politicians, including the former attorney general of Colombia.

What is the objective of LEAP? We want to curtail death, disease, crime, and addiction. Complications, spin off, blowback that are higher not because drugs exist but because drug prohibition exists. Prohibition creates all these problems then people in authority—the DA who wants to build a bigger jail, the congressman who wants to build more prisons—use prohibition's blowback as justification for more drug war.

Over the lifetime of this drug war, we have given well over one trillion dollars to law enforcement in the name of stopping the flow of drugs, protecting little Johnny, and keeping our neighborhoods safe. Yet the problems have gotten worse and worse and worse.

Through this drug war, we have created the reason for which most of these violent street gangs exist. It's the reason children have access. It's the problem itself, but law enforcement and prosecutors use this situation to justify asking for more money. Whether they succeed or whether they fail, they always need more money. A lot of damn money wasted that could be building our infrastructure, that could be going to schools, that could be funding health services for the people of this nation.

Public safety is jeopardized by the drug war because we mandate that our law enforcement community focus their attentions on drug users, sellers, and traffickers. We waste millions of man-years looking under car seats, under dashboards, and in trunks, searching for the motherlode of dope that brings a rise in rank, a fatter paycheck, and department stature to an otherwise thoroughly distracted policeman. End the drug war, and law enforcement can go back to doing what it does best: protecting our communities from those who would do us harm.

PETER CHRIST

In 2002, Peter Christ, a former police Captain, founded Law Enforcement Against Prohibition (LEAP), a drug policy reform group of current and former members of law enforcement modeled on Vietnam Veterans Against the War. Christ has spoken before hundreds of civic, professional, educational, and religious organizations, plus television and radio interviews in dozens of markets. This is from November 3, 2013.

DB: Where are we headed, what's going on at this drug policy conference?

PETER CHRIST: I've been coming to these conferences since 1990 so I've seen a lot of things happening. There's a lot of people who are very excited about the cannabis issue which is not really a LEAP issue. There are successes. People are feeling energized. You can see that. They are feeling changes coming, so I think it's empowering a lot of people.

It's, again, not changing my argument; in fact, I often like to say my big fear is that if we legalize cannabis, if the government takes cannabis off of Schedule I tomorrow and moves it to Schedule II, two years from now we're at the next DPA conference we're going to have far fewer people here because the marijuana people aren't going to be here.

Then in our country we're going to go through about a two-year lull and then we're going to start hearing this, "Wait a minute. You said that if we legalized this stuff the violence would end but we still got the gangs, we still got the cartels, we still got the violence." Then we're going to have to regenerate the discussion all over again and get back to the policy of prohibition and that is where the fault of our system is.

It's not in marijuana prohibition or even drug prohibition. It's when you send armed law enforcement into the streets to enforce one group of peoples' impression of morality that is not a function of law enforcement. That is a function of church, education, and health care and the family. It is not a criminal justice function. This whole type of policy, no matter what it is whether it's drugs, gambling...we used to arrest people for being gay in America. That's another morality law. That is not function of law enforcement.

There's a guy by the name of Robert Peel. Lord Robert Peel created the London police department back in the early 1800s and that was a model for all the police departments in the free world that we use today. When he set that up he said in his writings that he wanted to put a group of people in the community that would protect people from each other not from their own moral indiscretions. That is what we are supposed to do and that is what we need to return to doing.

DB: There are many, many instances of corruption in border patrol, law enforcement, any and everywhere the oversight is supposed to protect us, where it has actually fallen into the hands of criminality, where too often cops become the criminals. You and I, with law enforcement experience, cringe at that thought that our profession has been stained by this situation.

PETER CHRIST: Absolutely. In fact it's interesting. I have never heard of a case of police corruption that the cop who was paid off was paid off by the local rapist or the cop was paid off by the local bank robber or the local house burglar. It's always these consensual crimes—prostitution, gambling, drugs.

There was a drug bust in the late 1960s in New York City—a huge drug bust. In fact it was such a big deal that they made two movies out of it. One was called "The French Connection," and the other one was called "Panic in Needle Park." That movie was about the shortage that was on the streets of New York for about a month and a half of heroin because of this huge drug bust. That huge drug bust was 9 pounds of heroin—9 pounds of heroin. Now the reason I make a point of that is we are seizing these drugs now by the ton, and there's never a panic in needle park. There's never a shortage on the street. That's where we have come from the late 1960s trying to follow this policy.

It is simply dysfunctional. It does not work. In fact I talked to my harm reduction friends in this movement and I often say to them if you're honestly going to talk about harm reduction the first thing you should talk about is the harm that the policy of prohibition is causing because most of the problems we have are caused by the policy of prohibition not by the drugs. So let's get the cops out of that.

I don't think we'll ever be loved as much as we love firefighters, but if we go out there and all we're doing is protecting people from other people doing them harm, I think people will actually start to like us a little bit.

JACK COLE

Jack Cole, a retired Lieutenant from the New Jersey State Police, was my first interview with a LEAP speaker. First broadcast November 25, 2003.

JACK COLE: Our organization is Law Enforcement Against Prohibition or LEAP. It was created to give voice to all the current and former members of law enforcement who feel like the War on Drugs is a dismal, abject failure and who would want to support alternative policies, policies that will do four things; lower the incidence of deaths, disease, crime and addiction by ultimately ending prohibition.

DB: When you and I first met I kind of showed a little bit of incrementalism—one that talked more about medical marijuana, perhaps, but you guys are for ending prohibition outright. Is that correct?

JACK COLE: Outright, yes. That can only mean one thing. It means legalizing all drugs—legalizing them so we can control and regulate them and keep them out of the hands of our children—something that the War on Drugs has been incapable of doing for 33 years at the cost of one-half of a trillion dollars. [We're now over 40 years and a trillion dollars.]

DB: You gave me a bumper sticker a little earlier that said, "Drugs are too dangerous to leave in the hands of criminals."

JACK COLE: That's exactly what our thought is. Drugs are too dangerous to leave in the hands of criminals and right now they are in the hands of criminals. At LEAP we feel there are only 3 possible models of who can control and regulate drugs in the United States. There's a government model. There's a free market model, and there's the Al Capone model. It's been the Al Capone model that we've been using for 33 years. The Al Capone model is basically donate 400 billion dollars a year to your local gangster, murderer and terrorists because that's how much money is spent in the world on illicit drugs—400 billion dollars a year.

DB: Yes, sir and the government is now trying to draw some sort of involvement if you use drugs you support terrorism but is it not the policy itself that lends support to the terrorist?

JACK COLE: That's exactly what it is—certainly. They would like you to believe that it's some little kid who smokes a joint is supporting terrorism but the true people who knowingly or unknowingly are, in my estimation, supporting terrorism are the people who either pass the legislation or vote for the legislation that keeps the War on Drugs continuing as it is. If we ended the War on Drugs today and legalized all drugs there wouldn't be a terrorist in the world who would make a single penny on them.

DB: I heard an earlier discussion of yours and you talked about in the early days as the War on Drugs was ramping itself into full existence that there was some fudging of data, etc. that you guys did.

JACK COLE: I like that, Dean—fudging of data. What we did basically is we lied about everything. The War on Drugs was a lie to begin with. It was created in 1968—coined and created by Richard Milhous Nixon. It had almost nothing to do with drugs. It was created in order to garner votes for him to run for the presidency because he felt that if he were running as a strong, anti-crime person that would get him a lot of votes but if he could be in charge of a war and it worked, of course, as we all know he was elected. In his first year in office he managed to get congress to pass massive funding bills to give tremendous amounts of money to any police department willing to hire officers to fight his War on Drugs.

To give you a slight idea of how massive these were, the New Jersey State Police at the time had 1,700 people in their organization. We had a 7 man narcotics unit when I went in in 1964. In 1970 when I went into narcotics myself I went in with a whole lot of people because in October 1970 we went from a 7 man unit to a 76 person bureau—overnight, one step—and it was all done on federal tax dollar. Not a single penny came out of local or state government which meant tremendous amounts of money and power going into the administrators of these police departments.

DB: It is kind of mind boggling the amount of money that through the decades that we have spent on this—not just given to the drug lords (as you said earlier) but that we have spent giving to law enforcement.

JACK COLE: We need to follow that thread if I may. Due to that fact when we hit the streets we were trained for 2 weeks and then they designated one-third of the 76 of us as undercover agents, and I happened to fall into that. That's where I spent most of the next 14 years of my life.

When we hit the streets we were supposed to arrest people for selling drugs. That's what we were out there for. That was a very hard job in 1970 for a couple reasons. First reason was we had no idea how to fight a war on drugs and neither did our bosses, but our bosses did know one thing—they knew how to keep milking this federal cash cow in their own barnyard because now that they had hired 76 people they had to pay them every year forever. Since this was all federal money they had to show how this war was absolutely necessary in order to keep this money coming in.

Let me tell you what the War on Drugs was like in 1970. We didn't have much of a drug problem at all in 1970. It was more a nuisance, really, than anything else. Certainly nothing that I think should have had police intervention let alone a War on Drugs. I was thinking about it today and what I mean by that is, for instance, deaths caused by the drug culture. In 1970 you were less likely to die as a result of the drug culture in this country than you were to die from falling down your own steps in your own house. Less likely to die of the drug culture than you would choking on your own food at dinner. As far as I know we haven't started a war on stairways or dinner, yet but, who knows?! We still have time.

This wasn't really much of a problem but it was a problem to us because when we hit the streets there weren't a whole lot of drug dealers out there. The drugs that were out there were almost entirely what we called "soft drugs"—marijuana, hashish, LSD, psilocybin—that type of thing. Hard drugs like methamphetamine, cocaine, heroin were practically non-existent in 1970—certainly non-existent compared to what they are today. So this caused us quite a dilemma. How are we going to show that this war is an absolute necessity so our bosses can keep this money coming in?

Our bosses had the answer to that—as you say, they said fudge a little. They said maybe we can inflate these statistics a little. They gave us every go ahead to lie and lie we did. We lied about everything we did in the first year. We inflated everything we did. Let me explain how we did that. First we were looking for drug dealers and since we couldn't just find a whole lot of drug dealers what we did is send our undercover people in to infiltrate small groups—friendship groups—10 to 15 people maybe in college or high school kids or kids in between. Back then we had a lot of hippies around and they were all using soft drugs. They were also doing something that the administration didn't like at all—they were protesting the Viet Nam war. We could pretty much do what we wanted to with those folks. What we did is infiltrate those groups.

I remember one of the first ones that I infiltrated and everybody was doing this. I was working about 30 miles outside of Manhattan. Back then Manhattan was the main place you went to get drugs because they just weren't everywhere like they are today.

The idea of an undercover agent is not this romantic thing that you see on television and in the movies. An undercover agent's job is really pretty despicable because my job, every agent's job was to do...when we're targeting against someone our job is to do whatever is necessary to become that person's closest friend—their best confidant so that we could betray them and send them to jail. As soon as we finish with that one, we're off to the next.

Friendship, betrayal, jail over and over and over again—repeated hundreds and hundreds of times. Over a thousand young folks went to jail as a direct result of my undercover work. People went to jail for nothing more than the fact that they wanted to put something in their body that I didn't want to put in my body.

Let's go back now to how we did this. We got this group of 10 to 15 people and come Friday night they were just like other people. Somebody says, "Hey, you want to get high?" If some of them answer yes, then one of them will say, "Well, I've got access to the family car. I'll make the run to the city tonight. You all give me your money. Give me a list of what you want me to buy, and I'll buy it and bring it back." Somebody might ask for a couple joints or a dime bag of pot or get me a couple mushrooms or whatever, and I'd put in my order, which was just as small and give them a few bucks, and this person would make the run to the city. When they came back they would just hand it out.

Now they didn't get money for this. They probably didn't even get gas money. They just figured this is a friendship thing. A week later it might be person B that did it and a week after that person C and a week after that person D. Well, I hung around until I had them all.

We were infiltrating groups like this everywhere in a community. After a couple months we'd have maybe 90-95 people that we had gotten drugs from. By the way, they didn't even have to do what I just said. Just the mere fact that they would, as a friend, (and we know drug use is a very social thing especially soft drugs—take two tokes and pass it on) if they passed it to me I would pretend to take a toke, knock the flame off the end of that joint and put it my pocket and then that night it would be submitted as evidence and they would become a drug dealer.

DB: Distribution.

JACK COLE: That's right. By the end of a couple months we would round these people up. We'd have maybe 90-95 of them, and we would send in 350 cops at 5 o'clock in the morning, kick their doors down, and we did it for a purpose. We did it because this was very important to us to show them street justice—to frighten them away from using drugs because, after all, the courts were not treating them nearly harsh enough.

We would kick their doors down, drag them out in chains, and back then they were charged with distribution of a controlled, dangerous substance, which in 1970 was exactly the same charge because we didn't have weights attached to it or anything attached to it as far as which substance was which. They could have sold me a kilo of heroin, and they're getting the same charge. The charge would have put them in prison for 7 years. By the end of the first year we had all kinds of drug dealers that we were releasing to the media. They looked like this was the worst problem in America, right?

It wasn't just that that we lied about we also lied about the amounts of drugs that we seized. The way we did that is back then, as I told you, hard drugs were almost non-existent so a decent seizure for a local police department or state police department might be one ounce of cocaine or one-quarter ounce of heroin—believe it or not.

But when we'd go in and we'd seize one ounce of cocaine in the house we'd look around to see if there was any kind of cutting agent there—quinine, milk sugar lactose. If we found any cutting agent somewhere between where we seized the ounce of cocaine—say we found 4 pounds of cutting agent—somewhere between where we seized the cocaine and the state lab that magically all became cocaine which is very simple. You just accidentally drop the small package into the big package and shake it once. As far as the state's concerned that is all cocaine.

Our bosses are very happy. We're happy. Everyone goes home happy except maybe the poor slob that just got arrested.

DB: You used the word and I'm going to use it here. This behavior is despicable. What can they do to help end this madness?

JACK COLE: What can I tell the police? I could tell them that first off you have to treat these people as human beings because that's exactly what they are. We were trained with this metaphor of a War on Drugs so we were trained as officers to go to war. When a person is trained to go to war the sad thing is they have to have an enemy. The enemy becomes the citizens of the United States—the population of the United States. It truly is the population of the United States because according to the government statistics now they say 87 million people in this country above the age of 12 have used an illegal drug so every one of those is vulnerable to arrest.

So the enemy is us. This is not a War on Drugs this is a war on people. This is a war on our children, a war on parents, a war on ourselves.

NEILL FRANKLIN

The Executive Director of Law Enforcement Against Prohibition is Major Neill Franklin, a 34-year law enforcement veteran of the Maryland State Police and Baltimore Police Department. During his time on the force, he held the position of commander for the Education and Training Division and the Bureau of Drug and Criminal Enforcement. This first interview with Neill was while he was still wearing the badge as a working cop yet speaking boldly for LEAP and before he was appointed the second Executive Director of LEAP.

Cultural Baggage, December 17, 2008

DB: You had an OpEd published in the Washington Post. I want to start at the top here. "Legalize and regulate the drug trade" regarding the December 4th article about Mexican drug cartels sends a message of chaos and death and your response to that was, "This mayhem occurs as a direct result of, and not despite, increased enforcement of senseless policies that make drugs illegal." You want to elaborate on that, Sir?

NEILL FRANKLIN: It's like what we say as we go back and compare to what we're facing now with drug prohibition and compare it to alcohol prohibition of the roaring 20's. We've created the perfect atmosphere for, what I refer to it as, the perfect storm for criminal enterprise and it's not just criminal enterprise here in the states but, it's international. Because of the proximity of Mexico to, of course, to the states here, they're one of the countries that are severely affected by our policies. Our failed policies as it relates to drug prohibition. By creating that perfect storm for criminal enterprise. It's all about money for those folks and until we take the money out of it; until we develop and create some policies that work, it's not just going to continue but, it's going to get worse.

DB: Let's talk about your career. Tell us about your experience.

NEILL FRANKLIN: I started with the Maryland state police back in 1976 and I spent about 23 to 24 years with the Maryland state police before I retired in 1999. Now, most of that time I spent in the narcotics or criminal investigation fields. In the early 1980's, it was about 1980, that's when I became a narc for the Southern Maryland area. That's the borders of Washington D.C. Prince George's county, for those that may be familiar with this area, and yeah. I just want to say that when I first started as a narc, in 1980, I was a member of a 6 person team and we worked four counties in Southern Maryland. We would go out by ourselves. I mean, we each had a county. We would go out by ourselves. We would develop our own cases. Work by ourselves. Many times we were unarmed. Because, even though the illegal drug trade was there, it was not nearly as violent as it is today.

Today, you don't let a narcotics officer work a case by themselves, go out by themselves or even unarmed. I'm going to get to a very important point, as it relates to the violence. I then went on to command seven task forces. Now, these are multi-jurisdictional task forces in the Western part of Maryland, involving federal agencies as well as local towns and so on. I then moved to the Northeast part of the state and commanded about 12 to 13 task forces, both criminal and narcotics work on that side, before I ended up commanding a training division for the Maryland State Police prior to my retiring.

I had a young man, a trooper who worked for me, many of us considered him the best narcotics officer that Maryland State Police had ever seen, his name was Edward Totely. Edward Totely joined an FBI task force, working the Washington D.C. area. I went on to Baltimore, to the Baltimore Police Department then and I was commanding their academy during this time. It was the year 2000, October of 2000. Ed Totely was working a somewhat of a mid level dealer, in the Washington D.C. area. That night, late one night in October in 2000, with back up from other members of the task force that he was assigned to, when the person he had purchased the drugs from came back out to the car, to deliver the package, he was assassinated, point blank, from the driver's side of the car.

DB: And for what? That's really the question.

NEILL FRANKLIN: Right. For what? For what? Two sons and a daughter... and a wife, are now without him. Now, that's just one case. We know that this happens across the country. In Baltimore City, we know that officers are being shot at on a daily basis from members of the illegal drug trade. Because we, with our policies, have created this atmosphere, for this to take place.

DB: This boon, this granting of the ability to make money, to turn weeds into hundred dollar bills so they can afford that weaponry. Is that right, Sir?

NEILL FRANKLIN: That's it and 'course... oh, that's another point, oh, God. Even with the advancements that we have made, as law enforcement officers with a higher quality of fire power that we have, we still can't match what they have. It's just become so dangerous for our men and women who are out there on a daily basis in any one of these cities or towns and their just chasing... It's like a dog chasing it's tail.

DB: Now, I want to... you know, you send your friend or someone sent your friend out to do this task, to curtail the supply, to make a difference and yet, we have never made a difference. Have we?

NEILL FRANKLIN: It has gotten worse. We haven't held the line. We haven't pushed the line back. We're losing. We're losing ground. The numbers are increasing in every size, shape and form, mainly when it comes to people dying.

When I say, 'people dying' it's not just one group of people. It's not just the people who are involved in the game. It's, as we just talked about, it's law enforcement officers, it's innocent bystanders. In Baltimore here we have a number of children that are caught in the middle, on a monthly basis. We have a very high juvenile homicide rate, here in Baltimore.

It's even for those who are addicts. Because of the non-regulated supply of drugs that they get, the poor quality of drugs that they get, the change in quality and purity of the drugs that they get and the stigma that's attached to being involved in illegal activity, they don't get the help that they need. They're dying at alarming rates.

Cultural Baggage / March 3, 2013

DB: We've seen not just the benefit of marijuana but the horrible blowback of the policy of prohibition.

NEILL FRANKLIN: I want to talk about a couple of things. The prohibition of marijuana and what it does to our communities, to our states, to our country, globally to Central America and other places, because basically what we've done, similar to alcohol prohibition, is we've taken a commodity and made it extremely valuable and it's being peddled at the hands of criminals—organized crime, cartels, neighborhood gangs. These proceeds they use not just to survive off of but to wreak havoc within our communities. Our communities have become extremely violent as these gangs compete with each other for market share, for corners basically. Guns have become the tools of the trade. Guns that were initially used just to manage the business of illegal drug trafficking are now used to settle just about any dispute—even a simple dispute of disrespect. It's how they handle business today in general. It's become very costly for us financially as a country. It's become very costly for our police departments and where they focus their energies and their time. That equates to less resources being used for violent crime—for rape, for domestic violence, murder, burglaries, robberies.

If we were to just legalize marijuana alone the limited resources that we could then redirect to violent crime are significant. It would make a huge difference in the communities—especially our impoverished communities. So that's a little bit about prohibition but I want to also talk about the legalization of recreational use and medical marijuana. Some people see them as one in the same but they're not. They're distinctly different. Medical marijuana has its own unique place. The research…the importance of research so that the different strains of marijuana of which I'm beginning to learn a lot about the benefits of medicinal marijuana and how it is used to improve the quality of life for people who have different ailments. I'm learning about the cannabinoid system and how that works. The medical marijuana industry and the research that needs to be done in its own special unique place and the different strains depending on what the ailment is. All of that is important.

The recreational use of marijuana is completely different. That's similar to the alcohol industry where people drink and consume alcohol for enjoyment purposes. That's the recreational side. Along with that comes regulations and control. Age limits—how do we keep marijuana away from our children. We would do it similar to how we do it with alcohol and tobacco. Under our model of prohibition where we currently are there's more access. Drug dealers are on just about every corner. If they're not on the corner they're around the corner. They don't just sell to kids because they don't ask for ID but they also recruit kids to sell to other kids. That means we have more marijuana, more drugs available to our kids. It's so easy for them to access it today. Under a model of regulation and control we move it from the street corners into a licensed establishment where there are quality control measures, where they card people—they want to know if you're 21 or not. They don't hire kids to peddle their products.

STAN FURCE

This is an edited transcript from my television program Unvarnished Truth, edition #19 from August 30, 2013. It was a debate panel featuring Stan Furce, head of Houston's High Intensity Drug Trafficking for the DEA. Michael Ronan with Houston Community College was moderator. The topic of discussion was "Are we winning the war on drugs?"

STAN FURCE: I'm going to give up and legalize drugs. There is no War on Drugs. There never has been a War on Drugs. We agree on a lot of the same things. The only message I'd like to give this audience is to approach it with pragmatism and reality. That's all I'm asking you to do.

Look at my opponents viewpoints. Look at our viewpoints and before you read or digest anything and say this is the truth—research it in its entirety. If there was a War on Drugs we would have won years ago if we had applied all our resources but we never have and we never will be.

Joe Biden says the War on Drugs is kind of like his lawn. The lawn is going to continue to grow and unless you mow it consistently it is going to become a jungle. What we do in narcotic enforcement on supply reduction is we try to keep the supply down by mowing that lawn.

I don't know if you've ever been to New York City, for example. If you've been to New York City you can imagine the amount of garbage that they generate every day. Nobody ever pays attention to the garbage man until he goes on strike.

There's another anecdote on the legalization thing and I used to use this when I used to teach about drugs. Transform yourself back in time as a troglodyte walking through the jungles with you knuckles dragging and for the first time you encounter a chicken. You've encountered many other animals but here is your first chicken. All of the sudden something drops out of its butt. Now, you know what drops out of most animals' butts. Now what would make you go over and eat that thing? In this case it's an egg.

What I'm saying by that analogy is people will try to do anything. Who was the first person who dried a marijuana leaf and smoked it? Who was first person who took Xenia seeds and tried to get high from them?

What do we legalize? Do we legalize everything? And if we do legalize things do we put any kind of parameters on them? Will we give it to anybody? Can a 3-year-old go in and buy marijuana? I would think not in this country. As long as you instill or put some kind of parameters on any kind of legalization you're going to have a black market.

In the early days of my career when I arrested somebody coming in at the port of entry into the United States it wasn't for possession. It was a failure to pay the tax and we got him almost like a Revenue Agent. Think about legalization from that aspect of it. There will always be something that somebody wants to use. Are we going to legalize everything and if we do legalize everything are we going to put any kind of attachments to it? There is no War on Drugs. It's an ongoing thing.

STAN FURCE: If you look at who was arrested for marijuana you have to look at a couple things. Were they on probation or parole? Was it a reduced sentence? Was it part of plea bargaining where this person may have done something else and it was mitigated through the courts to just pleading guilty to the plea bargain rather than the original offense.

When you are looking at "we have incarcerated all of these people for simple possession" I think you have to look beyond that. I would suggest that you go to our source who's really in prison for marijuana.

MICHAEL RONAN: Next question. Who benefits from the War on Drugs?

Mr. Furce.

STAN FURCE: No War on Drugs. It's just a business. I work 9 to 5 and it's a business. It's a business not like Mr. Becker said that we're in it to make money. We don't build prisons to make money. We don't have pharmaceutical houses that dispense illegal drugs.

Who benefits from the War on Drugs? If there was a War on Drugs I think the society benefits from it. We have to have sanctions on our society because if we don't, we have anarchy. One of the things that you've asked this government to do through your voting rights is to have people like me out there like the garbage man in New York. So the people that benefit from the supply reduction are you. The people that benefit from our moneys that go to treatment are the people who need it. The moneys that go to prevention go to people like Miss Baker and provide you with the message.

We have to have a 3 prong approach. You have to have supply reduction. You have to have prevention, and you have to have treatment. You have all three. The most important of those is prevention.

MICHAEL RONAN: If drugs were to be legalized what do we legalize and for whom would it be legal?

STAN FURCE: And those were my questions. Those are the ones that I posed. What do you legalize? I ask you at the beginning of this to be pragmatic. If we legalize everything...this is the United States of America—what are we going to do? Are we going to put sanctions on it? Are we going to say 18-year-olds can have it or 21-year-olds can have it?

Are we going to have a purity level? Are we going to tax it? In this country you bet your life we're going to tax it. Guaranteed. If we put any of those sanctions on it, any of those sanctions whatsoever, there is going to be a black market. There's going to be sales to minors. There's going to be smuggling. There's going to be illegal manufacture of something that I can get around without having to, for example, he said that Merck would make all the good methamphetamine. Well, yeah, Merck would make it. Would it be as good as the stuff I can make in my backyard or cheap? No.

We're always going to have some kind of illegal market. No matter what you do you are going to have me around in supply reduction. You are going to have me as a revenue agent or you are going to have me as a possession agent so it's not going to go away.

What's vogue today will not be vogue tomorrow. There will be a new drug on the market. The FDA won't approve it, and who is going to legalize it? The FDA will go through this big thing and say, "OK, we're going to legalize it." It's not going to happen.

My last thing is what do we tell our children? What do you tell your children? If we are trying to make a conscious decision as an adult with a kid not to smoke, behave responsibly with alcohol and, by the way, you can take all the heroin, cocaine and marijuana that you want. Doesn't make any sense to me.

The last thing on that list would be what do we tell the other countries that we signed the treaties with saying we won't legalize it? We signed this treaty in 1961, the Single Convention, and we're signators of that. What do we tell them?

RUSS JONES

Russ Jones, with 30 years experience serving the US government in the drug war, is the author of "Honorable Intentions: The Odyssey of an American warrior who kept his eyes wide open and is willing to stand up and pull the veil away on what is really happening." Cultural Baggage / December 11, 2011

DB: I think in so many cases people want to serve their country and oft times the country is not serving its people.

RUSSELL JONES: I think that's what I'm trying to point out in the book, "Honorable Intentions." Our men and women are serving honorably. They served honorably in Viet Nam. Of course I was involved in Iran-Contra. Our men were serving honorably down there.

I was involved in the War on Drugs in my police work. I worked in the Soviet Union and in China. Everywhere I went the people on the front lines were serving honorably and today our law enforcement officers, our narcotics detectives, our DEA agents—they're out there serving honorably. But this is a failed policy, and they're dying for this failed policy. Not only are the civilians dying but we've got law enforcement personnel who are giving up their lives for this absolute failed policy.

DB: Let's talk about your involvement in Iran-Contra. A lot of folks probably have heard the term but how did you participate?

RUSSELL JONES: I was involved in what was called the Southern Front. That was working out of Costa Rica. The Contra war down in South America was Nicaraguans who were fighting to free their country from a socialist dictator at the time, Ortega. The United States was supporting them but were not getting the funding so people were taking it in their own hands to raise money in various ways. Now Iran-Contra was the way that became world public and we all learned about the sale of missiles to Iran. The money from those missiles was being used to fund the Contras. What was less known—although it came out in hearings they managed to do a better job of keeping it a secret—was that drugs were also being run, brought into this country, flown into Mena, Arkansas, flown into Florida to raise money to support the Contras. Of course I was involved in trying to find out where the small arms were coming from but within the course of that I also came across this drug-running that was going on.

DB: That was not necessarily from President Reagan's office but there were some indications that he know about it and approved it.

RUSSELL JONES: I don't know how far up the chain it goes. I do know at the lower levels, we know this as a fact, this came out in the Senate hearings, that people in the government, the CIA and other agencies, knew that drugs were being run from Central and South America into the United States and that those funds were being used to support the Contras. We also knew that some of those funds were being diverted for personal reasons, but people were looking the other way.

I should point something out. In World War II, it was called the OSS then, was working close with the mafia because the mafia was fighting Fascism and Nazism in Europe. The OSS knew that the mafia was raising money through the sale of drugs in order to fight Nazism and Fascism. So this isn't new. This looking the other way isn't necessarily new. I'm not condoning it either. I'm just saying this is a fact. This is something that happened. And we need to be aware of it. We need to learn from it.

DB: In the U.S. we've invested hundreds of billions in "stopping the flow of drugs" and yet we don't seemed to have stopped them, have we?

RUSSELL JONES: No. That's a known fact. Facts are interesting things—they just are. And the fact is that we have not reduced the flow of drugs. We surely have reduced the price of drugs—that's come down. The purity has gone up and the rate of addiction has pretty much stayed constant since the beginning of the War on Drugs. Statistically we've accomplished nothing in the War on Drugs.

LEIGH MADDOX

Leigh Maddox joined the Maryland State Police in 1989 and retired with the rank of Captain. He teaches at the University of Maryland, School of Law. Cultural Baggage / July 10, 2011.

DB: Leigh, I want to ask kind of a touchy question here. I see the acceptance, the positioning of police lying to suspects. Trying to get them to, you know, "You go first and it will go easier on you." And, in so far as the drug war—this nation is awash in a sea of snitches, isn't it?

LEIGH MADDOX: Well, it's always been OK for the bad guys to lie to the cops and the cops were taught, on the back end, that it's OK for the cops to lie to the bad guys. Now, obviously, there's a line there that crosses from black and white into grey that you don't want to cross. You don't want to do anything that's not ethical but, you know, it's kind of a give and take. The trouble we see today is because it's gotten so dangerous you don't have the cops initially going in and actually doing the drug deals. We rely on these people who we pay good money to, day in and day out, to go in and tell us who's doing right and who's doing wrong in the communities. And, based on their opinions (and we protect them because we don't want them getting killed) based on their opinions we're putting people in jail for a really, really long periods of time. As long as the cops are really clear about…and have a heightened sense of awareness about what it is they're doing and as long as the snitches are acting with good intentions it works. But, if either one of those two people in the dance, if you will, are operating from a plateau that is not good intentions, then it's very, very problematic and destructive to society. I think that's a lot of what we're seeing now.

DB: Some 39,000 SWAT raids per year are staged against people on a drug charge because the theory is they'll flush the drugs before they can get in, right?

LEIGH MADDOX: Yeah. It used to be I didn't have a problem with this. I thought that our slow militarization of our police forces was a good thing because it made me feel safer as a police officer. I used to predict, years ago, that we would have a National Police Force and I thought that was a good thing. I have now the hindsight of a lot of years in this business, and I'm seeing that my idealistic frame was really out of whack. And, in fact, the local police departments are accepting a lot of money and a lot of training from federal agencies that has resulted in extreme militarization of our police agencies and a lot of that is centered around the drug trade.

I still have sympathies for the cops on the street because they feel a whole lot better when the SWAT team dudes decide to go ahead and do the raid because they're not the ones that have to knock on the door. They're not the ones that have to stand there and wonder if the pit bull is going to come through the door or if a shotgun blast is going to come through the door and take them out. Now they're not going to have to be so worried if they are going home to their wife and kids at the end of the day because the SWAT team guys, the one's with the charging rams and the bullet-proof vests and the helmets and the cameras and everything else they have, all the tools we've enabled them with and, quite frankly, a lot of the times they are very much needed. But, for your "average Joe" cultivating an ounce of hemp plants in his basement, yeah, it doesn't seem like it's a good marriage.

DB: I've talked to many law enforcement officers and the question I ask is "Which would you rather do: go to bust a drunken fight or a pothead?" And, of course, the answer is always a pothead. He's not going to throw up in your car. He's not going to create a fight. It shows alcohol is more dangerous.

LEIGH MADDOX: Right and we've never had the level of violence associated with marijuana that we see with alcohol. And, we've made a lot of mistakes with how we've regulated alcohol. I think that if you're going to look at a model that's currently working fairly, look at tobacco. We keep it away from kids. We're limiting the time, place and manner, you know, restrictions. We're taxing the hell out of it, and we're following that money with education so the usage rates have dropped off like 40% across all socioeconomic lines. That's the great American success story right there—not alcohol.

JOSEPH MCNAMARA

Joseph McNamara, has thirty-five years experience as a law enforcement officer including Police Chief of both Kansas City and San Jose, California. He's written extensively about the harms of the Drug War and is a research fellow at the Hoover Institution. Century of Lies / August 01, 2010.

DB: You were there when President Nixon declared "War on Drugs" and when Ron and Nancy "Just said No". What has this done to our nation? What has prohibition done to the world?

JOSEPH MCNAMARA: Well, raising the drug issue to the presidential level has really changed things dramatically. I must say that as a result of that we have spent billions, hundreds of billions of dollars, locked up millions of Americans and yet the violence and the corruption and the level of drug use is probably far greater than when I became a New York City policeman way back in 1956.

DB: Chief McNamara, in all your years in law enforcement, how many times were your officers called to settle a public disturbance where the only drug in play was marijuana?

JOSEPH MCNAMARA: I don't recall that that ever happened because the fact is that marijuana seems to make most people mellow. I have to confess that I have never smoked any cigarette or tobacco. I have certainly never taken a hit from a bong and I doubt if I ever will. Having said that, I'm not advocating the use of marijuana or judging whether people should use it or not because I think there's so many differences of opinion medically and socially, that people need to make up their own mind. While I wouldn't use it personally, I don't think I'd want to live in a country where you become a criminal, merely because you're behaving in a way that a police officer doesn't think you should.

The result of criminalizing marijuana has really been a disaster for our country because we have made many millions of otherwise law-abiding citizens into criminals, simply because they use a certain substance which we don't think is good for them. The result is that we have an extremely profitable black market coming from the fact that the drug marijuana, cannabis is illegal, giving best profits to illegal gangs and cartels. It's creating enormous violence and corruption and I think, increased marketing of cannabis.

DB: Chief, I wanted to ask you, of the new complaints that we now hear about, that are in regards to Cannabis dispensaries in California, Colorado and elsewhere, we most often hear about the robberies of these dispensaries. Would this or other scenarios be solved or exacerbated via legalization?

JOSEPH MCNAMARA: Well, the answer to that is that, when was the last time you saw a Budweiser dealer robbed or involved in a drive-by shooting? If you legalize it, you won't have this kind of crime. You'll immediately, like in California, reduce crime enormously by many millions of crimes, millions every day because the conduct that's today criminal will cease being criminal. When we take away the black market it will be just like the alcohol industry. It's harmful to some people, but it seems like over 90% of the people really benefit or enjoy alcohol and it's a thriving industry.

DB: Well in this time of, I'll call it "Fiscal Fiasco" all across this nation, it does make a great deal of sense doesn't it?

JOSEPH MCNAMARA: Especially now that when during this present recession, law enforcement is really hurting because of cutbacks in funding. So, it's imperative that law enforcement be part of the efforts to reduce expenditures and to use resources more wisely. The public is not terrified over pot smokers. I can tell you as a lifetime policeman. They would love to see the police spend more time on violent crime and burglaries and other crimes that affect them and their children. The fact is, in California we have about 60,000 serious and violent crimes that aren't solved every year but we're making more than 60,000 marijuana arrests, mostly for simple possession. So, I can say as a policeman who worked ten years in the highest crime areas in New York City that, at that time, no self-respecting cop would make a marijuana bust.

There is no doubt that we are using tremendous resources in this war against marijuana. People don't realize that the police officer who makes a marijuana arrest, spends a lot of time—and the law enforcement agency—a lot of time in processing and analyzing the evidence and in preparing the various reports for prosecution and court testimony. In addition to which, there are enormous costs for public defenders, for prosecutors, for our courts and for our correction agencies. Our prison system is very troubled in California but I think it's fair to say that the parole revocations of people on parole are incredibly high. The majority of parole revocations are for possession or use of drugs and no other crime. So, we are reprocessing people through a revolving door for parole violations, as well as taking up court time and police time.

When you take the whole situation and we see the fact that the illegal drug market for marijuana provides most of the profits for the drug cartels in Mexico, where the violence is absolutely incredible with more than 20,000 people killed in recent years, including soldiers, police officers, judges and other government officials. The whole government of Mexico and the whole country of Mexico is endangered and the instability of a huge country of a hundred million people just south of our border is a great danger to the security of the United States.

So, this spills over internationally and creates enormous problems for our country that come about because we refuse to get real and face the fact that perhaps we don't personally feel that people should be using marijuana, that nevertheless, there are millions of Americans that are going to use marijuana and willing to spend billions of dollars that go to criminals to further their purchase of deadly weapons and stimulate the violence that occurs.

People have to remember that the violence is not occurring because people are using marijuana, it's occurring because of people dealing in marijuana shoot each other and endanger innocent bystanders. Also, even the law enforcement with the primary duty of protecting human life is taking human lives in some dangerous drug raids.

When you think back to the prohibition of alcohol, Al Capone and the gangsters and bootleggers weren't machine-gunning each other and innocent bystanders because they drank too much booze themselves. They were committing this violence and the murders because it was an illegal business with vast profits and they were in competition with other violent gangsters. The result was a period of lawless violence and the creation of widespread disrespect for the law. One estimate is that 1/3 of the people in California tried marijuana last year and this year the impossibility of labeling 1/3 of your population as criminals should make us recognize that this is a very damaging and unrealistic approach to government.

I'd like to remind people that our last three presidents, President Clinton, George W. Bush and Obama, by their own admissions, indicated that they used marijuana during their wild and reckless days of youth. If any of them had had the misfortune to be in the wrong place at the wrong time and been busted for marijuana, they would not have had successful lives, let alone become President of the United States. So there's a huge cost in turning people into criminals who are essentially good citizens and going to be leading productive lives. It's way past time to recognize that marijuana should not be criminalized.

NORM STAMPER

Norm Stamper was a police officer for 34 years, the first 28 in San Diego, the last six (from 1994-2000) as Seattle's police chief. Norm is the author of *Breaking Rank:A Top Cop's Exposé of the Dark Side of American Policing*. Century of Lies / August 14, 2011.

DB: Numerous organizations are coming out for ending the drug war: the NAACP, the Conference of Mayors, the Global Commission on Drugs, but, the government just doesn't want to do that new analysis.

NORM STAMPER: Well, let's go to some of those other reasons. Let's assume that you've come out of a career in law enforcement, you're steeped in drug policy traditions and vocabulary, and I think there's a tendency on the part of those who preside over U.S. drug policy, willfully or unintentionally, to succumb to all of the moneyed interests that are associated with perpetuating the drug war. I refer, of course, to the prison industrial complex. Nothing more pernicious by way of aspects of that complex than the increased privatization of American prisons, which makes it a profit-motivated enterprise, relying on per diems, building and filling as many prison cells as possible. That's a very, very powerful lobby in this country.

The law enforcement narcotics industry is also a big part of that. And, it could be argued that the pharmaceutical companies and a variety of others have interest in perpetuating the drug war. I think it's safe to assume, as one who's on the outside looking in now, that one of the reasons they don't want to talk to us is a fear that even being seen with us or were the American public made to understand that there's been a sit-down, face-to-face, honest, grown up conversation about U.S. drug policy, would put them at odds with all those people who are supporting the drug war.

DB: Recently Obama set the hatchet team against the La Familia, one cartel in Mexico and not bringing that same focus on the other cartels. Your response.

NORM STAMPER: Let's assume for the moment that in targeting La Familia we are achieving some level of success, conventionally defined. What we've really done is strengthen the other cartels. I think it's safe to assume, and we have ample evidence of this, that every time we take down a drug kingpin or one of his lieutenants we have created an employment opportunity or a promotional opportunity for somebody in the ranks of that cartel to move up. And, these are people who have learned from the history of their own syndicated criminal enterprises that the way you expand or protect your profits is through escalating levels of violence and more and more imagination being applied to kidnappings and to torture and other forms of really unspeakable violence in Mexico.

So, I think it is very short-sighted of us to target a single cartel. On the other hand the argument could be made that we should realize how big the problem is in Mexico and how ineffective it is to spread our resources and go after them all. In fact, bottom line, we'll never win that battle, we never should have engaged in it in the first place and it's time for us to withdraw from the Drug War. Declare a victory if necessary or a truce if that's more politically palatable but recognize that adding to our failed policy year after year after year and dollar after dollar after dollar is just utter folly.

DB: This leads me to one last thought that I want to examine. And that is that there was a high lieutenant used by agents of the federal government to point at other cartel efforts to, in essence, be their informant. And for that they were allowed to smuggle tons of cocaine into these United States. We had the gun smuggling into Mexico where the ATF allowed that to happen. How criminal must law enforcement be to win?

NORM STAMPER: I've written in my book that of all the major scandals involving U.S. law enforcement in the last several decades, virtually every one of them is traceable to drug trafficking. It is an enterprise created through prohibition which is the organizing mechanism behind U.S. drug laws that guarantees not only violence but corruption. It guarantees over zealousness, violations of the 4th amendment for example. And as it relates to the specific issue that you've raised, it guarantees that we will as a government, because this is how law enforcement functions, we will favor one breed or brand of evil conduct over another in order to grab what we perceive as the larger level of evil.

And what that means, and we've seen this in the history of the Central Intelligence Agency, DEA and the like, buying off people in effect allowing them to continue their criminal enterprise in order to go after a bigger fish. There's something just unholy about that. I don't consider it to be honest and honorable police work. Police work, for example, the kind that prevents people from hurting other people. Police work that actually makes a positive difference in the lives of people who in many cases are terrified of crime, who change the way that they live as a result of that, but we have found ourselves preoccupied with these strategies and these tactics that ultimately undermine police work and public confidence in police work.

And having spent 34 years as a cop I can tell you that it's an absolutely essential, indispensable line of work; it's an honorable profession; but when we engage in those tactics, we dishonor it. I'm not rejecting my own history and my own background, but there are plenty of occasions where we develop snitches who help lead us to the prevention of homicides and robberies and burglaries and the like. That's been a part of police work from day one and it will always be a part of police work. But we always kind of prided ourselves as those who formulate sound rules and live by them. It's when we deviate from those rules, it's when we create rules, if you will, that are beyond the spirit of the Constitution of the United States, that we find ourselves in big, big trouble. And it's just not worth it. There are ways to do police work and there are ways to do police work. And unfortunately under the Drug War we have found lots of reasons to violate if not the letter then certainly the spirit of the Constitution.

LARRY TALLY

Larry was a US Navy Intelligence Specialist who is now retired. While stationed in Panama, Larry deployed frequently to various locations in Central and South America in support of counter drug operations, where he formulated and implemented eradication strategy in conjunction with the Drug Enforcement Agency and with many countries in the region. Cultural Baggage, August 1, 2010.

LARRY TALLEY: I'm a Texas native and I came home after retiring, after a stint of twenty-one years in uniform. I joined the navy back in 1986. I joined the military here to serve my country but from the very first day when I got on board my very first ship, I found myself involved in a Drug War.

My very first ship, I landed myself on board the USS John L. Hall, which was a small fast frigate doing what they call "Law Enforcement Caribbean Drug Operations" for drug interdiction operations in the Caribbean Sea. I hadn't been in navy but a few days and we made a nice nineteen-ton marijuana bust. We pulled the skiff, got all of the pot off the skiff, sank the skiff, arrested the really bad, mean, horrible Rastafarians and drug heads that were trying to get that stuff to market, and this is what we did.

My very first port of call was Curacao. We had basically starved the people on this island because their main source of income was the exporting marijuana. Understand, in the 1980s that Reagan was in power, "Just say no to drugs" was a really big marketing campaign in this country. In reality, there were billions that were injected into our military. Let's make this clear, military, not law enforcement, military enforcement in law enforcement operations doing drug enforcement operations.

We would set up basically naval blockades to try and interdict this stuff and we starved some islands. These people had been exporting marijuana for generations, for generations, for almost a hundred years. For as long as they'd been there, that's what they had made their money on, so then they were starving.

Being the gracious country that we are, we put the Peace Corps in there to build them huts and things and bars. So that when we anchored off of their island, we brought them liquor and then we made it a port for us to go drink off of. We literally delivered them the liquor and the beer so they could build a bar then it became a sailor hangout.

Now, so skip forward, twenty years later, this beautiful native culture, Rastafarian environment has now been inundated with private culture and land developers and alcohol and addiction rates. These things, I watched it occur, right before my eyes. I thought from the very beginning, "Wow! Why are we doing this? This doesn't make sense. We're poisoning these people with alcohol." It doesn't take a college education when you first see something like this and realize what's wrong, what's ethical and what really isn't ethical.

DB: Nineteen tons of weed is a pretty good haul, I would think. Then again, it really doesn't make a difference, does it?

LARRY TALLEY: No, it makes no difference at all. I skipped ahead a number of years. I lived in Panama for a lot of years. We did drug interdiction operations in South America. I worked for Special Operations Command Unit, a naval special worker unit that was down there and we were dropped to or subordinate to General Barry McCaffrey. A lot of listeners may recall that name, General Barry McCaffrey, later became the Drug Czar. So I worked with him in South America. I interfaced with him. I got to brief him and had a very casual conversation. He probably wouldn't remember me. I remember him certainly because he was "The Man." He was the guy in charge of every asset in South and Central America. Every CIA, DEA agent, FBI agent, every asset that's down there, he belonged to him. It was choppy. He was in charge of every black force in every operation that existed.

It's real interesting because he's the one that really led the charge against the cartels, the cocaine cartels. The army people believed that they could change the course of Drug War, so what they did is cut of the heads. They disabled and dismembered these huge cocaine cartels from the days of Scarface. What picked up in their place were these politically motivated organizations that then become pseudo-terrorist organizations that were then financed by the illicit black market. That's what we have today. They are very fragmented, so now we created fragmented organizations where we can't possibly ever control it. It was futile to think that we could, in retrospect.

JOHN URQUHART

John Urquhart has been in law enforcement for more than 35 years and is the elected Sheriff of King County, Washington. As Sheriff, he serves as the chief county-level law enforcement official for 1.9 million people and oversees the 1000+ employees of the King County Sheriff's Office. Sheriff Urquhart was called before the US Senate in September, 2013 to testify regarding the legalization of cannabis in Seattle. Century of Lies / December 22, 2013.

JOHN URQUHART: As sheriff I am the top law enforcement official in the largest jurisdiction in the country that has legalized marijuana. I've been a police officer for 37 years and I was elected at King County Sheriff last year. During my career I've investigated everything from shoplifts to homicides. But I've also spent 12 years as a narcotics detective. My experience shows the War on Drugs has been a failure. We have not significantly reduced demand over time, but we have incarcerated generations of individuals, the highest incarceration rate in the world. So the citizens of the state of Washington decided it was time to try something new. In November of 2012 they passed Initiative 502, which legalized recreational amounts of marijuana and at the same time created very strict rules and laws.

I was a strong supporter of Initiative 502 last year, and I remain a strong supporter today. There are several reasons for that support. Most of all, I support 502 because that's what the people want. They voted for legalized marijuana. We—the government—have failed the people and now they want to try something else. Too often the attitude of the police is "We're the cops and you're not. Don't tell us how to do our job." That is the wrong attitude and I refuse to fall into that trap.

While the title of this hearing is conflict between state and federal marijuana laws. I don't see a huge conflict. The reality is we do have complementary goals and values. We all agree we don't want our children using marijuana. We all agree we don't want impaired drivers. We all agree we don't want to continue enriching criminals. Washington's law honors these values by separating consumers from gangs, and diverting the proceeds from the sale of marijuana toward furthering the goals of public safety. Is legalizing and regulating the possession and sale of marijuana a better alternative? I think it is, and I'm willing to be proven wrong. But the only way we'll know is if we are allowed to try.

In closing let me make one thing absolutely clear. What we have in Washington State is not the Wild Wild West. And as Sheriff, I am committed to continued collaboration with the DEA, FBI, and DOJ for robust enforcement of our respective drug laws. For example, I have detectives right now assigned to Federal task forces, including a DEA HIDTA Task Force. It's been a great partnership for many years and that partnership will continue.

Furthermore the message to my deputies has been very clear: You will enforce our new marijuana laws. You will write someone a ticket for smoking in public. You will enforce age limits. You will put unlicensed stores out of business. In other words, the King County Sheriff's Office will abide by the standards and laws voted on and adopted by the citizens of the state of Washington, and the guidance provided by the Department of Justice on August 29th.

HOWARD WOOLDRIDGE

Howard Wooldridge, a former police officer, now heads up the organization Citizens Opposing Prohibition. Century of Lies, July 3, 2011.

DB: The Global Commission on Drugs released their report and there was a storm of media coverage and yet we've heard very little from the halls of congress.

HOWARD WOOLDRIDGE: In the background, of course, is the fact that the federal government is broke and they're still spending about $15.5 billion dollars chasing Willie Nelson, Charlie Sheen, Rush Limbaugh and the rest of them.

DB: Wait, that's at the federal level, right?

HOWARD WOOLDRIDGE: That's just at the federal level, about $15.5 billion in the fiscal year 2011. And, now, from my sources fiscal year 12 will be the same thing. My colleagues, the lobbyist for the Sheriff's Association, Fraternal Order of Police, etc., are pressuring the congress to continue that money…keep that money coming in so that they get that good overtime check flying around in helicopters looking for a green plant.

DB: Yeah and something that's been overlooked is they did away with most of the…I think it was the Byrne Grant money which funded the drug task forces but in the early part of Obama's administration they brought it back, right?

HOWARD WOOLDRIDGE: Yeah, the Bush administration had asked for it to almost be zero-ed out and then, of course, the police lobbyist said, "Look, we want that money. We love the overtime. We love the job security. We like flying around in helicopters." And they were able to reinstate it back up to the half-billion mark. So the lobbyist for the police and whatnot basically blackmail your congressmen to say, "Either you vote for this money for us or we will tell the folks back home that you're soft on drugs, soft on crime." and endorse their opponent. It's straight-forward blackmail, Dean.

DB: And, let's remind folks. This is the type money that funded that sting, operation there in Tulia where 40 black folks were basically arrested, none had any drugs or money or guns…

HOWARD WOOLDRIDGE: Right. These are the task forces the Byrne grants, the HIDTA grants that basically target people of color. I just came back from LULAC convention—that's the League of United Latino American Citizens, and they understand that if you're white you have to be as stupid as a fencepost in Texas to be arrested for drugs, but if you are Latino or black, just wake up in the morning, and you will be busted. I mean, they understand the racist elements of this, and they're starting to come around saying, "You know what? Maybe this isn't such a good idea."

DB: You've traveled extensively looking for information, looking for facts. And you made a couple trips to Switzerland, have you not?

HOWARD WOOLDRIDGE: I've been to Switzerland three times now. I've spoken to people at the Swiss Health Ministry about their Swiss program for heroin addiction. I've been to the heroin clinics a couple of times, talked to the doctors who run it, seen the patients come in for their daily shots of heroin, and seen the overwhelmingly amazing results—now 16 years running—where they reduce crime, death, disease and drug use by allowing some of their heroin addicts to have access to legal, government-controlled and regulated heroin. Overwhelming success.

DB: And, was it just about one year ago that the Swiss actually voted nationally to institutionalize or make that their standard, right?

HOWARD WOOLDRIDGE: Exactly. They voted 68-32 to make heroin, government heroin, available to their addicts as part of their normal body of laws. What was interesting, Dean, the Swiss are not some "wild and crazy" people. At the same time they are being so conservative. They voted to keep marijuana illegal 67-33. So while they legalized heroin distribution by the government, they also kept marijuana illegal. The Swiss are very, very practical. They're very, very sharp on what's effective and what works and how to save money, and that's why they legalized and regulated the distribution of heroin for their addicted population. Treatment on demand, and if you can't stay on methadone, if you're not successful, they actually allow you heroin, pure heroin, twice a day. This has been very successful—now copied in 6 countries.

Slamming the Cell Door

"You can get over an addiction, but you will never get over a conviction." —Jack Cole, LEAP

The United States is the world's leading jailer, by far. By percentage or by outright numbers behind bars, we're number one. Among the states, Texas is always battling California and Louisiana for the title of number one in the US. Per-capita, Louisiana often leads, but in overall arrests, year in, year out, Texas usually outdoes California as well. A few years back, CBS television reported that Houston is the world's number one on drug arrests. Why is Houston the number one in drug arrests? Ignorance. Bigotry. Tradition.

In 2007, the Texas legislature passed and Gov. Perry signed a law that allows district attorneys to no longer arrest or jail those found with 4 ounces or less of marijuana or for graffiti and other crimes of less than $500 damage. Only Travis and Hays county DA's have chosen to make use of this law. In Houston, our district attorney continues to invite those arrests, to fill those jails at a cost of millions of dollars per year. We must not, cannot, lose sight of the fact that the drug laws are used predominately against our black and brown citizens.

But it's not just Houston. The United States leads the world in drug arrests, arresting 8 times more people of color (per capita) than did South Africa under apartheid. Hell exists today, right now, for more than 2 million, mostly young black and brown citizens of this nation behind bars, the largest portion there because of this eternal war on drugs.

A prime example of how a minor pot bust can affect one's life can be derived from examining what happens to pot smokers caught with a small bag of weed in Houston/Harris County, Texas.

First, if you are black or Latino, chances are near 100% that you will be arrested, taken to jail, and denied a public recognizance bond. If you have no money for a bail bondsman, you will sit in the County Jail for a few weeks or even months before you go to trial.

If you sit behind bars till the trial starts, you will be given the option of pleading guilty, accepting a sentence of time served, paying fines, being placed on probation, perhaps sent to mandated drug treatment sessions, and perhaps lose your driver's license. Because those found in possession are now convicted of a drug charge, they will soon find they are no longer eligible for government loans, public housing, credit, or even a job. Today there are more than 7 million Americans in prison, on parole, or probation—people who cannot vote, cannot afford an education, cannot get a loan, housing, or credit. Only the black market, the world's largest multi-level-marketing organization, awaits them with open arms. What else are they supposed to do?

NORA CALLAHAN

Nora Callahan is executive director of the US-based November Coalition, which she co-founded in 1997. The coalition publishes *The Razor Wire* and is the #1 voice of the drug war prisoner. www.november.org. Recorded April 29, 2009.

DB: The nature of the drug war is subject to a lot of investigation and change at this point, is it not?

NORA CALLAHAN: It is. Well, part of it, if we're real honest about where things are at, the economic boom having ended and now gone bust, we don't have the ability to pay for so much injustice. When we're cutting back school budgets and teacher's salaries and medical care to the poor, states are finding it isn't economical to take the non-violent drug offenders and give them long prison sentences. So we will probably, in prison stats in the near future, see a leveling off compared to what we've been doing for thirty years.

We have a terrible cash crunch in America to where they can't afford the large policing they have. But I think that sometimes alarms are sounded. I remember years ago when there were tax changes in California and people were saying, 'Houses are going to burn down and violent crime is going to go up,' and those things actually didn't happen.

What I think we're seeing is state legislators looking at drug laws because so many studies have come out to say, at a certain point, when you imprison these people, you're doing much more harm than any good to society over all. Because we can't forget that the one thing we know prison does, is it destroys a person's ability to live in a free world. So leaders are willing to look at that for the first time and say, well, we can't put this good money to do something bad. We are having, like in Washington State, a lot of changes even in the way some cities are looking at, well, we're going to stop making this a crime. Instead of giving them a full-blown criminal record, we'll give them a citation. We're seeing a move away from criminalization of non-violent people. It's probably all a good thing. I wouldn't worry about burglars going free because I don't think that's where we're headed. For one thing, they put so many non-violent prisoners into prison that every state could afford to take their prison population down by 25%, off the top, without suffering any violent effects on the street as long as communities can help. Instead of building prisons, build sustainable economics where people live.

DB: Let's talk about the November Coalition.

NORA CALLAHAN: We were founded in 1997 because the prisoners of the drug war in federal prisons realized that they didn't have a voice in calling for change, and people on the street didn't really know about the laws they're subject too. They didn't understand them. It's been hard to explain federal drug laws to people. That was the desire, that we would begin the education of the public, so that they understood the drug laws, so that they could say 'yea' or 'nay' to them.

People that don't understand something have a tendency to ignore it, so we wanted to explain how a person who was involved peripherally or low-level involvement or even no involvement, an innocent, could be subjected to decades to even life in prison for a non-violent drug offence. We needed to explain to the public and it involves the use of informants rather than physical evidence. The Sentencing Reform Act of 1986 was the culprit for these dramatic changes in sentencing and that's where we got the United States Sentencing Commission, who have power over many areas of Federal criminal justice, beyond sentencing.

DB: On november.org there's a story about Lawrence Garrison, one of two twins who were sentenced to twenty-plus years for cocaine conspiracy, but they were found without drugs. Without guns. Without money. The guy who informed on them got three years behind bars.

NORA CALLAHAN: Yes. That's how it works. When people are arrested by the Federal government and they are taken in for their "free talk"—they have different nicknames for it—they tell them, 'You're either going to get charged and you can face thirty years to life or you need to tell us everything you know.' If a person says, 'Well, I don't know anything,' then they might offer to let them wear a wire and go out and learn things and give information. In other words, you can work off your sentence by the entrapment of others, if you can entice others into drug crime or give the police information about a lot of people you know that might be involved in illegal drugs. So, people do time, especially in the federal system on the 'word' of the people trading these words for their freedom. Yeah and freedom, what's that worth? Yeah, way more than money, and people respond to that.

We think it's a form of mental torture. The idea of detainees and rendition have been part of the drug war since day one because so many people, especially again in the federal system, are denied any bail. So, they have to stay inside because they say they're more of a flight risk, in part, because they are threatening them with life in prison. People who are threatened with life and who look at the statistics, see the feds win. Ninety-seven percent of the time they get a conviction, whether it's by plea agreement or trial. They win. So people are more likely to abscond, perhaps.

Many drug offenders, I think it's thirty-five percent, are held before they've been convicted. You know that period where you're presumed innocent? They have to stay in jails, and these county jail situations and detention centers are always terribly overfilled, often filthy with the sewage problems and the lights on and the screaming and the rape and all those things that break a person down psychologically. So, when you ask, 'Well, how did a person give up their mother and do that to them?' It's because they were tortured.

DB: There's so much comparison to the inquisition of old, involved in this…

NORA CALLAHAN: Or the KUBARK program of the 1950's where psychologists designed ways of breaking people without leaving physical marks. Torturing people in their head, so that they could never be brought into a court and say, 'Yeah, they put electricity to my genitals.' You could put sewage on the floor and have somebody have a 'mad and overcrowded' jail, and you can get a better effect than if you break somebody's leg, and they know that now. For sure, they know that because we took it globally. They go from freedom one day into this cesspool of life. The informant system works really well, because people break down very quickly.

We're trying to change that. November has been one of the groups, one of many, who took the constituency affected and said, 'Well, instead of just enduring this, we're going to start trying to teach others what we're going through,' because people didn't see the hidden problems of imprisonment, and drug war imprisonment particularly, only the propaganda on TV. Now, for instance, one of our legislators who was lobbying here, appealing to her other co-legislators in Washington State said, "When we talk about those people in prison, who are we really talking about? We're talking about Uncle Larry. We're talking about our cousins. Our sister. Perhaps our parents. Those people are our people." For a legislator to say that, in a debate on a bill, it's pretty cool. But that's sad also, because that's how many people have been criminalized. Everyone knows someone who's been directly affected by drugs and/or illegal drug problems and/or imprisonment.

I used to scream it from the Hempfest stages and all around communities and in Unitarian Universalist Churches and Baptist Churches, asking people, "Are we so evil?" "Are we that bad?" "How can we have only five percent of the population and twenty-five percent of the world's prisoners?" I have a brother twenty years down now on drug charges, and still we have a lot of years left. So, it's imperative to reunite families. This idea of torturing people for a mistake in life is incredibly painful.

TOMMY CHONG

Half of America's best-known comedy team of Cheech and Chong, Tommy Chong was busted in 2003 for having his face pasted on the outside of glass pipes. After spending 9 months in a Federal prison, he became a strong advocate for ending the drug war. Recorded September 11, 2011.

DB: Tommy, you see a big difference, I would imagine, in the attitudes and the goings on from California coming to Texas. We got good people.

TOMMY CHONG: Oh, very good people.

DB: We got some bad laws, though.

TOMMY CHONG: Yeah, always have. I think Texas is probably the "home of the bad law." I remember years ago reading about the Mexican migrant worker doing 10 years for one joint.

DB: Well, close. There was a gentleman here in Houston, his name was Lee Otis Johnson, and he got busted for one or two joints and sentenced to 10 years.

TOMMY CHONG: And the worse thing about pot is they call it a "recreational drug." The constitution is actually written to protect our right to have recreation, freedom and pursuit of happiness. Lou Dobbs is on TV talking about how marijuana is more dangerous now because it's more powerful than it was during the Cheech and Chong days. I mean they actually said that, and it's ridiculous. Whenever I talk to these people, I ask them, "Well that means you've smoked it." And they go, "Oh no…no, no, no…I haven't smoked it." So then I say, "Well how in the Hell do you know what you're talking about? You don't know what you're talking about then."

DB: They don't. The Drug Czar says the same thing, "This is not your Cheech and Chong marijuana. This is industrial-strength or whatever…"

TOMMY CHONG: Like he would know! And then they don't take in the possibilities … it's like beer. You know you can have alcohol, 100 proof. You obviously don't drink a 100 proof glass of liquor the same way you would drink a 4% can of beer. No, you sip it. And it's the same thing with pot. If you get some killer weed that could knock your socks off if you smoked a whole joint, guess what?! You don't smoke the whole joint.

DB: The other day on the Lou Dobbs Show they had a gentleman talking about after 20 years it seems to have some sort of effect. And if that were true, folks like you and me—we'd be in the hospital or in the ground. I mean they have no legitimacy.

TOMMY CHONG: It's more lies, more lies. This law was enacted in the middle of the night because, and I quote excerpts from the Library of Congress where it said, "Marijuana tended to make black jazz musicians horny for white women." Now, that's true. Back in day that was against the law. But now-a-days, you know, if you look at Project Runway and you see that beautiful Heidi with her black musician husband –it's legal. It's legal to mix up. And these people, man…it's just so annoying. But, I got to give them one thing. If it wasn't for them—I wouldn't have a career..

DB: You've tried to get into commerce. You and your son, I think, were producing the bongs, smoking instruments.

TOMMY CHONG: We sold them all over the country, yeah. They were a great product, too. And now they're worth a lot. It was actually my son's business. I just put my face on the bong. I went to jail for it. In fact, it was Arlington, Texas where the DEA had cameras, and they followed me around the head shop in Arlington, and they used that as their evidence that the pipes we were selling weren't just for "tobacco use only". They were actually made to smoke marijuana. Can you imagine that?!

They've been programmed in a certain way—the Christian Right or whatever—they've been programmed. Then, all of the sudden, they smoke a joint and they look around and the sunset is more beautiful, and the music is clear, and the water tastes fresh, and the food tastes sweet. Everything is good, everything is wonderful, and it freaks them out. Because they've been conditioned all their lives to not enjoy themselves but to ... like slapping themselves with chains... Because they're not supposed to enjoy themselves in this life and no one else is supposed to enjoy this life, you know. If you see a guy sitting in a corner with red eyes listening to music—oh, arrest him; put him in jail because he's a danger to society. Because, and you know what they say? "We're unproductive." That's what they say.

DB: It's beyond reason. They use the results from what happens from their policy as justification to continue their policy!

TOMMY CHONG: That's what they're doing. The DEA, there's another great organization. When I was in jail I had the privilege of being in jail with some very beautiful, smart people, and I was in jail with a lawyer from Colombia, South America. His only crime was knowing stuff about the cartel and the collusion between the cartel and the DEA. He said that he's seen an air field in the heart of Colombia where the DEA flies in and out of. They fly out of Colombia without any checks. They don't have to go through Customs. And the planes are loaded with "guess what?!" and lands somewhere in America because that's the biggest dealer. Those guys are the biggest dealers in the world. This guy knew about it and so rather than kill them as they would normally, they give him a chance to do a prison sentence and get out of the country. So he was in jail where I was, serving his time.

DB: It's the international implications of this...The Iran-Contra affair, swapping drugs for guns back then. The Vietnam era, bring heroin back in the body bags.

TOMMY CHONG: Look at the Afghan...

DB: Ho, more heroin than the world's ever seen...

TOMMY CHONG: And that's on the surface—that's just on the surface. Can you imagine what's you don't see?! This is surface—what everybody sees. And isn't amazing that the war is still going? The countries are falling apart because it's this chaos that allows these criminals to keep working. You can't police under chaotic situations so that's how these people work.

The money is so huge, you know?! You think about America—we should be in a recession with the war and everything else. We should be hurting economically, but we're not. And you know why?! Because there is a product, an agriculture product that is the number one cash crop in the world. Let's not just talk about America—let's talk about the world. This cash crop is keeping everything afloat because it grows. It's cash growing out of the ground, not being taxed except by the DEA when they bust people with the dope and the cash.

DB: Cheech and Chong, you guys were two hippies having a great time in this world but the DEA kind of changed that for you a few years ago, did they not? Change you into more of an activist?

TOMMY CHONG: The humor…with me it started with Lenny Bruce. Lenny Bruce used to say, and this was in the 50s, he says, "By the 60s pot will be legal because there is so many lawyers in law school smoking pot." And that was in the 50s. And here we are in 2007 and the pot laws are worse than ever.

MARC EMERY

Marc Scott Emery (born February 13, 1958) is a Canadian cannabis policy reform advocate, politician, and media publisher as well as a former cannabis seed seller. He started Marc Emery Direct Marijuana Seeds in 1995, which he ran until it was closed by a raid by the Vancouver Police Department acting on the request of the United States Drug Enforcement Administration (DEA) on July 29, 2005. He is currently serving a five-year sentence in a US federal prison for selling cannabis seeds via the internet and US mail. Century of Lies / January 8, 2008.

MARC EMERY: On January 21st I have an extradition hearing and its all expected that they'll rubberstamp the U.S. extradition request, and its possible that in six months to a year I could be being taken by force to the United States to stand trial for what I did, which was sell seeds to consenting adults, ultimately shipped over an invisible line called the U.S. border, so that's as much as I've ever done. I provided seeds to people so they could be self-sufficient in marijuana, and these were all consenting adults, people who wanted to do that, and people I encouraged to do that. I mean being self sufficient and growing your own marijuana is a great goal of mine for the people of the United States and the world so they wouldn't have to be dependent on schwaggy pot and paying outrageous sums of money for bad marijuana. Thousands of people over the years I did this with were very desperate and in bad need and in terrible physical and mental health, and the marijuana was very helpful to them. They didn't have to buy it or go into the inner city or buy it on the street or support terrorists or anything like that. They were able to grow it themselves in the United States for their own benefit, and for that I am being persecuted by the United States Justice Department.

DB: How many million pounds did they say you're responsible for?

MARC EMERY: Well, the DEA on Lou Dobbs went on and said I'm responsible for a hundred thousand pounds of marijuana for each year I was in the seed business. I was in the seed business 11 years so that would make it 1.1 million pounds of marijuana, which is, you know, a lot of marijuana to be responsible for when you're brought before the U.S. criminal justice system. The high end of the potential punishments that they're going to give me is anywhere from ten, twenty, thirty, forty years in jail, possibly for the rest of my life, all for the simple act of distributing seeds to people who wanted the seeds to grow their own marijuana.

DB: The truth of how you went about your business model is you wrote "Marijuana seed distributor" on your income tax forms, whereby you paid hundreds of thousands of dollars to the nation of Canada, and they never objected until the U.S. DEA got involved. Right?

MARC EMERY: They never objected, they certainly took the money, they always took it. They were glad to get it. I negotiated with the income tax people frequently about how they could get more money from me. They were always well aware of where all my cash went and everything to do with my business. They were aware of it. I told them. It was very transparent because I was paying personal income tax on this money, I was declaring it. I didn't ever want to be accused of income tax evasion or avoidance or have these kind of things, so I made a point of paying all of my taxes.

Remember the whole point was to raise a lot of money and give it away, so we did. From 1995 to 2005 we gave out over $4 million to groups advocating peaceful democratic change in the world, to drug addiction clinics, to just so many wonderful things. It was never meant to provide personal wealth for me or to give me some kind of great standard of living personally. It was never designed for that. It was designed to have money raised to be given away for the movement, and that's what it was. That's what we did with it.

We did wonderful, wonderful things. We paid for class-action suits against the U.S. federal government, a Supreme Court challenge. We paid for ballot initiatives in Washington, Arizona, Colorado, Alaska, and various states. The money was used to pay for the global marijuana march around the world, finishing posters in several languages, distributing them around the world, and so over a period of ten, eleven years we gave away over four million dollars.

I'm proud of what I did. I'm proud of everything I've stood for. I'm proud of all the thousands of people I've helped who are crippled up and sick and infirm. I met more people who needed medical marijuana than almost anybody who's ever met them. Tens of thousands of people over the years have written me, and I was there to provide it for them. I'm really happy about that. I'm really proud of it, and no matter what happens to me, if I get put away in jail for many, many years, I know I've helped thousands and thousands of people and done great things with the money people sent me. I can't say that I'm contrite or regretful or in any way want to turn back the clock. I don't.

JODIE EMERY

Jodie Emery was already a political activist and speaker, but as Marc's wife she is now an owner of the Cannabis Culture Headquarters store, *Cannabis Culture Magazine*, Pot TV and the BCMP lounge. Century of Lies / January 20, 2013.

DB: Tell us what happened to Marc. Why is he in US federal prison?

JODIE EMERY: That's a kind of story that people should google Marc Emery and watch the "Prince of Pot" documentary made by Canadian Broadcasting Corporation or any of the many movies or interviews or CNN, *National Geographic, 60 Minutes.*

Marc Emery is a freedom and liberty activist who has fought for various causes for freedom since his earliest years in London, Ontario—his hometown out east in Canada. He brought cannabis magazines such as High Times and the book The Emperor Wears No Clothes into Canada to sell them and promoted them in the newspaper because those kinds of literature were illegal. He wanted the police to arrest him so he could challenge the law to make marijuana literature legal in Canada.

He has had civil disobedience in his life for many different causes. He moved to Vancouver in 1994 and decided to open up a hemp shop called Hemp B.C., which would sell bongs and pipes and all the marijuana paraphernalia which were not available in Canada at that time. In the 80s all the head shops had been shut down.

Marc decided to start wholesaling to different stores across Canada so that they could open up and sell hemp and cannabis-related material to people who wanted them. He started selling marijuana seeds at the same time saying that he would send them to anybody in the world because the money they sent him for buying those seeds would all be spent on legalization activism. To that end, from 1994 to 2005, he spent over 4 million dollars. He gave to the marijuana movement, to the U.S. Marijuana Party, to ballot initiatives, to medical marijuana court cases, to well-known activists and organizations throughout the United States. He helped finance NORML and the Marijuana Policy Project, political parties in New Zealand and Israel and all over the world. Marc Emery was the leader in financing and activism. He started Cannabis Culture magazine, Pot TV (one of the first video-streaming websites). He was the leader in the marijuana movement and called the "Prince of Pot" by CNN because he was so recognized and so well-known.

He was always arrested but continued to do what he was doing because he knew it was right and because nobody else had the balls to sell the seeds and make the money that he did. He paid taxes on all the seeds though. He ran for office on every level of government. He financed the B.C. Marijuana Party campaign. He appeared in media regularly. He was very reachable and in contact for anyone who wanted to reach out to him.

He was arrested by American agents in Canada with Canadian police on July 29, 2005 even though he had never left Canada and gave away every dollar. He only had 11 dollars in his bank account the day he was arrested. The DEA admitted that all of the money was given away and that he had nothing left to his name. They admitted that they went after him because he was financing the legalization activists in the United States and in Canada and around the world and that was the only reason they went after him. The stole him from his home country of Canada, gave him a 30-year minimum sentence (30 years to life) in U.S. prison even though he had never gone to the United States and only gave money and seeds to Americans to help them "overgrow the government." That was his slogan: Plant the seed to overgrow the government! They came up here when they were tired of it, in 2005, and had him facing 30 years to life in prison. He accepted a 5-year plea deal. He was extradited in May of 2010 and is currently serving his sentence in Mississippi.

A lot of times we forget that prisoners are still there. There's a lot of sympathy, compassion for medical marijuana patients, for a lot of people whom obviously suffer injustice and arrest but there is a lot of prisoners who aren't ever ....it's hard to fight for prisoners. It's hard for politicians to work for prisoner's rights. Oftentimes they are the forgotten ones. I always remind people let's not just jump ahead to how we regulate marijuana—let's talk about calling an amnesty. Let's talk about releasing all the prisoners who are in prison right now. If we're talking about this law being unjust and changing, then let's release everybody who is suffering under that law as it exists. If people are interested in finding out about that, we've been covering it a lot at cannabisculture.com and pot.tv.

If people stop fighting for those who are locked up or those who will be locked up or those who ever were locked up—if you stop fighting for them, one day you might end up locked up, and who is going to be fighting for you? I see it as an obligation that if you live somewhere that you're celebrating cannabis, you have access to it, you get to use it—if you have that sort of freedom and access and lifestyle, you owe it to those who don't to not stop fighting until everybody has the same freedom.

JAIME FELLNER,

Jamie Fellner specializes in US criminal justice issues, including prison conditions, the incarceration of the mentally ill, sentencing, the death penalty, and drug law enforcement. From 2001 to 2007, she was the first director of Human Rights Watch's US program, supervising research and advocacy on US counterterrorism policies, immigration, and the criminal justice system. What follows are excerpts from two interviews. Cultural Baggage / July 01, 2009.

DB: You have been involved in trying to re-frame our prisons and our justice system overall, for well over a decade. The Houston Chronicle ran an oped you wrote titled: "Jails Must Take Measures to Stop Prisoner Sex Abuse." Let's talk about the magnitude of that on a national basis first.

JAMIE FELLNER: Prison rape, whether it be committed by staff or by other inmates, is an appalling crime. For too long, though, this country has treated it as the subject of jokes or the subject of indifference. Finally, I think, we've seen a real change in public attitudes and in the attitudes of correctional officials to realize that when someone is sent to prison, rape shouldn't be part of their sentence. The loss of liberty is the punishment and nothing further. But too many people have, in fact, been abused. Now, we are still trying to get at the actual numbers. The Bureau of Justice statistics has done a survey and came up with 60,000. This doesn't count juveniles who have a higher rate of abuse than adults, but we think even 60,000 in the last year is under-reporting because too many prisoners are still wary of acknowledging that they have been abused. In fact, under-reporting has always been a huge problem.

DB: Isn't it also true that in many instances they may remain silent because they know not much will happen.

JAMIE FELLNER: Well, you are absolutely right. Many prisoners don't report because they think nothing will happen. But, worse, many prisoners don't report because they think there will be—you know, really strong problems will follow that reporting. Either, they will be retaliated against if they have reported a staff member, or let's say they reported another prisoner who happens to be a gang member; either way they may face retaliation and they don't believe that the prison officials will protect them. Or, the protection will amount to being put into isolation, which is the same thing you do when you are punishing somebody in prison. So, you know, here you are the victim and you are being isolated. Finally, you know nobody wants to be known as a punk in the prison culture and there's the belief that if you report you will get labeled and officials will not keep your victimization secret and then you have all the consequences of being called a punk, which invites further attacks by—especially if it's by—inmates.

The conditions inside US prisons are pretty damn bad quite frankly. Partly because we are sending too many people so they are over crowded. There's not enough staff. There is not enough treatment. And, whatever the purpose of prisons is, in theory, has been obliterated in practice because there these swollen, barren warehouses crammed full of people. So, you know, you sort of need to proceed on both fronts at the same time. You can't really solve the problem of what goes on inside prisons, fundamentally, until you reduce the number of people being sent to prison.

But, that being said, prison officials have an obligation to ensure the protection of those individuals who are committed to their care. That is a fundamental legal, moral, ethical and human rights obligation, and too many prisoners in this country are not protected and that is just totally unacceptable. Officials around the country, because of the Prison Rape Elimination Act, are taking it much more seriously. And the good news is the steps that they take to address prison rape—especially if they adopt the commission's recommendations—our standards—will not only help reduce prison rape, they will help improve prison management and protect prisoners more. That is what I think is tremendously exciting about the standards that the commission came up with: that it offers sort of a toolbox for better run prisons that are run in the sense of being safer, more humane—both for prisoners as well as staff because staff are at risk in a badly run prison, too.

I have always found it hard to understand why people think that a person is their neighbor as long as they live next to them and a member of the community, but when they are sent to prison, suddenly they are not part of the community any more. They are still part of your community. They are still someone's brother or mother or daughter or cousin. So the public that remains outside needs to care about how they are treated. It's not just the responsibility of the officials, and it's not just the responsibility of inmates and staff to follow the law and treat each other with respect. It's also the responsibility of the public to care about what goes on and to insist that those who break fundamental rules are held accountable.

These cases from Florida, you'll have prisoners in their cells, they cannot harm anyone, they are in their cells, but they are yelling, and they are banging, and they are making noise, so they get tasered. I mean, there is absolutely no excuse for tasering someone in their cell, yet this happens. Or, they get chemicals sprayed on them, because staff use force instead of using... You know, how with kids, we tell them, use your words? Use your words; don't use your fists. Well, I think too many staff aren't taught how to use their words to manage inmates.

Too many prisons aren't operated on systems of mutual respect, meaning that staff have to respect inmates as human beings just the way inmates have to respect staff as human beings. There is kind of this loss of understanding of each other's humanity that goes on in all too many prisons.

Century of Lies / December 8, 2013

JAMIE FELLNER: There are a lot problems with the U.S. criminal justice system long before anybody is even sent to prison. One of those is the plea bargaining system which resolves most cases. In federal drug cases, for example, 97% of all cases end with a plea agreement. Only 3% of defendants go to trial. The reason there is so few trials is fairly obvious. Defendants don't want to take the risk of a much, much higher sentence if they go to trial than if they plea. Prosecutors armed with mandatory-minimum sentences can essentially force defendants into accepting a plea. As the Godfather would say, they make an offer you can't refuse. You can either take a plea for 10 years or you can go to prison for life or you can take a plea for 10 years or go to prison for 45 years.

What the mandatory-minimums do, among many other things, is they transfer sentencing power from judges to prosecutors. Prosecutors dictate your sentence by what they charge. They can say, "Look, if you don't accept this plea we're going to increase the charges." Congress has given them plenty of ways to do that so, yes, judges are essentially bystanders in a criminal justice system that is run by and dominated by prosecutors.

DB: You've got a report that says the average sentence for drug offenders who plead guilty was 5 years 4 months; for those convicted after trial the average sentence was 16 years.

JAMIE FELLNER: Yes, that's just for the average sentences—an 11 year difference—which is just astonishing. One of the things that's quite troubling about this is when you have a criminal justice system in which 97% of the defendants plea and across the country—even in all state cases as well as federal it's 95%—prosecutors don't ever have to be put to the proof. It's an unhealthy system that puts so much power in the hands of prosecutors and yet doesn't have their confidence, in essence, tested before a judge, before a jury in a trial setting. There's a real lack of incentive for prosecutors to make sure they've marshaled all the evidence lawfully and legally and that it's all there because they know the case is going to plea out.

DB: Jamie, the U.S. Attorney General, Eric Holder, has made some rather profound statements in the last year or two talking about the need to rein in the prosecutors and try to deny some of them from using the mandatory-minimums so severely, correct?

JAMIE FELLNER: Yes and no. He has focused on two things. One, really low-level drug offenders who fall within a certain category shouldn't be charged with offenses carrying mandatory-minimum sentences but there are plenty of loopholes that prosecutors can use to avoid that directive. The Attorney General has also said that prosecutors shouldn't seek sentencing enhancements to increase those mandatory sentences unless the severity of the case warrants it.

Again, there are so many loopholes in the over broad language that any prosecutor who wants to seek a sentencing enhancement can. There's no remedy if a prosecutor doesn't follow directives. You can't say to a court, "Hey, in this case the prosecutor is charging me with something that Holder wouldn't approve of." The judge can't do anything about it. Holder has not spoken out about the need to curb prosecutorial discretion in the context of plea bargaining. He has not acknowledged what is I think acknowledged by everybody in the system that there is this huge gap between the sentences if you plead vs. going to trial and that there is no way that that gap can be justified.

KAREN GARRISON

Identical twins Lawrence and Lamont Garrison were inseparable. They attended Howard University together. Both worked part time to help pay their tuition—Lamont for the Department of Justice and Lawrence for the Department of Energy. Good students and aspiring lawyers, the twins graduated together in May 1998. A month before their graduation, the police came to the door of their house one night and arrested Lawrence and Lamont. They were charged with conspiracy as part of a 20-person cocaine operation, implicated by a target of the investigation. In court, they maintained their innocence and would not accept a plea bargain. Although no drugs, paraphernalia or drug money were found in their house or on their person, they were separately convicted of conspiracy to distribute powder and crack cocaine. Cultural Baggage / November 14, 2007.

DB: Karen, I hesitated to invite you because I find this so heart wrenching. Tell us about your sons.

KAREN GARRISON: My sons Laurence and Lamont were convicted of one count of cocaine conspiracy. There were no drugs, no guns. I think they had like $14 between them when they were arrested.

They arrested them in April. They graduated from Howard University in Political Science in May. In June they went to trial and September they were supposed to be sentenced but I thought it would be better to get a paid attorney because the two court-appointed lawyers literally did nothing.

They rescheduled it for October. In October they were sentenced to 15 and one-half years for Laurence and 19 and one-half years for Lamont. They were only supposed to get ten years.

DB: Very industrious young men certainly didn't need the drug trade to advance in life did they?

KAREN GARRISON: No, they loved school. Their ideas were to go to school to be attorneys. They wanted to be lawyers to work in their community to help people out in situations that they never thought would be their situation.

DB: Let's talk about the case itself. There were no drugs, no guns, no appreciable amounts of money and yet they were caught up through the conspiracy aspect of this law.

KAREN GARRISON: Conspiracy is the worst thing because it's built on "he said" and it was just one guy that said the boys did business with him for a span of 10 weeks or so and they were there all the time. It was impossible for them to be there all the time and graduate from Howard University at the same time with good grades.

The professor testified that they were always there. They know that their lunch was in the trunk of the car. I used to pack their lunch and put it in the cooler in the back of the car so that they wouldn't lose their parking space, and they would wait for each other and eat and didn't leave the campus all day. It was impossible. I know he wouldn't risk his profession to lie for my sons and say they were there if they weren't there, and all the other teachers passed them.

DB: There has been a lot of discussion about the informants that work for the government. This gentleman who ran an auto body shop who was actually the king pin of all this; he got 36 months because he testified. He could find people to testify against, and it reduced his sentence. Your thoughts on that?

KAREN GARRISON: I think that if he was going to be an informant that's fine but they should have investigated the things that he said. No one investigated.

They said there were conversations and phone calls. My mother was wondering why her car wasn't ready at the car place next door so we called this guy, Tito's Auto Body, to ask him if the car was ready.

No one checked the phone calls for content. They just said these phone calls went on. No one checked what the professor testified—that my sons were there at school every day and at the law library at night. No one checked any of his stories out, any part of his testimony which would have shown that it couldn't have been possible. They took all of his words as truth and that's what put my sons in prison.

Nobody goes and checks anything. The judge has nothing to do but sit there and make sure they're all there. The first day both of the attorneys went to sleep at the table—right in front of the judge, right in front of the marshal and nobody said nothing.

I see that jail has done nothing for them but harden their hearts. They thought this system worked. Now everything is not going to always be perfect and they understood that. But to go to jail for something that you're not guilty of, and then 19 and one-half and 15 and one-half years? People don't believe it, but they're doing it mostly with the crack to the African-Americans. If you don't believe it go visit the prisons.

I just want to tell everybody if your loved one is in prison they need your support. Don't forget about them. Some people get so embarrassed because their people are in prison but the embarrassment is not on you. The embarrassment to me is when you do nothing. When you do nothing and you give up and you don't show love because that goes a long way.

RYAN KING

Ryan King is a policy analyst who has conducted criminal justice policy research for The Sentencing Project since 2001, and is the author of many research and policy reports. King's expertise focuses on a broad range of criminal justice issues, including the effects of sentencing and incarceration on individuals, families and the community. His publications include an analysis of the media coverage of methamphetamine issues, an examination of disparities in marijuana arrests, a statistical profile of state prison inmates incarcerated on drug charges, and a study of the localized impact of felony disenfranchisement laws. Cultural Baggage / October 8, 2008.

DB: You guys had a recent report dealing with voter disenfranchisement; why don't you summarize that for us.

RYAN KING: We tried to take a positive angle and looked at the legislative changes in disenfranchisement policy in the last eleven years just to sort of take a step back. In 48 states, and the District of Columbia, a felony conviction can result in the loss of voting rights, for people who are incarcerated.

Maine and Vermont are that only two states in which individuals in prison are permitted to vote after felony convictions. Probation and parole, 35 states being under supervision of probation and or parole can result in the loss of voting rights, and there are 10 states in which a felony conviction can result in a lifetime loss of voting rights.

The impact nationally is about 5 million Americans are currently disenfranchised as a result of a felony conviction, and it has a disproportionate impact in African American communities. So that's the concern about the policy. Our report was to take a look at the last 11 years since 1997.

Since then it has received a much higher profile, whether it be through reports and research and public advocacy or a lot of the razor thin margins of elections at the federal, state and local level that have brought people to think more about voter registration, voter turnout, purging, etc. And so our report, actually, from a positive side, shows that, despite the fact there still are estimated to be about 5 million Americans who can't vote, in the last 11 years policy changes in 19 states have resulted in the restoration of the vote to about 760,000 people across the country. So there is a silver lining to an otherwise dark cloud.

DB: You guys dispelled the rumor that once you've been incarcerated you can no longer vote; many prisoners think that's the case, right?

RYAN KING: I think for most Americans, in a culture of tough on crime, mandatory minimums, life without parole, capital punishment, drug war arresting hundreds of thousands, millions of people over the course of years, most people would say, "Yeah I presume that I can't vote."

And they don't bother to ask the question, and frankly a lot of surveys of election officials show that even the state officials and agencies aren't aware of what the laws are. So most Americans are eligible to vote even if they have a felony conviction but aren't aware of what the law is, and that's a second layer of a tragedy of a really wrong headed policy.

DB: Lets talk about the racial disparity.

RYAN KING: We did a report looking at the racial disparity at different city levels from 1980 to 2003, looking at FBI data, and we found, I think quite surprisingly, that the disparity in drug arrest in 1980 was not particularly significant. But fast-forward to 2003 and that ratio between white and black drug arrest rates had really skyrocketed. And that was because in 1980 under the Reagan administration there was a real commitment to the war on drugs. There was a commitment of federal funding. And the result of that was that there were many, many more arrests for drug offences from low level all the way up to higher level.

And they happen disproportionately in African American communities, despite the fact that what we know from both drug sale data as well as house hold survey data on drug use is that African Americans do not disproportionately use drugs, do not disproportionately sell drugs, but they certainly are disproportionately arrested, convicted, and sentenced to prison for drug offenses.

DB: Zogby International released a poll which indicated 76% of Americans think the drug war's a failure. Yet I called up their PR guy and he tells me that I was the only media to call him in that regard.

RYAN KING: There's a real fatigue around a lot of these issues and it's something that we certainly think about here daily at the Sentencing Project, which is ways to continue to keep people thinking about this. The struggle with the war on drugs, the struggle with racial disparity in the incarceration system has been to try to overcome the fatigue that I think a lot of the public feels, which is that "We've known about this for a while, and nothing's really changed." And frankly when we issue reports, one of the first things we'll get from a newspaper journalist or an editor will be, "Well you know why, why do I need to pay attention to this? We already know this." That to me is what's dangerous, because whether you think you know it or not, the fact is that the policy's still there.

Policy makers apparently are not getting the message that the public is fed up with these policies. So, you know, I put the burden, I turn that back upon the public, as I said earlier, change has to come from the ground up.

EDDY LEPP

Eddy Lepp is a Rastafarian Minister and Vietnam War Veteran in his 60's currently serving a 10-year mandatory minimum sentence in Lompoc Federal Penitentiary, in Southern California. Lepp had a large-scale farm in Lake County, California where he grew medical marijuana for hundreds of patients in Northern California. All local officials were notified. Lepp provided medicine at cost or free of charge to anyone in need and used any proceeds from medicine sales to support local organizations, provide food and shelter for whomever needed it, charities, and a church in Lake County. The DEA raided Eddy's Medicinal Gardens in 2004; he was sent to federal prision in 2009. Cultural Baggage / November 12, 2008.

DB: Eddy, you have stood forth for marijuana as a sacrament, and you worked with local officials to bring medicine and sacrament to those people in your area and yet it has fallen down upon you. Please tell us about your situation.

EDDY LEPP: Well, as you were alluding to, I've been a minister for many, many years now and quite a few years before 215 was actually passed, my father passed away, due to cancer, and we used marijuana to get him to eat because the last three or four months he was alive, he couldn't even force down the Ensure. So, I used the marijuana and his doctor told me, at that time, that he knew I had added several months to my dad's time, being able to get him to eat. I've known for many, many years before 215 was passed, that the healing powers of this sacred plant and so when 215 was passed, it was very easy for me to step forward and start telling people the various stories about how I'd seen this miraculous plant work and help people.

I went from that to becoming the first person arrested in the state of California, under Proposition 215. I was later acquitted and became the first one arrested, tried and acquitted completely under the umbrella of 215. From there Linda, my wife who sadly passed away last year, and I started having huge clinics where we would help people get their recommendations, anywhere from 150 to 500 people a weekend. Once a month. That went on for several years until it became more mainstream and more doctors were willing to write prescriptions. As this progressed, we tried to help more and more people, and ultimately I ended up putting in a garden with 32,524 plants that the federal government took exception to and consequently turned around and arrested me. I believe that I'm still scheduled to be sentenced December 1st, up to two life sentences, for helping sick and dying patients. The other side of that is, is that with Obama being elected and a whole bunch of other things that have happened politically and a whole lot of things that we've done ourselves, it appears that I probably am not going to go to prison for the rest of my natural life. Which is really good news for me.

DB: Eddy you, as you've said, you've been a minister for, I guess, decades, at this point, and we have seen, you and I, the benefit; the positive, that this sacramental use can bring to the individuals, right?

EDDY LEPP: Well, so many times it's not even funny, Dean. Like you said, you and I know firsthand the benefits of this sacred plant. You see people out there all the time saying, 'Oh Jesus, that's terrible, it's going to kill you, it's a gateway drug, yadda, yadda, yadda.' It goes on and on and on, and they're just horrible, and then all of the sudden, somebody in their family gets sick, and they turn to marijuana, and it saves their life, and that same person that before was telling me what a no good SOB I am, how I'm turning kids onto drugs and ruining the world, comes to me and tells me, 'Eddy, my God, you're a hero. What a great man. I'm so sorry, I didn't realize what you were saying when I heard it the first time.' So, it's definitely one of those things that, if you see it and experience it firsthand, it completely changes your attitude about it, because it does work. My dear friend, Jack Herer, has said for many, many years, "Hemp will save the world."

Do the politicians we have in place truly want a better world or do they just want a better world for the one percent? Religion is much like the government. They seem to function best and have their best results when they've got everyone living in fear. Hey, they tell you these stories about how you're going to go to Hell and burn in a handbag and all this other bull that they tell people and it's ridiculous. The bottom line is, there's really only one thing God wants out of any of us, and it really doesn't matter if you're a Muslim, it doesn't matter if you're Christian, it doesn't matter what faith you follow. All God wants from any of us, is on the day that we die, is to be able to stand in front of Him, look Him in the eye and say, 'You know what? I honestly believe that I lived my life in a way that You would find pleasing.' Now, if you can't look Him in the eye and tell

Him that you lived that kind of life, then maybe you better change the way you're living your life, to be good people. To live our life in a way that He would be proud of. If we do that, we're all going to Heaven.

We can get through this in a peaceful co-existence, where everybody is equal and nobody suffers. There's no reason in the world for anybody in the world right now to be starving. There's no reason right now for anybody to not have medical care, and yet millions don't, and there's no reason for it. It's right now a world controlled by greed and Babylon.

ELIZABETH PATTY LUGO

Rachel Morningstar Hoffman was a 23-year-old Florida State University graduate who was murdered while acting as a police informant during a botched drug sting on May 7, 2008. Her body was recovered two days later near Perry, Florida. She was under drug court supervision for possession of 25 grams (0.9 oz.) of marijuana during a traffic stop on February 22, 2007. On April 17, 2008, a search of her apartment by Tallahassee police uncovered 151.7 grams (or 5.328 ounces) of cannabis, and four ecstasy pills. The police pressured her to act as a confidential informant in a drug sting operation in exchange for avoiding additional drug charges. This interview is with Rachel's friend Elizabeth Patty Lugo on the 5 year anniversary of Rachel's death. Century of Lies / September 29, 2013.

ELIZABETH PATTY LUGO: My name is Elizabeth Patty Lugo. I'm one of Rachel Hoffman's best friends. I met Rachel through my husband. They lived in the same apartment complex. Rachel was murdered five years ago. I was less than a mile away from her and about five minutes away on the highway to see her when she was shot five times point blank with a gun she was ordered by police to buy. Ever since that day I would definitely say my life has been completely affected by that. Every day has been different since then. I always tell people that that was the day that I lost all my innocence and my naivete. There is not a day that goes by that I don't think about her. She's influenced most of my life to the better. I live life to the fullest because every day could be your last. It's been really hard without her around. It's been especially hard for her family.

DB: Let's talk about the situation. Rachel dabbled a little bit with drugs. She got caught up for those small amounts. She was given a penalty more severe than prison by becoming an informant, correct?

ELIZABETH PATTY LUGO: It's not unusual for people to become informants regardless of the amount of drugs they have or whatever police activity is involved. People become informants for a number of reasons. Informants are a fairly important aspect of police work. A lot of crimes do get solved using confidential informants. Rachel was selling marijuana out of her apartment in Tallahassee. I always tell people I will never dispute that what she was doing was illegal. She should not have been selling marijuana because she was breaking the law.

After she was caught by police selling marijuana instead of getting a court sentence that a lot of us are used to she was offered a deal by police to become a confidential informant and then she wouldn't be charged with the marijuana that they found in her apartment. That's kind of how all that happened. She was selling small amounts. There's no disputing that that was illegal but the police had her purchase—after they caught her—two to three ounces of cocaine, 1,500 Ecstasy pills, and a handgun.

Rachel was caught with a little under a 1/4 pound of marijuana, which may sound like a lot to some people. It's about a gallon ziplock baggy full of marijuana. I read about a bust a few days ago that was 500 pounds, so at this point we're quibbling sizes, but one-quarter pound is as punishable as 500 pounds. I just don't think that her punishment fit the crime. She'd never been charged or accused of having cocaine. She'd been caught with two Ecstasy pills and they asked her to get 1,500. She had never once in her life fired a handgun. I don't even think she'd been around them. Whenever the conversation of firearms was brought up in her house, she was very much against firearms. She was very much into gun regulation. For her to be asked to the things that she was asked to get, based off of what she was caught with—it's just asinine. It doesn't make any sense.

DB: The day she was murdered, I hear there were a dozen cop cars that were supposed to be backing her up, a helicopter was involved and, yet, somehow they lost track of her. Tell us how that unfolded.

ELIZABETH PATTY LUGO: The day of Rachel's operation she went to the Tallahassee police department in the late afternoon. She was wired by a member of the police force who was not cleared with wiring and how their audio-visual technologies worked for tracking informants. She was wired improperly to begin with. She was given $13,000 in marked bills to go meet with two men whom she had never had any previous contact. She'd never purchased any amount of drugs from them before. She had said hello to them once because she was introduced to them by a friend. The police had her meet these two targets with $13,000 in her purse by herself with the faulty wires. That day there were 19 law enforcement officials involved in her operation including one DEA plane which was to be flying overhead to track Rachel.

The area where Rachel's buy/bust operation was supposed to go down is a heavily wooded area of Tallahassee. Tallahassee has a lot of Spanish Moss, big oak trees—there's a lot of canopy. Tallahassee is kind of famous for it. The DEA plane was basically useless because they couldn't see through all the heavy tree cover. When Rachel went up to this park, which was about 20 minutes northwest of Tallahassee, the wire failed and police could not hear her through the wire, which is what they were expecting to do. Even if they had been able to hear her through the wire, one of the lieutenants at the Tallahassee police department who was tasked with monitoring her wire testified that she was distracted during the hours of Rachel's operation and was not fully monitoring Rachel's wire. It was a moot point since her wire failed anyway, but even if the wire hadn't failed she still wasn't listened to.

Rachel was told that she was going to have line-of-sight on her at all times by a number of law enforcement officials. There were 19 involved that day. They had assured her time and time again that she would be watched at all times. If anything would go wrong they would be right there. They told her the worst thing that could possibly happen is that they would have to fake arrest her as well just to make it look like she wasn't in on the operation and then they would drive her home. In her mind that was the worst that she thought could happen.

She gets up to the area of northwest Tallahassee where the buy/bust operation is taking place and police lose sight of her. In the Grand Jury report and a lot of the legal documents it's not really clear why they lost her. Rachel went to turn into one park where the buy was supposed to happen and she missed that turn and continued on but for some reason law enforcement officials did not monitor her after she missed that turn.

She had missed one turn previously and was alerted immediately that she had made a wrong turn, but then she missed another turn and for some reason police were not able to track her after that. This area of Tallahassee is sketchy for cell phone reception, so she didn't have a lot of reception. They were unable to get her on the phone. Somehow all of the 19 law enforcement officials that day lost visual sight of her. Rachel went to meet the two targets by herself at the end of this secluded area where police lost her. Granted the buy/bust operation was supposed to happen in a park where there were tennis players, there were families of all ages. It's kind of a very "Leave it to Beaver" kind of park. It's very family-orientated. I'm surprised that they set up a buy/bust operation in that park. To begin with an ABC correspondent said that the park would have been fine if it was just a drug deal, but the fact that there was a weapon involved was a very poor choice made by TPD. The location of the buy/bust operation had been changed no less than 5 times, and each time the location had been changed by the target, which is a violation of Tallahassee Police Department protocol—something that the Grand Jury noticed several times in their panel report.

The Grand Jury report noted that Rachel Hoffman had no way of knowing that the audio equipment had failed. She had no way of knowing that the law enforcement officials who were tasked to monitor her had lost sight of her. The Grand Jury report says, and I quote, "Rachel Hoffman cried out loud for help as she was shot and killed, and nobody was there to hear her."

DB: Sadly that's all too common. Hers is the most notorious of them all, but this story plays out across America on too regular of a basis. Your closing thoughts?

ELIZABETH PATTY LUGO: There was a wonderful article in the New

Yorker by a woman named Sarah Stillman. The title of the article is "The Throw Aways." It's one of my favorite pieces that someone did about Rachel. It's a beautiful piece by a very gifted writer. It profiles not just Rachel's story but the stories of other people across the country who are coerced every day into becoming a confidential informant.

I always say that I feel like Rachel was emotionally blackmailed in this situation because she was given the options of either go to prison for 4 years or she could become a confidential informant to work off her charges. Given those two choices I guess you could say she chose to be an informant, but what type of choice is that for a 23-year-old to make? She was specifically told by the Tallahassee Police Department not to tell her attorney that she had been arrested and she was being used as an informant. Rachel's rights were violated because she was never officially arrested on these charges. She was never read her Miranda rights. Rachel was basically just a pawn who had no rights and was being used.

The piece in the New Yorker profiled people who experience that every single day. Some people say that the reason that Rachel's story got so much attention is because she was an upper-middle class, white college graduate. That might be true.

When we think of confidential informants maybe we think more of minorities or we think of hardened criminals who are flipping on the person that they trafficked heroin for or something like that, but Rachel's story hits home for a lot of people because it could be anybody in this situation. Sadly minorities are used as informants way more often than non-minorities. It can happen to anyone. It just needs to get the story out there. You can say no. If you have been arrested for a crime, the first thing you need to do is contact an attorney. Don't let anyone tell you that you can work off your charges. The only people that can lessen your charges in a court of law are a prosecutor or a judge. The police cannot promise you a reduced sentence.

The reason I speak out about Rachel's story is because you have the right to say no. Your life is at stake here and that's why I always talk about her. Everybody could be in this position. I've done some things in my youth. I could have very easily have been her. The person down the street that you know could have been her or it could have been your daughter or your son or your best friend. It happens more often than we think.

GEORGE MARTORANO

In 1983, George Martorano was a small-time drug dealer, buying a bag of weed and selling perhaps half to his friends. Georges' father was part of the Philadelphia mob, and federal prosecutors thought they could get to the father by busting the son. Over a period of just a few months, DEA agents supplied George with three, multi-hundred pound batches of cannabis, first providing the money, then the weed. Upon the advice of his attorney, because it was his first conviction and thinking he would get perhaps a 10-year sentence, George pled guilty. In 1984, the judge sentenced him to life, without parole. Since then he has written more than 30 books, as well as short stories, screenplays, and poems. Through a special arrangement with his warden, I was able to interview George behind prison bars. Cultural Baggage / February 17, 2004.

GEORGE MARTORANO: I'm the longest non-violent, first-time offender serving time in the federal prison system. I have no other prison record at all. My years of criminal activity were less than three for marijuana. I pled guilty to the offence assuming I was going to get 10 years, but at the time there was a lot of political rhetoric going on in Philadelphia, and I fell right into it. Instead of getting the 10 years, I was sentenced to life, no-parole—the fourth person in America at that time, and the first person in the state of Pennsylvania.

After spending a year in solitary, getting the sentence I thought that I would finally go to an institution where I would be in population. Instead I was sent to the most severe prison in America and that was Marion. I wrote a little bit about that. It's called "The Role of Words and Walls." I'll just read the first few sentences. It was for Professor Ian Ross, who writes a lot about prison chronology in America.

"No one knows what goes on in a body under the skin when sentenced to die within walls. I know. I was sentenced twice. Twice to come home in a body bag."

The reason I was sentenced twice is because I had the sentence vacated in 1986, but I was unfortunate to get in front of the same judge. His AKA was "Hang 'em High Hannem," who is now deceased. Also there was a lot of media on him at the time due to the fact that while I was fighting for my life in court, my then-lawyer, Robert Samone, was indicted by the IRS and facing 20 years in prison. I didn't know that during this trial his main character witness was going to be my judge. It was the first time in history that the judge actually walked in through the door where prisoners were escorted into the courtroom in his robes and took the stand as the main character witness. Samone gets found not guilty but the press had a field day with the judge and Samone relationship. 60 days later, instead of getting the 10 years, because of the bad publicity I get life without parole.

There was a clandestine deal made. I was supposed to get the life and hire a certain lawyer, and the life was supposed to come down to maybe 20/30 years. When they made the deal in the shadows no one told me. The certain lawyer I was supposed to hire I didn't hire. I hired a lawyer out of New York, Jerry Shagale, a very prominent appeals lawyer there, and the judge thought, I guess, that I had double-crossed the deal because the deal was never told to me.

I'm not bitter, but all I want is freedom. I pled guilty to the whole indictment figuring I was going to get 10 years. If you were to add up every gram of marijuana in my case, under new law I would get 15-22 years. Well, I did that. This is why webelievegroup.com is there fighting for my freedom.

DB: You say you got life without parole but it is my understanding that you pled guilty. How in the hell can that happen?

GEORGE MARTORANO: All these years I've been trying to get this lawyer, Samone, to come clean. Incidentally he gets indicted again in 92 for RICO. Two of his counts were that he took $30,000 that was owed to me for a pot bill and never told me, pocketed it, so why would he want me in during the trial where that would have been revealed. The guy he took the $30,000 from was an un-indicted co-conspirator. Also he was indicted for a conspiracy to murder my father.

DB: Along that line, George, is there some innuendo of why they applied these laws to you, in particular? Is it because of your family?

GEORGE MARTORANO: Yes, we want to be totally truthful to the audience because I respect this interview. At the time in Philadelphia (the early 80s) there was a mob conflict, and a lot of guys were killed. It had nothing to do with me or my father. There were no arrests being made. The violence got so bad I believe from research that I've gathered the fallout even came from Washington, D.C.—"What's going on there? Not one arrest." The violence went on for years. Here comes me, this young guy who falls with the pot case, and they finally thought they had someone who they had inroads with and they started squeezing me. When I'm there for sentencing, nothing was mentioned about the pot case. They all went on these other spiels about the violence and Nicky Scarfo.

Right in front of me I have my sentencing minutes. Here's one sentence: "We also have on the record an indictment that goes in alleged pattern of racketeering with Nicky Scarfo as head of the mob in Philadelphia in 1996. We further have intelligence information that if this defendant was willing to cooperate and testify truthfully that he would be able to help us." When I was indicted for this marijuana conspiracy there was no mention of mob. There was no mention of my father. There was no mention of Nicky Scarfo, and there's no violence. There's no violence in my case at all.

DB: Then the rationale by which they were able to sentence you to this lengthy term revolves more around the fact that it was an enterprise not a violent...

GEORGE MARTORANO: The CCU statute was devised back in the 50s but they never started using it until the Reagan administration laid heavily on the drug war. It's called the CCE 848. Because the sentence was so severe they didn't want to bring it into the courtroom.

The government actually brought the marijuana into Philadelphia and had me sell it. To make it CCE 848 count you must do that three times. So the government brings the marijuana into Philadelphia three times, and I sell it. They could have arrested me the first time, but they wanted to apply pressure. You got to remember I never was in prison. I basically worked all my life. I paid taxes all my life, so they figure this is a prime candidate to squeeze.

DB: The DEA or the local drug task forces are more than willing to make you wealthy for a short time in order to bust you in the long run. Am I right?

GEORGE MARTORANO: Oh, yes. I think the amount of what we sold—what the lawyers all ended up taking would have been over $300,000. That money was, like I said, the marijuana was brought in, was sold and all our guys split it up. Incidentally, all of us pled guilty because we were all first offenders, and none of us had records. I said, "Listen, we got caught. Let's plead guilty. Most of my co-defendants were all sentenced from 35 years and down and no one did more than 10 years. They're all out.

DB: In a third of their time.

GEORGE MARTORANO: I fell under this whole political trap. When I was sentenced I was sentenced to Marion—the most secure prison in America. I pull up in front of Marion escorted by two marshals with two other prisoners. We were all chained together by the waist and by our legs. There was a whole regiment of guards and lieutenants waiting for us. I was the first prisoner ever brought directly from the courtroom to Marion, because under that policy, lock down policy—23 hour lock down—you only went there when you were extreme risk to other prisons for escape and violence. I pulled up there and I was refused, so the Marshall's didn't know what to do, so they called some other county jails while I'm sitting in the car almost two hours waiting for them to accept me. No county jail wanted me due to the fact that Marion prisoners at that time had a very bad reputation. How they got me through the door is the marshals wound up faxing Philadelphia, and the U.S. Attorney there put max security on me, and that's when they walked me through the doors.

DB: If you could speak to the president or your local representatives, if you could educate anyone in government what would you tell them about those people that you see in that prison with you?

GEORGE MARTORANO: I've been a teacher for many, many years—over a decade. It seems now with this minimum-mandatory sentences, I get these young guys...I got classrooms of up to 30 and life, life, life. The educational lessons that I teach in creative writing and wellness and mentoring them is only part of it—now I have to instill hope. If not, these places will be unbearable to live in. No one's taking a good look at what's going on.

If they are going to let me languish here, let me do some good. I'm man enough to take whatever they dish out. Chain me up. Bring me to these county jails where these young kids are coming in for the first time. Let me do some good there. If they want me to die in these places, let me be a deterrent. I lost my poor son in 2001 in a motorcycle accident. In 2000 I lost the mother of my children to cancer. In 2002 I lose my father in the streets of Philadelphia to violence. I think that made me nail it down and look at the walls in a very different light. So, if you're going to keep me here—I just want to be more help to the guys coming in.

ROBERT PLATSHORN

Robert Platshorn is the author of "Black Tuna Diaries," the story of his marijuana smuggling operation. After 30 years in prison, he now tours retirement homes holding seminars about how marijuana can benefit old folks. Cultural Baggage / December 9, 2012.

ROBERT PLATSHORN: I'm the man who spent more time in federal prison for marijuana than anyone in the history of the United States. I did 30 years in federal prison for a non-violent marijuana offense. I used to be a smuggler. I tell my story in my book, "Black Tuna Diaries," which has gotten great reviews. You can learn about me in the movie "Square Grouper" which is now on Showtime and available on Netflix, iTunes or Video on Demand.

The reason I'm here is to promote the Silver Tour. After being on the road for the book and the movie for over one year, I realized that we were all preaching to the choir. No one was actually going out and trying to reach the public with information about medical marijuana, the safety of marijuana, the efficacy of marijuana. All the groups like NORML, ASA—they preach to the choir. When I go to Hempfest, Hempstalk and of course I go to all the High Times Cannabis Cup events. I write for High Times. I do a senior medical column for High Times. You're still preaching to the choir. I felt I had to do something to reach out to the public especially because the senior vote is so important and has been so ignored.

I watched Prop 19 in California and there was a tremendous amount of money spent on publicity to overcome the negativity of the growers and the dispensaries who didn't want to see legalization because they thought it would affect their income. It occurred to me that most of those people don't vote. The growers and the people around the growers are all ghosts. They don't want to vote, but the only people who went to the polls—and that was a bi-election—90% of the attendees at the polls were seniors and Hispanics.

No one was talking to seniors except the beer lobby, and all they had to say was, "You don't want stoners on the road." And seniors are easy to scare. But they were the people who defeated Prop 19. That's my generation. We invented marijuana on the mass scale that it is known today. Before that not many people were smokers—jazz musicians, ethnic groups—but there was no widespread availability or demand for good cannabis. My generation made it happen and we never bought the government's story. We never bought the negativity that the government had been spreading for years.

In the beginning they said, "It makes white women chase black men." Henry Anslinger said, "It makes negroes think they're as good as white people." And, of course, "It's the cause of all the greatest evil in America. It's the cause of jazz and jazz is an evil music." That's how they sold prohibition. The real reason, of course, was to stop the hemp industry.

No one was talking to them about marijuana today and its medical uses. No one needs it more than the seniors, and no voting group is as important as the seniors. Seniors can make or break an election in almost every state—certainly in California, Arizona, Florida—any place where there is large retirement communities. Without the senior vote nobody gets into office.

So I started something called the Silver Tour. I go around and put on a show. It's not a lecture. It's not a seminar. It's not a panel or any of those other things that tend to put you to sleep. It's a show. I'm an old pitchman. I worked on the boardwalk with Billy Mays and Ron Popeil. If you've ever read my book, "Black Tuna Diaries," there's an inscription by Billy Mays that says, "Bobby Platshorn was a legend in the pitch business—one of the greatest." Well, if I can pitch Vitamixes and Ginsu knives, and I was the first guy on TV with Ginsu knives, I can certainly pitch cannabis.

So I go around, and we have a doctor who tells them about the medical uses, the safety. He assures them it doesn't interfere with their medications, which is one of the great fears. We explain that you don't have to smoke it. That's the other great fear. A lot of seniors don't want to smoke, but they have no conception of edibles, oils, tinctures, extracts, ice cream—all the ways they can do cannabis. They don't know about vaporizers. Now we've given them a variety of ways to get it. Then there's usually a lawyer who will get up and explain the legal situation in that state or how to change the legal situation. At many of our shows we have a congressman who actually speaks to the audience and tells them they're entitled to get cannabis. There's no reason they shouldn't. He tells them how congress works and what to do specifically to change the laws.

It's a great show. We don't encourage activists to come to the show. This show is for the uninitiated. We go into senior communities, clubhouses...I'm not talking about nursing homes. I'm talking about places where people still play golf, go swimming, play tennis—have an active life. They've got the time and the inclination to go after their legislators and get them to change things. We go into the clubhouse. We give them a big, free buffet. That fills the seats. Seniors love free food.

If you've seen the piece that CNN did, you know they interview the people coming in, all of whom said, "Well, I'm here out of curiosity. My nephew sent me. My grandson sent me. My neighbor was coming, so I rode with her." Then the interviews at the end were unanimously in favor, "I want to try it. Maybe I can get off of some medications. I think I'm old enough to make up my own mind." The press coverage has been national—CNN, Newsweek, next week the Wall Street Journal. They did a fabulous piece. They even did live interviews which will be on their website.

Next week I have a show. Because of the national publicity here I got a call from the biggest channel in Australia that covers the whole country—TV 7. They've already flown in a crew who are going to video my show next week with Irv Rosenfeld. It looks like Bob Melamede is going to be my medical expert.

The congressman is going to be there, and we're actually attracting attention all over the world. Because this will be on prime time in Australia it will echo right back to the states, so we'll get even more national publicity.

To the best of my knowledge there is no one else who is reaching out, educating the public and turning them in our favor. We made so much progress, and we are so close to being able to push it over the edge or get pushed back. Now it's got to be one or the other. In California when Prop 19 didn't pass I knew sure as could be that the DEA and FBI would take that as a mandate from the public to go ahead and start closing down dispensaries, go after growers, and now this year Colorado, Oregon, Washington…so something has to push it, and the Silver Tour is the answer, because seniors vote.

RICHARD WATKINS

Harry J. Anslinger, our nation's first more or less drug czar proclaimed: "the primary reason to outlaw marijuana is its effect on the degenerate races." The design and implementation of these drug laws was/is/will always be about subjugating minorities and the poor. The stats from the jails, prisons and court rooms of America bear this out, obviously, glaringly every day of the year. Within my band of brothers, Law Enforcement Against Prohibition, we have no confusion regarding the nature and intent of these drug laws. Our current director, Neill Franklin is a black man with decades of law enforcement experience. Back in 2008 I spoke with a former board member of LEAP, another black man, Richard Watkins, who was the warden of the Holliday Unit, a Texas prison. Century of Lies / June 24, 2008.

RICHARD WATKINS: I was with the prison system in Texas for over twenty years, but about ten years was spent as a warden in the system, and I had an opportunity to see a variety of offenders come into the system, most of them drug related in some way, which caused concern for me. I subsequently had an opportunity to do more investigating and check on the reality of this so-called drug war.

DB: Our prisons quadrupled during that time frame, right?

RICHARD WATKINS: You bet. I saw the prison population go from approximately 18,000 incarcerated at that time to over 150,000. And you talk about a real escalation, and the drain on our state and our communities and just an awesome negative part of our society.

DB: George Will of the Washington Post was talking about how the incarceration rate was a good thing and how it actually, to paraphrase him, was better than creating universities. But it's totally misguided, this policy, is it not?

RICHARD WATKINS: The only good thing about it was for those companies that captured that opportunity to make money on incarceration. But as far as our society, the individuals involved, the families on the peripheral, it was a real, real liability. You see, locking up people is not a solution. I mean, we've done that, as you've pointed out, to a great degree and it's just really been such a drain on our society. As a matter of fact, we've spent more money trying to lock people up, actually locking people up, with the old mentality 'lock them up and throw the key away,' we've spent more money on those folks than we have on educating our kids. And, to me, that's just real backwards, you know, as far as priorities go.

DB: You have spoken to many organizations, churches and so forth, about this. What has been the response from the audience?

RICHARD WATKINS: It's really been awesome. Just real gratifying to me because a lot of people had made up their minds about this drug situation based upon hearsay and mistruths, but when they had an opportunity to be able to be exposed to the truth of the matter and the reality of this so-called 'drug war' then the responses were really, really amazing. I mean, it came from members of the community to include district attorneys, sheriffs, chiefs-of-police, judges, folks who have had an opportunity to see this great explosion in incarceration and to recognize that this so-called 'war on drugs' just has not worked. When reasonable people look at the reality of what has happened in this country, they recognize the truth.

The unfortunate thing is that so many people in positions of authority who themselves have benefited from this war on drugs have portrayed locking people up as equating to safety in our society. That has not been the case. It's been just the opposite, as a matter of fact, because when individuals are locked up—and so many of them have been locked up and are still being locked up for minor drug charges—it puts an 'X' on their back for the rest of their lives. They will never, ever have an opportunity to be good productive citizens again.

And I suggest to you that many of them were good, productive citizens before they were charged. These were people who owned their own businesses, who were professional people, who had jobs. They took care of their families, and they paid taxes, and they did all those things. But when these folks were locked up, Dean, it just reduced their station in life to being dependent upon the rest of us as opposed to being good, contributing citizens, because, like I said, they have that 'X' on their back, and unless they run into a very unusual situation, they will never again have an opportunity to be good, productive citizens.

Thank goodness that I recognized early on that this so-called 'war on drugs' just had not worked, and it was such a liability to our society. It's just been so clear that prohibition of alcohol, all it did was generate a criminal environment. We didn't learn, this nation didn't learn that prohibition on alcohol didn't work, and now we're doing the same identical thing with drugs. Talk about an industry that's producing wealth for itself—when you lock these folks up, those people who benefit are those people who are actually involved in incarcerating individuals and it just brings about a greater drain, not just non-productive but just really detrimental to our society.

I joined LEAP when I was still working as a prison warden in the state of Texas. You know, a lot of people called me crazy, but I just, I will not agree with that. I felt so strongly after I saw the reality of what was happening in our society that I felt a need to be a part. So many good people sit on the periphery and hope that somebody is going to do something to help turn bad situations around. I think we, as individuals, have to look for an opportunity to serve wherever we can to help bring about the truth in this situation, because I also suggest that it's probably one of the greatest liabilities that we have in our society in this country now. I mean it's not just Texas; it's every state in the Union experiencing the same kinds of effects. The only way things are going to change is that we do what we can, where we can, when we can.

#1 SUCCESS OF THE DRUG WAR

*"If you look at the drug war from a purely economic point
of view, the role of the government is to protect the drug cartel."* —Milton Friedman, Nobel Laureate economist

There is a very important group that benefits from the drug war: the politicians. Democrat or Republican alike, they all benefit from the drug war.
They no longer even have to campaign as tough on drugs because we already have in place an eternal jihad on drug users. Mandatory minimums, three-
strike laws, urine testing, probation and parole, all serve as everlasting inquisitors
on their behalf. The politicians now have but to simply maintain the status quo.
Those who originally stood for ever-lasting, ever-escalating drug war cannot now
back down from their stance taken, can never say they were wrong to destroy
the lives of millions of Americans by virtue of these drug laws, and will do everything possible to prevent the opening of the mass graves of drug war inquisition
that would expose their "morals."

I don't think too many of them consciously know they are working for the
cartels, but every time politicians vote to escalate the drug war, they are ensuring
profits for insurgents, terrorists, and bad guys all round. They are crafting scenarios that lead to increased overdose deaths, children killed in crossfire, corrupt
law enforcement, more AIDS and Hep C cases, and billions of our tax dollars
being continuously flushed down the drug war toilet.

The people know the truth; even the politicians, pundits, and doctors know.
The problem lies in the criminal justice community, whether that is the patrolman
on the beat or the district attorneys focus, the financial machinations and requirements of the probation officer, or the need of treatment providers to fill their beds,
it's the "authority" and bully pulpit of those who benefit the most from this drug
war, that continually pervert the truth so as to perpetuate this madness (and make
that mortgage payment).

I've tried so many times to find one high-caliber drug warrior, brave enough,
intelligent or stupid enough to defend their policy of eternal drug war on the
radio, to absolutely no avail. They hide their sins behind feigned ignorance,
psuedo-superstition or simple "bully pulpit" bluster. For too long their attitude,
their out of control policy, in and of itself has barred the discussion which will

force us to repeal these unconstitutional laws.

As a speaker for LEAP and as host of weekly radio shows broadcast on dozens of affiliate stations in the US and Canada, I have for years sought the answer from major public officials to the simple question: "Can you name the number one success of the drug war?"

There is not one person in public office willing to answer such a basic question. There is not one top cop, DEA agent, drug czar, or elected official willing to spend 30 minutes on the airwaves, defending this policy. Their beliefs are superstition, and their faith comprised of air.

The drug war has been handed down from generation to generation, from one group of elected officials to the next. Nobody bothers to investigate the racial bigotry involved, the lack of substantive data, and the ever-escalating costs. The effort wasted on this drug war is enormous, outrageous. Cops, sheriffs' deputies, DEA, CIA, FBI, justice department, state police, rangers, US military, Interpol, customs, border patrol, IRS agents, forestry service, the list is endless of those involved in "fighting" the first eternal war, the war on drugs.

Meantime, the child molesters, the rapists, the murderers, and the terrorists only have to worry about the few members of law enforcement not currently engaged in drug traffic control, an ongoing bust, escorting pot possessors to jail, testi-lying in court, or working on some 18-month undercover drug sting.

Behind closed doors, these politicians, judges, and law enforcement personnel agree that the drug war is a failed, hopeless policy. Yet when the corporate media puts that microphone to their mouth and that camera in their face, they revert to cannibalism. In order for them to thrive, they insist on maintaining the lie (can't back down now), and so they continue devouring our children's lives for making the same mistakes they made in their youth. (Right, Mr. Obama?)

Those who support drug prohibition are the best friends the drug lords could ever hope for. Drug warriors stand in eternal support of Al Queda and worldwide terrorism; they are the wind beneath the wings of the barbarous cartels in Mexico and serve as home boys to the violent gangs that run roughshod in our neighborhoods. Drug war proponents have crafted policies that ensure ever increasing numbers of deaths from overdose, more street corner shoot outs and more deaths from diseases that could have been prevented via a more intelligent policy.

Those who thrive on eternal drug war refuse to debate me, to submit to an interview on my radio shows, to email or write me or to even talk with me in public. They live in a world of lies, a mutual absolution society. There is no truth, justice, logic, scientific fact, medical data or any legitimate reason for this drug war to exist. The main reason it continues is the silence of the lambs, the populace so afraid to speak, so paranoid of the glaring truth that surrounds us that they remain in the grip of a taboo so powerful that they stand helplessly while the drug war devours our Constitution, fills our prisons with our children, empowers criminals worldwide, and wastes hundreds of billions of our tax dollars.

To encourage you to grasp this truth, to make the leap of faith and take the initiative to DO SOMETHING to make the drug war dry up and blow away, following is a snapshot description of the evil these bastards bring to the table every day of the year:

Government—The arrest each year of 1.5 million, non-violent US citizens. The destruction of many of these 1.5 million individuals' families, fortunes and futures often follows closely behind. Racial bigotry and racial profiling, so much a part of the drug warrior tactics have now made it possible to place more than 1,000,000 black Americans behind prison bars, more black's than lived in the south during the Civil War. The FDA is a quasi-corporate joke; the DEA is a certifiable threat to our nation; HHS mimics the lion from Oz; Congress too is full of cowards; the President is a walking billboard for success after drug use, and yet the Controlled Substances Act remains a screed for the new inquisition.

Corporations—The "Partnership for a Drug Free America", the corporate-sponsored castle crafters of the drug czar, was originally funded by the alcohol and tobacco industries and to this day receives funding from pharmaceutical houses, media, and energy companies. The death, disease, and destruction wrought by their policy increases each year, all according to their plan.

Cops, Doctors, Scientists, and "Experts"—Those in ancillary positions of authority, the "working man" of the drug war, make sure their mortgage payments are met and their retirement assured by joining in the feast. Their meat is spewing tales of dread and woe, knowing full well their lies will pay the bills, and the agony that spirals from their "intervention" will be disguised to support their contentions regarding the "harms of drugs."

There is not one in government, corporate planning, out walking the beat or "testi-lying" in court who deserves a moment's grace. They are all aware, full-knowing, and guilty as hell. It is our job to drive these gross and evil sinners down to the river of reform for baptism, forcibly if need be. It is our job to sing "hallelujah" to the end of drug war, to preach, reach, teach, and, if necessary, to impeach these politicians.

JOHN CONYERS, US REPRESENTATIVE

I seldom get politicians, especially working politicians to come on the radio with me. This is one of the few instances when a US Congressman visited us. Cultural Baggage / May 24, 2004.

DB: Each year here in the US we arrest 1.6 million people for drugs and the predominant numbers of those arrested are blacks, Hispanics and then whites at least in their correlation of their representation. Many have said the drug war is a continuation of slavery or the poll tax or it just the best means available to continue white supremacy in this modern era. Your thoughts on that, sir.

JOHN CONYERS: The fact that there's a racial factor to who's arrested, locked up, gets the long sentences, the death penalties, the most brutality, the most abuse of process is clearly race-based. I can't deny that. The question is how are we going to marshal the forces to do something about it against those who say, "Well, so what?! They did something wrong—lock 'em up and throw the key away."

I don't think that's any longer an acceptable approach to our criminal justice problems.

DB: Just as in New Jersey they had this modus operandi and they said the practice of racial profiling was not being used but their method was actually found to be institutionalized and taught around this nation. Can we not see a correlation, another type of bigotry being practiced in Iraq, Afghanistan and Guantanamo Bay?

JOHN CONYERS: Sometimes it's religiously motivated. Sometimes it's ethnically motivated. Sometimes it's motivated against nationality. We need some sociologists and psychiatrists to help us out.

DB: I wanted to close this out with one last question. Harry J. Anslinger, our first Drug Czar, he and William Randolph Hearst made sure lots of stories (I call it propaganda) were published in trying to get marijuana made illegal. Mostly they eluded to the fact that many of the users of marijuana were black musicians. To further demonize these users they were sure to point out that it was jazz musicians. Your thoughts on that, sir?

JOHN CONYERS: I'm disappointed to know that that happened but I can't say that I'm surprised. Racism is not a logical operation.

VICENTE FOX, FORMER PRESIDENT OF MEXICO

Vicente Fox is a Mexican businessman who was President of Mexico from December 1, 2000 to November 30, 2006 under the National Action Party (PAN). He is also the co-President of the Centrist Democrat International, an international organization of Christian democratic political parties. The first section is from a speech at Texas A&M, followed by answers to my questions. Century of Lies / April 10, 2011.

PRESIDENT VICENTE FOX: We have problems right now in Mexico, but it's not our problem. It is what happens in Mexico and why so much killing was going on there. What are they doing? Well, we're trying to stop the drugs from crossing the border, so you it doesn't reach you or young people in the States or Houston or drugs in the States. That's what we're doing because we are not a drug consumer nation. So we, in a way, are doing the job for the United States. We don't produce drugs in Mexico, very little. California, where I am coming from today, produces more marijuana than what is produced in all of Mexico. California, a state right here in this nation, and the rest of the drugs come from Bolivia, from Ecuador, from Columbia and from Venezuela. We are not consumers and we don't produce drugs. Then why the problem? Because we are in between the producing nations of the South and the consumer market in the North, and we are used as a way of transit, to bring the drugs.

What happened when those cargo loads cross the border? Right here, very close to here. Maybe at this very moment cargo is crossing the border. Well, it's up to Mexicans to stop it. Why doesn't this government and its security agencies drug enforcement agencies stop it at the border? Who takes that drug from there? From Chicago to Seattle to New York to Washington, to everywhere in the states? Who takes it there, and why is it not stopped? Who delivers? Who collects? And what is collected is billions. Big, grande, big B, billions. Billions of US dollars that are collected here, that are laundered here, that are taken back to Mexico and that money is used for three things: to bribe Mexican officials and police and to buy weapons. And guess where? Here, right here. The weapons, the ammunition are bought in United States with the money that drove addicts and consumers to pay for the drugs, and with that they buy the guns.

Finally, that money is used to contract thousands of kids, 14 years old and 25 years old, which are working for the cartels and not working for maybe a $1,000 a month. Every day they go out, and they take the risk of dying or killing. 40,000 have died in the last 4 years, but another 40,000 killed them, and today there are many, maybe another 100,000 are working for the cartels. So, we took about 200,000 kids in Mexico that could and should be in universities, could and should be having a job and an income, but unfortunately they don't. They were not born criminals, believe me. They were not. We are treating them as criminals, but they were not born criminals. It is not in their genes to be criminals. So, there we have a huge opportunity to work. That money is used for paying that payroll with those kids. So, how are we going to solve this? And this is maybe were we can discuss how can we solve this. Because we are trapped.

In the meantime, Mexico is paying in the toll in blood and death. In the meantime, Mexico is losing tourism and visitors and income that we used to have. In the meantime, foreign investment is not flowing into Mexico because the decision makers now say that right now it's not a good opportunity to invest. Look at the hundreds and the thousands of relevant and non-relevant businessmen from all of the north of Mexico that have transferred their families to live in San Antonio, in Houston, and San Diego and everywhere around here. Look at your compañeros, ask those who come from Mexico if they are thinking once they finish, once they get their degree, if they come back to Mexico. They'll say, "No, for the moment, I am going to stay here for a little bit." The loss and the cost is terrible for Mexico. We have to get out of that trap. So, maybe we have enough.

Following his speech, President Fox took questions.

DB: Mister President, given the horrors we inflict upon ourselves, empowering the cartels and the thousands of US gangs, what is the benefit? What positives have we derived from this policy?"

PRESIDENT VICENTE FOX: Nothing. I am supporting legalization.

I don't take drugs because they are harmful to my health. So, why are we demanding the government stop the supply of drugs, protect our kids so they cannot have access to drugs?

Many drugs are the very last frontier of the prohibitions. I cannot think of anything else that is prohibited today. Abortion is perhaps legal in many nations. It's led to the free choice of people. Alcohol, cigarettes are now legal.

So, I think the responsibility lies on the person, on the consumer and the family and the home and the kids. Governments will never have the opportunity to cut the supply of drugs. They will always be there. So, we better prepare our kids, our citizens not to consume drugs because of their own free will. Don't do it.

We have to separate the health problem from the violence problem and deal with it. By legalizing it you terminate the amount of income the cartels are taking.

We all have beliefs, beliefs that were created or that we learned over all of our lives. We have many good beliefs but we have many limited beliefs. If we had adjusted those beliefs, if they were adjusted like in the case of alcohol in Chicago, a hundred years ago with prohibition, we might not have this prohibition. Prohibitions don't work. It started with the Garden of Eden, with the apple. Adam and Eve ate the apple and then they went forth. So, I am promoting that and I think that many things will change.

GARY JOHNSON, FORMER GOVERNOR OF NEW MEXICO

Gary Johnson served as Governor of New Mexico from 1995 to 2003 as a member of the Republican Party, and was the Libertarian Party nominee for President of the United States in the 2012 election. Governor Johnson and I have been friends for more than 12 years. Gary was one of the first to volunteer to guest on the NY Times Drug Policy forum at my request. He has been our guest on air at least 8 times. April 22, 2012.

DB: If I recall right, you vetoed dang near every bill that your legislature put before you because you didn't see the fiscal balance there, correct?

GARY JOHNSON: I vetoed 750 bills which may have been more bills than the other 49 governors in the country combined. It saved billions of dollars, I think, when it came to the government telling me what I could or could not do in the bedroom. It enhanced the drug penalties. That came to an end, certainly, I wish so many of the drug laws would have been repealed. I would have loved to have signed those.

DB: Under your leadership the process in New Mexico was begun whereby the Good Samaritan Laws came into effect. What was that harm reduction scenario?

GARY JOHNSON: What we really care about when it comes to drugs is reducing deaths, disease, crime and corruption. There were a couple of pieces of legislation that passed that exemplified that. One was indemnifying law enforcement from administrating the anti-heroin drug, Narcan, it just indemnified them. The notion was that police would be looked upon as helpful and to be sought out and for those that seek the help they wouldn't have reciprocity against them. So, anyway, it worked out.

DB: President Obama said no to the Latin American leaders who are wanting to talk about—just talk about—ending the drug war. He's afraid that some cartel will take over countries once it's legalized. Your response, sir?

GARY JOHNSON: That's just ludicrous—absolutely ludicrous. You know one thing I'm asked about all the time is immigration. I think, number one, we should not build a fence across the border. That would be an incredible waste of money. And then make it as easy as possible for somebody who wants to come into this country to work to get a work visa. Not a green card. Not citizenship. Just a work visa that would entail a background check and that's what we really care about.

I think that legalizing marijuana would reduce border violence by 75%. The cause of violence is prohibition. The disputes that are being played out by guns rather than the courts. Let's get these disputes in the courts and out of the streets. You know, dead people laying in the streets.

GROVER NORQUIST

Grover Norquist is an American political advocate who is founder and president of Americans for Tax Reform, an organization that opposes all tax increases. A Libertarian-leaning Republican, he is the primary promoter of the "Taxpayer Protection Pledge," a pledge by lawmakers who agree to oppose increases in marginal tax rates for individuals and businesses. Cultural Baggage / October 6, 2013.

DB: You spoke to a large gathering of Students for Sensible Drug Policy about the difference between federalism and states' rights in regards to the marijuana laws. Could you briefly summarize that?

GROVER NORQUIST: What we're looking at is some people have talked about states' rights. That's when George Wallace said that he can beat up somebody in his state if he wants and nobody can get in the way. Federalism was what Reagan was for. Federalism is we want 50 states to provide 50 different competing visions of how to provide the best government at the lowest possible cost.

People move to well-governed states. They will move to low tax states. So I think it is extremely helpful step by step to allow states to take different approaches. We like competition. When you have an issue as difficult and as ingrained in people's habits as drug prohibition if you are going to discuss ways to reduce the harm of drug prohibition it's probably a good idea to try it in different states and then other people can say, "Oh, that seemed to work." Or "Here was a problem." If you pass one law for the whole country you don't know good or bad things that flow were really from that law or whether it was just something affecting the whole country.

DB: I wanted to point out, too, that often those that are jailed are unable to make bail for these minor charges and they are often held in jail longer waiting for a trial than they would if they were found convicted and had to serve that time. I was wondering your thoughts there, please.

GROVER NORQUIST: That is a real challenge. I think everything that we can do to speed up the criminal justice system, to make it simpler and more transparent...One of the questions you have to ask is how many people do you really want in prison? How much time and effort and money are you willing to spend putting people into prison? Are there ways to do this less expensively?

DB: Recently Senator Grassley held some hearings. The first one was dealing with marijuana, the second more with mandatory-minimums and sentencing. This is a good sign. Politicians are starting to wake up to that need to re-address this. Am I correct?

GROVER NORQUIST: Oh, yes. There have been a number of definite steps in the right direction on mandatory-minimums. I had dinner last night with Rand Paul, who has legislation along with Senator Leahy to give judges more discretion and get around mandatory-minimums. The administration has said they are going to ignore and go around some of the mandatory-minimum laws. I'm more comfortable actually passing a law and reforming the laws than have a President go, "Well, I won't enforce the laws as written because I don't like them."Because the next President might turn around and decide to enforce the laws. I think it is a lot healthier to change that.

DB: What do you think it might take to get the Republicans in Congress who say they are in support of the 10th amendment to apply those same principles in support of legalizing marijuana?

GROVER NORQUIST: I think what you'll have is states like the 21 states who have passed rules that liberalize medical marijuana and the two states that have decriminalized marijuana period, and people will look and see what happens. Some folks who are advocates of prohibition say you're going to have all these problems. Others say look at all the problems you avoid by getting rid of prohibition, and, just as with concealed carry permits, there were people who said, "This will be a disaster." Well, it wasn't a disaster. Those people are a little discredited. There are people who said, "Here are the benefits that will flow from this." They turned out to be correct. It helps to have the different states so that we can learn from them to see what happens, what works best.

Obviously politicians tend to shy away from issues that they are unsure how the electorate is going to respond to them. That's why everybody who voted to end drug prohibition in Washington State and in Colorado and those politicians who support it get re-elected. Then politicians in other states will be more comfortable moving in that direction. If they don't get re-elected then the movement will go the other way.

DB: Currently we arrest more drug users than we do violent criminals. I see this as a huge squandering of resources, a waste of our tax payer dollars and especially our police resources.

GROVER NORQUIST: One of the arguments for ending drug prohibition or certainly reforming significantly is that it's very expensive. It's expensive to put people in prison. It's expensive to chase after people and arrest them and convict them. If you're not sure that you really want to do that, spend the money, if you do really want to encourage somebody to get drug rehabilitation if they're addicted to something, perhaps there are places other than prison to do that.

DB: In order for these drugs to move from the hands of say the Mexican cartels to the hands of our children the obvious fact is that it requires pervasive corruption of border guards, of cops, of banks and, in fact, our whole society suffers because of this corruption. What are we to do?

GROVER NORQUIST: Whenever you have laws that people are uncomfortable obeying—like liquor prohibition—then you have a situation where people want to buy liquor and they are not comfortable with the laws. They don't turn in people who break the laws. They do break the laws themselves. It leads to corruption because politicians take bribes. Terrorists at the borders have always been a source of bribery. Government licensing of businesses has always been a source of bribery. Prohibition has been a source of bribery.

DB: Because of our mandate to the world, the Mexicans try to enforce these drug laws and they suffer. In Guatemala, Nicaragua, Honduras, it's even worse. Can you talk about the international ramifications of this policy?

GROVER NORQUIST: Obviously drug prohibition has effects not just in the United States but internationally. By making certain things illegal you dramatically increase their price like drug crops overseas and then people will kill each other to have control of those. It's not just an American problem it's also very much an international problem. Latin American politicians are often talking about their view of how prohibition harms everybody.

DB: Kids who get busted with a small amount of drugs get convicted and then they're barred from education, housing, employment, credit...the list goes on. Many of these ramifications are lifelong.

GROVER NORQUIST: One of the challenges we have with our criminal justice system is when you make someone a felon it's a tattoo, it's a mark, it's something that people carry around for the rest of their lives. When you're doing that you're not just putting somebody in jail for a short period of time you are affecting them for the rest of their life. That can be a little bit rough and tough for kids who make a mistake at a young age to turn around and do better.

DB: What might you say to those recalcitrant and often misinformed supporters of the drug war?

GROVER NORQUIST: I think people need to look at what's working and what's not working in the various states. Let's look at those states that are dealing with medical marijuana, that are doing drug courts rather than prison, that are thinking about ending prohibition—states like California, Alaska as well as Oregon, Washington State and Colorado. Take a look at what works and feel comfortable when you see things working.

DB: Do you believe in the legalization of drugs or at least the control and regulation?

GROVER NORQUIST: I run a taxpayer group so I don't have opinions on everything, but I'm open to the idea that with the 10th amendment the 50 states should take a look at what works. I look forward to seeing how reducing or eliminating drug prohibition works in the states compared to the ones that have it. I'm certainly aware that while there are costs to society of drug usage there are very definite costs to society for drug laws. The costs of drug laws are not zero and not negligible so we need to take a look comparing the costs and benefits of prohibition.

BETO O'ROURKE, US REPRESENTATIVE

Beto O'Rourke was elected to represent the people of the 16th District of Texas in November of 2012. Prior to his Congressional service, he served two terms on the El Paso City Council and has been deeply involved in civic, business and community efforts in his hometown. Beto is co author of *Dealing Death and Drugs: The Big Business of Dope in the US and Mexico*. Cultural Baggage / September 29, 2013

DB: The drug war is a much larger problem than most elected officials are willing to admit. Am I right?

BETO O'ROURKE: You are definitely right. But there are some really amazing current members of Congress who have been there, in some cases, for many years that have been working on this issue. I was very pleasantly surprised when I got to Congress to find people like Jared Polis out of Colorado, Earl Blumenauer out of Oregon, Steve Cohen who I think has just been bucking the trend from representation of southern states on dealing with this issue.

On the other side of the aisle you have people like Justin Amash from Michigan and others who all see the futility of the current War on Drugs and this idea that you're going to be able to get to these desired outcomes of reducing drug use and availability especially amongst the most vulnerable among our society like children, that you are going to be able to reduce drug-related crime, that you are going to be able to reduce profits going to crime bosses...on all those counts we have failed miserably prosecuting a policy for now more than 40 years.

You ask the people in Congress who "get it" and they're not just open to doing something differently they are authoring legislation, they are trying to build coalitions. I have faith that they are going to be able to make something happen. Just to start things on a positive note, that's been the big positive surprise so far in Congress.

DB: Well, certainly and we've had the pronouncements by Cole and Holder and the senate hearings about the drug war and about marijuana in general. There is some hope on the horizon.

BETO O'ROURKE: There is, and it doesn't mean that there still isn't a lot of work to do. You've been really kind in allowing me to be on your show now for over two years—maybe three. Just that there are people like you who have been persistently advocating on this issue is really making a difference. It is building awareness. It's holding people accountable who are in positions of public trust. It's creating the opportunity for people to do the right thing.

I'll tell you this and this is an educated guess—I would wager that the vast majority of certainly the Democratic members of the Congress and I would say the vast majority of members of Congress know that the drug war has failed. They know that we need an alternative. They just are not so sure that it's politically viable. The more that we hear from constituents throughout the country and from people like you who are advocating on this issue I think the easier it becomes to do the right thing.

DB: I perceive a little bit of anti-war stance in some of your position. These soldiers go to war based on false premises put forward by these other officials. They do their duty and they deserve respect for having done so but you also are calling for bringing our troops home and getting out of some of these involvements.

BETO O'ROURKE: It ties back to a subject that you and I have spoken about on a number of occasions and that is this War on Drugs. I think the more powerful we have become as a country the easier it's become and the more readily we have been to react to threats or needs in the world with military force or through an enforcement-only policy. It's the War on Drugs and everything that we do here in the US and everything that we promote and push down through Latin America and other parts of the world. It's meeting the perceived threat that Saddam Hussein posed by military intervention. It is the war in Afghanistan which is now the longest war this country has ever fought. It is response to the crisis in Syria from the administration to pursue a unilateral military strike. Thankfully that did not happen and hopefully will not happen. I do think that as a country we need to rethink how we respond to the crises that arise or we perceive to arise. I think we would benefit by looking at some non-violent and perhaps non-traditional means of responding to these threats.

DB: One of the issues I saw on your website dealt with the militarization on the frontier. I'm assuming that's the Mexican border and how it is disrupting lives, commerce, etc., yes?

BETO O'ROURKE: I'm glad you asked. There are 6 million US citizens who live on the US side of the US / Mexico border. That's every community from Brownsville through the California/Mexico border, all of the Arizona communities like Douglas and Nogales through New Mexico down through Texas.

Six million people and that part of our country is far safer than the rest of the country on average. In fact, El Paso, Texas—where I live and have the honor of representing—is the safest city in the United States today for three years in a row. San Diego is the second safest city and the rest of the border follows very closely. This idea that we need to further militarize our border, put up more walls, double the size of the border patrol (and these are all proposals that have passed the US senate), the idea that we need to do this when we are already as safe as we've ever been on the border, when we're already spending 18 billion dollars a year to secure the border in a time when net migration from Mexico is zero—I think it begs the question, "What are we really talking about here?"

I've pushed for a more humane, rational, and fiscally responsible approach to border policy. That certainly pertains to immigration and not continuing to build these fences and walls and militarize. It pertains to our trade relationship with Mexico, which is connected to more than 6 million jobs in the US. It's also connected to our drug policy. It's something that we, in El Paso, have been talking about now for many, many years. These very well-intentioned drug enforcement policies that originated in Washington, D.C. are largely carried out here in communities like El Paso or on the U.S./Mexican border, and they really diminish our quality of life. I think we can argue that we don't pose a real threat to the homeland. I think if we can work on things like passing comprehensive immigration reform, substantially and meaningfully reform our drug laws, we then allow our country to focus on those real threats that are, in fact, out there.

There are human smugglers who are, in some ways, not too far from slave drivers. People bringing in other people to work in a constricted fashion—sometimes without any pay—which is, to me, the definition of slavery, being held in bondage. There are people who are trafficking in children. There are people who are trafficking in weapons. There is the potential (although we haven't seen it on the southern border) there is the potential that terrorists will see this as a gateway into the country. If you can more rationally respond to those other perceived threats of immigration and drugs, I think you can focus very limited resources on the real threats that are out there.

DB: They intercept perhaps 10, 15, 20% of the drugs being brought across the border. These Congressmen, these senators who basically stand with "reefer madness" hundred year old propaganda—they've never really taken a look at this information or they've not wanted to see what's before their eyes. Your response?

BETO O'ROURKE: I think you are 100% correct. I'll tell you it doesn't come out of any maliciousness. It really comes out of ignorance. .I can speak a little bit to this from my 9 months on the job—it really comes from the fact that you are asked to vote on and respond to so many thousands of issues every year that you are in Congress and there are a limited number of those that you are going to be a subject matter expert on or really have much expertise at all.

For many members of Congress the drug war and its terrible unintended consequences and effects (like the fact that we imprison more of our own population here in the US than any other country in the world, that we've spent over one trillion dollars since 1970...etc. etc.)...You know, they just don't know these things and in not knowing about them and how these policies affect their constituents they just don't care. I think if they were able to better understand all of this I think they would be more open to doing the right thing. Going back to what you do and your program and others in the advocacy community, that work is so important to generate interest and attention and focus and help educate those members so that they can make the correct decisions and do the right thing.

But, as you know, a lot of the people that we're talking about, a lot of those people can't vote after they've been in prison and a lot of those people don't get involved in the public process and they're not at town hall meetings and they don't really apply any pressure on those elected leaders. They're really a constituency without representation in the highest levels of government. I think it is then ever more important for you and others, people who are listening to these programs to be the voice for those who are essentially shut out of this system. I think the more we are able to do that successfully, we'll be changing opinions and building the consensus in Congress to get something done. I do think positions that the majority of members of Congress have taken come out of ignorance more than anything else.

What will really be decisive, in my opinion, is to have the constituents, the voting constituents in those districts pressure their members of Congress because if a member of Congress perceives that the pressure is coming from outside of his district it's really not going to be much pressure at all.

I can point to immigration reform. It's something that most of the country wants to see happen and it is something that after the 2012 Presidential election every pundit and analyst said had been decisive in Mitt Romney losing to Barack Obama. The fact that Barack Obama was able to connect on this very important issue and that connection, especially among Hispanic voters, provided a decisive edge. Everyone's conclusion from that is that if the Republican party is ever going to truly be a national party and have a chance at winning the White House or controlling the senate, it is going to have to act on this.

And yes, despite that, in the House of Representatives you've seen absolutely no movement towards comprehensive immigration reform. I think that has a lot to do with the fact that the Republicans were the majority in that House and are really beholden to their constituents and are very focused on winning the next election and especially the next primary election. In some ways they couldn't care less about the national prospects for their party. What they really care about is maintaining their seat. If there were that kind of pressure around the reform of our nobly-intended drug laws but disastrously enacted drug laws—if there were that kind of pressure around that kind of change I think you would start to see a lot more openness.

I'll tell you there is a meeting of the minds in the Democratic party and some elements in the Republican party. We're seeing more and more Democrats who for social justice reasons and making sure that we're doing the right thing by the most vulnerable in our communities and Republicans for almost Libertarian reasons of keeping big government out of your life and whatever you choose to do that is non-violent and it doesn't harm anybody else you should be allowed to do is something that I hear from many of them. You're seeing these two groups come together around this issue of drug policy reform. To me it's really exciting. I'm not a hyper-partisan person. I don't operate that way. I'm truly pleased to see people from both parties coming forward, leaders in both parties and influential people in both parties.

It will require a really unique coalition to make progress, but that's essentially what we saw with the repeal of prohibition in the 1930s. You had the most unlikely of coalitions come together and finally admit that this very noble experiment to try to improve human behavior, to try to limit lawlessness and vice was a complete failure that created far more problems than it ever resolved. I think many of us have reached that same conclusion about the War on Drugs.

RAND PAUL, UNITED STATES SENATOR

Here we tune into an October 2013 US Senate Panel where the Tea Party favorite Rand Paul called for immediate changes to our nations drug laws, sounding for all the world like a member of Law Enforcement Against Prohibition. Cultural Baggage / October 6, 2013.

RAND PAUL: If I told you that one out of three African-American males is forbidden by law from voting, you might think I was talking about Jim Crow 50 years ago. Yet today, a third of African-American males are still prevented from voting because of the War on Drugs. The War on Drugs has disproportionately affected young black males. The ACLU reports that blacks are four to five times more likely to be convicted for drug possession although surveys indicate that blacks and whites use drugs at similar rates. The majority of illegal drug users and dealers nationwide are white, but three-fourths of all people in prison for drug offenses are African American or Latino.

Why are the arrest rates so lopsided? Because it is easier to go into urban areas and make arrests than suburban areas. Arrest statistics matter when applying for federal grants. It doesn't take much imagination to understand that it's easier to round up, arrest and convict poor kids than it is to convict rich kids.

The *San Jose Mercury News* reviewed 700,000 criminal cases that were matched by crime and criminal history of the defendant. The analysis revealed that similarly situated whites were far more successful than African Americans and Latinos in the plea bargaining process. In fact, "at virtually every stage of pretrial negotiation, whites are more successful than non-whites."

I know a guy about my age in Kentucky, who grew marijuana plants in his apartment closet in college. Thirty years later, he still can't vote, can't own a gun, and when he looks for work he must check the box, the box that basically says: "I'm a convicted felon and I guess I'll always be one." He hasn't been arrested or convicted for 30 years-but still can't vote or have his Second Amendment rights. Getting a job is nearly impossible for him.

Today, I'm here to ask you to create a safety valve for all federal mandatory minimums. Mandatory sentencing automatically imposes a minimum number of years in prison for specific crimes—usually related to drugs. By design, mandatory sentencing laws take discretion away from judges so as to impose harsh sentences, regardless of circumstances. Since mandatory sentencing began, America's prison population has quadrupled, to 2.4 million. America now jails a higher percentage of its citizens than any other country, at the staggering cost of $80 billion a year.

Recently, Chairman Leahy and I introduced the Justice Safety Valve Act. The legislation is short and simple. It amends current law to provide "authority to impose a sentence below a statutory mandatory minimum." In other words, we are not repealing mandatory minimums on the books—we are merely allowing a judge to sentence below a mandatory minimum if certain requirements are met. There is an existing safety valve in current law, yet it is very limited. It has a strict five-part test and only about 23 percent of all drug offenders qualified for the safety valve.

The injustice of mandatory minimum sentences is impossible to ignore when you hear the stories of the victims. John Horner was a 46-year-old father of three when he sold some of his prescription painkillers to a friend. His friend turned out to be a police informant, and he was charged with dealing drugs. Horner pleaded guilty, and was later sentenced to the mandatory minimum of 25 years in jail. Edward Clay was an 18 year old and first time offender when he was caught with less than 2 ounces of cocaine. He received 10 years in jail from a mandatory minimum sentence. Weldon Angelos was a 24-year-old who was sentenced to 55 years in prison for three marijuana sales.

Federal Judge Timothy Lewis recalls a case where he had to send a 19-year-old to prison for 10 years for conspiracy. What was the "conspiracy?" This young man had been in a car where drugs were found. The judge said, "I don't know about you, but I'm pretty sure one of us might have been in a car in our youth where someone might've had drugs."

Imagine this...and I'm glad the President has such great compassion because he's admitted like a lot of other individuals who are now in elected offices that at one time he made mistakes as a youth. I think what a tragedy it would have been had he gone to prison. What a tragedy it would have been if America would-n't have gotten to see Barack Obama as a leader. I just don't know why we can't come together and do something about this.

Each case should be judged on its own merits. Mandatory minimums prevent this from happening. Mandatory minimum sentencing has done little to address the very real problem of drug abuse while also doing great damage by destroying so many lives. I'm here today to ask you to let judges start doing their jobs. I'm here to ask that we repeal mandatory minimum sentencing. I'm here to ask that we begin, today, the end of mandatory minimum sentencing. Thank you, Mr. Chairman.

PATRICK LEAHY: Thank you Senator Paul. This is a public statement that you are making here but you've talked to me many, many times about this. I don't question your sincerity. I know the Sentencing Commission found that African-American and Hispanic offenders constitute the large majority of of-fenders subject to mandatory minimums. As a result African-American offenders make up 26% of drug offenders convicted of drug crimes but they account for 35% of mandatory minimum sentencing. Those statistics are very clear on this. They are also very clear that this hasn't really done anything to protect us or make us safer.

KURT SCHMOKE, FORMER MAYOR OF BALTIMORE

Kurt Schmoke, former mayor of Baltimore and now a leader in calling for the end of drug war, is currently Dean of the Howard University Law School. What follows is from his remarks to the Caravan for Peace. Cultural Baggage / September 16, 2012.

KURT SCHMOKE: Good Afternoon. I am very sorry that I cannot deliver this speech in both Spanish and English but I am so pleased that we have friends that will be supportive and help me out in this regard. I want to not only thank the Caravan for Peace for bringing this initiative here to Baltimore but thank you for your efforts to lift up the issues of the War on Drugs, why it's a failure, what it has done in our communities not only in the United States but throughout the world. It is very important work that you do and it is work that unfortunately will have to continue for several years to come.

In 1914 a law was passed in the United States called the Harrison Act. That began what we currently call the War on Drugs. In 2014, unfortunately, we will be celebrating the 100th year of the War on Drugs. It is my hope that, at least, in that year we can have peace and not continued war. I mentioned to you that the War on Drugs in the United States started in 1914. I want to highlight for you a comment by a man who was a police chief and the president of the International Association of Police back in 1936. His name was August Palmer. He was an outstanding, progressive law enforcement official and he said at that time and I quote him, "Drug addiction is not a police problem. It never has been and never can be solved by policeman. It is first and last a medical problem." That was in 1936 and yet we are still continuing to fight the battle today of trying to get our country and our policy makers to understand that the War on Drugs is complicated. It is not a single, silver bullet that will solve it but, most importantly, it is a health problem and not a crime problem.

You bring to our attention—and I know that our hero Señor Javier Sicilia has understood this—that it is an international problem and not only international but interconnected. That is, what happens in this war in one country affects what happens in the War on Drugs in another country.

We have seen the terrible, terrible impact of the War on Drugs in Mexico recently. Not only in the large number of deaths, the rise in the cartels but unfortunately in watching American policy, particularly the so-called "Fast and Furious" policy of selling weapons and trying to track those weapons—a very bad policy that has done more harm than good.

We have seen what has happened in Colombia with the United States policy of so-called "Plan Colombia" that was supposed to help that country but, in fact, all that it did was to buy large numbers of helicopters that could be used by the military not only to attack civilians but to spray poisonous material in the areas of civilian populations.

And then just yesterday I pick up the *New York Times* and I cut this article out that says, "United States suspends its anti-drug radar sharing with Honduras." What had happened is as a part of the War on Drugs the United States sold technical information and intelligence, so-called spying operations, to the government of Honduras and was supposed to be used to help fight the War on Drugs but the Honduran government ended up using it to shoot down civilian aircraft of people who were deemed suspicious by the government.

Now I want to point out there have been very positive things with respect to international involvement and our interconnectedness. Caravan for Peace for coming here and explaining to people in the United States how we share the agony in the War on Drugs is very important.

Here in Baltimore many years ago we tried to make an improvement in fighting one aspect of the drug problem which is the AIDS problem—the spread of AIDS. We wanted to do that by having a sterile syringe exchange program. We were not very successful in getting the public to understand it until friends from overseas, from the Netherlands, came over and explained. It was law enforcement officials, it was public health officials from the Netherlands that came over and explained how the needle exchange program could help reduce the spread of AIDS without increasing the criminal aspect of the War on Drugs. I was the mayor of this city for 12 years and I was so proud of our community for being creative in trying to make sure we did more to treat those who had been drug addicted and allowing us to do the needle exchange program that helped so many

AIDS victims. I'm very proud of Baltimorians to be creative, but I've been so disappointed at the national leaders. Not just the Republicans—it's been the Democrats also. I thought that the Republicans would just look at the money that's being wasted on the War on Drugs—they care so much about balancing the budget and doing efficient things with money. The War on Drugs is an absolute waste of dollars, and it should be converted from heavy on law enforcement to more on public health. But they didn't do it. And then when the Democrats came in, I thought, well, maybe there would be a change there, but, as I said, we had this "Fast and Furious" policy, and then, unfortunately, our President decided to attack medical marijuana in California for reasons that I simply don't understand. Let me pause—I do understand.

This is a very political issue, and when you look at the War on Drugs going over for the last 100 years, you have to ask yourself, "Don't people understand the definition of insanity?!" That is, most people understand that if you do the same thing over and over and expect a different result, that is one definition of insanity. But with the War on Drugs we continue to do the same thing over and over and expect a different result. Why? Why is that? Because the War on Drugs is mostly about money and power. This is not just about people being addicted to drugs. It is also about people being addicted to drug money. You say, "Who's addicted to drug money?"

Well, look who benefits by the current policy that we have. People make big money on prohibition. Prohibition failed in the 1920s to make ours an alcohol-free America and prohibition is failing today to make our a drug-free America. But many people are making a lot of money. Drug cartels, of course, but financial institutions, many financial institutions, private corrections (people who make money building jails are very happy with the War on Drugs as we have it today) and many, many who receive money for military misadventures also are happy. So it's money and power, and we have to break the grip of that.

It is my hope that efforts like Caravan for Peace will do that. In the United States, our key to starting a new approach is starting to accept the definition of our problem as it was laid out by a great American professor, David Musto, who wrote a book that described the drug problem as, "the American disease."

Think about it. Think about it. The problem, he is saying, is this is primarily a health problem. Addiction and AIDS, which are related to the War on Drugs, are health problems. Ladies and gentleman, you don't arrest your way out of a disease. You don't prosecute your way out of a disease. And you don't incarcerate your way out of a disease. You have to come up with different strategies. Let us start by redefining this as primarily a health problem and not a crime problem. We know the criminal justice system has a role to play—it's just not the primary role. It is the public health that should lead the way. I'm asking you, as we welcome our friends from the Caravan for Peace and all of the friends who are considering doing something different about the War on Drugs, to think globally but act locally. Think globally but act locally.

We know that this problem is an international problem. Our elected officials at the highest level are not about to do something about it, so we have to do something at the local level. What is that? We and the city and the state and the private sector and our individual citizens have to carve out ways in which we can work together. We can expand treatment for those who have been addicted. We can expand rehabilitation. We can also make sure that we are doing what some of these organizations are doing, which is to try to make sure that when people get arrested and serve their time, they get to wipe that off their record. That they expunge that and get a fresh start. We need to give people a fresh start, because there's so many young people that get involved early and yet want to go on and live wonderful and productive lives.

When George Bush, the President, was asked whether he ever did drugs as a young person what he said was, "When I was young and irresponsible I was young and irresponsible." He never admitted what we know he did as a young man but he was able to get a fresh start. He was able to change and society supported him in his fresh start. I think that's what we owe our young people.

Finally, because of my concern about involvement in citizenship, we ought to do all that we can to eliminate the laws that prevent people who have a criminal conviction from being able to vote. Right now there are so many laws that restrict the ability of people to vote and it makes such a huge difference. In 2008 in the Presidential election 13% of African-American men who by age were eligible to vote in that election were prevented from voting because of something that happened when they were very young. 13%—just think about that. The difference that could make in an election.

Well there's much more that we could say and I know you will hear from the panel and hear from those who have been victimized but I have just come to say that we all should be hopeful. We can make change. It may be slow and we know that progress is sometimes very difficult but I do believe that in 2014 we will no longer be using the term war as it relates to drugs but by 2014 we will, indeed, be talking about peace.

CLIFF THORNTON, GREEN PARTY

Clifford "Cliff" W. Thornton, Jr. is an American drug policy reform advocate and Green politician serving as one of the seven current co-Chairs of the Green Party of the United States. Century of Lies / July 1, 2008.

CLIFF THORNTON: There are two questions that I always ask the audience when I'm speaking before a group of people and the first one is: Do you think what we're doing with the war on drugs is working? And the second one is: Do you think people are ever going to stop using these illegal drugs? The overwhelming response is 'no.' And before we can go anywhere else we have to answer those questions in their entirety. And that promotes a very vigorous conversation amongst the audience. What I like to do is, rather than lecture, I like to engage the audience and let them come up with their own solutions. And it seems to work very well.

DB: You ran for governor, and you've had access and conversations with many other politicians in this regard. Why can none of them ever speak up? Why can none of them ever call for an end to the drug war and to destroy the cartels?

CLIFF THORNTON: There's a couple of things that I think we should realize. The drug money that is taken from the drug sales, a lot of this money, somehow, some way, gets back to the coffers of the people that are running for office, and they're not going to come out against the drug war. Secondly, the fear of the politicians is that if they propose something like legalizing drugs, they fear that they would not get elected. And it makes a lot of sense to me, because the general populace, first and foremost are not what I call well-educated, and they don't seem to want to be educated on the particular subject. But we don't realize, as a country, that this drug war, as I've said many times, many ways, is sucking this country dry. We can start to look at our health system, our education system, and economic system and see that for the past almost a century, drug prohibition has been a steady drain on the money for things like education, health care, and our economic system. So we're heading down the road of catastrophe. The United States is really an accident waiting to happen.

DB: Why do people cling to this idea that it's going to work?

CLIFF THORNTON: People don't cling to the idea that it's going to work. Like I said earlier on, the very first thing I ask are those two questions: Do you think the drug war is working? And do you think people are ever going to stop using these illegal drugs? And overwhelmingly the response is 'no,' and those people that say 'yes,' the people in the audience, I let them do my bidding, they tell them one reason or another why it can't end.

But when it gets down to the real hardcore stepping up to the plate, those people that agree with me on both questions, they're not willing to put forth the effort to end this drug war for fear of some type of ostracization. You've got to understand that people fear for their personal welfare when they go up or against the drug war, because the drug war is a money maker, not only for the drug cartels and drug dealers but also for people who build prisons, people who have made their living off of prosecuting drug dealers and drug cartels. It's like Sanho Tree says over and over again, the drug war is like the balloon effect. You stop it in one place, and it pops up in another. And that's been going on all of my life.

So things are not going to change until we get a politician that has the gumption and the wherewithal to take this to the next level. It's not going to happen at the UN. It's not going to happen at the federal level. It is only going to happen at the state level. During my run for governor, what I found is that seventy percent of the people in the state legislature are for some type of regulation and control or bringing drugs within the law. However, of that seventy percent, only thirty percent of them within the state legislature are going to actively pursue changing of the drug laws, such as voting and promoting the medical marijuana thing.

Where we have to go to really show that the drug war can be controlled is to put in things like heroin and cocaine and meth and ecstasy type maintenance centers that have been proven to be effective all over the world. At this present time, at Columbia University in New York, they are running those type of programs, and hopefully they won't be sabotaged by the governmental authorities.

DB: We have in Colombia, where union officials are being killed by the dozens and yet we're teaming up with them to 'squelch' the flow of drugs and in Mexico journalists are being gunned down. Police and military being gunned down. The unintended consequences, as you said earlier, impact every aspect of our lives, right?

CLIFF THORNTON: The drug war is two degrees from everything in society. There is no subject that you can bring up that you can't directly or indirectly connect it to the drug war through economic reasons. The humanitarian side of it, the people are not going to act until it hits them in their pocket economically. You see this type of gas crises, that we use for our cars, we're going through in this country, and people are up in arms with that. Somehow, someway, you're going to have to show the people how they're affected economically. In the state of Connecticut, there has been a surplus of funds for the last four or five years, but now we're slowly but surely entering into that deficit process, and it can be directly attributed to the spiraling costs of incarceration within our prison system. Connecticut has a population of about 3.5 million people. And we spend, every year, anywhere from $600 to $800 million a year just on the operations of our prison system. Now that $600 million would be a tremendous boost to giving health care to every single individual in the state of Connecticut. But people don't want to look at that for what it is. And it's going to take time, but things are going to change really drastically in the next four years to push us into looking at, seriously, how we're going to regulate, not just marijuana, but all of these drugs.

See, people don't understand. In 1996 the UN said that world terrorist organizations derive thirty percent of their funds from the sale and distribution of illegal drugs. Now, you've got to look at that and really understand what's going on. Thirty percent of their revenue, for world terrorist organizations, comes from the sale of illegal drugs.

So, we have been really stupid on crime, not smart on crime, for the past four decades. It is a huge mess, and I don't foresee within the near future that the drug war is going to be successful. Because in order for it to be totally successful we would have to have a police officer on every single corner and every single country store in rural America. What people have to understand is that we have to ring this country with border guards, not only around the Mexican border but also the Canadian border. What that means, nothing comes in but, obviously, nothing is going to go out, so we're not going to put up with that either.

So we're doomed, the drug war is doomed to failure. But this is the big thing for me: Drug dealers and drug cartels tell you readily they can afford to lose eighty percent of their product and still make a huge profit. That is astounding.

DB: And when you get right down to it I don't think they've ever had more than about a fifteen percent interdiction rate over the life of the drug war,

CLIFF THORNTON: You're absolutely correct. We have been in a downward spiral, and as the drug war fails more, the more this country goes downhill. It's plain and simple. I've watched my native Hartford go downhill for the past four to five decades, and right at the core of this decline is the drug war.

Hippocratic or Hypocritical

"Give one of these Mexican beet field workers a couple of puffs on a marijuana cigarette and he thinks he is in the bullring at Barcelona."
—South Dakota legislative hearing, 1936

We must expose the drug war addicts, to force them to explain their horrible, destructive habits. Today, the Drug Czar and his minions have determined that not even doctors can be trusted to make medical decisions for the citizenry. Bands of gypsy snitches roam the countryside, pretending to be in pain, begging good doctors for pills to alleviate their suffering, only to appear in court, fit as a fiddle and thus "exposing" the good doctor's intentions as evil, their prescriptions as willful violations of law and their practice to be trafficking in drugs.

I despise and want to destroy the black market in drugs, to deny the terrorists funding from turning flowers into weapons, to destroy the barbarous cartels in Mexico and elsewhere and especially to eliminate the reason for existence of most of the violent US gangs. These bad actors are actually just trying to make a living. Mostly, I blame those in government, in positions of authority, whose ignorance, lack of common sense, of history, has given us nigh unto a hundred years of barbarism and overdose deaths, street corner shootouts, children dying and international fiascoes. Millions of lives have been destroyed as a result of these proponents of drug war, the cheer leaders of prohibition who bear the blame for this cluster flock. Those who believe in drug war are akin to dim witted hillbillies and fundamentalist freaks.

The constant refrain of drug warriors is that the use of drugs will stifle your career and leave you homeless in the streets. Perhaps these pro drug war advocates should educate themselves before sticking both feet in their mouth. A prime example of the hypocrisy of such statements can be found in the life of "the father of American surgery," Dr. William Halsted, one of the founding members of Johns Hopkins University who was a daily user of morphine for several decades. Edison, Freud, and Einstein were also occasional users of cocaine and morphine, and why not, for it was perfectly legal at that point in time.

It must be pointed out that chief among those responsible for this drug war are those whose intellect, and knowledge is supposed to lead us in the right direction; scientists and doctors, treatment providers, the people whose knowledge could redirect and absolve the mindset and direction of our elected officials and thus counter the implementation and continuation of laws designed for eternal failure.

DONALD ABRAMS, M.D.

Dr. Donald I. Abrams is a cancer and integrative medicine specialist at the University of California, San Francisco Osher Center for Integrative Medicine and chief of Hematology and Oncology at San Francisco General Hospital. He is an executive committee member of the UCSF Helen Diller Family Comprehensive Cancer Center and is co-chair of the center's program in Symptom Management, Palliative Care and Survivorship. Dr. Abrams specializes in complementary and alternative therapies including mind-body treatments, botanical therapies, medical use of marijuana and traditional Chinese medicine herbal therapies. Dr. Abrams, who has been in the forefront of HIV/AIDS research and treatment, stepped down from the HIV Clinic at San Francisco General Hospital in August 2006 to devote more time to integrative medicine and oncology. The interview was recorded in 2008 at the International Conference on Cannabis Therapeutics.

DB: You conducted the first clinical study on how marijuana affects the human immune system. What did you discover?

DR. ABRAMS: What we found in that study was that patients who were either smoking cannabis or taking the pill, compared to placebo, had no change in the level of the AIDS virus in their bloodstream, no significant change in the level of the AIDS drugs in their bloodstream, and if anything, the groups exposed to the cannabinoids may have had some improvement in their immune system. We also found weight gain in both the people smoking and the people taking the dronabinol which, previously dronabinol had been shown to increase appetite but not weight, but this study was really too small and was not powered for that as an endpoint.

After that first NIDA study, we were fortunate to be funded by the University of California Center for Medicinal Cannabis Research. The Center for Medicinal Cannabis Research allowed for funding of studies that may show that cannabis has a medical benefit, which NIDA, the National Institute on Drug Abuse, is really by a mandate of Congress is not allowed to fund. They can only study substances of abuse as substances of abuse and not as therapies. So with our funding from the Center for Medicinal Cannabis Research we did a randomized, double-blind, placebo controlled trial of cannabis, smoked cannabis, in patients with the AIDS related peripheral neuropathy, which is pain or tingling from nerve damage either from HIV itself or from the anti-viral drugs that we use to treat it.

In this study we enrolled fifty patients: 25 smoked cannabis and 25 smoked placebo cannabis and we found that there was a reduction in pain from the peripheral neuropathy in the cannabis smokers compared to the placebo group. And we published that last year in the *Journal of Neurology* and that, I think, now makes it impossible for people to say that there's no randomized placebo controlled clinical trial that shows that smoked cannabis has a medicinal benefit because that clearly shows it.

DB: There are those actors who roam the country, for instance Mr. John Walters, our nation's drug czar, who ignore these stats and, as you say, indicate there are no recognized studies indicating positive benefits.

DR. ABRAMS: Having worked now in this medical marijuana arena for the past 15 years, I'm not ever surprised that science does not win in the fight against politics. We're fighting a war on drugs in this country, and it's a shame that, unfortunately, we also are combating patients who need the drugs at the same time. So we knew that, even if we showed that cannabis was effective for medical indication, that people would still say, 'Well gee, patients don't smoke a medicine.'

So another study that we completed that was published last year in *Clinical Pharmacology and Therapeutics* was a study in healthy marijuana smokers, aged 25 to 40, comparing smoking cannabis to vaporization, using a product called the Volcano Vaporizer. This was the easiest study we ever enrolled because we paid these, you know, 25 to 40-year-old marijuana smokers $600 for spending six days in our general clinical research center at San Francisco General and allowing them to either smoke or vaporize half of a NIDA cigarette on each day, three different strengths. What we found in that study was that, checking the level of THC in the bloodstream, it was really comparable in the patients who smoked compared to those who vaporized, and the patients who vaporized had much less expired carbon monoxide, which is a marker for noxious products of combustion.

The interesting thing was that we also found that patients had very similar levels of the so-called 'high' and when we were getting the paper published one of the reviewers wanted to know how we measured 'high' and if there was a validated instrument for measuring 'high' and what the gold-standard was, which I thought was quite funny. We just asked people to rate their 'high' on a 1 to 10 scale and, you know these reviewers are always interested in validated scales and what you compare it to. We also found, and again this is using NIDA marijuana which is low potency and also freeze-dried so it needs to be rehydrated, that out of the eighteen participants, fourteen actually preferred vaporization to smoking.

So with that data we're now doing a study, which I think is really the sort of the end stage of the evolution of the studies that we're doing and I think may be one of the most important ones, and that is looking for a potential interaction between cannabinoids and opioids. We're taking patients with chronic pain who are on a stable dose of either morphine or oxycontin and we're bringing them in to our general clinical research center at San Francisco General Hospital and we're drawing on day one the levels of the opioid, the oxycontin or the morphine, in their blood stream and then we're having them vaporize cannabis three times a day for four days and at the end of that period we're again checking the level of the opioids in their bloodstream to see if there's any interaction between the cannabinoids and the opioids.

Our hypothesis is that there will be an interaction and that, in fact, the cannabinoids will hopefully, or I think, will boost the levels of the opioids in the blood stream because anecdotally and in pre-clinical models people have suggested that cannabinoids and opioids work synergistically, that is the sum of the two is greater than additive, so you get a significant benefit to the pain relief from opiods if you combine it with cannabinoids. In this study, again, we're using vaporization so that we don't have to deal with peoples' concerns about smoking. We've demonstrated that vaporization delivers equal amounts and is less toxic.

DB: You mentioned the use of the vaporizer and there are also the edibles to cut down on the toxins, if you will, of normal smoking, but it seems to me it's all kind of hypocritical when you think of the damage done by the tobacco smoke in this country, the 400,000 people that die each year. Have you ever heard of a death from the use of marijuana?

DR. ABRAMS: No. In fact I've been a doctor now 31 years, and what I always say is, working at San Francisco General Hospital where we see a lot of the ravages of people who are abusing substances, that I have admitted many, many patients due to consequences of the use of tobacco, alcohol, crack cocaine and heroin, and in my life over these past 31 years as a physician I can remember one patient admitted during my internship who had a complication from smoking marijuana that was laced with PCP, phencyclidine or angel dust, and had sort of a psychotic break. But other than that, you know, I have not admitted a patient. Nor have I seen, as a cancer specialist and somebody working with immune-compromised patients with HIV, any risk of aspergillosis, which is the fungal lung infection that people always tout may be a risk of smoking marijuana--I think that might have come from the old days when marijuana was imported from Mexico on ships in pallets, the marijuana was sprayed with water to decrease the volume and put under tarps and was prone to get fungus at that time--but I don't think that's how most people are obtaining cannabis as medicine nowadays.

DB: If you would, talk to those doctors out there who may not be aware of marijuana's efficacy, who may not be aware of the potential to cut down on the use of opiods and some of these other more harmful drugs. Give them a little pep talk. There's information out there that might help them change their mind, right?

DR. ABRAMS: So I've actually, myself, clinically stopped taking care of patients with HIV, and I'm currently back to my roots. I'm taking care of cancer patients, and what I do particularly is what I call integrative oncology. I finished a two-year program in integrative medicine from Andrew Weil's program at the University of Arizona where I learned much about nutrition, physical activity, botanicals and supplements, traditional Chinese medicine, mind-body medicine, the role of spirituality, so I see new cancer patients at our Osher Center for Integrative Medicine at the University of California, San Francisco, and I speak to them about integrating all of these other modalities into their cancer care.

So very often I see patients in the beginning or the middle of their chemotherapy who are suffering from nausea, from vomiting, from weight loss, from pain from their cancer, from depression, from insomnia, and it shocks me how their regular oncologist has failed to even suggest or comment that cannabis, one medicine, might be able to speak to all of these problems that their patients have. I think, as far as a drug for symptom management, certainly in oncology, we don't have much better than cannabis.

MITCH EARLEYWINE, PH.D

Dr. Earleywine received his B.A. in Psychology from Columbia University in 1986 and his PhD in Clinical Psychology from Indiana University in 1990. Following his clinical internship at the University of Mississippi Medical Center he was an Assistant Professor from 1991-1997 and Associate Professor from 1997-2005 at the University of Southern California. He came to the University at Albany in 2005, where he currently is Professor of Psychology. Dr. Earleywine is author of *Understanding Marijuana, Substance Use Problems*, and *Pot Politics and the Costs of Prohibition*. Cultural Baggage / January 27, 2013

DB: The LA Times had an editorial that basically called the DEA childish children. They won't recognize the science in regards to marijuana that's been brought forward and then they deny any further studies into it. It's a real conundrum isn't it?

MITCH EARLEYWINE: It's kind of reminiscent of Mike Gray's book, *Drug Crazy*, where once the cannabis laws change you start to realize the number of hard drug users in the United States isn't all that large, and then it's kind of hard to justify an enormous budget for the DEA if, in truth, the magnitude of the drug problem isn't as large as they say, and that approach isn't the way to go. We could imagine a wonderful world where all that money essentially went to treatment, and suddenly we're treating this as a health problem instead of kind of a legal way to put people we don't like in jail.

DB: Recently I had a gentleman on to talk about the accumulation of more than 700 studies which have been conducted on medical marijuana and not one of them was all that negative, most of them quite positive. I guess what the DEA was demanding is that somebody invest...what does it cost to bring a drug to trial? 100 million?

MITCH EARLEYWINE: It's sad but true. It can approach that. When my book "Understanding Marijuana" came out in 2002, I had 550 studies. You'd think that would have been enough. Unfortunately, no drug company is going to invest that, or it's extremely unlikely just because why would they do that when it's a plant we can all be growing in our backyards? So it's this oddball "catch 22" where if you don't have the data, you can't have the marijuana, but if you don't have anybody to invest in medical marijuana, then you'll never have the data.

DB: Major players have gotten involved in the cannabis industry. GW Pharmaceuticals has put out a product called Sativex which is half THC and half CBD. Talk about that situation, Mitch.

MITCH EARLEYWINE: GW Pharmaceuticals started over in the United Kingdom and they're basically doing their best to make cannabinoid medicine as accessible as possible. They have a spray that essentially goes in a patient's mouth. It has cannabidiol and THC in various concentrations. They have really compelling data that suggests that it's superb for spasticity associated with MS and certain spinal cord injuries. It's wonderful for insomnia. It seems to be ideal at the appropriate dosage for pain. The funny thing is, though, all of these findings should generalize to the plant, so in some ways it seems like they're making as good an argument for medical marijuana as they are for the Sativex itself.

DB: I've heard it said that if Marinol, which is just THC, or the GW product Sativex are legal, then it's like comparing orange juice being legal and oranges being against the law. Your thoughts, sir.

MITCH EARLEYWINE: I think that's a reasonable way to think about it. In fact, I know people are concerned about respiratory irritation that comes from smoking cannabis, but two papers out of my lab show that with the vaporizer you can certainly use cannabis without any respiratory irritation. Those long-term data gathered by Tashkin out at UCLA suggests that there really is no elevated risk for lung cancer for folks who smoke cannabis and only smoke cannabis. All in all, there aren't really any big concerns about this. The edibles created either through tincture or some of the notorious cookies and brownies and things like that actually have no respiratory effect whatsoever because there's obviously nothing inhaled.

This is hardly a big deal when you think about the things that are available for prescription now. So despite what everybody thinks, cocaine is a Schedule II drug, and marijuana is a Schedule I drug, meaning cocaine has approved medical uses as part of eye surgery and a few other procedures, so pharmaceutical cocaine is actually something that exists, but pharmaceutical marijuana does not at the federal level?! That's just absurd.

Obviously morphine is as strong an opiate as anything we've pretty much ever seen. Adderal, which is prescribed to little bitty kids, is basically speed. The fact that we can trust a physician and a patient to discuss drugs like this and not cannabis—the irony of that is just too painful. Oxycontin and Codeine and things like that where you really do develop tolerance very rapidly and they have some cumbersome side effects that people don't like to talk about, and the withdrawal from them is very genuine, whereas combining that with cannabis means the dosage stays lower, the rate of toxin development is markedly lower, and you don't have these adverse side effects. Suddenly not only are you saving your HMO money, but you're saving human life. You're really saving the quality of human life for these individuals who were often really suffering in ways that it's hard to imagine, if you've never experienced chronic pain.

Quality of life is the key issue. It's not that we just want to prolong someone's life while they're suffering. We really want to make the time all of us have on earth as productive and as enjoyable as possible. Cannabis is not the cure to all that ails humanity. It is, however, really ideal for AIDS-related wasting, cancer chemotherapy-related nausea, any kind of appetite suppression problems, and all these big issues with pain that we've been discussing. So, by all means, let's make sure that this is available in that armament of all the different tools we have in medicine.

DB: I wanted to ask you, what are some hot buttons that maybe I haven't touched on?

MITCH EARLEYWINE: We keep seeing the media persevere on this idea that cannabis is somehow going to create mental illness in folks. I, of course, don't say that it is a good idea to use cannabis if your brain hasn't fully developed, you're too young to really make good decisions on that sort of thing, or if you're suffering from a psychotic disorder—cannabis is not the plant for you.

But this bell ringing and alarmist focus on the idea that marijuana produces schizophrenia in non-schizophrenics is just really inconsistent with the data, and I hope folks when they read those types of newsletters or see things like that on the web really interpret them with a big grain of salt, because it's just not the case at all. If you look at rates of schizophrenia across the United States across all of history, they're completely independent of what cannabis use was in the same eras and in eras previously. If you look across different countries, the base rate of schizophrenia are pretty much all just a little under 1% whether it's Jamaica or Singapore, where people can go to jail forever for cannabis. I just want folks to really use their heads when they're making those kinds of decisions.

This assumption that marijuana is going to produce lung cancer which I'm still hearing and still occasionally see in print. We now have one of the best long-term data sets ever by Don Tashkin at UCLA, with over 20 years follow up now, that shows that cannabis is clearly not creating lung cancer in folks who smoke cannabis and only cannabis. Bob Melamede actually walked through the pharmacology on that. It's pretty obvious that THC is completely unlike nicotine when it comes to the creation of tumors in the lungs.

I thought this would have died by now, but it just hasn't, and that's this idea that marijuana is supposed to increase violence or aggression somehow. Anyone who has ever used it has to find that kind of laughable, but it does seem to come up. The original studies were done back in the 70s. Folks who smoke placebo or real cannabis and then had some stooge come into the lab who was working with the experimenter try to irritate them. It was the folks in the placebo group who got more angry and hostile, not the folks who used cannabis, and I think they were just disappointed that they got the placebo.

The bottom line really is the harms caused by cannabis are certainly really, really minor, and the percentage of folks who run into trouble with the plant is really small and certainly not enough to justify putting anybody in jail for owning what is essentially hay.

GEOFFREY GUY, M.D.

When I learned of the enormous cannabis grow houses in the UK operated by GW Pharmaceuticals, I knew I had to interview their chairman, Geoffrey Guy. Their cannabis medicine Sativex is now legal in most of Europe, and in late 2013 the FDA approved an experimental protocol for use of Epidiolex, a purified CBD extract, for children with severe epilepsy. GW has been conducting some of the only clinical human trials on cannabinoids as treatment for Multiple Sclerosis and cancer pain. Cultural Baggage / September 16, 2003.

DB: Today we'll learn about a new and exciting cannabis product called Sativex. It's made by GW Pharmaceuticals out of Great Britain and it's going to be distributed by Bayer Pharmaceuticals.

Our guest for the evening is the Executive Chairman of GW Pharmaceuticals in the UK.

GEOFFREY GUY: I'm Dr. Geoffrey Guy. I'm a pharmaceutical physician. That means I spent about 23 years in chemical research in the pharmaceutical industry developing drugs. I founded GW Pharmaceuticals right at the end of 1997 and the beginning 1998.

I founded the company in response to a debate that was beginning to become more pressing in the UK during 1997 and that was mainly that a number of patients were finding themselves in front of judges in court having used cannabis (marijuana) for certain debilitating conditions—mainly Multiple Sclerosis, spinal cord injury and other neurological conditions—but the courts weren't taking pity on them and letting them off. This presented a quandary to the British government and certainly the civil servants at home office because the law was being brought into disrepute.

Therefore a solution was sought to find a way in which the patients could be treated but with a legal prescription pharmaceutical. I led that program and developed the plan which was then accepted by the UK authorities and the UK government.

DB: I understand that you have developed a couple of products under the brand name of Sativex.

GEOFFREY GUY: Sativex is one particular product and that is a cannabis-based extract which is made from the extract of two cannabis plants. The plants are being bred to specifically represent one specific cannabinoid in abundance.

One plant exhibits very high levels of THC and the other plant exhibits very high levels of CBD, which is cannabidiol. We make pharmaceutical grade extracts from these plants and then we blend them in certain ratios. In the case of Sativex the ratio is approximately 50-50 so that we have this equal quantity of THC and CBD in the material. The reason we did this is this very much mimics the sort of cannabis that is found in Europe derived from northern Africa, for example, where the CBD content is much higher than the cannabis that would be found in the U.S.—certainly 5 years ago.

DB: You have done tests, you have done studies on these products. Could you tell my listeners what those studies have shown?

GEOFFREY GUY: First of all the tests and research we do were initially to be able to grow the two plants consistently, make consistent extract and produce pharmaceutical-grade material. Our approach was quality. It would be pointless to proceed with safety and efficacy studies with an extracted material if it were to change each time we made it. So the early research was to ensure that we were able to produce a material which was highly consistent and of appropriate quality.

We then went through a number of clinical trials which initially allowed us to establish appropriate dose levels in patients which would allow patients to gain relief from symptoms without necessarily suffering from any of the side effects of excess dosage. This gave us what we call a therapeutic window for the patients to be able to treat themselves and maintain side effects at a very low level.

Once we had done that in a number of what are called phase 2 studies, exploratory chemical study, we moved on to more involved studies where we exposed a much larger number of patients and now our trials are approaching over 1,000 patients in our trials overall.

Those are the trials, four of which were completed at the end of last year. We were able to show a relief of symptoms in patients with Multiple Sclerosis—mainly neuropathic pain in Multiple Sclerosis and that is nerve damage pain—spasticity, spasm, and in a wide number of patients a relief in sleep disturbance which is very troubling to these patients.

We also carried out studies in a very rare condition called brachial plexus avulsion where the nerves feeding the arm are damaged during trauma. This usually occurs in young motorcyclists—almost exclusively males. They are left with very, very painful arms. We thought this was a very good model to look at just how potent the cannabis extracts could be in treating this neurological pain, this neuropathic pain. We were able to demonstrate benefit in these patients.

We also carried out studies with patients with pain of general neurological cause. Those would be patients with spinal cord injury, with peripheral neuropathy and other neurological conditions. We were able to show benefit in those studies. What is notable is that in all these studies the patients were considered to be intractable—in other words, the end of the road with regard to their therapeutic options. And, indeed, during the clinical trials the patients remained on all their other medicines which would include opiates, gabapentin, and a range of other pharmaceutical products. Therefore any benefit that we were able to show in those studies was over and above these conventional treatments.

DB: For the distribution of your products I understand you've entered in agreement with Bayer Pharmaceutical Company. Could you explain that arrangement for us?

GEOFFREY GUY: Yes, indeed. We are a research and development company and essentially our job stops once we have a product to be approved in a variety of countries throughout the world. We would continue to research our products to extend the initial indications, the initial conditions for which the product would be approved. But we commercialize our materials by entering into distribution arrangements with pharmaceutical companies that have established capability in selling and marketing pharmaceutical products. During the course of this summer we entered into arrangements with Bayer from Germany to cover our first product, Sativex, in the United Kingdom. Under that arrangement Bayer will have an option to expand the territory from the United Kingdom to other countries throughout Europe, to Australia, New Zealand, and Canada. We are currently in discussions with Bayer to consider which territories are most appropriate for them to be our distributor outside the UK.

DB: I understand that the Netherlands has allowed for the distribution of cannabis products through pharmacies, that Belgium is considering following suit, that we know now that Canada distributes medical marijuana to their patients and I was wondering if you could give me your take on the situation in America.

GEOFFREY GUY: Obviously I should be very careful in giving my opinion on policies of different countries. First of all I think we can comment on the Dutch and Canadian experience. I think the Dutch solution is a very Dutch solution and has really followed on from a series of liberalization measures that they have taken over a number of years.

The patients are still required to pay for these medicines and the medicines come in the form of herbal cannabis which can be dispensed by the pharmacist. For the doctor in Holland and, indeed more appropriately in Canada, a lot of doctors are not very happy that they do not have a product which has been tested rigorously in the way that every other medicine that they would prescribe has been tested. So they have a situation where a patient is taking a range of medicine because in complex conditions like Multiple Sclerosis or spinal cord injury or rheumatoid arthritis patients will be taking a range of medicines and all these other medicines will have been tested to appropriate standards of quality, safety and efficacy. But the doctor will not be able to rely on that rigorous testing for the herbal material.

I believe that this approach is an interim approach until pharmaceutical products are available and certainly when one listens to the news from Canada the Canadian Medical Association is not in favor of doctors prescribing herbal material of unknown provenance where I understand the major insurers that insure the doctors for malpractice have indicated that they are not happy to be insuring such practice. I think that these measures are interim measures that demonstrate how carefully each of the countries has viewed this very, very difficult situation. These countries have dealt with this matter compassionately in their own way.

We are in the business of developing pharmaceuticals. A pharmaceutical is able to yield profit to each shareholders so we can put more money and resources back into research. Throughout Europe I think the preferred method for the medical professional and for patients would be to be able to have a product prescribed, reimbursed by the national health care or equivalent agencies throughout Europe and to know that there is of assured quality, safety and efficacy.

Now the U.S. is very different insomuch as the U.S. really hasn't embraced the debate in regard to the need that patients have. This has been a very much unmet need. It's been unmet by conventional pharmaceutical products and medicines and that has been very well recognized in the United Kingdom, in Canada, Australia, New Zealand and throughout Europe. I think the U.S. has yet to embrace that the patients have a very, very serious need, that they're being exposed to some very potent conventional pharmaceuticals which are giving help, no doubt, in a number of cases but also are accompanied by quite serious side effects. When one considers the extracts or the components of the cannabis plant in comparison to some of these other very potent medicines then the cannabis plant and its extracts provide a very favorable comparator in terms of fewer side effects and in terms of relative benefit. So one would hope the lessons that are being elsewhere learned will fall upon receptive ears in the years to come, but from my position I can only see that this will be a rather slow and very resource-intensive process.

DB: I recently received a couple of pictures of your production facility. As I understand it you have a very precise, very repeatable process to obtain the exact specifications for your products. Given that is an exact process, that the components of each plant is repeatable would it not be possible to use those products with a vaporizer to avoid the particulates of smoking?

GEOFFREY GUY: We have done a lot of research with vaporization and a lot of our research has to do with vaporization of specific extracts of cannabis. It is very difficult to create a constant temperature through a vegetable material. As you know, dried cannabis will contain some amounts of water in it. The delivery efficiencies from vaporizing herbal cannabis are very variable. Whereas that may satisfy a vernacular use of the material, one would not be able to satisfy the regulators in terms of product consistency. One would have to prepare the materials in a way that you get a very consistent substrate for that vaporization and then by adding energy at a predetermined fashion, and we do this in a computer-controlled fashion then you would be able to produce vapor of all the cannabis constituents in a reproducible and consistent fashion.

In attempting to vaporize herbal cannabis it is inevitable that carcinogens would still be released in hot spots within the material and stopping hot spots within the material is very difficult to do. We've spent a lot of time looking at the heat dispersion throughout surfaces and surfaces that have cannabis on them. So in pharmaceutical terms, vaporizing a vegetable material is not a very satisfactory route to move ahead; however, vaporizing a consistent extract of that very same material which will contain all the same active components probably would represent a very advantageous route for the delivery of materials.

DB: Would you discuss the process of growing the plants?

GEOFFREY GUY: Yes, obviously it's not my role to provide a growers' guide for marijuana, of course, that's not why we do the research. What we had to do was choose varieties of cannabis that would yield for us the correct components of the active ingredients. We would stress that there are a range of active ingredients and they work best when they are in the right ratios as presented in the plant. We believe that the whole is greater than the sum of the parts and a lot of our research is now able to show that.

We have therefore bred plants and controlled the genetics through breeding. There's no genetic modification or modulation here. This is purely through breeding in the old Mendelian sense. Something like 15 years of breeding has gone into the program to produce plants that have a predefined cannabinoid ratio.

That is one objective but, of course, the plants have to be robust. They have to be pest resistant, disease resistant and they also have to be open to economical growing. To grow the plants economically we wanted plants with short cycles of harvest. You mentioned a plant 26 feet tall but I'm sure it didn't get there in 13 weeks. We want a plant that is not too sticky so that it can't be handled properly. We want a plant to provide a reasonable canopy to absorb the light but not so much that there is increased humidity below the canopy so that we get an increase in botrytis, for example.

We researched all of these elements over the past five years now—we've grown probably approaching 300,000 plants now—and we feel that we have an optimum approach which provides us with a very consistent end product which can be subjected to economic growing at very, very large volumes now and that we've been able to actually transfer that technology out of our own glass houses in the past 12 months to one of our contract growers and the very first crop that they grew met all of our very rigorous specifications. We've now been able to bring the varieties that we use in line with economical agriculture practice. We are able to produce a very consistent end product.

DB: Here in America they talk about the harms of marijuana. They continue to demonize it every chance they get. In your studies have you had any instances where people wound up with kidney failure or liver damage from using your product?

GEOFFREY GUY: Certainly not. There no basis for considering or imagining that they even would. There are no recorded deaths from the ingestion of cannabis alone in the last 100 years. The chairman of the American Medical Association 1998 published the Therapeutic Index, which is the safety ratio of materials, to be something like 20,000 times. That means one would need to take over 20,000 times the therapeutic dose before the product would kill you. Compare that to just a couple dozen in products like morphine or acetaphetamine.

In pharmaceutical terms these are very safe materials. They are of no organ toxicity. They are very well tolerated by humans. That has been witnessed by many, many thousands of years of human coexistence and ingestion of these materials. So there's no basis, no reason to believe that liver failure or renal failure would be caused by taking these materials. Indeed our clinical trials have brought that out. We have seen some side effects which, of course, one would expect, and they are those that you would expect to see and that is the patients will have some feeling of intoxication. I must stress this is not patients being high or stoned as we often explore the appropriate dose. They will begin to feel intoxication which they very readily recognize and are able to curtail that dose to maintain their therapy below those levels. Patients also found that they had dry mouth which is a very well reported side effect of the use of cannabinoids. We see some increase in heart rate in the very early days when the patients are first exposed to the materials, which, again, are very well reported, and if patients do take too large of a dose sometimes we see a fainting ordeal but that's also been very rare indeed.

The main side effects that we have seen in our clinical trials are those that could have been predicted from the vernacular or common use of the materials. I think that it is simple scurrilous to suggest that these materials could cause liver failure or renal failure. There really is no supporting evidence in the science anywhere for that kind of side effect.

DB: Where would you send doctors, clinicians and government officials to learn the truth about cannabis?

GEOFFREY GUY: I think that they could probably sit in their offices and read the appropriate text, which is now becoming available in the journals. It is true to say that over the last 20 years most of the information on cannabis has populated the journals having been supported by various agencies that probably have as their prime objective the highlighting of the dangerous aspects of cannabis. I think that the literature when you look at it over the last 20 years is very much slanted towards looking for the side effects and looking for the dangers of the material. When one reviews that literature (and we have recently reviewed over 13.5 thousand papers) you find that there is very little evidence or very little in the way of convincing evidence to say these materials are harmful and damaging but what one actually does find is that there is very good evidence in the literature to say that there's an extremely good basis as to why people in medical research should look at the use of these materials for a variety of different conditions.

I think that as more and more research like our own and that supported by the

British government in the Methods research, Council research and studies being done in Canada and elsewhere as more of these studies are done and people take a more pragmatic and sensible approach to cannabis and not demonize it and not be paranoid about it I think the message will come through.

If the doctors and opinion leaders did want to find out a little more, then the International Cannabinoid Research Society meets once a year. Last year it was in Canada. Next year it is in Italy. That's extremely instructive. There is a *Journal of Cannabis Therapeutics* which has some very good articles in it. I think the literature is now becoming well populated with a more balanced approach to this and I think that we'll find hopefully that U.S. clinicians and U.S. scientists will be able to look towards the European and Canadian, Australian, New Zealand literature for the answers they may seek.

CARL HART, PH.D.

Carl Hart is an associate professor of psychology and psychiatry at Columbia University. Hart is known for his research in drug abuse and drug addiction. Hart was the first tenured African American professor of sciences at Columbia University. His latest book is *High Price: A Neuroscientist's Journey of Self Discovery That Challenges Everything You Know About Drugs & Society*. Cultural Baggage / June 9, 2013

CARL HART: It's a coming of age story and being a black person coming of age in the state sometimes means being caught between two worlds. I hope I did a good job of explaining that. I talk about having a scanty education or poor education in high school—barely literate, quite frankly. The only reason I stayed in school was to remain on the basketball team and really didn't see the value of an education.

Then I went into the Air Force and learned some things that I didn't know— some things that I didn't even know that I didn't know. Then I found out the importance of an education, the value, the power of education. I committed myself to education just like I had previously to athletics. In doing so it meant that some of the people, some of the things I was once into I was no longer into and sometimes people may feel slighted when, in fact, it's not really about them it's about me. Those were difficult waters to navigate.

DB: We all run into those kind of familial situations. Now the focus of the book deals with the drug war interweaving itself into life here in America, right?

CARL HART: Yes. It is a difficult book for some people to wrap their heads around because it's a memoir but it's also a big ideas book. It's also a science book. It's also a policy book—policy being drug policy. All of those things are who I am and they make up me. I thought that the only way for me to tell my story was to talk about science, growing up in the 'hood, to talk about my disgust with the current drug policy, particularly as one tries to wrap their head around the science and how inconsistent what we are currently doing with drug policy is with the science.

DB: You've done the investigation on people using methamphetamine and I want to speak on that because I had about a 2 and one-half year dalliance with methamphetamine myself. It started with the Air Force by the way who handed it out like candy in the beginning and it became "methamphetamine or life" and I chose life because too many people get caught up in chasing down those drugs and finding the drugs and spending their lives chasing drugs. I think that's the biggest failing, if you will, of methamphetamine users.

CARL HART: One of the things I try to do in the book is point out that most of the people who use methamphetamine don't have that type of relationship with the drug. There are, of course, people who do have that relationship, but the problem for me is most of attention is focused on people who have trouble with the drug—people who have a pathological relationship with the drug when, in fact, the majority of the people don't. The folks who have a problem with the drug, we certainly want to pay attention to, certainly want to make sure that we help them to the best of our ability, but we shouldn't be making policy based on a select group who has a problem with the drug when the majority of the people don't.

Now that is not to say that methamphetamine does not have the potential for harmful effects to those individuals who use it, but if we think about another drug that we are all familiar with—let's say alcohol—there is 10 to 15% of the people who use alcohol who have a pathological relationship with that drug, but you don't see the society making laws based on that 10 to 15%. We tried to do that in 1919 with prohibition until 1933, but the other 90 / 85% was like, "Hey, I don't have a problem with this drug. I know how to use it and I'm fine. I know how to enhance the positive effects and minimize the negative effects. Why should I be punished because of that?"

In the book I'm trying to get the public to realize that's what we have done with cocaine. That's what we have done with methamphetamine. That's what we have done with heroin. It doesn't mean that we can all of a sudden change the way we are regulating those drugs today. It means we need to change the way that we are educating about these drugs and then think about changing the way we regulate these drugs. I put forth that we should decriminalize all these drugs first and then have the sort of corresponding increase in education, and then if people want to think about legalizing all of these drugs that's fine. But first we have to be re-educated, because currently we're talking to the country about drugs like the whole entire country are adolescents. I'm trying to have an adult discussion about drugs.

DB: So many people think they know the truth about drugs, and they stand adamantly opposed to any changes, but there is much they "know" that just ain't true right?

CARL HART: That's absolutely right. We just have been mis-educated, misinformed about what drugs do. I guess some of the most detrimental education surrounding drugs has been doled out by law enforcement. People turn to law enforcement, for example, for educating people about drugs. That's one of the most ridiculous things I've ever heard. What we have to do is make sure any-body—whether it's law enforcement, or somebody like me, a scientist—we have to make sure that whatever they are talking about as it relates to drugs has foun-dations in real evidence. Ask people the question, "What's the evidence to support your position?"

If people say, "Well, my Uncle Jack told me…" That's not evidence—that's anecdote. Anecdotes, oftentimes, are not even representative of the real situation. So anecdote might be fine to illustrate a point, but please make sure that it is grounded in evidence. What's the evidence to support that anecdote?

DB: All the time people take the words of cops and people in the criminal jus-tice system and use their words as evidence to continue this policy even though these people have absolutely no medical background.

CARL HART: In chapter 17 of the book I really deal with that issue because it has disturbed me as well, precisely how you pointed out. Law enforcement offi-cials don't have any training in pharmacology. They don't have any training in the behavioral sciences. They are trained very well to deal with people who are criminals. Now when you're dealing with people who are criminals, people can act bizarre in the presence of law enforcement simply because they are afraid be-cause they've done something wrong and you can get a lot of bizarre behaviors.

Oftentimes that bizarre behavior is attributed to a drug when, in fact, there's no drug on board—or there is a drug on board like alcohol. It may be that the person has some sort of psychiatric issue but drugs are typically scapegoated in those situations. Long before we even know if drugs are involved or if drugs aren't involved, we still say that drugs were involved. That has gone a long way for perpetuating myths about drugs.

DB: There is a very current situation that touches on what you are talking about. A crane operator is accused of manslaughter because he was high on mar-ijuana and codeine. Now the codeine was mentioned in the earlier stories but it's being focused on marijuana now. I guess the point I'm trying to make here, sir, is whether it's marijuana, codeine or whatever, it's blaming the drugs rather than waiting for an investigation.

CARL HART: You just described it beautifully. I don't know the contributions of codeine. I don't know the contribution of marijuana. I don't know the contri-butions of this person's psychiatric history. It would be nice if we could tease apart those things and figure it out before we disseminate information that's not complete, but certainly we do that too often in this society.

I'm trying to ask people to be more careful, more critical because it's not neu-tral when we perpetuate these myths about drugs. If it was neutral then it wouldn't be a big deal, but the perpetuation of these myths about drugs have extremely negative effects on our citizens—particularly our poor, minority citizens because it creates an environment in which the society goes after certain types of drugs (marijuana, cocaine, methamphetamine) all of these drugs with such zeal. They go after these drugs at any cost to those in the communities and those communities pay the price. They pay the price with increased arrests, increased prison sentences and also increased death. If we think about Trevon Martin. What the person who killed Trevon Martin thought was that he was on some drug. That's the excuse that they've given. This excuse has been given often times when drugs weren't even involved. As long as society or people in authority are allowed to believe that drugs somehow create these monstrous effects, we are going to get this excessive force from law enforcement and security officers, and that's why I am so concerned about the myths that we have perpetuated about drugs.

DB: I wanted to come back to the mention of alcohol. I mentioned that it complicates, expounds the problem with the use of other drugs. Let's talk about that for a moment.

CARL HART: One of the things I try to be careful about doing in the book is I don't want to vilify one drug for another. Alcohol, for example—we know that there are lots of crimes and those sorts of things that may be associated with alcohol, things that concern us as a society. I don't want people to get the idea that I think alcohol use should be restricted. I think that the vast majority of people who use alcohol do so safely without problems and responsibly, so I don't want to restrict alcohol. But I do want people to understand that no matter what the activity is in society—whether it is drinking alcohol, using cocaine or driving your automobile—whatever it is, there is the potential for danger so we cannot be so naïve to think that we're going to prevent every accident, every sort of tragedy. That's naïve. Any public policy that is based on that is not realistic and it will be wasteful. Yeah, there are problems related to alcohol but those problems are actually minimal or minor or relatively low compared to the vast numbers of people who use that drug.

The same can be said for cocaine. The same can be said for other drugs if we enhance our education surrounding their use. We know a great deal about methamphetamine's effects that we could tell people who are using these drugs to keep them safe. We know a great deal about heroin's effect which could keep people more safe, but often the public health message is "Heroin caused this overdose and killed this person." While heroin overdoses are possible, they are highly unlikely, and they are rare. Seventy-five or more percent of the people who die a heroin-related death die because of the use of heroin in combination with another sedative like alcohol. So the public health message should be screamed out, "Do not use another sedative when you're using heroin." If we do that we can prevent a number of deaths but we don't do that in this society. Instead we just blame heroin so people who are using heroin don't know this information. Just tell them, "Please don't use another sedative." And keep people safe.

DB: You talk about in the book that there is this idea that drug users have this uncontrollable craving, but you've conducted studies which show that to be less than true.

CARL HART: There's this belief, for example, when you take a drug like crack cocaine there was myth perpetuated in the mid-80s that one hit from crack cocaine and you're addicted for life and you're only driven by going to get that drug. You have these cognitive impairments—a wide range of sort of negative behavioral effects that we have been led to believe and it's simply not supported by research.

Data from research does not support those notions. Data from my studies as well as other people's studies show that people who use crack cocaine are not cognitively impaired. They respond just like you and I would to various options. OK, if you have a choice between a nice dose of cocaine and nothing—what would you do? Well, you'll probably take the crack cocaine, but if you give them a choice between a hit of crack cocaine and let's just say 5, 10, 20 dollars or something like that, they will choose money. That's how most of us would respond. Or if you give them a choice to pay a bill that will help your children out, they'll choose the option that helps their children out, and not this sort of myth that we've all been taught about. It just simply not supported by evidence from research.

DB: The New York Times kind of did a mea culpa (that didn't say as much) but they were talking about the crack baby scare and how untrue that was and, once again, we have to be careful about what we know to be true, right?

CARL HART: The New York Times, like you said, did run that piece about a week and one-half ago but they had run a similar piece maybe a year and one-half/two years ago about the sort of crack baby epidemic that wasn't. They have been on it sort of in the past several years. That was all part of the whole crack hysteria—part of these myths that led to those awful laws surrounding crack cocaine versus powder cocaine as you know.

In 1986 we passed these laws that punished crack cocaine one hundred times more harshly than powder cocaine. In the book I clearly show why that was unfair because the two drugs are essentially the same drug. They produce the same effect but the media hysteria surrounding crack cocaine in the mid-80s made the public believe that crack was a completely different drug.

The difference, of course, is that crack is smoked whereas powder cocaine is snorted and injected. When you look at the effects, no matter what route the drug is taken, the effects are virtually the same, particularly when you compare intravenous cocaine administration and smoked cocaine administration. They produce the same effects, and I clearly show this in the book.

In August 2010 President Obama signed legislation to decrease the disparity between crack and powder cocaine from 100:1 to 18:1. That certainly was a step in the right direction, but I have been arguing that it needs to be 1:1 because it makes no sense when the two drugs are the same. It would be like punishing people who smoke marijuana more harshly than those who take marijuana via a brownie. It's just not fair.

DB: I want to address the appeal in this book to just take another look at this drug problem, right?

CARL HART: One of the things I want people to see that I'm a regular person. People who grew up like me really have been punished and they really have been shut out of mainstream society. I want people to see that we have wasted large human resources by our drug policy. If we think about what happened to my friends and the people that grew up with me (this is one of the reasons I told their stories) that could have been me. That could have been ...that would have been a loss to our society.

I have made scientific contributions. I have made a number of contributions not to mention that I pay my taxes, trying to do my part to contribute to society. The folks who look like me, who grew up like me, many of the guys my age— they are not. They haven't made those contributions because they got saddled with a criminal record related to a drug charge, related to drug possession charges and those sorts of things. The society loses. The society loses their taxes. The society loses their other contribution and so I hope that reasonable people, reasonable Americans will see that this is so un-American and so unfair and realize that we have to do something differently.

The following is excerpted from a speech given at the Texas Drug Policy Conference. Cultural Baggage / January 26, 2014

CARL HART: Sometimes people ask: what can they do. Everybody kind of knows about the injustice but few of us actually know what we can do. I hope today I leave you all with something you can do. Mainly the take home message is that you can challenge some of the assumptions that people make about drugs because most of them are incorrect. Today I'm going to talk about some of the assumptions that I challenged in my research not knowing that I was challenging them.

My research deals with methamphetamine these days. Just to let you all know what I do is I actually bring people into the lab and we give them drugs, and we test the effects on behavior, brain activity and a wide range of things. When I talk about what drugs do it is from an empirical perspective. We bring people into the lab and they live with us for about 2 to 4 weeks. They can't go outside. They stay locked in this laboratory. After their 8-hour shift they have access to a recreational room where they can play video games, watch video-taped movies and interact with the other participants. We went from studying 5 and 10mg orally to studying as large as 50mg given intranasal. A 50mg dose of methamphetamine is a really nice dose. It's a dose that is related to abuse.

What about cognitive performance? In the lab we certainly test these sorts of things. Participants in these studies complete a wide-range of cognitive tasks under the placebo conditions, baseline conditions. Then they receive methamphetamine and we test these cognitive functions again repeatedly throughout the day to see how the drug altered performance, if it altered performance.

We were expecting some destructions particularly when we gave the drug at large doses. When I think about all the studies that we did and I reviewed the literature studies that have used doses larger than 20mg and have given the drug smoked, intravenously or snorted, none of those studies have reported disruptions in cognitive performance after taking the drug. In fact, the studies have reported improvements in cognitive performance when you give these larger doses.

This is not a surprise. Amphetamines are used for that purpose. Amphetamines are used to help people who have cognitive issues like Attention Deficit Disorder. So that's not surprising. What is surprising are the sort of mythologies surrounding methamphetamine cognitive impairments. My point here is that we have exaggerated the extent of harm associated with methamphetamine. I worry about people and sleep disruption. I worry about them not eating. You make sure that you have culture norms around that. You teach people how to do it right. If you take care of people's eating and sleeping with methamphetamine your problems go away.

So, with that, I will leave you with my take home message. Many assumptions about methamphetamine are simply not supported by evidence from research but what methamphetamine does nicely is it shows a nation how to launch a worldwide drug menace. If you want to know how to do that just follow the methamphetamine story right now. It was crack-cocaine in the 80s but now it's methamphetamine. One thing we have to be cognizant of as well is our current knowledge about methamphetamine as well as some of these other drugs is incomplete. We don't know everything about it. We may learn new information but we still have to act in terms of education, treatment policy. We make some mistakes. It's not a crime to make mistakes. We are making mistakes now. But it is a crime to make mistakes and get new information, better information and not alter your course.

JOEL HOCHMAN, M.D.

Dr. Hochman was my doctor till his passing a couple of years ago. As much as I wanted and he wanted, he still never could bring himself to write me a medical marijuana recommendation in Texas. Century of Lies / June 14, 2009.

Dr. JOEL HOCHMAN: The issue of drugs is a very complex issue. You're talking about teenage, adolescent experimentation. You're talking about the symptomatic use of medications that are appropriate. You're talking about addictive disorders and, by the way, the instances of addictive disorders has not changed for seventy-five years in this country, so that's a whole separate issue in itself.

The whole 'supply side' strategy of approaching drug issues; drug problems is, I think, a calamitous mistake. It's never worked and it will never work. What we have to do is succeed on the 'demand side'. On the demand side, we need to, number one: Make every child, in the United States, knowledgeable and wise, about substances; drugs, particularly dangerous drugs or potentially dangerous combinations of drugs. I think that the so called National Prescriptive Drug threat that Kerlikowske was announcing in early April, is an exact example of the wrong direction to be going.

Being the kind of person that I am and the training I have, I went to his actual sources, data sources, that he cited in the press releases for that, and did a very detailed analysis and discovered that the data that they themselves cite as justification for their campaign; their 'prescriptive drug threat' campaign, simply does not support the claims that they're making. There is not an epidemic of diversion in drug abuse.

If one assumes that all eight thousand plus overdose deaths in the United States last year were caused by prescriptive drugs, diverted, when there's a great deal of doubt about the accuracy of that statement—then you still have to compare that to the fact that there were one hundred fifty billion doses of pain medications prescribed last year. So, what is the likelihood of someone killing themselves with a prescribed opioid? Eight thousand four hundred fifty-one over one hundred fifty billion. That is an infinitesimally insignificant probability.

So you're not really talking about the whole picture of prescriptive drugs. What you should be talking about is that super small sub-set of kids who haven't got enough sense to know what they're doing, so they end up killing themselves. It's not going to do the job of trying to restrict the availability of these drugs to the population, who have a legitimate need for medication.

I was talking to Dr. Douglas Throckmorton who is head of the FDA, in charge of this Risk Evaluation Management Strategy Proposal that they have. In response to a great deal of political pressure from hysterical parents, they have proposed putting some very strict limitations and restrictions on who can prescribe and requiring all kinds of additional training.

To further restrict physicians in their availability of these prescribing substances is going to just cause an even greater crisis in the management of legitimate medical pain, in the United States. Anybody who's in pain, or has had pain for as long as five minutes, knows that the whole notion of learning to live with pain, is an oxymoron.

Nobody can tolerate pain. They have to do something to get out of it, so there's alcohol. There's street drugs, particularly heroin. There're all kinds of things that people will do to try to get out of pain. If we deny legitimate pain management, what's going to happen to all of these people is very predictable. They're going to do whatever they have to do and go wherever they have to go to try to do something about reducing their suffering.

DB: The vast majority, ninety plus percent I think, of people who use, or abuse, these sometimes dangerous drugs quit on their own and go on to lead lives without the involvement of government or a treatment agency. Is that a fair assumption?

Dr. JOEL HOCHMAN: Well, that's certainly what we've discovered at the UCLA project. We discovered that the two groups that most frequently utilized Cannabis, were the very best students and the very worst students. At the end of five years, the very worst students dropped out or flunked out and the very best students had gone on to graduate with honors and eventually most of them gave up drugs because they simply weren't that big a part of their life, to begin with.

It was a part of a phase of their life and that because they were intelligent rational people and made good decisions and learned how to make proper decisions, it just simply wasn't important to them anymore and that's how things went for them. Which is the way I think it goes for most people in our society and that's the reason I put together this guidance for overdose victims and for their parents.

I felt that it was really important that instead of being hysterical, I thought that it'd be important to give some kind of rational guidance to both the potential drug overdosers and their parents. The idea came to me from talking to Dr. Throckmorton, who said he understood it was not rational to make public policy on the basis of the behavior of drug abusers, but on the other hand he had a thirteen year old and he's concerned about his own child.

So this is my guidance for would-be overdose victims: If you were considering using a drug to change your mood; to get high; because your friends are doing it; in combination with other mind altering substances, particularly alcohol; to cope with stress; to escape; in a party situation; alone, with potential help unavailable; for the first time and you are unfamiliar with this drug, or at a dose higher than you are use to or you don't know how strong it is; when you have health issues, that might affect your breathing or your ability to metabolize the drug; and for opiates, you don't know about Naloxone and it's not available anyway; then the possibility that you may kill yourself is very high.

Proceed at your own risk and do not blame the drug. You took it; it didn't take you. Relax. If you kill yourself, your parents will blame the drug, not you and they will think about you every day for the rest of their lives.

For the parents my rational advice is as follows. Do not pretend that your child will never be involved in drugs. Assume the drugs are everywhere and will always be available. Supply side strategies have never succeeded and will never succeed. Make sure that your kids are factually educated about every drug. If you misinform them or give them propaganda, your credibility and authority with them is over. Share your personal experience and knowledge with them. Do not be a know-it-all, because you don't. Accept the fact that they may be smarter and more knowledgeable about drugs than you. If you are going to keep medications in your home, keep them absolutely locked up. No exceptions. Do not expect that they will not try to defeat the security. Be informed about the symptoms and signs of intoxication and / or overdose. Have an overdose plan. Know what to do, who to call and what to say. Do not blame the drugs. Your kid took them; they didn't take your kid.

Expect that your kids will experiment; you probably did. Make sure that they know what to expect and what to do if they get in trouble with a drug. Tell them you really love them, will miss them the rest of your life, if they kill themselves and you would really appreciate it if they didn't. Don't do anything to convince your child. It's too risky, to tell you the truth.

PHILIPPE LUCAS

Philippe's current research interests include the use of cannabis, ibogaine, and ayahuasca in the treatment of addiction. Additionally, Lucas is the CEO of a research and public health consultancy called Compassionate Consulting, and has acted as a court-recognized expert witness on medical cannabis criminal cases. This work draws on his years of experience as a medical cannabis researcher and federally authorized cannabis patient and medical cannabis producer. Century of Lies / December 9, 2012.

PHILIPPE LUCAS: I'm a Research Affiliate with the Center for Addictions Research in British Columbia.

DB: You and a group of associates have put together a study regarding the use of cannabis as a substitute for alcohol and other drugs. Outline that for us.

PHILIPPE LUCAS: The study is the survey of 404 medical cannabis patients at four dispensaries in British Columbia—three of them in Vancouver and one of them in Victoria. It's a study designed to specifically examine a phenomena called substitution effect, and in this case cannabis substitution effect in which medical cannabis users would find that their use of cannabis would lead to a reduction in their use of alcohol, illicit substances, or pharmaceuticals.

This is a phenomenon which has been identified at the population level for at least a decade. Myself and other researchers in North America have been studying in regards to both the medical and recreational use of cannabis. Just to nutshell it, this would suggest that as people would increase their use of cannabis you might see a subsequent reduction in the use of alcohol, tobacco, illicit drugs and pharmaceutical drugs and that might have a positive—both personal and public—health impact because the fastest rising rate of addiction that we see in North America right now is to pharmaceutical opiates and as a result of that we've seen an incredible increase in the amount of morbidity and mortality associated with pharmaceutical opiates as well.

DB: This really rang a bell with me. May 8, 2013 will make 28 years for me without alcohol. Prior to that time I had a severe problem with it. I want to thank the good folks at Alcoholics Anonymous for welcoming me and helping me to begin to unravel that predicament. The fact of the matter is after about 6 months I happened to mention that I was still using cannabis and that I thought it was helping me to stay away from the alcohol, and they kind of kicked me out of the building. What is your thought in that regard?

PHILIPPE LUCAS: My experience is quite similar to yours. I was diagnosed with Hepatitis C in 1995, which I got through the tainted blood system here in Canada in 1982, when I was 12-years-old and went in for an operation. The physician I was working with didn't know much about Hep C at the time—in fact no one did in 1995. It wasn't even called Hep C at the time. It was non-Hep A / non-Hep B. The one thing that he could tell me is that I should really consider quitting alcohol and tobacco.

Now alcohol had always been my drug of choice. I really wasn't a cannabis user or a regular cannabis user through high school or even through my early academic university studies. My family had struggled with alcoholism, and I think it's fair to say that I felt I might be on the same path as well. So I started using cannabis as really a substitute for alcohol in order to not have alcohol worsen my liver condition. It was only through doing some research over the ensuing months and years that I realized that the cannabis was not only helping me stay off of tobacco and alcohol but was also having some positive impacts on both the symptoms associated with Hep C and the progress of that condition as well. For those so many years since 1995, I've been using cannabis essentially as a substitute for alcohol and also as a treatment for my Hepatitis C.

DB: We often hear from Drug Czars and government representatives that all of this information is anecdotal and it means nothing, but the truth be told, this is a scientific study. Where was this published?

PHILIPPE LUCAS: This was published in the *Journal of Public Research* and Theory. It's a well-regarded journal. This study was certainly not the first of its kind to identify substitution effect, but it is the largest study of substitution effect to date. What we found was quite fascinating. The results suggest that over 75% of respondents use cannabis as a substitute for at least one other substance. 41% of respondents say that they use cannabis as a substitute for alcohol. 36% said that they used cannabis as a substitute for illicit substances and 67.8% said that they used cannabis as a substitute for prescription drugs.

That may have some significant impact on health care costs. If people are using less pharmaceutical drugs and suffering less from the potential addiction and the health impacts associated with pharmaceutical opiates, this could not only improve their health but significantly reduce the cost of treating conditions like chronic pain. If we also see a reduction in the use of alcohol and the use of illicit substances, we can also see some significant public health and personal health impacts as a result of those. With the recent legalization initiatives in Colorado and Washington, I think that this may have some really profound effect on what we're going to see in a legalized cannabis atmosphere.

Looking at the available research and what we know from other jurisdictions who have either de facto legalized or decriminalized cannabis, I think that we will see in Colorado and Washington State probably a minor increase in cannabis use, but I think as we see attached to that a reduction in the use of pharmaceutical substances as well as illicit substances and, most significantly in terms of public health and safety, we may also see a reduction in alcohol-related hospitalizations from alcohol-related accidents and alcohol-related drinking and driving incidents. I think that if we saw a reduction in alcohol-related property damage and domestic violence as well, the net impact of seeing a slight increase in cannabis use in those states may be balanced off by seeing a similar reduction in the use of alcohol and illicit substances. I think from a public health point of view, that may mean that an increase in cannabis use would have positive public health impacts if it is tied to a reduction in these other substances.

DB: Tell us who else was signed on to this report. What other researchers were involved?

PHILIPPE LUCAS: This was a community-based study, so it was great. I initially contacted the four dispensaries and was able to train four representatives from those dispensaries to both hand out and collect the survey in a way that would follow scientific protocol. The four dispensaries were the Vancouver Island Compassion Society, the British Columbia Compassion Society, the Vancouver Dispensary Society, and the Green Cross Society of B.C. Then I had a lot of help with doing the data input and data analysis of our findings by my friends and fellow researchers Amanda Reiman and Mitch Earlywine, who are U.S.-based researchers who have some familiarity with the concept of substitution effect. In fact Amanda Reiman is one of the foremost researchers of this, as well.

DB: In the past I've been lucky to have several conversations with Dr. Tom O'Connell in the United States who has done some research in this area. It seems that the truth is just too difficult to ignore in this regard, right?

PHILIPPE LUCAS: What we're seeing right now is that there are credible biological mechanisms behind these results. What I mean by that is that there are a lot of reasons why cannabis may be helpful in helping people deal with addiction or with the reduction in the use of pharmaceutical drugs, alcohol, and tobacco. The evidence suggests that we really need to move to the next level of research when it comes to cannabis substitution effect, including randomized clinical trials on cannabis substitution for problematic substance use. In other words I think we need to start looking at cannabis not as a gateway drug leading to addiction but potentially as an exit drug for problematic substance use and potentially as a treatment, a specific treatment for problematic substance use.

Now I want to be clear—I readily acknowledge and truly believe that there are some people who have developed a dependence associated with cannabis use. The evidence suggests that 1 in 10 regular users will develop some kind of dependence on cannabis that will cause problems in their lives. But I think from a harm reduction point of view and with such a low percentage of regular users developing problems of dependence, the use of cannabis as a tool in the arsenal to deal with addiction should be seriously considered.

I also think that from a population point of view, any changes in our current laws or regulations that would lead to safer use of cannabis and potentially to an increased access to a safe source of cannabis may have the potential to reduce the harms associated with the use of alcohol and both the legal and illegal use of pharmaceuticals and other drugs and tobacco as well.

DB: The changes in marijuana law in Washington and Colorado, how do they resonate in Canada?

PHILIPPE LUCAS: It's been remarkable and it's truly, truly changed the discussion here in Canada around legalization. Our federal government for years and years has been citing that we really can't consider changing our cannabis laws or liberalizing our cannabis laws because of the backlash that would come from our biggest trade partner and neighbor, the U.S.

But now with so many U.S. states decriminalizing cannabis and two U.S. states having full on legalized it, I think those arguments from the government fall flat. It's worth mentioning that here in British Columbia there's a group called Sensible B.C. that's trying to get a referendum on our current cannabis laws that would effectively de-penalize adult, personal use of cannabis. I think that's what's happened in Washington State, which is literally our border state with British Columbia, has really added some momentum to that drive.

I was an elected official at the municipal level. I was a city councilor in Victoria for the past three years. At the municipal level, a group called the Union of British Columbia Municipality has recently supported basically the decriminalization of cannabis at their annual meeting. So at all levels of government right now in Canada I think that people are looking at our cannabis laws and seeing how they might be improved and how they might be fixed to better reflect what the people of Canada want themselves. Recent polling suggests that a tax and regulate model here in Canada has about 70 to 75% support of the population and that our current War on Drugs simply isn't supported anymore by the Canadian populace.

Unfortunately at the federal level, we've got a government that literally the day after the federal election in the U.S., finally had the enactment of a bill called C10 that they'd been pushing for that puts in very harsh mandatory-minimum sentences for even minor cannabis production—and I'm talking about producing 6 plants or more leading to a 6 month sentence here in Canada. So while the U.S. has been moving to fix the harms that are clearly associated with mandatory-minimums and with harsh penalties associated with illicit substance use, in Canada we've really swung in the other direction and have increased the penalties associated with illicit cannabis and drug production as well as distribution. So sadly at the federal level we're not seeing a lot of movement in the progressive direction, but at the provincial and municipal level here in Canada I can't overstate how much the changes in Colorado and in Washington are influencing our current direction.

I think that ultimately, like so many bad policies, it's going to be a culmination of the public no longer tolerating the impacts and detrimental effects on their personal freedoms along with a compelling argument to reexamine our current approach to illicit substance use. I think that substitution effect speaks to both of those. I think it would be very hard to condemn someone who has moved from an addiction to pharmaceutical opiates or to alcohol and the associated health and public safety issues and who has been able to reduce that by the use of cannabis. I think that we lose the momentum to punish the cannabis use when we see that it's actually potentially improving the lives of some individuals. I think that at the same time, the associated cost savings at a time when we're all under very tight fiscal pressure suggests that our War on Drugs is not evidence-based. It's no longer supported by the public, and it's no longer defendable in any basis in any jurisdiction. It's just time for drug laws that are based on science, reason, and compassion rather than fear, prejudice, and misunderstanding.

ROBERT MELAMEDE, PH.D.

Dr. Melamede is a professor at the University of Colorado, Colorado Springs and has a Ph. D. in Molecular Biology and Biochemistry from the City University of New York. Dr. Melamede has authored or co-authored dozens of papers on a wide variety of scientific subjects and is recognized as a leading authority on the therapeutic uses of cannabinoid. He serves on the Scientific Advisory Board of Americans for Safe Access, the Unconventional Foundation for Autism, The World Aids Institute, Board Tim Brown Foundation (The Berlin Patient), Phoenix Tears Foundation. He is also CEO of Cannabis Science Inc. Cultural Baggage, February 13, 2008.

DB: There have been over-the-years so many studies, I think a hundred and twenty plus in the last ten years, that talk about the positive, or at least the non-dangerous, aspects of marijuana, and yet the government goons travel the country saying, 'There is no legitimate use, there are no positive studies.' How can they ignore that truth for so long?

DR. MELAMEDE: Well, there's so much more studies than what you indicated, because what you now have to include is not studies specifically on marijuana but studies on a broader topic known as the endocannabinoid system. Because marijuana has the effects that it has just because it happens that that plant uniquely has the ability to touch on the way our bodies function. And we function by producing these marijuana-like compounds called endocannabinoids, 'cannabis from within,' and those cannabinoids literally regulate everything in our bodies.

So when they first legalized medical marijuana in California the government out there and law enforcement were freaking out...'old people are going to be using it for headaches and for this and for that and for everything...' well you know what? It works for all of those things because that endocannabinoid system is so pervasive and so controlling in our body of so many aspects of, not only our lives, but how we interact with others. Our immune system, our digestive system, our cardiovascular system, our nervous system, our excretory system, our reproductive system, all organized entities like that are in fact balanced, which we call homeostasis, by our endocannabinoid system.

So imbalances are what our illnesses are. And in many cases those illnesses are now recognized to, in part, be manifest as cannabinoid deficiencies, things like migraines, multiple sclerosis, and in varieties of illnesses are imbalances that can best be corrected by imitating how the body tries to do it, and the body does it through cannabinoids. But to go further now and try and explain insanity. One of the things that our endocannabinoid system regulates, as indicated by mouse models, we have to put in that qualifier, is what we call open-mindedness. So if you think about what open-mindedness is, it's the ability to take in new information and change your old ideas. That seems pretty straightforward.

So there is in fact a mouse model for being able to effectively rewire. And what it's based on is that you can make mice today, with modern biotechnology, that are lacking a particular gene. So the gene that we're interested in seeing the effects when it's missing is what's know as the CB1 receptor. And that's the receptor that's most involved with getting high. Our brains are loaded with it. And in this one particular example they took what we call 'knock out' mice that don't have that receptor, and they put them in a water maze. So mice don't like water, and they swim around, and they freak out, and eventually they find that there's a platform. So once they've accomplished that they learn the direct route to the platform. And you can take normal mice, scientifically known as 'wild type' mice. You can take 'wild type' mice or these CB1 'knock out' mice and you put them in to this water maze and they both will learn where the platform is and directly go to that because that's the quickest way to get out of the water.

Now if you change the position of that platform to a new place, essentially they have to relearn the maze. They put both mice in; they freak out because the platform isn't where it used to be, and then they start searching and exploring as they learn the maze again. The 'wild type' mice do that very effectively. You take them out, you put them back into the maze, and they go right to the new position. They've relearned.

You do that with the CB1 'knock out' mice, and they only go back to the old position. They're not able to rewire. They're not able to learn. And I believe the human equivalent of that is what we call open-mindedness. And pretty much everybody who has consumed cannabis knows that it tends to make you open-minded. So, here we have this situation where cannabinoids are regulating everything in the human body and we have this mouse model for a particular behavior.

Well, what is inevitably true is that in our population, in all populations, you're going to have people who are more or less endowed in cannabinoid activity with respect to a particular functionality, be it how it modulates your blood pressure or how it helps prevent auto-immune diseases, or how it helps reverse arteriosclerosis, or how it helps protect against Alzheimer's disease. And some people are going to be deficient in particular areas.

So what's inevitably true, in my mind, is that there are going to be people who are lacking cannabinoids with the result, the consequences, that they are not open-minded. Now that has a lot of implications because people who are not open-minded don't particularly like to look into the future because the future means you have to learn new things and they don't have the biochemical equipment to effectively do that. So those people tend to look backwards in time.

Well, there are consequences to that. If you have a group of people who are looking backwards in time, they're going to tend to agree with one another because they're looking at what's already happened, whereas people who tend to be forward looking people, they're going to, at best, agree to disagree because nobody knows what the future holds, and everybody has a different vision and being open-minded they don't want to necessarily say, well, 'my vision is correct'...you know, let's work together and see what the future holds.

Well, the implications of these two, cannabinoid endowed versus cannabinoid deficient, people are very profound, because by the deficient people looking backwards and agreeing with one another, it is my belief that they are going to naturally tend to gain power and therefore get in government. So what I think has happened is we have cannabinoid deficient people who are narrow minded, close minded, running the government and making laws that essentially are attacking those people who have different genetics, those people who are genetically pre-disposed to open mindedness and being creative and embracing the unknowns of the future. So I think that's my explanation for this whole insane war that goes on and on with cannabis. And you can trace the same kind of thinking back to things like racism, people who are afraid of things that are different because, again, that requires embracing change.

Nothing is all good and nothing is all bad, and what might be good for one person might be bad for another person. So, with respect to the cancer story, I find that one particularly offensive because there is significant amounts of peer-reviewed scientific literature that very clearly documents anti-cancer properties of cannabinoids in the plant, not just the THC, but non-psychoactive ones like cannabidiol which we are also not allowed to grow. I mean you could grow hemp plants that wouldn't get you high that would be very rich in cannabidiol that would have profound anti-cancer activities, and that's also illegal, so you got to really wonder what's going on with these people. But the cancer story is pretty impressive. Cannabinoids do have anti-cancer activity for breast cancer, brain cancer, prostate cancer, lymphoma, leukemia, thyroid cancer, melanoma, skin cancers in general.

I mean there are just so many interesting studies because what the cannabinoid system seems to do, and this is how I view it and how I put it simply to people, is I call it the 'oil of life.' And what it does is that it reduces the friction of life. And what is that friction? The friction is basically free radicals. We all make free radicals because we eat and burn food. And those free radicals are very reactive and they essentially act like biochemical friction, they deteriorate the quality of our biochemistry, and it is known that these free radicals are essentially what's behind aging and behind a lot of age-related diseases. So what are the age-related diseases? Cognitive dysfunction like Alzheimer's, auto-immune diseases like diabetes, multiple sclerosis, Crohn's disease, and cancers. And all of those illnesses are inhibited or can be treated with cannabinoids. So we essentially have an anti-aging drug that has been outlawed.

Tod Mikuriya, M.D.

Dr. Tod Mikuriya was the first doctor to specialize in cannabis consultations. He's also the founder of *O'Shaughnessy's: the Journal of Cannabis in Clinical Practice*. Cultural Baggage / January 12, 2007.

DB: Dr. Mikuriya, this issue of *O'Shaughnessy's* is a special issue. If you would, give us a quick run through of what's in this Spring 2007 edition.

TOD MIKURIYA: This is a tenth anniversary commemorative issue of the passage of Proposition 215, the California Compassionate Use Act of 1996. This issue contains both historical perspectives and chronologies of the different dispensaries that have grown in number and also the clinical summaries of physicians and the kinds of cases that they've treated and found cannabis useful for.

DB: If you will tell us about your practice and your article within this issue.

TOD MIKURIYA: My practice contains roughly 9,000 patients that I've seen over this period of time. It attempts to innumerate the different diagnosis that I've encountered. I've attempted to categorize them, and roughly there are four categories of a traumatic, auto-immune immunomodulator cases. That is to say where there has been no trauma but chronic inflammatory symptoms have been treated or controlled with cannabis. Also chronic spastic disorders, as well as diseases like migraine headaches and common back pain, usually due from trauma, but there have been also some very unusual auto-immune diseases that responded to cannabis that have not responded to anything else.

DB: One stat that caught my attention was the fact that those who found relief through cannabis, 95% + had been prior users. Your thoughts on that, sir?

TOD MIKURIYA: In my practice, they've been over 99% previous users that have spontaneously made the discovery that cannabis controls their symptoms better than any kinds of medications on the market.

DB: Many of these people are having to take opiates, sleeping pills, other muscle relaxers, etc. that have what can be egregious side effects, but through the use of cannabis they are able to diminish or even eliminate the use of those hard prescription drugs. Your thoughts there, sir?

TOD MIKURIYA: Indeed. This is one of the most promising, exciting findings that people who have been using medications with adverse effects when used chronically, are able to kick the habit and improve the quality of their lives. This is especially true about opiates that have been utilized to manage chronic conditions. With the opiates there's the difficulty with the chronic sedation, demotivation, mental dullness, depression, and really a closing down of their lives and withdrawing. Their lives are given back to them when they are able to discontinue these medications. This is especially true with opiates but also strikingly true with sedatives and the anti-seizure medications that are given to manage chronic conditions without any kind of rationale. I think this is one of the most disturbing findings that I've had of the number of medications that are irrationally prescribed that not only do they have no efficacy but they have a bunch of adverse effects. When they ask to discontinue these medications, they're fighting the misinformation of the prescribing physician who really can't describe the thinking behind prescribing these drugs in the first place. This is not just my finding but in a recent issue of Psychiatric News over three-quarters of patients are prescribed medications that are off label, that are not recommended specifically for use. This results in a lot of pharmaceutical sales but really no relief to the patients who take them.

DB: Is there a lack of oversight in the control of these pharmaceutically produced drugs?

TOD MIKURIYA: Not only is there a lack of oversight but an unhealthy involvement with the Patent Office and the worship of pharmaceutical industries of patentable compounds rather than the interest of the patients themselves. As a result, we have a giant, out of control industry that is striving to increase the number of drug seekers through direct television advertising.

DB: A moment ago you were talking about the list of improvements, better situations created through the use of cannabis. I know there are ongoing studies now on the cannabinoid system regarding homeostasis. Would you mind explaining that to my audience?

TOD MIKURIYA: Homeostasis is my term that I'm applying to the effects of cannabis and also my belief that cannabis has been improperly classified and should be reclassified as an unique medication called easement that unlike all the other psychotropics, cannabis uses the fat system to circulate and is not soluble in water. This has created a totally new root of effectiveness that goes way beyond the specific locations of receptor sites in both the GI tract and the brain to affect the gland and prostaglandin system, which affects the inflammatory process throughout the body.

DB: Denis Peron is a brave fellow. It takes a person with knowledge and courage to do something like he did. What are your thoughts to the others around the country and maybe even in Canada about that courage and that initiative?

TOD MIKURIYA: I was with Dennis when he decided to start the medical marijuana movement through the San Francisco Cannabis Buyers Cooperative. We were attending the Drug Policy Foundation meeting in Washington, D.C., and we got word that the Food and Drug Administration had closed down the Compassionate Use Program for AIDS patients, denying them access to cannabis because of the warped and twisted fantasy of Dr. James L. Mason, Assistant Secretary of Health and Human Services, where he rationalized that making cannabis available to the "queers" in San Francisco would just encourage uncontrolled sex in the streets and be a great menace to society. This is typical of the homophobic, irrational thinking of the ignorant that had no direct effects with cannabis.

I can make these statements because once upon a time, as first director of the Marijuana Research Program under the National Institutes of Mental Health, I discovered that cannabis was on the market for one century, available to physicians, and that it was taken off the market because of the intervention of Harry J. Anslinger, who personally strong-armed the chair of the Pharmacopeia Committee to take cannabis out of the formula areas. We lost cannabis to the initiative of an ignorant cop who just wanted to make a propaganda point and propel us further into a dark age with regard to cannabis by substituting incorrect police argot for medical intelligence. It started this long period of ignorance. What other place do you find that police dictate health policy? That's a sick idea in itself. It's a general social pathology of the preponderance of a sick "call a cop."

DB: The Drug Czar knows all, sees all and he's perfectly willing to kill you to keep you safe from drugs.

TOD MIKURIYA: It's just pure propaganda and the culture of lies that people who had direct experience with the effects of cannabis especially the other physicians you saw described in *O'Shaughnessy's* have found differently. This is not the kind of information that people want to get out because it will threaten their power and their control. This includes the pharmaceutical companies but also part of the criminal justice system and the Prison Guards Union and other camp followers to the police.

DB: As a medical user myself I find that in my case I'm an alcoholic. I haven't had a drink now in 22 years and I won't say I owe it all to cannabis but it certainly has helped along the way. I want to thank you California doctors for having the courage to stand up.

TOD MIKURIYA: Well, you joined 500 other alcoholics in my practice that have gotten their lives back and saved their families from a never ending cycle of violence and childhood abuse.

Tom O'Connell, M.D.

Doctor Tom O'Connell, an 84-year-old retired Army thoracic surgeon, is my medical marijuana doctor who writes my recommendations when I am in California. Century of Lies September 1, 2013.

DB: You've been doing a lot of work, a lot of investigation about how this medical marijuana situation has unfolded.

TOM O'CONNELL: Really surprised to find myself in this position. I never intended to become a "pot doc" in my medical career, but I became one after Prop 215 passed in California. What I now realize is, after 215 passed nobody knew exactly what to do with it. The Drug Czar had threatened the license of any doctors who dared to speak to a patient seeking a recommendation. That chilled the atmosphere for a while. Fortunately the Supreme Court shot him down on First Amendment grounds. Gradually a small amount of physicians began writing recommendations for applicants who were all pot smokers. That set up a demand for outlets where people could buy cannabis, and it attracted money, investment capital, and the first so-called "buyers' clubs" were established.

I wasn't invited to become a "pot doc" until 2001. I really had never been a pot smoker in my early life, and I was unaware of what now is called the movement. The first thing I learned is pot smokers were of a certain age. Almost all of them had been born right after World War II—they were baby boomers. I've since figured out it took a critical mass of Baby Boomers who had along the way become pot smokers before the medical marijuana tactic was employed by what we now call reform. These are organizations like NORML, Americans for Safe Access, and several others that now exist all over the country. It's a grassroots (pardon the pun) movement supporting use of cannabis.

I didn't know a thing about medical use when I started interviewing patients. I knew I didn't like the drug law and knew the drug war was absolutely stupid because I had edited an online newsletter between 1997 and 2001 in which I had to review hundreds of news items every week. That was my undergraduate education. I got my medical education when I started talking to patients. To tell you the truth, the drug war in the trenches turns out to be a lot worse than it is in the newspapers because you're talking about real people with real problems, and they're being harassed and frustrated and blocked.

My profession to its great discredit has been passive. Worse than that, the psychiatrists, as a group, almost to a person, support Nixon's law so that they have classified "marijuana use disorder." The problem with psychiatry is they're wandering in the desert. They don't have an organized, coherent plan for the conditions that they attempt to treat. In some respects I've come to think that this is Nixon vs. Darwin, which is utterly simplistic, but it's the difference between enlightenment and enforced fascism, because our drug laws are fascist.

The domestic marijuana market in the United States, which has been underground since 1937 and which didn't really start to grow until the mid-60s, is now enormous. How big is it? We don't know. The government doesn't know. Nobody knows. Why is that? It's a drug that doesn't have to be imported from the Middle East or from Colombia. It can be grown at home, and it is far more beneficial medically than most of its supporters even realize because it treats the mind and the body. The government is preaching against the use of marijuana. They have no idea what goes on because they haven't talked to pot smokers like I have.

The same kids who are trying weed also try alcohol and tobacco. How do I know that? I ask them about it. 96% of my applicants tried cigarettes by inhaling at least one cigarette and 100% of them have tried alcohol by getting drunk. Most of them got drunk enough to get sick. The ones who liked alcohol and were on their way to becoming alcoholics changed that behavior once they became pot smokers. So pot is not a gateway into trouble with drugs, it's a gateway out of trouble with drugs.

I've got a panel of drugs that I ask everybody about. It includes LSD, cocaine, MDMA, meth and heroin. That's a pretty good panel for looking at...it profiles pot smokers by the intensity of their need. When you know that somebody's tried all the drugs on my list and is now applying for a pot recommendation I can tell how intense their emotional trauma was, because why do people use illegal drugs? Why will they try drugs at all? It seems to be that they've been traumatized as children. That's a general rule.

The biggest source of that is (and this surprises a lot of people. It surprised me when I stumbled into it) absent fathers. If your biological father was unknown to you during childhood, you are a prime candidate to try drugs. It doesn't matter what color you are, what your cultural level is—this is perceived as a trauma. It's not recognized, obviously, but it makes perfect sense because childhood is when we develop our emotional intelligence. We are emotional creatures long before we are rational creatures. Rationality begins sometime around 11, 12, 13, but before that we've been conditioned emotionally. A major influence is our parental acceptance. In that group it seems that "daddy" is very important. One of the most common reasons to be gone is early death or early divorce. The clue is people who were adopted who didn't know either parent—they stand out in my database like a sore thumb. Their emotional needs were obviously great.

One such person who is very famous and recently in the news is Steve Jobs. Steve Jobs was a very successful guy. He was born to a couple of graduate students at the University of Wisconsin in the early 50s. His parents had wanted him to be adopted by people like themselves who had college degrees. For that reason his mother traveled to San Francisco and had Steve in San Francisco. Amazingly the couple that had agreed to adopt him had decided at the last minute that they wanted a girl. Since Steve wasn't a girl, he was rejected yet again. An adopted kid is rejected, but he wasn't aborted—a mixed blessing. His adoptive parents were found. They were both high school dropouts, as a matter of fact, living in Mountain View, but they supplied Steve with a loving home. They nurtured him. Obviously they were successful, because he became one of the richest men in the world. When his biography became available, I bought it as soon as I could because I knew Steve would have been a pot smoker for sure, and it was also a good guess that he used LSD. He was a hippie. He toured India with a friend of his called Dennis Cocky. Steve could be very cruel. He was an erratic guy. He was impatient with people who he thought were bozos. He was not a kind man or a particularly friendly one, but he was incredibly successful.

ALEXANDER SHULGIN, PH.D.

Alexander "Sasha" Shulgin is a chemist and author credited with introducing MDMA ("ecstasy") to psychologists in the late 1970s for psychopharmaceutical use. He discovered or synthesized over 230 psychoactive compounds. He is author with his wife Ann Shulgin of the books PiHKAL and TiHKAL about Phenethylamines and Tryptamines. Sasha Shulgin has been called the "godfather of psychedelics." Century of Lies / May 6, 2008.

DB: Today, we're honoring the passing of a great man, Dr. Albert Hofmann. I want to get your recollections, your thoughts about Dr. Albert Hofmann.

SASHA SHULGIN: Mine are very, very positive. We actually got to really know each other meeting at Esalen. I knew him from way, way back when he had first worked with LSD and other things of the ergot world. But I really got to know him quite well in Esalen some two or three decades ago and really spent time with him in a quiet way that was very nice. Subsequently both Ann and I had visited him at his home near the French border in Switzerland.

ANN SHULGIN: That was on his one hundredth birthday.

DB: That sounds like a wonderful opportunity to talk with the man. As I understand it, he lost his wife just about six months ago.

SASHA SHULGIN: Yes, just the end of last year.

ANN SHULGIN: That was a very, very long and solid and very loving marriage so we're not exactly surprised that he didn't stay around very much longer.

DB: Yes, Ma'am. Now Dr. Rick Doblin told me that he was glad that the Swiss have decided to begin new studies of LSD and that both Dr. Hofmann and his wife were able to learn of that information.

SASHA SHULGIN: Yes, that's very nice. We met at his home and I remember very well the fact that Hofmann, at one point, sort of wiggled his fingers and asked me to come back into his office for a few minutes. And I had no idea what he had in mind and I did that and he said 'Sit down. I have had many, many consultant meetings with people, this newspaper and that journal and that writing, but I have not had a chance in a decade or two to talk a person who's a chemist.' And he said 'I'd just love to talk a little bit of chemistry.'

DB: Well, between the two of you I can't imagine the rest of the world even stacking up.

SASHA SHULGIN: (laughter) But it was delightful. We just exchanged comments on FM2 reactions and other strange little things known only to chemists. And he was very happy with that, and he went out and joined the small party he had in the living room.

ANN SHULGIN: I'd like to tell a quick story about Dr. Hofmann at Esalen. When he first got there I remember it was evening and he was dressed like any Swiss gentleman with a suit and tie and white shirt. And these young, nubile, very eager, pretty young girls rushed up to him and took him by the hand and one would say 'Dr. Hofmann, you shouldn't be wearing a tie. This is a very, very relaxed place. Come, let me take your tie off.' And he would grin, and the girl would take off his tie. And he seemed to come back the next day with a tie back on. And we finally caught on to the fact that he was just waiting for the pretty young girl to come rushing up to him and take his tie off. (laughter) He was a scamp.

DB: He sounds like quite the raconteur, I suppose, as you say, Ann. I think we should celebrate the man's life. He has left so much for us.

ANN SHULGIN: Absolutely. Very much so. I don't know how to explain to anyone who's not familiar with the world of psychedelics and psychoactive visionary plants how important Dr. Hofmann was. He was a ground breaker, and LSD has been very much maligned, but it is one of the most extraordinary compounds ever discovered. And we have him to thank for that.

DB: I know in the 60s and 70s it was truly an awakening for me. It helped mold and shape my personality and perhaps my perseverance.

ANN SHULGIN: Oh that's great. That really is very good to hear. Oh, one of the funny things that happened at Esalen was that we, we and several other people, introduced Dr. Hofmann to MDMA, which is sometimes called ecstasy, but that's a name we never use, and he loved MDMA.

SASHA SHULGIN: In fact he asked for a sample to take home to his wife. (laughter)

DB: Any thoughts on the future of psychedelic medicine?

SASHA SHULGIN: We just hope that eventually it falls out of the control of the government illegal side of things and gets into medicine. That's what I like very much about the way it's going in Switzerland. They have their drug problems, but to them, all these materials that are psychedelic are medical problems and medical concerns and not legal ones. Hence, the research is going on with Swiss support. It is not going on in this country.

ANN SHULGIN: For people like me, LSD and other psychedelics and visionary plants are tools for spiritual searching and that is not the easiest path in the world but it is the spiritual path that many, many thousands of people all over the world follow. And someday that will be respected.

SASHA SHULGIN: It will someday, I know.

Donald Tashkin, M.D.

Donald P. Tashkin is a pulmonologist at UCLA Medical School. In 2006, he was in charge of the biggest case-control study done by the National Institute on Drug Abuse on cannabis, which took in total of 2,200 subjects. We recorded during the Cannabis Therapeutics convention. Cultural Baggage / April 9, 2008.

DR. DONALD TASHKIN: Tobacco smokers are at risk of developing COBD, Chronic Obstructive Pulmonary Disease. This is manifested by an accelerated rate of loss of lung function over time as you grow older. We failed to find a similar relationship with marijuana. So that was one finding.

We are also interested in investigating the possibility that marijuana smoking might lead to lung cancer. Now lung cancer is mainly attributable to tobacco smoking. And since marijuana and tobacco share similar ingredients including a number of carcinogens, it's a reasonable hypothesis that smoking marijuana, at least heavily, over a long period of time could predispose to the development of lung cancer, maybe not to the same extent as tobacco but to a greater extent than if you didn't smoke any marijuana or tobacco at all.

So we did a very large study which we call a 'case-control' study. And in that study we identified 600 patients who were diagnosed with lung cancer. An additional 600 patients or so were diagnosed with neck cancer, throat cancer, lip cancer, or tongue cancer, and over 1,000 control subjects who did not have cancer. And then we administered a detailed questionnaire to all of these subjects including questions about marijuana use and tobacco use and family history of cancer and other putative risk factors that could predispose to cancer and the results were entirely negative--if anything, the risk for developing lung cancer was slightly less in relation to marijuana than no marijuana although not statistically significantly so.

Despite the fact that the study was designed as well as we could possibly design it and it included a large number of subjects, over 100 of whom smoked marijuana heavily, both among the cases and the controls, I think we can say with some confidence that there just is no evidence of an association between marijuana use and lung cancer.

On the other hand, very recently, earlier this year, another paper was published by New Zealand investigators who claimed that there was a positive relationship between marijuana smoking and lung cancer. Now they studied far fewer patients than we did who smoked marijuana less heavily. In fact there were only about 79 cases of lung cancer and a few hundred controls. Their control subjects actually smoked less marijuana, about half as much marijuana, as our control subjects. Yet they came to the rather amazing and implausible conclusion of a positive-- quite a positive--association between marijuana and lung cancer which is similar to the association between tobacco and lung cancer, which is quite difficult to believe. For example, in continuous analysis of their data they found that for each joint/year of marijuana, that is a joint a day for a year, the risk of developing lung cancer is increased by 8% over not smoking marijuana and it's, the increase is similar for each pack/year of tobacco. That means there, according to them, there is an equivalence between 365 joints and over 7,000 tobacco cigarettes with respect to the impact on the risk for developing lung cancer. I find that to be implausible.

DB: We are attending the International Conference on Cannabis Therapeutics and there are many here who think the government has, over the years, focused in the wrong direction--trying to impugn the good name, if you will, of marijuana and yet there are so many studies--even the American Academy of Physicians recently came out for changing our stance in that regard. Your thoughts, Sir. Has some of it indeed been propaganda over the years?

DR. DONALD TASHKIN: Well, I can say that the government agency that I deal with is a funding agency, it's called the National Institute on Drug Abuse, and their funding policy I believe is quite fair because they have an independent body of scientists, for example my peers, who evaluate my research solely on the basis of science rather than on some agenda, some political agenda. So I think it's fair. Now that doesn't say that there isn't propaganda from other agencies of the government but the agency that I deal with I think is fair.

DB: Tthe FDA has dropped the ball in many instances in the last few years. Has it been a situation that the Administration has not focused so much on science and true regulation?

DR. DONALD TASHKIN: Well, that certainly is true of the present Administration which is the most disastrous Administration in the history of our country. (laughter) I'm going to get into trouble for this. (laughter)

DB: You are here to speak to this conference on cannabis therapeutics. Can you give us a quick summary of what you'll present?

DR. DONALD TASHKIN: Yes, actually I'm going to be presenting some of what I've already mentioned. I'm actually going to review the evidence regarding the question as to whether or not regular smoking of marijuana leads to Chronic Obstructive Pulmonary Disease--that consists of chronic bronchitis and emphysema, it's the fourth leading cause of death in the U.S. and the world--and whether or not regular marijuana smoking leads to lung cancer, primarily. And also there's another question: does regular marijuana smoking predispose to pneumonia. We know that tobacco smoking does. And I could tell you that our own findings, our own findings from our own research, indicate that the answer to those three question appears to be negative.

MEDICAL CANNABIS

"Marijuana in its natural form is one of the safest therapeutically active substances known to man. By any measure of rational analysis marijuana can be safely used within the supervised routine of medical care."
—DEA Administrative Law Judge, Francis L. Young

Modern science and common sense have shown that the laws against cannabis use are based not on fact but rather are, quite simply, tools of oppression. The oppression is becoming more obvious as each day passes. Governments of Mexico, Central and South America, Canada, Switzerland, Holland, Germany, Italy, Belgium, Australia, New Zealand, and other nations have seen the folly that is a result of the failed U.S. policy on cannabis. Many of these countries have changed or are changing their laws in regard to cannabis possession; only their fear of losing US preferential treatment or the breaking of international treaties forced on them by the US government prevents the complete reversal of their cannabis laws.

For some, the use of cannabis can be a moment of enlightenment, an epiphany, or a moment of communion with their creator. It is a fundamental right of each US citizen to be allowed this moment of peace and serenity without the threat of government interference. It is therefore necessary this day that we stand together and deny the government authority that would prevent use of a sacrament, the cannabis plant.

For many, the use of cannabis is necessary for life, pain prevention, or maintenance of other disabilities. Knowing that the real truth about cannabis is aligned with benefit and relief rather than the supposed government truth that speaks of death and destruction, we must again deny the government authority that would prevent the use of cannabis for relief of pain or for other medical reasons.

For all people, certainly for US citizens, there are certain inalienable rights, and among them is the pursuit of happiness. Again, because the government laws against cannabis have minimal basis in reality, and because they are designed to prevent access to a certain level of contentment that may at times be available through the use of cannabis, we must once again deny allegiance to government authority that would unduly prevent the pursuit of a level of happiness as guaranteed in the Declaration of Independence.

The heart of this deception is a small, at one time insignificant lie around which all the other lies are able to exist: MARIJUANA IS EVIL! Around this thought were designed propaganda films, books, and a million speeches to proclaim the use of this weed would lead our children to insanity, criminality, and death!

The deception made use of the ignorance of the American people, who were at the time quite comfortable with the use of cannabis and hemp. Our government proclaimed there was a new threat, from south of the border, a menace named marihuana that with just one puff could destroy the lives of our children and the future of our nation.

Vaporizers are on the market to eliminate the smoke in smoking marijuana, cannabis throat sprays are coming to market from Bayer, and the American Cancer Society is funding a "cannabis patch" (think "nicotine patch"). Does it make sense to have Gil Kerlikoske, the ONDCP's Drug Czar of the America's, a law enforcement officer, speak on the medicinal efficacy of marijuana? Not really. According to DEA Law Judge Francis L. Young: "...[for] those with AIDS, or who are undergoing chemotherapy and who suffer simultaneously from severe pain, nausea, and appetite loss, cannabinoid drugs might offer broad-spectrum relief not found in any other single medication."

In 2004, a coalition of scientists sued the U.S. Drug Enforcement Administration, U.S. Department of Health and Human Services, National Institutes of Health, and National Institute on Drug Abuse for obstructing medical marijuana research in violation of federal law. Even though numerous, in-depth studies, including one US President sponsored study, (the Shaffer Report) have been conducted over several decades, and even though each and every one states that marijuana is much less dangerous than alcohol and less addicting than coffee and that we should stop arresting people for its use, the prohibition continues against marijuana or any real study of its properties.

The drug czar and all those who thrive from drug war will never admit they are wrong. Scientists from around the world know the truth; many of them focus their work on ending the myriad harms of this drug war. Nowhere are the harms and the hypocrisy more obvious than in regards to disallowing sick and dying patients the right to use medical marijuana. Doctors in California and the 20 other states that allow for medical marijuana dare to recommend marijuana to their patients. The American Nurses Association, some 6 million strong is for medical marijuana. Even the Texas Medical Association is in favor of doctor/patient discussions about marijuana, and they have called for more studies ASAP. Surveys done in every region of America indicate that 70 to 80% of US citizens are in favor of legal access to medical marijuana.

Informed scientists have filed suits against the government "suits" for years, battling for the right to produce a better quality marijuana, a better mechanism of delivery, and a means to soothe suffering and pain. Patients simply want their medicine now, while they are alive, while they are ill or in pain, and yet the government continues to do everything possible to thwart studies of and access to this herb.

NORTON ARBELAEZ

During the Drug Policy Alliance 2013 International Reform Conference in Denver, Colorado in late October, 2013, Norton Arbelaez, the General Counsel of River Rock Wellness Center, took us on a tour of the grow facility which features warehouses and outdoor facilities with thousands of cannabis plants.

NORTON ARBELAEZ: So, we are here at River Rock Wellness Center. We have two licenses in the city of Denver and also our optional premise cultivation license which is basically a manufacture license, the grow license. As the law stands today we have a system of vertical integration in the state of Colorado which mandates that one cultivates a minimum of 70% of what is sold in the store. That's important for any number of reasons. The real goal of Colorado's regulated model as explained by the Colorado code which passed in 2009 is to really have the supply chain of cannabis controlled from seed to sale.

When California passed its Compassionate Use Act in 1996, it was a huge step for the movement that really lit the fuse for the rest of the states over the last now almost 20 years. We are dealing now with controlling the production. California's done a fair job of controlling the points of distribution. They have the municipal level of laws concerning cameras and distance requirements but really unfortunately California has never been able to get its arms around the control of the production side of it, the manufacturing side of it.

How can we ensure that the product that is being sold legally was cultivated legally? Manufactured in a way that doesn't hurt public health, that hasn't used private lands or public lands for example. We see that there is an environmental consequence to illegal grows in the forest. Here in Colorado what we wanted to do was really focus on the backend of production so we can ensure that this is a legal product that is being sold in a legal manner. It really isn't the hard part to control. The hard part to control is how much are you producing, where are you producing it, in what manner are you producing it. Is it free of pesticides, is it free of things that will hurt the patients and the consumers?

Our philosophy was that we would rather err on the side of caution and have more requirements so that we have that leeway and that time to prove ourselves that this is a system that is feasible, that can be responsible, and that can be accountable and that can work within our system of federalism. By virtue of operation we have disclaimers, we have waivers, we have ingredient lists, we have license numbers, expiration dates. We know exactly under what circumstance the product was produced and the potency of the product.

We put about 2 and one-half million dollars into this building. This is not a "get rich quick" scheme. It's far from it. There are easier ways to make money.

There are much easier ways to make money. But we're legal. We're doing this sort of social entrepreneurship. This economic ripple effect is huge. It's not just the 85 employees. It's not just the 700,000 dollars in state and local taxes or the 41,000 per month that the landlord gets or the 26,000 dollars a month that Excel Energy gets. It's the CPAs. It's the highest paid person in the company last year was the electrician. The main guys that are responsible for taking care of the plants are making 80,000 dollars per year.

When it's in soil it gives it a depth of character that hydroponic cannabis doesn't have. This is a lot more like a small craft brewery style. We do have some scale in the back as you'll see. We're really focused on pharmaceutical grade cannabis. That means the most interesting and effective cannabinoid profiles on the particular plants. There's an esthetic component to it. There's smell, a taste, a flavor and there's also an effect.

We don't have to continue to go down the same path of prohibition that inordinately affects minorities, Latin American youth and African-American youth who are branded as criminals for the rest of their life because they get caught with a joint when they are 18 or 19-years-old and get denied federal funds for education.

It's not just about business. As I said earlier, this is sort of a social entrepreneurship. We are unleashing the powers of the free market into this particular regulated space. We want a safer society. We want a society where it's harder for children to have access to not just cannabis but tobacco and alcohol and anything else that is going to hurt their development and their prospect going into the future. We know that the supposed cure-all of prohibition causes more disease and more rot within our society.

The states are innovating new approaches because of the inactivity and negligence of the federal government in this regard. It's hard for them to even keep their lights on and to keep the government open much less revisit cannabis policy. As sovereign states with their own constitutions and their own regulatory powers and our own police powers for law in our own states, we have the capacity in the state of Colorado, within the state of Washington, within the state of New Jersey to say, "Enough." We will not collaborate with the federal government anymore.

MARY JANE BORDEN

Mary Jane Borden is a public policy advocate for safe, legal access to medicinal cannabis in Ohio who has participated in running non-profits, crafting legislation, meetings with numerous state legislators, hiring professional lobbyists, and hearings for three bills. Recorded March 31, 2013.

MARY JANE BORDEN: About 3 years ago in 2010 we formed an incubator for a constitutional amendment to legalize medical marijuana in the state of Ohio. What we have going now in the Ohio Rights Group is the outgrowth of the formation of that think tank. It was formerly under the name of the Ohio Medical Cannabis Association. In January we re-formed under the name of the Ohio Rights Group.

DB: Tell the folks why. What was the main reason?

MARY JANE BORDEN: Well there are a number of reasons the least of which was that ...if I could backtrack just a little bit so people can understand this in context. We're on our third initiative. We had one submitted in September 2011 that was way too long.

For two years we were working with this as our bull's eye target. Little did we realize in 2012 how much air a national election sucks out of any other advocacy. I realize Colorado and Washington passed but so much is taken up by the presidential election. All the dollars on the media had already been committed. We had 5 little months to get this on the ballot. It just became particularly apparent to us that the stars were simply not going to align.

In June we had a reorganization of the board and I became treasurer and I go to Chase bank and say, "Hi, I want to put my name on the account." I've done this with many organizations before. They said, "No you're not because we're going to foreclose your account."

"Why are you going to foreclose our account?"

"Because you have cannabis in your name."

I was absolutely stumped. One of the requirements for valid initiatives in the state of Ohio in terms of a statewide issue PAC is it has to have a checking account. When a bank forecloses your checking account you can't do business as a PAC.

I think that led to our inability to make the 2012 but, without doubt, the last nail in the coffin was when Chase foreclosed the account.

DB: Because the word cannabis was written on the account it's almost as if it's illegal as the plant itself.

MARY JANE BORDEN: It's a true story. You can't imagine how shocked I was as treasurer. I had heard about this but thought it was something that happened to other people. We are a political organization. We are in the business of passing ballot initiatives. We're not dispensing any Schedule I substances. By extension to say not only will we foreclose a dispensary even though they're operating legally in California but we're going to foreclose the account of a political organization to me is an assault against free speech.

DB: I spoke earlier with Chris Goldstein. He was complaining that in New Jersey it has taken years to unfold, to slowly make its way into existence and even now some several years later it's severely limited in the amount of patients it can serve and the amount of cannabis it can provide. It's another example of fear getting in the way of progress isn't it?

MARY JANE BORDEN: There's a stopping block put every step of the way—if it's not the U.S. Attorneys going after the dispensaries in California forcing them to close by going after their landlords. Or say you have this issue with the banks not providing services. I was reading the other day about the EPA trying to apply environmental law to marijuana. I don't think it's fair at all. I think it's this grind of the drug war. We are certainly trying to stop it but I think it's really the grind of the drug war.

DB: Looking at your website I see you guys want to hear from the veterans because they are very instrumental in helping sway public opinion and they are the people who I think often need this most.

MARY JANE BORDEN: That's right. I had the blessing of receiving a lot of the messages that come into our website. I'm kind of the point person for reading them and then sending them off to the person most capable of responding to them.

Within the last 3,4, 5 or 6 days we've had many veterans…I actually printed off a couple of these if you could give me a minute to read one of them. Here's Nick…He says he's a veteran of the Operation Iraqi Freedom with a 30% disability rating. He writes: "When I left the Corps I came home to a strange and unfamiliar world. I have only found one thing that calms me down without making me lethargic—one plant that diminishes the threat lying around every corner." People are writing this stuff to us all of the time.

If I could read another one here. This is Jeff. "We set out for a mission that night." He's talking about being in Iraq. "Everything went according to plan but on the way back to the FOB my driver ran over a roadside bomb instantly killing him and leaving myself and my truck commander severely injured." He goes on and says he's been on the road to recovery. He's been on everything – all kinds of morphine, antidepressants, sleep aids, therapy. "You name it. I began to feel like a mindless zombie. I went over to a friend's house and he offered me some marijuana. Thinking what else do I have to lose I gave it a shot. 15 minutes later I felt like a little school boy again. I was laughing, socializing, the pain had dwindled, thoughts of my accident had diminished. I thought the last time I felt this way was before I deployed. Medical marijuana is a God send."

That's a true statement. That's a person that just sent this message in the last day or so. That is a human being out there who is suffering and found the ability to alleviate his suffering with this miraculous plant.

DB: It's an example of countless people – veterans or not—people who suffer debilitating conditions and maladies. It doesn't take away all the pain. It doesn't put you into some sort of zone – zombied out. It just helps you to diminish the pain, to push it away a bit, to keep it at a distance so that you can live a more productive and useful life, right?

MARY JANE BORDEN: That's exactly how we approached it in our ballot language. I don't know how many mentions we have of this, but the alleviation of suffering is key to this. We are giving patients the right to use this to alleviate their suffering and to possess an amount of cannabis sufficient to meet their therapeutic needs and alleviate their suffering.

VALERIE CORRAL

Valerie Corral is the Executive Director and Co-Founder of "WAMM", the Wo/Men's Alliance for Medical Marijuana and Raha Kudo, Design for Dying Project. Cultural Baggage / August 3, 2007.

DB: A lot of people make fun of marijuana but it can be a very serious concern for people who need it for medicinal properties. Am I right?

VALERIE CORRAL: That's absolutely true. A lot of people make fun of a lot of things that they don't understand don't they?

DB: Yes, they do. Let's talk about WAMM. Tell us about your organization.

VALERIE CORRAL: A brief description is in the early 70s I was in an automobile accident that rendered me with a brain trauma. At the time I was in college and had up to 5 grand mal seizures a day and was taking a myriad of pharmaceuticals some of which I became addicted to. As was the case with me, about 25% of epileptics do not respond to pharmaceuticals as a useful treatment.

My husband, Mike, read in a medical journal in the early 70's that marijuana could be successful used (at least in a rat model) to treat laboratory induced seizures. We really didn't quite believe that it was possible that that could be so but quite desperate as I really lived a muddled life – very, very confused by the effects of the pharmaceuticals. They didn't help my seizures. They didn't reduce them.

We started a pragmatic and methodical approach by using marijuana to see if it, indeed, would help. Lo and behold and, honestly, literally surprised it worked. In the early 90's my husband and I were arrested for growing 5 marijuana plants and I was the first patient in the state of California to challenge the law on medical necessity. The reason is I knew it worked and was a medicine is because of my own personal experience. It's difficult to speak about another person's experience but to have that experiential acquaintance leaves us with very little room for doubt.

That started a long journey through the courts. We won. We were re-arrested...well, before we were re-arrested we were contacted by patients in our community asking if we could help them – people with cancer and AIDS, 6 month prognosis, pancreatic cancer, metastatic bone cancer, brain cancer – what do you do? Do you say no?!

Anyway that's how WAMM began. The genesis of WAMM began from the community reaching toward us and a humanitarian response. We'll try to figure it out together. In 1993 we began an outreach program into our community. On the steps of the county building we said, "We're going to work together with other people who are sick. We're not going to sell anything. We're not going to buy drugs. We're going to create our own little communal garden and people that can work and can help will do so or their caregivers will help. We want notes from your doctors. We want you to prove that you have an illness."

During the processes of going into the judiciary I realized that it is very important to have your physician understanding. At the time there's no such thing as a recommendation for marijuana. Doctors were writing on their prescription pads saying, "Yes, this patient might be a candidate for your organization." We applied for non-profit in 1996 right after California Proposition 215 (which is the medical marijuana proposition) passed. The day after we got our non-profit – that was a state non-profit. The feds refused to grant us non-profit so we had to go through another court battle which we did not win. We've been in the courts ever since.

DB: Let's talk about the people who "qualify" to become members of WAMM. These are not skateboard injuries or that sort of thing...

VALERIE CORRAL: I'm going to have to say something. You brought up skateboarding. One of our members was paralyzed from the neck down in a skateboard injury...

DB: Oh, my gosh.

VALERIE CORRAL: That man was coming down a hill, saw a car coming so he took his board into some bushes. He tripped up on the curb and went head first into a rock and became paralyzed. He's a quadriplegic, beautiful young man, amazing intellectual being – quite remarkable.

DB: It makes me feel ...

VALERIE CORRAL: We work with people who are seriously ill. Right now the only people who can get into our organization—because of our difficulty to be able to provide free medicine to the number of people who need it in our community – we work with only the terminally ill presently. It's a quandary and one that we are hard pressed to make those choices. If only we could serve everyone...if only we could feed all the hungry children, right?

DB: I have egg on my face about that skateboard....

VALERIE CORRAL: No, no, no – don't say that. Sometimes people think...you think a kid is just abusing it and then you look into a child's life or into their eyes and you meet their parents. One of my most dear friends, a young man 19-years-old, Riley died recently from metastatic sarcoma. It's a very aggressive childhood cancer. Doctors from Stanford contacted us and said, "What can you do to help?" His parent does drug counseling in high schools throughout the county so you can imagine his concerns. We had long talks and they would come to the meetings.

We have a weekly meeting. We all come together at that place. We don't smoke in the building. That's not what we do. We come together to talk about our troubles, how to resolve them, what family needs a refrigerator or a babysitter. It's part of the education. The children come. We speak about medicine not about abuse. Without education we lose our children no matter what the story – whether it's historical, the future, medicine, math, quantum physics – we have to teach our children the truth because they'll find out. They will not believe us if we don't speak truth and set boundaries.

We have a remarkable community of people who are heroes and masters— masters because that if they face death they learn that we are learners. We are in the position to learn. We're the servants. The children are sometimes our great teachers because they bring the questions to us that really rock our world, that open our eyes to help us to be more cautious and more aware.

DB: I appreciate your understanding of that passage into death. You've seen it. How many of your members have passed on?

VALERIE CORRAL: As of two weeks ago 190 in 14 years – a little more than 1 per month.

DB: And yet the federal government a few years back came to your garden. Tell us about that day.

VALERIE CORRAL: That was one of the scariest days of my life and also one of the most profound. It was early in the morning. I heard some stomping on the deck. The kind of stomping that nobody arrives if they are friends and if they are robbers they certainly come in with more stealth. I heard that noise and I jumped out of bed and said, "It's the DEA." I sneaked around and I managed to surprise them because of the way the house setup and I opened the door on them and said, "What are you doing in my home. Get out!"

It is not a wise thing to do with the DEA. They yelled, "Get down! Get down!" They pushed me to the ground, put a gun to my head and a boot to my back, hand cuffed me. We had been up late that night making plans for the hospice that we opened. I say hospice but what it is very loosely is we offer in-home care to our members and we're just trying to make a way that we can serve people who are dying in a manner in which they require and request. It's a hospice not a facility but assistant hospice care. We do the 24 in-home care. We do the freshen IVs. We do the medicines – a lot of loving care, we're servants. Many of our members do this for one another.

That day something came...I have to tell you this. I want to say this. Something happened inside of me that day that was the peace of which I speak is profound. It's that place that's deep within every being and every being. Some people call it soul. It's that knowing of knowing inside. That place of peace that each human being...the part that no matter what else is going on there is a place within us that knows. I was fortunate to be able to touch that place with that boot in my back and that gun to my head. I understood at the moment that I didn't feel necessarily faith I felt....pure, clean and not righteous but right. I knew that the work was profound and perhaps I could start speaking to these men – these 30 agents – I could touch their hearts. Now I'm not going to teach them anything but just open them to looking at our work as human beings working in a different way.

We were up late. We were up until 3 o'clock in the morning talking about how we were going to set up the hospice and finally, alas, some years later we have it. We always did the work but we didn't actually have a name. We spoke to many of the agents and some heard us. After that day, some 8 and one-half, 9 hours later, one of the agents actually said that he was thinking about getting another job sometime soon. Why would somebody do that? Well, because maybe it's soul looking at soul – human beings seeing human beings, recognizing that in every human being is the potential to suffer and with that understanding there is the potential to relieve some of that suffering.

It was so powerful. Well, in the meantime, though, they swept us away. A couple of our friends had not left. One was Susan Fyle who had been there with us. She was on an assisted breathing device. She is crippled, mind you, but she does use a wheelchair. They were yelling at her to get out of bed. Her blood pressure spiked dangerously high. They were only there to get me and Mike. They allowed another of my friends to drive her off. We have in place a 24 hour response team. It's a team that no matter what situation arises we have a way to respond to it whether it's a child needing to be picked up from school or the DEA coming in to bust us.

We are a community. Seriously ill people are often marginalized and isolated. That's one of the things in our little community that we try to serve. We serve one another. It's a "barn raising." You know what I mean? How do you get the barn up if you don't have any help. It would take you forever so we do it together.

It's pretty amazing. In 2002 the DEA had a gun to my head and 2 weeks ago I was invited...it was the first time that this has occurred and I don't know why they asked me of all people but I was invited to congress by the House Judiciary to the Subcommittee on Crime, Terrorism and Homeland Security because that's where marijuana falls under.

I was asked to testify before the Judiciary. What a great opportunity. I can't say my heart wasn't pounding when I sat at the table to testify by two DEA agents and 30 agents sitting over my shoulder. The last time I saw 30 agents it wasn't the greatest meetings on the planet although it changed my life significantly. What happened as a result of that is congress opened their ears. It's you, it's every single person that says, "Wake up Representative. Wake up Senator. I want your ear because if I don't get your ear I'll have your job." Everybody is worried about their jobs especially today, especially in America. Everybody is worried about their jobs and congress is worried about their jobs and they need to be.

They walked away asking for science. I asked them if they would go to a couple websites and not buy the nonsense that we were hearing from the DEA, "We can have a monopoly on growing marijuana in America. The only monopoly in America but it should be OK to have that." I asked them to go to the International Cannabinoid Research Society and the ICAM to look at the science that's happening all over the world. 400 research scientists belong to the ICRS bringing real science about marijuana. They have been for 14 years. It's remarkable. What they are finding is its usefulness. It's the properties that can relieve suffering and pain. They're speaking the truth because they can prove it. Now we know that if you don't ask the right questions you don't get the right answers. We know that if you're asking for something you're going to get it. There are many different ways to look at that but the point is this – there is a great deal of scientific data which is tilting the scales. It all aligns that marijuana is useful.

STEVE DEANGELO

Steve is co-founder and executive director of Harborside Health Center based in Oakland California. Harborside is perhaps the world's largest medical cannabis dispensary. Steve has almost four decades of activism and advocacy in the cannabis reform movement. His vision and leadership have been featured by news teams from around the globe. Steve has been featured by the *New York Times*, *Washington Post*, CNN, the Associated Press, *Wall Street Journal*, NPR, and the BBC. Steve afforded me the opportunity to do the first video tour of the facility in 2009. Cultural Baggage / March 4, 2009.

STEVE DeANGELO: This is the morning rush. There are two things that you see going on right now. Number one it's Tuesday. On Tuesdays we distribute our care packages to low income patients and that brings in about 400 low income patients just to pick up those packages.

Some of those people also purchase some supplementary medicine on top of that. We always do have a rush for the first hour that we're open. So you see a combination of those two things. It's not normally this busy here.

One of our most recent services that we introduced at Harborside is something called the Patient Activist Resource Center which we call "the PARC". The Patient Activist Resource Center is designed to teach patients how to become activists and fight for their own rights.

We have a designated fax, telephone and computer that we provide to patients along with instructions and talking points on how to be an effective citizen lobbyist. We teach them how to write letters to the editor. We put them in touch with federal prisoners of war who are locked up in prison. Patients will come in and they'll volunteer for an hour doing that kind of work and at the end of the hour we give them a gram of medicine.

What we've tried to do in addition just to teaching people how to defend their own rights is we've tried to create a situation here at Harborside so nobody who needs medicine need leave without it. If you don't have enough money you should be able to qualify for our low income care packages but if you're just running a little bit tight this week and you can't quite make it folks can come in and volunteer for an hour at the PARC and they can get some medicine that way. We don't ever want anybody to walk in here and walk away without the medicine that then need.

DB: I look at what's going on in California and I think if this could be packaged, if this could be exported to every other state in the Union, it would be over. People need to learn what you are up to because we all deserve the dignity that you're trying to afford, right?

STEVE DeANGELO: Yeah, one of the things that we try to do at Harborside is to help people heal not only from what illness they might have but also to help heal from the years that they've spent having to hide the fact that they use medicine, from all the years that they've had to be afraid of the police, from all the years they've had to be afraid that their children were going to be taken away from them if their medicine use was discovered. That's had a traumatic effect on many, many of our patients. One of the things we've done at Harborside it to try to create a warm, welcoming atmosphere and to make absolutely certain that every single person who passes through our door is treated with the utmost care and respect to help people heal from all of those years of oppression and misery.

DB: It seems absurd, just bizarre that the federal government would prefer that these people be out there in the alleys. They would prefer that they be denied or they get tainted or contaminated medicine. We own this moral high ground. It's just time to act, isn't it?

STEVE DeANGELO: Yeah, it's absolutely time to act. I think that the point that you made about California is a really good point. I've heard a lot of talk about people talking about the out of control situation with medical cannabis in California, how it's been exploited by unsavory elements. Where that has occurred, it's because there hasn't been effective local regulation. In every single city in California where there's been effective local regulation, what you've seen is legitimate, responsible collectives being operated in a manner that's respectful to patients and respectful to the community as a whole.

If you contrast the situation in California where at least half of the state has safe and affordable access to other medical cannabis states like Montana...there's a really sad story that comes out of Montana that illustrates for me the difference. In Montana there's a woman named Robin Prosser. Robin had lived for several years in California where she became a medical cannabis patient. Then as her disease worsened she moved home to Montana to be close to her family. Montana by that time had passed a medical cannabis law but Robin was unable to locate medical cannabis in Montana because there is no effective distribution system there. Robin, in desperation, had some of her friends from California send her medicine which was unfortunately intercepted by the DEA who then arrested her, prosecuted her, denied her her medicine. This was a woman who was already very, very sick. The pressure from the DEA and the removal of her medicine was really the last straw for her and she ended up committing suicide.

Now I know that there are thousands of "Robin Prossers" all across the country. So the people who say that California is a bad model for medical cannabis I have a question, "What about Robin Prosser? What about all the people like Robin Prosser who are living in states where they have the right to use medical cannabis but it's an empty right because there's no medical cannabis to be had."

DEBBY GOLDSBERRY

Debby Goldsberry has 25 years experience as an anti-prohibition activist. She is the 2011-2012 High Times Freedom Fighter of the Year and a columnist in High Times Medical Marijuana Magazine. Ms. Goldsberry co-founded the Berkeley Patients Group (BPG), Americans for Safe Access (ASA), the Medical Cannabis Safety Council (MCSC), and Cannabis Action Network (CAN). She is a former board member of Marijuana Policy Project, and was given NORML's Paula Sabine Award for Women in Leadership. Century of Lies / March 10, 2013

DEBBY GOLDSBERRY: I'm from Oakland, California. I'm with a collective called the CommuniCare Collective. We are working on opening dispensaries in a couple of cities in the East Bay and California – CommuniCare Centers because we believe that the community care is helping our members and we're a medical cannabis collective. We're making pure medicines from CBD and CB and THC medicines. We're really working on creating the best medicines to help the most people.

DB: We hear so many people – different states – trying to create those medicines that best suit the needs of various maladies, illnesses and injuries. Let's talk about how that's coming about and why and how effective it is.

DEBBY GOLDSBERRY: With medical cannabis right now we're kind of in a grey zone because we can't get standardized medicine. It's not like JC Penny's where if I run out of T-shirts I can just call up and say send me the purple T-shirts in size XL. The medicine supply is really varied. Even people that grow "Jack Herer" because of the changes in season and conditions the "Jack Herer" might be different from harvest to harvest even with the same cultivator. It's a real problem. We're trying to find medicines that help with specific conditions so if a patient can reliably go back to their dispensary or to their caregiver who cultivates for them and know that each time they are going to get the same medicine so that it will help them in the same way.

So we really have a problem making standardized medicine because we can't grow standardized cannabis yet because of the laws that make cannabis production illegal almost everywhere so it's really being done clandestine, underground, in back yards and closets. What we really need to do is create standardized medicine. We need to change the laws so that people can cultivate in a way that's safe so that we can really improve the science so we can have feedback loops between the cultivation facilities and the testing labs so that people who are cultivating can know the cannabinoid content of their medicines, can test it along the way for molds, mildews, pesticides and fertilizers so that at the end we can find out that the cultivators started with the seed, they planted it this way, they grew it this way, it turned out like this and then they did it again and it turned out the same way.

In most herbal plant medicines the medicine doesn't get to the patient until the cultivation is standardized, but in our industry, it went the other way. We have to backtrack now to create standardized medicines. Once we create standardized medicines, then we can really do the study with humans, so that we can give these medicines that are standardized so we can say it has this much THC, it is a pure medicine, it has this much CBD. We can take a small group of patients and in a scientific manner we can run a study to see how the cannabis is helping each patient individually. We can really collect the data to say this medicine under these standardized conditions with this patient member they felt this kind of relief from the medicine.

Nobody is doing that in our industry. It really needs to be done. My collective is working on the very first part of that – how do you standardize your medicines. Once you get your medicines standardized how do you standardize the research project with the patient members so that you can really make valid claims about how the medicine is helping people. It's not complicated stuff but it's stuff that's not being done in our industry yet.

DB: I would think that in a more rational approach that many of these safeguards you're speaking of would be handled by government, would have an oversight – nationally. Your thoughts on that?

DEBBY GOLDSBERRY: As far as government being the end regulators on cannabis – really in industries like pharmaceuticals the government doesn't oversee and regulate pharmaceuticals. The pharmaceutical industry is regulated by a 501(c)(3) non-profit organization that was established to regulate pharmaceutical drugs. They are called the USP – U.S. Pharmacopeia. So really the cannabis industry would be suited to self-regulate – to create the regulations ourselves, to hire the scientist to apply standards used in other manufacturing industries and other plant cultivation industries and other plant medicines to test out the theories, to develop the standards, to create proof that our handling processes are safe and then to self-regulate just like what's been done with pharmaceuticals.

For example, electricity is very dangerous yet it is self-regulated. Emergency rooms – very important, yet also self-regulated by a 501(c)(3) organization. The truth is the government doesn't want to regulate these highly dangerous substances or processes as long as there is a 501(c)(3) or regulatory organization that's standardized, validated that can be provable that regulates the industry. There really is a big self-regulation movement in the cannabis industry. I think that's the future.

DB: In your years of experience dealing with medical cannabis what have you seen that might support or refute the government's idea that it leads to psychosis or that there are components that may influence some people's mental capacity.

DEBBY GOLDSBERRY: First of all the government would like us to think that there is no research on medical cannabis but, in fact, at this conference yesterday we learned that there is 24,000 research projects that have looked at medical cannabis. That's about 2.3 research projects a day that are happening in our industry, so it's really big. There's been a lot of research in this.

If you look at cannabis and you compare it to other herbal plant medicines, you'll find that cannabis doesn't have any serious adverse effects. Serious adverse effect is a pharmacological term. If the substance has serious adverse effects, it will kill you, for example, and you really need to handle it in a different way than if it doesn't have serious adverse effects.

By reviewing the 24,000 studies and looking at 10,000 years of history, we can accurately predict that cannabis doesn't have any serious adverse effects. We can take it into another direction – into the herbal plant medicine handling processes, rather than through the FDA pharmacy process.

It does appear that cannabis is potentially counter-indicated for people that have schizophrenia. Potentially, in people who have a predisposition to that condition (which is very rare), it can create the first episode of schizophrenia. It's rare, and there's no real scientific data about this that shows us exactly how that happens, but there are a few counter-indications for cannabis use and mental health.

On the flip side, cannabis use has been shown to be incredibly beneficial for most conditions having to do with mental health. In fact the endocannabinoid system regulates mental health naturally in our own body and when you augment the endocannabinoid system (your body's natural THC system) with THC from plants it can really help.

For example, cannabis is really great for treating things like depression, bipolarism – a whole host of mental health illnesses. In fact we've found at Berkeley Patient's Group, that I help found, that a large group of people who were 18 to 24 or 25-years-old who had access to medical cannabis, as opposed to the group of people above them who had no access to medical cannabis because the implementation laws hadn't gone into effect yet, the people who are younger and had access to medical cannabis with mental health conditions, we're finding that they are not advancing to be serious medical conditions. They're not developing addictions. They're not developing alcoholic dependency. They're not developing addiction to pharmacological drugs. They're using medical cannabis to treat their condition effectively and it's really a very safe way to treat these conditions. So the counter-indications are very small thus far in the medical literature. Although we have to pay attention to those and learn a lot more of how cannabis works in the brain. But cannabis is incredibly beneficial as a pharmacological drug. A lot of people are using it to great effect.

DB: On television commercials you hear these pharmaceutical products advertised and then they list a host of horrible, debilitating spinoffs of what may happen to you if you take these products and then the list of potential harms from cannabis is miniscule in comparison. Address that thought, will you?

DEBBY GOLDSBERRY: Cannabis has been shown to have no serious adverse effects, so the side effects of using cannabis are pretty minimal. When you're watching TV it always cracks me up when they tell you this drug is going to be so great, you're going to have a great time and somebody is skipping through a field and then if you listen closely they're saying, "Oh, but you might die. You might get psychosis. You might have a heart attack. We're not exactly sure what is going to happen to you." Of course in such a pleasant voice you're like, "Oh, that's almost lovely to have a heart attack and die as a side effect of this drug."

The fact is cannabis doesn't have any side effects like that at all. It's never killed a single person. In fact it can't. It doesn't act that way on your body. It's a substance that our body produces naturally. Not only that, in the process of evolution, we have likely evolved with the cannabis plant simultaneously – the plant evolving and us evolving so that we have a symbiotic relationship and almost a need for this plant.

In fact, people who have lower amounts of natural endocannabinoids in their system absolutely need to beef up their endocannabinoid system by using the whole plant medicine cannabis, or they just won't feel right. They won't be as healthy as they could be, as productive as they could be. Cannabis is helping a lot of people that way.

DALE SKYE JONES

Dale Skye Jones, (nee Clare) is the Executive Chancellor of Oaksterdam University and an instructor in Cannabis Science, Economics, Civics 101 & 102, Politics and History. When Oaksterdam was raided and founder Richard Lee stepped down, Dale took over as President of OU to support sustainable growth with quality training for the cannabis industry. Important initial steps include establishing the political and social climate that will encourage cannabis policy reform. Century of Lies / February 24, 2013.

DALE SKYE JONES: The cannabis movement is growing into an industry. A lot of the self-regulation that has been attempted over the last few years has enticed folks like the unions—particularly the United Food and Commercial Worker Union who traditionally represents people like pharmacies, grocery stores, retail, agriculture which is simply a perfect fit for the cannabis industry.

Frankly we would have been unionized 40 years ago if only this had been legal, so with the introduction of hemp as an important agricultural opportunity the unions have even more opportunities with the southeastern states – particularly the tobacco farmers – to introduce a cash crop here to the US.

Meanwhile the mainstream folks – the people that are already at the top of their game in their own individual industries – are introducing "best practices" into the cannabis businesses, and that's not only improving confidence in the cannabis industry but also improving the policy around it and that's what most exciting for both patients and those that find themselves criminalized for behavior that's really one of the safest choices you can make as an adult.

DB: Let's talk about the possibilities of this plant – what it might mean to California where you live or to the nation in general.

DALE SKYE JONES: What's remarkable about cannabis is both its safety and its efficacy. The lethal dose has yet to be determined because it is so high. Cannabis is not a central nervous system depressant which is largely why cannabis can't kill you.

In fact the DEA Administrative Law Judge, Francis Young, stated after reviewing all the evidence that was available that it was, in fact, the safest therapeutic substance known to man. Ten raw potatoes can kill you, yet you would have to ingest 40 to 80 pounds of cannabis, and at that point it's a physical issue. It's more likely to split your gut.

What's remarkable also about cannabis are the many different ways that you can ingest it. The most popular way is smoking. Well that's been used for millennia; however, there are safer alternatives. I want to point out that when I say safer, there are valid studies that show that even smoking cannabis does not cause lung cancer, COPD, or emphysema; however, it can cause bronchitis. Anytime you set fire to plant matter and inhale it, you're going to irritate the lining of your lungs.

You can vaporize the material, which basically heats up or boils away the beneficial components (the cannabinoids, the terpenes) so that you can inhale and ingest the beneficial substances without actually setting fire to the plant matter. You're also not ingesting things such as lighter fluid, ash and tar that often happens when you're just using a pipe or, worse, smoking out of a blunt. Please, folks, no tobacco inside or as a wrapper.

All that being said, these different ingestion methods such as topical applications can show someone like your dear aunt Betty that cannabis is medicine that doesn't have to get you high. What's even more exciting is now that we're testing our medicine; we're not just cultivating based on how it made you feel. Now we're starting to test in laboratories for cannabinoids. We've discovered beneficial components like cannabidiol, known as CBD. Now we have farmers that are specifically growing high-CBD plants that will help specific sets of patients without the dysphoric effects of THC. In fact CBD mitigates the euphoric effects of THC. So for folks who really don't like the way that cannabis makes them feel—the THC is dysphoric instead of euphoric – you might try a high-CBD strain.

DB: There are many great people in Texas that work to change these laws and one of them saw a better opportunity and came to Oakland, California – Oaksterdam as he eventually helped get it renamed to – Mr. Richard Lee, founder of Oaksterdam University. He's now stepped down. Let's talk about how many people have graduated from Oaksterdam. What did they learn there?

DALE SKYE JONES: Since Richard Lee first opened the school in 2007 we have taught over 15,000 individuals. A lot of folks come through our programs – every race, age and background you can possibly imagine. That's what's so exciting. They are bringing the best practices from their own life into this industry. The folks that come to Oaksterdam University really come to us to learn best practices – how to do this well, how to work with their community and their local elected officials to make sure that they are the ones who get permitted and are able to open businesses. We also just teach patients – folks who want to understand different methods of ingestion, want to understand the rights and responsibilities under their local law and want to have successful law enforcement encounters.

First we teach politics and the history of cannabis prohibition so that you can speak to why we're here and actually understand your place within this movement in history. This really is part of the next civil rights revolution and first through the door, the brick wall tends to get the bloodiest. So the most important thing you might learn from us is what not to do.

There are definitely missteps that naïve individuals to this particular industry, the risks of this industry need to know before entering into it. You have grave responsibility to your family with respect to your home, your property, your children. You have to understand those risks and your responsibilities within this movement because until it is legal federally we're not truly an industry – we're still a movement.

So there's a responsibility when you enter this industry to keep pushing forward with good policy, good law and make sure that you represent the best of what the industry has to offer. We have to self-regulate until we're actually regulated on a federal level.

JEFF JONES

In 1998, the federal government prosecuted Jones for running Oakland's first medical marijuana dispensary. He fought a protracted court battle that went to the U.S. Supreme Court, but he lost the case. In the end, he was barred from ever running a dispensary again. Today he runs an Oakland-based medical marijuana ID card center and also works on behalf of the legalization efforts. He and Dale have two young children. Cultural Baggage / March 3, 2013.

JEFF JONES: I'm Jeff Jones. I work with the Patient ID Center as the executive director. I'm also one of the professors and a chancellor with the Oaksterdam University. We are both an educational and an advocacy organization to teach people about medical cannabis and about how to cultivate medical cannabis. The

ID Center issues ID cards and helps instruct patients on where to buy and how to grow cannabis. The Oaksterdam University teaches people about the industry, good practice standards, about what to do in and out of collectives that are dispensing and cultivating and also about the politics, history and the legal issues involved with our industry.

DB: You've seen the growth of the medical cannabis industry from day 1, basically...

JEFF JONES: I wouldn't say day 1, but I've been here for a long time. Dennis and Brownie Mary really laid the foundation level that I watched in the news about her getting busted and Dennis pushing open the first door in San Francisco for cannabis. Things have changed tremendously in the last decade, from being in the United States Supreme Court just a little over a decade ago with my 2001 decision saying there's no defense for medical necessity dispensation to now seeing a plethora of dispensaries in Colorado, Arizona, and here in Washington, D.C. start to open. Not to mention what just happened in Colorado and Washington State. I have to feel that we're in one of the brightest hours for cannabis reform that I've seen in my work period.

DB: What strikes me is the host of products ranging from salves to ice tea, from vaporizers to cookies. The point I'd like you to address is there are so many possibilities for commerce, for health, for positive change if we would just examine these laws and search for the truth of the matter.

JEFF JONES: I think the truth has slipped out underneath the canopy of the prohibition of cannabis in the last two years. We're seeing for the first time in our history a hemp bill introduced in our U.S. Senate and co-sponsored by Republican leaders for Pete's sake. I'm just pinching myself knowing that we're in a different era. To see that it is being pitched as a way to help the family farmer, when that's what we've been saying for years—it's as if finally as what we are backing is on the wall and they are reading it. It's validated the work that we have been involved in, the truth that we have been spreading for decades. It seems everything is starting to come together. I just hope that we don't squander this opportunity – that we don't miss this chance of changing things once and for all to bring this plant and the prosperity that it could bring both our economy and the ability for the U.S. to be a manufacturing country again.

We talk about things that we need to do here. I'm from the Midwest area, South Dakota, where there's a bunch of water and free farm land to grow things like this. My state is one of the number one eradicators of hemp in its natural, renewable state. I think that needs to be reversed and see South Dakota be one of the number one states to cultivate this plant and make it available in non-drug form for products to be processed and produced here in the U.S.

We are seeing one of the more interesting times in both the U.S. government and at local state levels related to cannabis policy. We're seeing a plethora of states question whether or not they want to make adult consumers legal in their states for use, cultivation and for commercial ability. It has gone beyond the medical question that we've been touting for over a decade. The compassionate access for patients and the need for this medicine and I just hope that that isn't lost as we move forward.

At the same time I feel it's going to help them a lot more by gaining access in a full more economical standpoint and in a safer fashion. They've had targets on their back. Every patient that's come out and talked about using medical cannabis in the last 15 years has been a target.

Now, as we bring adult consumers into that place where they're talking about their use, patients are no longer targets. They're going to be, hopefully, the spectacle of what we need to do to change our society to be better equipped to look after those who are hurt.

CATHY AND ROBERT JORDAN

In 2013, Florida State Senator Jeff Clemens announced that he was introducing a medical marijuana bill which would allow for the establishment of cannabis dispensaries. The bill was named the 'Cathy Jordan Medical Cannabis Act', in honor of a woman who has been openly using cannabis as medicine for over a quarter century, championing this cause from her wheelchair while living with an incurable condition—Lou Gehrig's disease. Her husband Robert has been growing two dozen cannabis plants to help with her treatment. One day after the state senator introduced the medical necessity legislation, publicizing her name and address, the DEA and Manatee County Sheriff's Office paid her a not-too-polite visit, raiding her home, dressed in swat uniforms, armed with machine guns and wearing masks, seizing her cannabis and arresting her husband for cultivation. Her wheelchair was no defense. Cultural Baggage / April 07, 2013.

DB: Cathy uses medical cannabis to help in living a more ordinary life. Is that right, Cathy?

CATHY JORDAN: Very much so.

ROBERT JORDAN: She has a little bit of trouble with her speech. As much as somebody can have a normal life with ALS it's all due to cannabis.

DB: On the day the Cathy Jordan Medical Cannabis Act was filed, what happened?

ROBERT JORDAN: That was February 25th. We got home from Tallahassee after the bill was introduced. Two sheriffs came up my driveway and they had their hands on their weapons and very aggressively. I went out to meet them to see what was going on. Words were exchanged and all that. I asked them what they were doing on my property and they said, "We got probable cause."

I said, "Probable cause for what?"

He said, "We have probable cause."

I said, "Where's your warrant?"

He said, "We don't need one."

I said, "When I woke up this morning I thought I was in the USA. What do you mean you don't need a warrant?"

He said, "We have probable cause. This is now a crime scene.'"

They wouldn't let us back in our home. They came on real aggressive and I went back at them real aggressive. I was trying to keep them off our property.

What had happened is I put the electric in my name at the property next door, and we ran an extension cord from that house to our house so we could get our electricity. Somebody saw the cord and thought we were stealing electricity, took a picture of the plants and sent them to the sheriff's office so the sheriff is saying he had no choice but to come and investigate.

Now how come they looked over the fence, that's up to the lawyers to decide. I'm just saying what happened to us. After that they called in the detectives, the undercover guys, and three guys came—two had ski masks on.

I said, "What is this?" A disabled Viet Nam Vet with a woman in a wheelchair.

Those guys were pretty good. They treated us real well. They came through and did exactly what they said they were going to do. They said, "There is one of two ways we can do this. Get a search warrant or we could do a walk through. If we get a search warrant we're going to tear your house completely apart and not put it back together or we can do a walk through."

I said, "What's a walk through?"

He said, "Just that. We know this is not a big grow operation."

I had a little 8 by 8 shed so it couldn't be for nothing more than personal use. They saw that, took the plants and left. They were perfect gentlemen. As a matter of fact they said, "We can't say that we agree with you but maybe we can say we don't disagree with you."

This whole thing just shows how wrong this whole situation is.

DB: Cathy, I was going to ask you. I did a little bit of study and I don't mean to sound macabre, but according to what I've read, about half of people with ALS only live for 3 years. Another 20% for 5 years and 10% for 5 years or more. You've had decades that you have persevered using cannabis. Your thought there.

CATHY JORDAN: If cannabis can be delivered to me in the brain then they can control ALS. That's what I've been trying to say for years.

DB: The science, the understanding is certainly improving despite the fact the government keeps trying to prevent any more studies from being done. Robert, the public has become aware of this. The media was just all over this and I think at least 99% on your side. Am I correct?

ROBERT JORDAN: We haven't had any negative press or comments. Since they dropped the charges one comment said, "If he can use it why not me?" And that's true – why not him? They were threatening me with 5 years and offered me a plea deal that I turned down because I wanted a jury trial. It says in this thing here and I talked to my doctor and they realized that they could not beat a medical defense so they didn't prosecute. I could have sat down and taken whatever plea they gave me and all that, but there's a time in everybody's life where you got to stand up. "No, I'm right and I didn't do anything wrong." What man who loves his wife and could grow something in his backyard to save her life wouldn't do that? I'm not doing anything any other man wouldn't do.

DB: Robert, I was going to ask you what are some of the ways you see medical cannabis benefitting your wife?

ROBERT JORDAN: One thing I got to say about her is she does more things out of a wheelchair than most healthy people do. The courage she shows in the face of adversity is unbelievable.

How it helps her is people with ALS have a drooling problem and anybody that's ever smoked cannabis knows it gives you cottonmouth so it dries up her mouth. It helps her sleep. It helps her muscle spasms. It helps with pain. It helps with appetite. It helps with depression. I told the police, "You give me something else pharmaceutical that will do the same thing the plant does and I'll use it."

There isn't anything else. It's amazing what this plant does. Without it…this came from when she first told her doctors that she used cannabis and it stopped her disease they wanted to put her in a mental ward because 5% of people who get ALS get dementia. He looked right over her like she wasn't in the room and said, "We might have to make different plans for her."

Now all these years later they're coming to her and saying, "What are you doing?"

We have this theory about the gluconate. The best way to explain it is like a spark plug going down from the distributor. If she wants her hand to move her whole arm will move. The signal won't get to where it's going because the coding is off the nerve. The cannabis seems to be protecting the nerve and what happens to her and what would happen in other patients in 2 to 3 months has taken 2 to 3 years to happen to her. It's slowed the progression down so remarkable. .

JUSTIN KOOZER

Justin Koozer's two-year-old child just started using cannabis for her epilepsy when we recorded this show. The family had to move from Tennessee to Colorado to access the medicine she needs. Cultural Baggage / November 24, 2013.

JUSTIN KOOZER: My wife and I have been married for some time now and we have a 2-year-old daughter who was born with Aicardi syndrome. Aicardi syndrome is…one of the major markers is she is missing her corpus callosum which is a bundle of fibers which connects the two halves of her brain. As part of that she has a severe form of epilepsy called infantile spasms and she's basically had multiple spasms every day of her life since she turned 3-months-old.

DB: Let's talk about the need to move to Colorado.

JUSTIN KOOZER: We were living in Knoxville, Tennessee and so we have been through 9 different seizure medications. We're on our fifth neurologist, and we have been told by three of them now that we have one other option from a pharmaceutical side of things and that option has a very high risk of liver failure. We started looking into alternative options and came across this group out here in Colorado that is using very low THC marijuana with a high content of CBD and they're having extremely good success with seizure control so decided in July of this year to pack up and move out here. We've been on what's known as "Charlotte's Web".

DB: Let's talk about your two-year-old daughter, Piper. She has had access to this for a limited time now and what have been the results, sir?

JUSTIN KOOZER: She's been on it for about four weeks right now. We've been increasing the dose that she takes every day and while we're not seeing complete seizure control but we are seeing some differences in her personality. She seems to be in a better mood most days. There have been a few days where she's had significantly fewer seizures throughout the day. We kind of like to reference that on her worst day ever, she was having over 400 spasms, and I think this past week there were two or three days where she had just two or three single spasms. We're starting to see things change in her. It's almost like a fog has been cleared from her mind. She's smiling and laughing a lot more. She seems to be getting a little bit stronger as well. Her sleep has improved.

DB: Justin, what you mentioned there at first is she is starting to recognize you, to be part of the moment. Am I right?

JUSTIN KOOZER: Yeah, it seems that she is just more aware. When we talk about developmental level for her she's about a 3 or 4-month-old. She's just now discovering...she's looking at her hands. She's playing with her toys like she never has before so it's pretty incredible to see the changes. We're a little reluctant on whether or not we're going to say that it's the results of the cannabis but the evidence is building up.

DB: I wanted to come back to the fact that you had to pull up roots. You had to move from Tennessee to Colorado because this medicine wasn't available in Tennessee. I guess I'm hoping that you and your wife had the type of experience necessary to get a job up there. That's been quite a chore in itself. Has it not?

JUSTIN KOOZER: We are very blessed in that aspect. We understand that we have had more support than a lot of other families. My job actually agreed when I approached them and said we wanted to move out here...the original intention was to move my wife and daughter out here and I would stay back home in Tennessee and my job was flexible enough to allow me to move out here with them. So it wasn't as difficult as a lot of families are having which is really unfortunate but, yeah, we did have to pack up everything and it really is a leap of faith. With her syndrome we're the first one to try this treatment. We feel like we're being pioneers in that kind of aspect. As far as jobs and everything the hardest part was leaving the family behind.

DB: The other thought that comes to mind is that you're blessed to be working with the Stanley brothers, their compassionate care outfit up there. Tell us about how that works.

JUSTIN KOOZER: The Stanley brothers have started what they're calling Realm of Caring. They've set up a non-profit organization that they're basically giving the medicine in an oil at their cost which is about 5 cents per milligram of CBD. The normal therapeutic dose is around 3 milligrams per pound of body weight. They're significantly cutting the cost. They have put their whole industry, their whole life into what they are doing now.

I know that Josh Stanley has been traveling all over the country trying to push for change in multiple states. I heard that he was in Utah 2 weeks ago and Pennsylvania and D.C. last week. What they're doing is incredible. They have a grow up in the mountains and they've slowly been adding more and more of this particular strain. They are also growing other varieties of cannabis for sale in their dispensary which they've used the profits from that to kind of help subsidize the non-profit side.

DB: When you start stacking it up with the tens if not hundreds of Gervais syndrome kids in Colorado and the hundreds elsewhere around this country it should be recognized for what it is. The science should come forward. What's your thought, Justin?

JUSTIN KOOZER: This is how science progresses. They look at what's going on in the patient population and then they take that and they study it with the scientific method. The problem is the federal government has not allowed that kind of testing to happen so that's all they can say now is that it is anecdotal evidence.

Now I know about the kids here in Colorado that they are doing a research paper on which we hope will lead to a clinical trial on the full plant extract but we also know that GW Pharmaceuticals is getting ready to start their clinical trial so things are coming. It's anecdotal at this point but the more the evidence builds up the local government especially will have to take a look at that.

Last week we had Utah—one of the reddest states, most conservative states in the U.S. – said, "OK, we're not going to totally legalize cannabis but we're going to allow these families to bring in this hemp oil." People are starting to realize that there's no side effects. It's not just a smoke screen for people to use it recreationally. It is something that can be used to help epilepsy, pain and nausea – the list goes on and on. We see more and more case studies coming out of Israel and other countries. I think we've hit a tipping point where people are starting to look at it in a more scientific perspective. Even if you look at the polling you see that 58% of Americans are for the legalization of medicinal cannabis.

DB: Is there a website where you might want to point folks to get more information in this regard?

JUSTIN KOOZER: You can visit the Realm of Caring website for more information. There are a lot of articles that are coming out now. There are a lot of documentaries. Currently there is a wait list for this particular strain but we're taking people off that list very rapidly. What I would encourage people to do is be very safe about this. If you're going to try it for your child, have your particular strain tested. There are some bad actors out there that are not extracting properly, and they're not testing properly to see the amount of CBD. I would encourage anyone that is doing this to do it alongside of a doctor, if possible. Try to be as scientific as possible.

MICHAEL KRAWITZ

Michael Krawitz heads up Veterans for Medical Cannabis Access (VMCA), which advocates for veterans' rights to access medical cannabis for therapeutic purposes. VMCA encourages all legislative bodies to endorse veterans' rights to use medical cannabis therapeutically and responsibly and is working to end all prohibitions associated with such use. VMCA is working to preserve and protect the ability to discuss medical cannabis use within the VA healthcare system without fear of punishment or retribution. Cultural Baggage / November 17, 2013.

MICHAEL KRAWITZ: We are a national organization working to defend our right to be able to speak openly with your doctor without fear of reprisal and working on access issues for veterans. We do one-on-one advocacy and we work within the VA. We're here kicking off a campaign where we're going to be down in Florida going from VA center to VA center meeting with veterans all the way through Gainesville and the Orlando area. If you're in that area check out the website, http://onehundredkstrong.net It's a wealth of information on how to use cannabis and how to navigate the VA.

DB: Michael, let's talk about the history of your work in support of veterans. It's been a long hard effort has it not?

MICHAEL KRAWITZ: Yes it has. I started out myself as a patient being handed a pain contract inside the VA and I was determined not to sign it. Since I refused to sign it they punished me. Since they punished me I was able to show the VA leadership eventually by working through the chain of command starting literally from my doctor and working one person at a time all the way to Washington, D.C.

It was amazing to me that it was amazing to them to see a veteran being denied treatment for this. These pain contracts in their opinion were only supposed to be a tool to help doctors communicate some of the ins and outs of narcotic treatment with their patients.

They never thought that it would be used as a blunt instrument to stop people from getting access to their pain treatment, but that's how it's being used. I fought that inside the VA for years. I give credit to Phil Smith of Drug War Chronicles. He wrote an early informative article on my pain contract work, and eventually that pain contract fight put me in a position to negotiate the first ever medical marijuana policy at the VA which you see as a big victory but actually is an interim victory.

DB: Right because in 20 out of our 50 states veterans are treated with more respect – with the other 30 not so much, right?

MICHAEL KRAWITZ: Not only is that true but the things that I am talking about are not just incidents that occur in the VA hospital. If you are ill and find yourself in pain and find yourself in a position where that pain does not go away and it becomes a long-term problem you are going to have trouble getting access to pain treatment and the pain contract is probably going to be the vehicle by which that trouble is going to present itself. This pain contract thing is more easily fought in some respects inside the VA but it's certainly not a veteran's only problem.

I'm really proud of the veterans that I work with. Veterans have made it an issue to pass the Massachusetts Medical Marijuana Law. It was a straight up veterans issue and then we passed the Illinois medical marijuana law. The governor signing ceremony was flanked by two veterans.

In our work since, we protected New Mexico's Post Traumatic Stress qualification which we had to fight to keep on the books since then we've added 5 more states. Now we have 5 states where veterans can legally use cannabis for Post Traumatic Stress and that hopefully is a trend. We're working four more states and three more states for legal cannabis for medicine. We're definitely on somewhat of a wave and we're hoping to make it even bigger.

Veterans out there have unique ability to bring this whole issue to a whole new level of understanding and a whole new perspective. It's not quite as dangerous anymore. I tell veterans you can come out of the foxhole – the coast is a little more clear now that we have the VA policy.

MARY LYNN MATHRE

Mary Lynn Mathre is a Registered Nurse, President and co-Founder of Patients Out of Time, a non-profit, educational charity dedicated to educating healthcare professionals and the public about the therapeutic use of cannabis.Cultural Baggage / August 21, 2011.

DB: Mary Lynn, as one of the co-founders of Patients Out of Time, you are called upon to speak to various organizations. You've got one such event coming up, do you not?

MARY LYNN MATHRE: Yes. It's the primary nursing organization for addictions nurses, the International Nurses Society on Addictions. And then for pain it's the American Society for Pain Management Nursing. They're coming together and the theme for their conference is "Managing Pain and Addiction."

DB: Tell us what you'll be talking about at this conference.

MARY LYNN MATHRE: I'll be doing a pre-conference workshop about the use of cannabis for chronic pain. My goal there really is to bring this issue in front of nurses and explain how the new science on the endocannabinoid system, let alone all our research on patients specifically and in animal research shows that cannabis can be helpful for chronic pain.

With the endocannabinoid system we understand how it's really involved in pain processing, especially neuropathic pain. So a lot of it is just to try to help nurses understand so that when they come across patients using cannabis they don't automatically assume substance abuse or people just wanting to get high. That this may, in fact, be a real serious issue.

Besides that workshop I'm going to do a concurrent session, a shorter session, on "To Test or Not to Test for Cannabis for Pain Contracts." And that one, I think, is really more interesting. I think patients everywhere who are chronic pain patients, if they're using opiates (morphine, Oxycontin, Oxycodone, the many, many opiate medications that are available for treating pain) they can be very helpful, certainly, but generally for long-term use patients need more and more over time.

Healthcare professionals get a little leery about giving them pain medication. So one of the things they do very often is have patients sign a contract. And part of that contract is … It tells them they can't be going to other doctors and usually it's something about, "You can't call in for your prescriptions early." "We're not going to acknowledge that you lost your prescription." Etc… And it will probably do random urine drug screening.

You know the whole idea, therapeutically, is to make sure that if they are giving them opiates the patients are using the opiates correctly and not mixing it with dangerous drugs. There are some federal issues that a physician cannot prescribe an opiate to an opiate addict. In the old days they'd say a "narcotic" addict. And so all the time the cops and even the docs would throw in marijuana when you say "narcotic" and marijuana/cannabis is not a narcotic.

What I'm trying to convey to the nurses is that if the patients are going to have a pain contract and sign that and are going to do drug testing with that, why include cannabis? In the states where cannabis is legal, pain is the primary reason that patients use cannabis. So it's overwhelmingly popular in those states.

DB: Mary Lynn, you mentioned that the amount of opiates tends to rise over a period of time and yet it has been found that through the use of cannabis people can more restrict their use of these dangerous opiates. Is that correct?

MARY LYNN MATHRE: Exactly, and that's kind of the point I want to make especially for those states where it's still not legal. They find the patients using cannabis, and very often the patient gets kicked out of the pain clinic or their opiate prescriptions get cut off. You know, "We're not going to write this prescription if you're going to use illicit drugs."

And my point to them is this is not good clinical judgment. "You're too concerned about these laws." I'm not telling nurses to break laws or anything like that but a patient who uses cannabis…I tell you, I would almost say 100% but clearly most of the overwhelming majority of patients because of the way cannabis works with opiates, they will cut their use of opiates. They won't have the problem of constipation. They won't have nausea that often accompanies patients who use opiates. And it actually helps with their depression.

So by using cannabis they decrease a lot of the other medication use and either get rid of their opiate use or cut it significantly. And they feel better. They feel more alert and they function better. So clinically it makes great sense to add cannabis for somebody with chronic pain. And yet what we see happening is patients going to a pain clinic. They get put on opiates. Then they get drug tested and if the cannabis/THC shows up in their urine, the next thing they know they're kicked out of the clinic.

It's because the clinicians are afraid of legal repercussions as opposed to really being open to the science and seeing what is good patient care. Granted, maybe they can't break the law, but, again the hope here is to, once they understand that use of cannabis for chronic pain is a good idea and often very helpful for a patient, they should be advocating to change those laws in the states that don't allow it. Frankly, all healthcare professionals should be advocating to get it out of Schedule I.

You know the fight goes on and on and on with trying to reschedule cannabis and every rational argument, every study with professionals who understand the science clearly know that it doesn't belong there. And yet the stubborn DEA continues to keep it in Schedule I.

Sometimes I've asked clinicians when they say, "Well, it's against the law." And I just look at them and ask, "But why?!" You know, stop and think. "Why are you just accepting this?!" "Your just thinking like it was always written in stone." That's one of the reasons we always use the word cannabis. I keep trying to tell healthcare specialists that this was a popular medicine. For centuries it's been a medicine. In the United States it was a popular medicine until "Reefer Madness" came about and they used "marijuana" and they've got it ingrained in our heads. Marijuana equals substance abuse.

There's no science to back that up. The whole marijuana prohibition was based on lies and racism so you just have to, hopefully, get people to stop and think about it. I was saying, you know, sometimes we make stupid laws for whatever reason and those laws need to be changed. This is one that, in general, people just think that there really must be a reason that it's illegal. It's got to be bad or the government wouldn't continue this. And that's just naïve thinking.

No, whether it be law enforcement, the DEA, as my husband says, "It's a jobs program." Keeping marijuana illegal means a lot of jobs for cops. We arrest, you know, how many people do we arrest every year for marijuana possession alone?! It's ridiculous.

The urine testing industry. Marijuana is probably the biggest one that gets used for that because it does stay in the system. There are a lot of people making a lot of money with marijuana being illegal.

Meanwhile the patients are suffering. For those using it recreationally it's a lot less harmful than the opiate epidemic we're getting now where kids are dying from overdoses. Or methamphetamine or other drugs that people get into recreationally.

So, from a harm reduction standpoint, we're making much ado about nothing. But from a patient perspective, this is really harming patients and yeah, I don't know either, Dean. It's just tough to break through people's ...The fact that they've grown up knowing it's illegal and they just want to believe it no matter what. They just can't fathom that we've been lied to all these years.

DB: Mary Lynn, as a recovering alcoholic, just over 26 years, my heart goes out to really millions of Americans who have a problem with alcohol and yet have a problem with drug testing and therefore they cannot substitute the use of alcohol, debilitating, physically/mentally etc., for just a bit of cannabis each day to kind of take away the nervousness and the need to reach outside one's normal existence.

MARY LYNN MATHRE: Well congratulations on your recovery. My background is Addictions Nursing and alcohol is a huge problem in the United States. And it doesn't mean that alcohol itself is bad but a lot of people have a problem with it. What we're finding too in some of those states where...the 16 states that do have laws for medical cannabis, some are keeping better track of it than others, and some of the dispensaries are keeping track of their patients...cocaine, methamphetamine, other opiates...they come in and they're finding the cannabis actually helps them get off those other drugs and stay off them.

Phillipe Lucas from British Columbia who ran the Vancouver Island Compassionate Society has coined the phrase that "cannabis is an exit drug" not a gateway drug. It helps people to get off of addictions rather than move you into stronger and harder drugs. I think that's a real important concept and that's another concept that's important for healthcare professionals to understand. If someone is going to be using something illicitly, they need to ask why. Asking patients, "Why are you using this drug and what is it doing for you." We can get an answer back.

Patients many times use alcohol for the pain. We can, at least, explain and show them how it is not a healthy pain remedy and that when it blocks the emotional pain it doesn't fix it. It doesn't make it go away. It's still there. And long-term, heavy use of it is going to destroy you mentally, physically, etc. We can show them that, and most alcoholics know they're having a problem with alcohol down the road. They just can't stop.

But with cannabis, it's kind of like you're trying to convince them that it's hurting them when a patient is only seeing that it's helping them. It's different things that I think healthcare professionals need to wake up and look at the patient and clinically help them see if it's helping or hurting them. If it's not hurting them and trying to convince them that they need to stop, it doesn't build a relationship between the healthcare professional and the patient,

ELVY MUSIKKA

Elvy Musikka is one of the few patients left in the Compassionate Investigational New Drug program. This is a United States Federal Government-run Investigational New Drug program that allows a limited number of patients to receive and use medical marijuana grown at the University of Mississippi. She gets 300 joints per month. It is administered by the National Institute on Drug Abuse. Closed to new entrants, there are four surviving patients who were grandfathered into the program. Cultural Baggage / February 24, 2013.

ELVY MUSIKKA: I am one of four people today who receives federally grown marijuana. It is grown at the University of Mississippi. It is part of a Compassionate Protocol Investigative New Drug program that has been going on since Robert Randall established it back in the 70s – this new drug research. Unfortunately the results never get published. I have maintained my interocular pressure under control for 38 years – the last 25 with the government supply of marijuana that grows at the University of Mississippi.

Before anyone could enter the program they had to prove to FDA, DEA, and NIDA that cannabis was the most efficient, the most reliable, and the safest part of our treatment. For that we had to have extensive medical records and reliable doctors to keep those records. Believe me, they did not want to hear the word marijuana when we got treatment.

First of all, my roller coaster ride began with a doctor telling me back in 1975 that I if I did not start smoking marijuana, I would go blind. I had been born with congenital cataracts. I had several surgeries as a child, but I lived a very normal life. We live with unstable vision but then, at that time, nothing but nothing that was available controlled it, except the marijuana.

I went home and showed them that I could come back 2 days later while eating brownies every 12 hours and pressures were 12 and 14. For me that was nothing but a show of a miracle. Unfortunately they were not impressed. They were unhappy because I had done research without them with an underground doctor, and they didn't like but he helped many people in Fort Lauderdale with my problem to maintain their sight.

I went on to let them try their experimental surgeries. Much to my dismay... I saw no reason to go onto surgeries, which even they told me that the best chance I had was 30% and a 70% chance of damage to the eye. Why would you want to go for such a surgery if you already found something that works? They wanted to do surgery in both eyes but I never let them except my better eye – the right eye – which had better pressures. That, of course, proved to be a disaster. After the second surgery I was unable to return to the bank to work so I became a tax burden for a while.

Then I went and worked for the state of Florida. It was when the urine test began. We knew we were breaking laws, so we made the doctors keep records, all of which came to light when I got arrested. I had said, "Keep my records, because I'm going to get arrested sooner or later. I'm doing something illegal and have to tell people in order to get the material."

So I was arrested, and it was like finding freedom for the first time ever, because I had no idea that we were arresting 200,000 people in those days. I thought marijuana arrests were rare. I certainly knew I had the right to use it because, by the time I was arrested, 12 years had gone by with the eye institute. I had lost the eye completely. I was depressed except when I had marijuana. I would write music and escape the depression that way. I was a pretty happy camper, but not having it always was really scary.

With the trial coming up, the support in south Florida was incredible. I was not prepared for that. It was wonderful. My children were in college so they couldn't threaten me with taking my custody away. We're not free to smoke marijuana as recreational or medical because we had children, we had jobs. We can get drunk all we want to when we get home from work and do other drugs but not the cannabis.

I won my trial, and the public support continued to be around me, and Robert Randall worked with me at the trial with my doctors for the papers. He was the lifeline along with my doctor and my attorney. All of them were brilliant. I was extremely lucky.

They put enough pressure on the federal government and threatened to sue them if I didn't get the federal marijuana, and I did finally receive it in November of 1988 – 25 years ago. I've been using it since then. Not only has it maintained my sight, but my sight actually improved for a period of time.

Last year the government was sending very, very bad marijuana. You can't call that marijuana. Of course that's not the right name of the plant in the first place. It's cannabis. They count on ignorance and prejudice to come up with a new plant that made people killers and you had to outlaw. Those kind of lies and misinformation and programming has been going on for one hundred years since 1913.

It's really too sad because since 1996 when we made marijuana legal in California I certainly had many opportunities to work with dispensaries helping other patients, growing the pot, but it was something I couldn't do because I really wanted to maintain my prescription. As long as I had my prescription, I can show you that my government lies because they know it's medicine. It's been my medicine, and I wasn't trading eyesight for brain cells as I was led to believe. I thought the only good thing about it was I was going to fade my memory, and I wouldn't remember any of it anyway. But, as we know, that's not the way it turned out and I thank God every day in the spirit of thanksgiving. I will continue to work to change the laws to end this blasphemous prohibition on the creator's work.

Come on let's get on it. Let no legislator not know what you are learning. Make sure that information is available. You've got to go see them. You've got to go talk to them. You've got to end the madness and you have to tell them that you will not continue any financial benefit to the party or to the individuals if they are so irresponsible as to continue to squander all of our resources in the manner that we have been doing for one hundred years and since the 80s more than ever.

IRVIN ROSENFELD

Irv Rosenfeld is a stockbroker in Florida who receives pre-rolled cannabis cigarettes courtesy of the US government. He's author of "My Medicine: How I convinced the U.S. government to provide my marijuana and help launch a national movement." Cultural Baggage / March 4, 2012.

DB: You're one of the few survivors of that plan whereby the federal government grows and supplies you marijuana, correct?

IRVIN ROSENFELD: It's sad to say there are only 4 of us left. That's it and I'm the longest surviving of the four.

DB: We've talked about it before but how many joints have they sent you?

IRVIN ROSENFELD: I'm up to about 130,000.

DB: Marijuana cigarettes provided by the federal government? And they send you...what is it 300 joints every 28 days, correct?

IRVIN ROSENFELD: Every 25 days.

DB: The University of Mississippi grows this stuff, right?

IRVIN ROSENFELD: They do and they supply it for the four patients and they also supply pharmaceutical companies to be able to synthesize different chemicals out of it so they can make potential other new medicines.

DB: So they have begun to do that – to make use of it for that purpose.

IRVIN ROSENFELD: Yes, which is sad because, again, the natural plant works great. Why synthesize it? Why bother? There were 13 patients getting marijuana when the federal government cut the program off. There had been another 28 patients who had been approved by all three government agencies – NIDA (National Institute on Drug Abuse), FDA and DEA – but they never received a shipment. It's an amazing medicine and the sad part is the "choir" knows but we have to teach our physicians. That's what we got to do. That's why this show is so important.

DB: Irv, I've got your book in front of me. We got the picture of you holding up that tin of pre-rolled joints from the federal government. It wasn't always that way. You had some difficulty in getting into this situation where the government provides it, right?

IRVIN ROSENFELD: It took me ten years. I started in 1972. I won it in 1982.

But, again, it was a 10 year struggle to try to convince the federal government that it worked for me and God was on my side. There were people put in place that things changed. I had the state of Virginia behind me. That state law changed. The University of Virginia Law School behind me. So, again, a lot of people—which you'll read in my book – that somehow helped.

It was step 1, step 2…step 20, step 30, whatever, but I finally won. Thank God I did because I've been able to help open up the entire nation and to help educate people to the benefits of medical cannabis.

DB: The government doesn't want to look at any positive at all, do they?

IRVIN ROSENFELD: No, not at all. Again, I'm living proof. I've been getting…They've been sending me marijuana for 29 years. They've never ever studied me at all. So what does that tell you?

DB: They don't want to know the truth, do they?!

IRVIN ROSENFELD: They do not and that's the sad part. I've always tried to be the moderate. I want to educate people. I want to try to bring the people who aren't on our side and educate them. But the people against us…if I'm at A and they're at Z, we can meet at M. That's what I'm trying to do.

The feds have never wanted to research me. The point is I'm in great shape because of medical cannabis.

DB: Let's tell the folks about your malady – why it is that you use medical cannabis?

IRVIN ROSENFELD: I have bone tumors. I have about 200 bone tumors in my body. They grow outwardly from the long bones of the body into the muscles and the veins stretching the muscles and the veins making it very tender and very painful. But, more importantly, if I were to tear those I could hemorrhage and a clot could break off from the veins and it would kill me.

So what the cannabis does is relaxes the muscles and the veins going over the tumors so I don't have to worry. It also keeps the inflammation of what's called a bursar over each tumor trying to protect the muscle and the vein less inflamed. It helps tremendously with the pain of my ankle.

The point is I'm able to do all this because I have the right medicine. Now they say the tumors should grow at any time and I've not had a tumor grow in 37 years…38 years. I'm getting older.

DB: Before the federal government supplied it to you you were having to obtain it clandestinely, correct?

IRVIN ROSENFELD: Correct. I did it illegally for 11 years.

DB: Eventually you and your doctors and everyone involved were able to convince this IND program to allow you to participate.

IRVIN ROSENFELD: I had a hearing before FDA and won those hearings in 1982.

DB: I realize the government supplies you with joints but have you ever had occasion to break up one of them and put it in a vaporizer?

IRVIN ROSENFELD: Sure.

DB: How did you perceive that?

IRVIN ROSENFELD: I enjoyed it. No problem but vaporizers are not portable. Plus I have to smoke so much that when I'm driving or working I have to be able to smoke.

DB: You find that it does not impact your perceptions...

IRVIN ROSENFELD: None whatsoever.

DB: And yet there have been a few times when a policeman has seen you smoking. What happens in that regard?

IRVIN ROSENFELD: They pull me over and I explain the federal program to them and then they go, "Well, you can't drive with this." I show my protocol which says I can as long as I'm not intoxicated and I go, "Am I?" And they go, "No, you're not." So the point is that having it in your blood system is not a definition of intoxication. What I try to tell other states is when they try to compare marijuana in you system I say imagine having alcohol stay in your system the same way marijuana does...

DB: 30 days.

IRVIN ROSENFELD: "So it's Sunday night and I had two drinks. Next Sunday night I get pulled over for whatever reason and they test me and the alcohol is still in my system and they accuse me of being drunk. Wait a minute. I drank last Sunday. I had two drinks but none since then. What do you mean I'm drunk?!

That's what they're trying to say with marijuana, and that's wrong.

PARENTS AGAINST PROHIBITION

"Mothers were instrumental in ending alcohol prohibition in the U. S. in the 30's because they wanted to end the loss of lives caused by organized crime, fueled by prohibition. Moms and concerned citizens can once again be instrumental in ending the 40 year failed war on drugs and the devastation that has been caused by it."
—Gretchen Burns Bergman, Director of A New PATH and lead organizer of the Moms United to End the War on Drugs National Campaign.

Each time I see stories of children who are able to escape at least a portion of the misery being inflicted on them by epilepsy, leukemia, and other maladies through the use of cannabis medicine, it infuriates and emboldens me to continue my efforts to thwart the efforts of drug warriors. In this chapter, we will hear from parents who lost their children to an overdose, to years in prison, or to the violence of the drug trade. We will also learn from parents who used medical cannabis to treat their children so that they could battle horrible diseases. The government's refusal to conduct or even allow for proper studies of the potential uses of cannabis for physical or mental issues, is itself corrupt and a truly great evil. If you have children, whether in diapers or grown, married and having children of their own, you must keep in mind that the drug laws are designed to take them away from your family for years, if not decades for possession or intention to possess plant products forbidden a century ago by ignorant, crazed zealots. Forty-five million arrests later, too many parents cling to the belief that some time in prison will set their drug using children on the right path. As has now been proven 44.9 million times, nothing could be further from the truth.

DENISE CULLEN

Denise Cullen's son died of an accidental drug overdose. She is now a Certified Grief Recovery Specialist and CEO of Broken No More. Cultural Baggage / February 5, 2012.

DENISE CULLEN: My name is Denise Cullen. My husband Gary Cullen and I are the founders of Broken No More named after our son because he used to call himself broken. And that is the drug policy arm of our organization. Within that is a grieving group, and that's called GRASP—Grief Recovery After a Substance Passing. We did not start that organization. Another couple did years ago, but we took it over January 1, 2010. Since that time, we have created a Facebook, online support for those who can't get to a group. We've also increased the number of active groups from 4 to nearly 50 across the country.

DB: Tell us about your son and what led you to this organization.

DENISE CULLEN: Our son, Jeff, died of an accidental overdose three years and six months ago tomorrow. He had a 12-year struggle with substance abuse and Attention Deficit Disorder. We tried everything as a family, never did the tough love thing. He tried everything. He would just relapse and get arrested, always minor and nonviolent offenses. He was in jail three times. The longest time was four months. He died two days after getting out of jail on that 4-month charge. He was our only child and the love of our life, and we just can't have his death be in vain. His life was never in vain. He touched everyone that he knew. He was very loved and a very important person on this earth, and now he's gone. Since that time, we have learned that so many, many other people have been through the exact same thing that we have, and we're just trying to offer help to them. We do this in Jeff's memory and his honor and feel him working side by side with us.

DB: Many parents or relatives of those who overdose somehow endorse or further support the drug war but that's not the path you've chosen. Tell us why.

DENISE CULLEN: No because it doesn't work. It's obviously failed. It's all a money-making industry for other people, and it doesn't help. I'm a licensed clinical social worker. I've worked with people addicted to drugs because I work in HIV and end-stage AIDS for many years at a university hospital. Every system that we tried to get help did nothing but make things worse for our son, which made him feel like a failure and unworthy. I would talk to him about what he needed to do. Maybe we should address his Attention Deficit, which is very connected in some people to addictive illness and the frontal lobe of their brain. He didn't want to do that. He said, "Mom, I'm just a junkie."

They brainwashed him into feeling he was unworthy. I have a picture of him with his first surfboard with a DARE shirt. The irony is just incredible. We believe that anybody with addictive illness needs to be treated as a public health issue not a criminal issue. The criminal justice system should not be involved in this issue at all. Not drug court—not anything. We just feel so strongly about that. How many lives would be saved if this was happening, and how much would be improved if we had harm reduction methods out there to teach people and to help them instead of scaring them?

I don't use drugs, but people who use drugs who are of age and adult and smoke marijuana...to me, alcohol and cigarettes are worse. Prohibition didn't work with alcohol, and it's not working with any drugs. It's also an issue of personal liberty. That isn't the main focus for us. We're parents who have suffered the ultimate loss of our only child. We won't stop until this is changed. I feel that it is moving in the right direction.

DB: You are involved with a couple of organizations. Please tell us about those.

DENISE CULLEN: The first one is the work we do with a New PATH (Parents for Addiction and Healing). That is run by Gretchen Burns Bergman and is based out of San Diego, California. From that organization, which has been around for 13 years as a non-profit, we are founding partners. We, being Broken No More, my husband and I, of Moms United to End the War on Drugs. We've done a lot of things so far and I've testified in front of the Senate and Assembly on some issues.

DB: Please share a website where folks can learn more details.

DENISE CULLEN: www.grasphelp.org. Our organization that's more focused on drug policy issues is www.broken-no-more.org.

DIANE FORNBACHER

Diane has been a tireless worker for NORML for about 20 years now, and in 2013 she began publishing what is now a very successful online magazine *Ladybud*. Recorded in Denver at the 2013 DPA Conference. Cultural Baggage / November 3, 2013.

DIANE FORNBACHER: Our primary focus is the NORML Women's Alliance Foundation, NORML and *Ladybud* are indeed the CPS, the Child Protective Services cases which are always trying to attack cannabis or even other drug use. What we want to do is to make people understand the overall drug war and how it's affecting families from the prison industrial complex to juvenile for profit facilities. For mere possession you can get a neglectment case against you and have your children taken away and God forbid your children are very young or infants you may never see them again.

DB: We had the case of baby Bree in Michigan. Her parents were legally growing/using marijuana not in the presence of the kids and yet somehow they've taken that baby from her parents.

DIANE FORNBACHER: If you have a CPS case the first impulse and legal advice you get is to not go public because you don't want to step on the fire ant hill of the CPS, because they can really come at you. We had a lot of cases recently, usually when these cases happen to activist families who are not quiet. CPS is not accustomed to that. The Green family is one of those families. They helped make the Michigan cannabis law. The mother is the caretaker, and the father suffers from epilepsy, so the judges basically want an epilepsy patient to stop using the very thing that keeps him alive and productive and present for his child. I really don't know about you but that just seems kind of crazy to me. That's really counterproductive. It's really just inhumane and cruel. It is unacceptable.

DB: Then there's that tragic case out of Texas where the 2-year-old girl living a happy life with her family. Her dad got caught with weed which triggered CPS to take that child and put it with a foster mother. Do you want to talk about that?

DIANE FORNBACHER: So the foster mother, unfortunately, killed this child. She died in foster care. The family that was taking care of this child was not vetted properly. A child was removed from a family who had a parent who consumed cannabis but was alive, growing, thriving. Now she's dead. How can I explain this? It doesn't make any sense. It's hard to wrap your brain around because it should not have happened. If cannabis wasn't illegal that child would be alive today.

The news that we deal with, the real news that we can concentrate on is very difficult, very difficult—it involves the death of children, it involves CPS cases, things that families find horrifying and don't want to think about but have to. http://ladybud.com

CHARMIE GHOLSON

Charmie has worked with Law Enforcement Against Prohibition, does constant battle with CPS efforts to take children away from pot smoking moms and dads and serves as executive director of Michigan Moms United. Cultural Baggage / December 15, 2013.

CHARMIE GHOLSON: We're seeing this wave of momentum, this wave of progress in reforms that are coming just since Colorado and Washington State legalized. More and more information is being elevated into mainstream consciousness of how this is a failed public policy that's done the opposite of what we want it to do, how it creates the problems that we are trying to fix. More and more people are beginning to grasp that. We're at a point right now where Child Protective Services is just a money-making scheme, but they do it with children's lives. I think this is how a lot of people are going to be waking up to the reality that their government is incredibly corrupt, because when they start taking our children, it doesn't matter who you are or whether you smoke pot or you're gay or you don't vaccinate your kids or you got a dirty house or whatever the ridiculous long list of reasons the state has for coming into your house with guns and taking your children. Trust me, now that they're actually doing this in a very widespread level—all across the country—people are waking up and saying, "If you take our kids we are going to revolt."

DB: Michigan is one of those states that has a type of medical marijuana law.

CHARMIE GHOLSON: We passed our medical marijuana law in 2008 overwhelmingly, just like in most places when given the chance people vote for drug policy reform. It went into effect in 2009. Our act does include protections such as if you are registered with the state and you've got these qualifying conditions they can't arrest you, they shouldn't prosecute you, no asset forfeiture, you can't fire us, you shouldn't kick us out of our housing, and you can't take our kids. Those things are very clear in the law; however, as you likely know when a state or municipality enacts drug policy reform, there is a backlash. You can count on a backlash most of the time.

I've been watching and fighting this backlash for the last 5 years. There is a strategy. I've actually seen it played out in several states, but there is a strategy to undermine medical marijuana acts, to remove the protections provided in the acts. Here in Michigan, medical marijuana patients and caregivers are still being arrested, still being raided by drug task forces. If there is a raid on your house, CPS is called right away, even if you're a medical marijuana patient.

On September 13th, Bingham County Child Protective Services took a 6-month-old baby, Bree Green, from her parents because the referee said, "You know, somebody might break into the house to try to steal the marijuana. That's an immediate problem. It's clear and immediate danger for the infant." So they came and took the baby.

Yes, if you want to gesticulate or wave your hand at how insane that is, go ahead. That's the beautiful thing. The state and the government acts in such a way that when the reporters finally hit on it, they're confused. That's the good news—the reporters and the media in Michigan have caught on to this, and they are going after these people. We made sure that there were video cameras there when they came and took Bree. That was a Friday, and then on Tuesday, I held a press conference outside of DHS, and I took many of the men who, as you know, will protect their families. I can't tell you how many big, hairy, strong guys I've held in my arms and cried since we started sending these clips of the state coming and taking babies out of people's homes. I took those guys who were really chopped up and emotional, angry, furious about what this beautiful baby and family had gone through, and I had them line the sidewalk outside of the Department of Human Services in Lansing, dressed in Veterans' regalia if they were veterans. I had them hold the space for us, and we lined up women holding hands and singing. We had strollers and pictures of Bree. I brought Tim Gehrach in from LEAP—a former prosecutor who is a LEAP speaker and board member. He had held Bree.

This is a family that formed the Human Solution Michigan Chapter. They provided Cannabis Court Crusaders for folks going to court for marijuana crimes. That baby had been all over the state. She's adorable. People love her, and that was incredibly helpful. Moving a community like that and being there for the community really paid off for the Green family.

We got so much media on this, and the media was confused and kept asking me, "Why are they doing this? Why did they do this?" They would ask questions like, "Well, Maria have you ever been robbed? Is that a real problem?" I would say, "The Greens were never robbed until the state came into their house and took their baby. Those are the bad guys."

There's no threat of someone breaking into the house to steal medical marijuana from the Greens. The Greens were not on trial in that courtroom. The entire Medical Marihuana Act was because of this orchestrated strategy to undermine the Medical Marihuana Act.

By the way whenever a judge or a referee issues a child removal order in Michigan it's like a $12,000 voucher—they get $12,000 for taking that child. Whenever they do that, a huge portion of those people are using marijuana. Why? A lot of people use marijuana - a lot of good parents use marijuana. Once they get their foot in the door, they can come after you for anything. They can monitor you, fine you. I know families in Michigan who pay to see their kids—50 bucks a pop. You got a visitation with your child? That'll be $50.

The judge in the Greens' case openly in court challenged the Greens' status as a marijuana patient. Steve Green has grand mal seizure, which he stopped with concentrated cannabis oil that the 34 pharmaceutical drugs he was taking were not able to do. He challenged his status as a patient. He wanted a board-certified neurologist to say, yes, he has grand mal seizures, and, yes, cannabis can help.

When you get the card, that's supposed to work for you. When you get pulled over by the cops, and there's your driver's license, they never say, "Is this valid?" It is issued from the state, but that's what they've been doing systematically in the courts—challenging every little bit along the way as they can with the hopes that it would get to the higher courts. We've had plenty of medical marijuana cases reach the Supreme Court and the appellate court in Michigan with the hopes that the higher courts will agree on their very narrow interpretation of our law and remove the protection. That's been an incredibly effective strategy. Most of the dispensaries have been shut down because of Supreme Court rulings. They just outlawed concentrates, butters, and all of those things in the appellate court. We're in very hostile territory here, and the family court system is not excluded from that hostility. They are working to maintain the status quo and keep the failed drug war gears in motion.

DB: This situation with young Bree Green is not the only one. What else can you tell us from around the country?

CHARMIE GHOLSON: It's not an isolated incident. In San Diego courts are continuing to take children from their medical marijuana patients. Certainly the beautiful little girl, Alexis, in Texas—a 2-year-old girl that was killed in foster care after they took her from her father who smoked marijuana. Baby Graham—beautiful little family. They had home-birthed children, organic gardening. The Butte Country Drug Task Force came in with guns. The SWAT team took her nursing infant from her breast and her 2-year-old and then took the next baby that she had. Just really horrific scenes all across the country. Here in Michigan, I've talked to 60 families just since September who are desperate for help. You might know that Ed Rosenthal has a fund for this exact thing. We are hoping to replicate that with the Free Bree Foundation. We're starting a foundation so that we can also find the ideal CPS case—medical marijuana or marijuana CPS case and get it to trial.

Prosecutors are out of control. They all have aspirations for getting a better status politically. If you have a prosecutor who is hell bent on going after you, you're screwed. We want to find the right case and put it to a jury trial so everybody can see their tactics and how unethical and, at times, illegal they are. We really, really want to change this in Michigan. We want to stop this abuse. We want them to acknowledge and adhere to the Medical Marihuana Act, and we want them to just leave us the heck alone.

It's a real war. This is a real war with real guns, real soldiers, real strategies, and real funding. My personal belief is if you are not ready to stand up and speak out, it's OK. I understand, but this machine is going to continue to spit out sausage and more and more victims.

DB: You work for medical marijuana in the state, correct? What is the name of your organization?

CHARMIE GHOLSON: I was the owner of the *Midwest Cultivator* for four years. I published quarterly this marijuana trade journal, and I traveled the state and delivered it and asked people how it was going and how the law enforcement was in their area. I was very, very blessed in that way that I was able to travel the state while I was working on the *Cultivator* and meet with people and get a client reading for how it was working in the state. I was a former staff writer for Law Enforcement Against Prohibition, as well. God bless those folks. They gave me my education in every single way about what's wrong with the drug war, how to fix it, methods with the media. Now I'm the founder of Michigan Moms United. I'm going to put a Speakers' Bureau up just like LEAP has done...women and families the resources they need to speak out in their region about whatever kind of issues they got going on with medical marijuana or in their lives. I also sit on the steering committee for the National Moms United to End the War on Drugs campaign. If you search Moms United to End the War on Drugs, you'll find something called the Empty Chair at the Table campaign. If you've got a loved one that is incarcerated due to the drug war, has died from an accidental overdose or isn't welcome in your home during the holidays because of the drug use stigma, you just put a picture of your loved in an empty chair and send it in, or just use the empty chair picture for your profile picture on Facebook. We really work to reduce the stigma of drug use and end the mass incarceration and the drug war.

MIKE HYDE, FATHER OF "CASHY"
AND DR. CHRIS CRISTENSEN, M.D.

Mike Hyde is the father of 3-year-old Cash Hyde who had brain cancer and passed from this earth in 2012. The interview with Dr. Chris Cristensen, a Montana physician who consulted on his case, was conducted before Cashy's death.

Century of Lies / July 24, 2011

CHRIS CRISTENSEN : My only role in Cash's medical care to date has been to see him on about three occasions. I first met the child with his mother and father when I met them and they became patients of mine. I met their child simply because he accompanied them. We discussed in rather general terms what they were facing with him in the way of proposed treatment out-of-state for his recently diagnosed brain tumor, and we had our first discussion at that time about whether or not there was any literature to support or suggest alternatively a negative impact of using cannabis to manage a malignancy in a child, because it was a presumed but proven malignancy at that time.

DB: Now I'm sure there are some folks out there listening that are saying, "Oh my Gosh. A 2-year-old using cannabis?! Isn't this dangerous?!"

CHRIS CRISTENSEN : Well, first and foremost, there is not a recorded fatality in any age group, to my knowledge, from any over dosage of cannabis in any form. The emphasis we place on medical use of cannabis or marijuana is on ingestion, oral ingestion, in some form where the molecules have been activated or extracted or both and the discussion we had about the potential use of cannabis in Cash's case was because at that point he was unable to eat, he had the gastric tube already in place—that's a tube through his nose into his stomach through which he was receiving tube feeding - and he showed little enthusiasm for even that form of nutrition. So our first discussions related to the need to increase his appetite, to get him relief of apparent distress, what one would assume was pain associated with the physical manifestations of physical discomfort and also to help him with sleep because his sleep pattern was almost non-existent.

Century of Lies / June 9, 2013

DB: Mike Hyde is the father of a young boy who lost his battle with brain cancer but persevered for a couple of years through the use of medical cannabis.

MIKE HYDE: Cashy was a beautiful little boy. When he was right around two years old, he was diagnosed with a stage 4 brain tumor. I found out 47 kids are diagnosed with cancer each day and 7 will pass away. Over 1,500 Americans die every day from cancer which means we have a 9/11 every other day in America and our terrorist is cancer. What I found is that 70% of these kids that are dying every day are dying of organ failure and drug overdose from the nausea and pain drugs that they are given. With cannabis oil not only is it one of the safest, most therapeutic medicines known to man it is a neuro-protector and anti-oxidant.

Cashy was prescribed Aderan, Zophan, Phenidren, Benedryl, Morphine, Methadone, Oxycodone, Ketamine and Dilaudid. They were given to him every day, all day long, one or the other. They just stagger it around. They call it the nausea and pain cocktail. It is one of the most horrific things you can watch. At the time when we decided to give cannabis oil to Cashy in 2010, the doctor and

I had a conversation, and I asked him if there was anything they could do to make his quality of life any better. The doctor said, "Mike, you're fighting stage 4 brain cancer. We're using high-dose chemo, bone marrow transplants. This is as good as it will ever get and it's probably going to get worse because we're looking at organ failure at this point. He hasn't eaten in 40 days. He's living solely off of a T panel of nutrition which destroys your liver. On top of that, he's getting all these different types of narcotics which are going to destroy his organs so really it's not if we can do anything to make him any better but we worry that it's going to get worse."

That's when I said, "I want you to start pulling him off this nausea and pain cocktail. I've looked at all the side effects from organ failure, respiratory failure, cardiovascular failure, hallucinations, depression, nausea. I think that you guys are making him sick with all these drugs." As they reluctantly started weaning him off all these narcotics, I started sneaking in cannabis oil into his G tube and over a two week period we pulled him off of all the nausea and pain drugs. The hospital of Salt Lake City charted. I have all the records. They pulled him off the drugs. They told me every day that they thought it was a miracle. They thought it was amazing. They were making him sick with all the nausea and pain drugs. They didn't know that he was on the oil. They just thought that by taking him off of all these drugs made him better.

So after we got him off all the drugs and I'm looking around the hospital... you become a family with all the families on the oncology floor. You know what's going on in all these rooms. You hear parents cry at night when they're kids pass away. It's very real. It's very dramatic. So I'm sitting there thinking to myself that all these parents need to know about this. I'm afraid if I tell them that they'll take the medicine from Cashy.

I had to keep my mouth shut. It really ate at me. I made this promise to myself that when we got Cashy home safe that I was going to tell the world. That way other parents would know that there was another option that wasn't being looked at. When I addressed Cashy's cancer with cannabis oil I wasn't even looking at as an anti-cancer. I was looking at it more as for nausea and pain. As I learned that stuff and I was like, "Oh my God we can pull him off the nausea and pain and give him a neuro-protectant and antioxidant and an anti-inflammatory and an antidepressant and I can't stop his heart."

I had watched them stop his heart. In 2010 I watched them stop Cashy's heart over 8 times at least when giving him Phentanol and Phenergan. There is nothing scarier than watching your kid 'code' and watching them resuscitate him. You're standing there on the sideline and you just watched them literally cause it. They just do it again and again until you look at them and say, "Stop putting that in my kid. You guys keep putting that in his body and his heart keeps stopping. How about you stop putting that in his body."

In Montana we were up against a big battle with our state legislature and our law enforcement . What they did is repeal our voter initiative and allowed the feds to come in and raid all the caregivers in Montana and actually take away our access. Within months of them doing that, Cashy's cancer came back. When his cancer came back the second time, not only was there nowhere to go to get any oil, if you could find it, it was very low. There wasn't enough oil around to actually fight cancer the way that we had learned that could possibly be better than radiation.

So as we went into our battle in 2011, we were only able to acquire enough oil to keep him between the 200 and 400 milligram a day mark, and over a 6 week period we were able to slow his tumor growth down by over 55%, which is huge deal, but at the same time, we couldn't get enough. The feds kept coming in and raiding everybody to the point where we had to leave Montana and go to California and start radiation. There was no more oil and the only thing left was radiation.

Watching radiation do its job was…with high-dose chemo it was a long-term treatment; it was 10 months. Radiation was an 8 week treatment. When we got done with radiation Cashy was in as poor of a state as when we got done with 10 months of chemo. The radiation just zaps you.

However when we got to California we met Ringo and he actually gave us a 90-day supply of oil that we were able to not let Cashy take any nausea or pain drugs the whole time he brain radiation. He was one of the first pediatric cancer patients to do full-body cranial, spinal radiation without any nausea or pain medication.

Every day we were out of the hospital—out patient. He went playing in the Ronald McDonald house because that's where we stayed, while all the other kids were stuck up on their floor heavily sedated with narcotics. His quality of life was different than the first battle even though the treatment was so hard. Ultimately I feel radiation is what consumed Cashy. As we got into 2012 and we were entering remission it was a full-time job just trying to rebuild his body to try to get him back up to running speed.

Right as we got there his cancer came back a third time and that's when we had to make a decision as a family, "Do we continue torturing Cashy with these medical treatments to keep him here another month or is it our responsibility as his caregivers to tap him out on that and not let him go back through all that again." It was a hard decision but the whole family made it and Cashy was part of that voice. He said he didn't want any more pokes. He was very set on not going back to the hospital and we made him that promise. He passed away at home in my arms.

I felt like I gave him a gift that a lot of parents can't give their kids. I felt like even at the end of the day if you're going to make a choice on how you live and how you die then that's the epitome of being a free human being on this earth.

MAIA SZALAVITZ

Maia Szalavitz is author of "Help Help at Any Cost: How the Troubled-Teen Industry Cons Parents and Hurts Kids."Cultural Baggage / May 13, 2009.

DB: Major newspapers, broadcasters, et cetera, are beginning to bring focus to bear. They aren't hitting it with a sledge hammer, but things are changing, are they not?

MAIA SZALAVITZ: It really does seem like there has been a sea change, especially with regards to marijuana. I think that people have realized that the idea that marijuana is more harmful than the already legal drugs is simply not true, and I think that the medical marijuana movement in California has shown people that having access to marijuana does not lead to a society in which everybody's stoned all the time.

DB: Hopefully some of these politicians will develop enough backbone to further address this and to take this forward, right?

MAIA SZALAVITZ: I would really like to see that. There has been a sad counter sign where the Obama administration has pulled back on needle exchange. So I am hoping that is not a sign of back sliding in this issue, but it does look like they have left the federal ban on needle exchange in their budget.

DB: It was what? Ninety-three years ago they passed the Harrison Narcotics Act and in so doing, they took away the rights of adults to choose for themselves. They handed it over to doctors to make that decision. But over the decades, it's now to the point where they won't even let the doctors make that recommendation, right?

MAIA SZALAVITZ: Yeah, I mean, there have been a lot of doctors who have been prosecuted for what they call over-prescribing of pain medication or prescribing to drug addicts. The thing is that you can't define over-prescribing because opiates cause tolerance, and so if you're going to be on opiates for a long time, you are going to need a high dose, and people who are large, or overweight, or have a fast metabolism may need doses that would kill other people ten times over, but that doesn't mean that they are drug addicts. But people don't understand the basics of pharmacology like tolerance and dependence.

DB: I think it's been three, perhaps four years ago, the DEA actually posted standards and then they realized that some of the people they had under indictment were within those standards so they took them down, right?

MAIA SZALAVITZ: That's right, and it was a real outrage because they had worked for a long time with the pain prescribing doctors, the patients, the people in the community — primarily doctors, actually — but to develop these guidelines, and then as soon as William Hurowitz used them in his defense, they immediately retracted them and said that they were no longer official and hadn't been approved. And it had gone through this long process of committees and arguments and back and forth and the whole bureaucratic thing, but suddenly it was no longer approved.

DB: You're the author of "Help Help at Any Cost: How the Troubled-Teen Industry Cons Parents and Hurts Kids." It's a gut-wrenching story, really.

MAIA SZALAVITZ: It is about the troubled-teen industry which is the group of tough love programs, including wilderness programs, behavioral modification facilities, and emotional growth schools — all kinds of different facilities that aim to reform teenagers through tough love. In the book, I show where this idea comes from, which is actually from a cult called Sinanon, and how it's completely not based on any evidence of what actually helps people, and how it's become a billion-dollar industry and has unfortunately hurt a large number of teenagers and their families. The sad thing is we do know how to help people with alcohol and other drug problems, but it does not involve being cruel to them, it does not involve humiliating them, it does not involve attacking them. It involves treating them with compassion and respect and treating addiction as though it were actually a disease, not a moral problem.

DB: I was talking to my engineer Laura, and she was telling me about a friend of hers who, in her teen years, was caught smoking a joint by her mother and was sent to one of these camps. They shaved off her long blonde hair and then dragged her through the mud. I guess tried to reframe her mindset. I'm not sure what they were thinking, but Laura said she came back and she was never the same.

MAIA SZALAVITZ: As far back as 1974, a congressional investigation compared them to North Korean brainwashing. We're hearing about these same tactics in the torture debate: sleep deprivation, food deprivation, isolation, extremes of temperature, and constant barrages of emotional attacks and sexual humiliation. One of the reasons I believe that the American public has not become as outraged as I believe we should be in the torture debate is because we have unfortunately said that this is OK to do to kids for years. So, if we think it's ok to do to kids, why wouldn't we think it's OK to do to people that we really hate?

So, it's really an extraordinarily sad situation, and yes, you know, when they do studies on what happens to people who have been through that, it can be incredibly damaging. It can demonstrably produce post-traumatic stress disorder and depression, and, ironically, it often exacerbates addiction. So, a lot of these kids go into these programs, they are smoking marijuana, and they're drinking, and they are telling their parents to "F" off, but they are not much different from any other of their peers. But they come out and they have been exposed, they have hours and hours of confessing, "I'm a drug addict, I'm a drug addict, I'm a drug addict," and they've heard from kids who have taken things like heroin or cocaine and who have been involved in things like injecting, and they are like well, "I'm a drug addict, so I guess I am gonna do drugs." And also, they have all the pain they are trying to escape from, so unfortunately it creates a self-fulfilling prophecy.

DB: Yeah, and sometimes humiliation can be a longer lasting pain than a bruise, right?

MAIA SZALAVITZ: That's absolutely the case, and unfortunately I think we also don't understand how the human stress physiology works. Humiliation, if you look at in animal models where you've got dominance and submission and you've got the animals that are the alphas who have very nice, robust stress systems that are doing well, and then you've got the ones beneath them that aren't doing well, and so when you sort of make that physiology active by humiliating people, you are creating real problems that can be very lasting.

DB: Your book talks about this organization called Straight. Who were the founders of that?

MAIA SZALAVITZ: The founders of Straight were Mel Sembler and Joseph Zappala. Mel Sembler became the campaign finance chief for the first president Bush, and under the second president Bush he was the ambassador to Italy. He most recently headed up the Scooter Libby Defense Fund and an organization called Freedom's Watch.

DB: So these people are not just some rebel, they are tied in tightly with many of the leaders of our government.

MAIA SZALAVITZ: Yeah, and I think that one of the things we have learned about these tough love programs is they've been very good with attaching themselves to local establishments and local politicians. In the past, there were some democratic people who supported Straight. But, they are very good at making themselves look like heroes. They go out there and they say, "Look, we take these kids who are so troubled," and the kids of course, when they are trying to get out, they are like, "Yes, you saved my life, you saved my life," and it looks very compelling. So, they have definitely insinuated themselves into the government and that's one of the ways that they've been able to survive this long.

DB: Now, I was at a conference where the Drug Czar said when he goes to these treatment centers, one of the things you hear most often is "The day I was arrested was the luckiest day of my life." Is that just people trying to get out the door?

MAIA SZALAVITZ: Yeah, and it's also reflects another phenomenon where if something terrible happens to you -- you get sent a concentration camp, or you lose your parents, some really bad thing happens to you -- people's natural instinct is to make meaning out of it. You don't want to think, "I just suffered through a meaningless two years or ten years or fifteen years in prison." You have to think, "This did something for me," for your own psychological health. Unfortunately that means people end up supporting their own oppression.

DB: President Fox of Mexico during a tour of the U. S. talked about the need to decrim, but decrim's really not going to help much in the long run, is it?

MAIA SZALAVITZ: Well, the thing about decriminalization as opposed to legalization in terms of drug strategy is that decriminalization only applies to possession, so it doesn't have any effect on the black market.

DB: Then we leave all the cartels and the street corner vendors in place.

MAIA SZALAVITZ: Right, so it doesn't do anything about issues related to purity or issues related to violence related to cartels and those kinds of things, because if you think about it, if you make possession legal, but you don't make the dealing legal, you still have the worst part of a black market. You know, a lot of people think that legalization means Philip Morris Crack, and I think that when people are considering alternate drug policies, they have to realize that there is a large range of options between Philip Morris Crack and sending people to jail for twenty years.

MONEY FOR NOTHING

"Pfizer and Merck kill more of us than the cartel's crap ever could. They thank us for our silence, each year's hundred billion dollars, and the chance to do it forever more."
—DTN Song, Eternal War

When we finally end this drug war, we will immediately reap huge financial rewards. The $70 billion squandered each year in waging this drug war could be used for health, education, roads, and bridges. With a small tax on these drugs, we could rake in hundreds of millions of dollars instead of constantly opening our wallets for more prisons, more welfare, and the destruction of millions of families every year, all over the contents of a baggie.

So what is it that makes this drug war work? Money. Taxpayer money, drug market money, money seized by police.

Millions worldwide profit enormously, continuously, from the drug war. It's not just the politicians and their perpetual "contributions leads to legislative payback machine." It's the stockbrokers selling prison builders stock and the piss testers of America. It's the foreign investor in the prisoner-made knickknacks and the prison guard unions who sells the prisoner's time for $0.40 and pay the prisoners $0.06. It's the local law enforcement departments and DEA offices who seize money, cars, and houses they say are connected to drugs.

We spend tens of billions of dollars each year trying to stop the flow of drugs worth at best 4 billion dollars at the farm gate, but because of our prohibition, we cause the final price to be 400 billion at the market gate.

The money, some several hundred billions of drug profits that have accrued to the major producers over the last few decades, is not sitting in gold bullion in some jungle cave. Many of those billions are back at work; in the stock market, in banking and industry, and in making political contributions.

In this time of corporate malfeasance and bankruptcy, for many Americans, prohibition now serves as the only means to place food on their table and a roof over their heads. But it's not just the sellers, growers, importers, drug lords, and political candidates who prosper from this war. No, the bankers and the insurance companies make billions, as well, from "don't ask, don't tell" money laundering. Some would say that without the skim from laundering, the stock market would tank so badly that the fall after 9/11 would pale in comparison. The black market rules from Bogotá to Matamoras, from Washington D.C. to San Francisco, and there is precious little that law enforcement can or will do to end the problem.

It is the prohibition law and its resultant enormous profits that bring drug violence to our communities. Drug traffickers are more than willing to break every one of the Ten Commandments in order to maintain their share of this multi-billion dollar black market. That they use extortion, murder, bribery of public officials, and other illegal tactics should no longer come as any shock.

With controlled distribution of cannabis, coca leaves and opium to adults, we could immediately end this drug war, bankrupt the cartels, save billions of tax dollars, cut down on overdose deaths, free up our prisons, and reconcile the distrust between the community and law enforcement. Who speaks against it? Those who enrich themselves on the drug war as it is.

SCOTT BULLOCK

Scott Bullock joined the Institute for Justice at its founding in 1991 and now serves as a senior attorney. In addition to litigation, Bullock works extensively on grassroots campaigns with homeowners, small business owners, and activists throughout the country to oppose condemnations for private use. Bullock directs the Institute's campaign against civil forfeiture, a nationwide effort to challenge the ability of governments to take property from owners without a criminal conviction. He is co-author of Policing for Profit, a comprehensive report published in 2010 documenting forfeiture abuse at all levels of government. Recorded April 4, 2010.

DB: The Institute for Justice litigates nationwide on behalf of individuals whose rights are being violated by Government. Is that a good summation of your work?

SCOTT BULLOCK: That's a very good summation of our work. We are a nationwide organization. We're located just outside of Washington. We have four state chapters and we're really suing governments throughout the country who violate Fundamental Constitutional Liberties.

We, just this week, released a study that really is the first nationwide survey that looks at the abuse of civil asset forfeiture. Civil forfeiture is a concept that some people are familiar with. But if they're not and you tell them about it, they are shocked. Because under civil forfeiture, police and prosecutors can take your property away from you without so much as charging you with a crime. In over forty states and at the federal level, police and prosecutors can then profit from the proceeds and property that forfeit from you. We think civil forfeiture laws really represent one of the most serious assaults on private property rights in the nation, today.

DB: The predominant use of this is in regards to suspicion of drug possession?

SCOTT BULLOCK: Oh, no question about it. It is oftentimes tied to the drug war. But it's not only related to that. They seize people's cars for DWI's. For soliciting prostitutes and other types of crimes, because civil forfeiture laws are written very broadly and one of the major problems with them, is that property can be seized merely on the suspicion that you are doing something wrong and one of the primary things that governments seize now is cash. If the police officer suspects that you have a 'larger than normal' amount of cash on you or in your vehicle, they can seize that saying, 'I suspect you of being a drug dealer or engaging in money laundering' and then once that property is seized, the burden is on you to try to get the property back. So it's really, as we call it, this upside-down world where rather than the criminal context, where the burden is on the Government to pursue you and prove that you're guilty beyond a reasonable doubt. In Civil Forfeiture, the opposite is true. The burden is on the individual to try to prove their or their property's, innocence.

DB: Guilty till proven innocent. Now, you have given grades to the various states, if you will, on their use of this policy. Correct?

SCOTT BULLOCK: That's right and unfortunately only three states received a final grade of B or higher and thirty-five states received a D or an F for their laws alone. So this is a nationwide problem and unfortunately most states and at the federal level, do not have adequate protections for property owners. Some of the worst abusers are in the South. But we also have states like Michigan that very aggressively forfeit proceeds, and this is not a very good track record nationwide. One of the things that the report points out and one of the things that needs to be reformed is that, even in states, for instance like North Carolina, that have pretty good Civil Forfeiture Laws, that do not allow the police and prosecutors to profit from forfeiture activities. What often times agencies will do there, is pass off forfeiture prosecutions to the Federal Government.

Then the Federal Government will prosecute the forfeiture actions and under federal law, the money goes right back to law enforcement. Up to eighty percent can go right back to local police and prosecutors. So this is really an end run around the wishes of the citizens, of a particular state, and it's one of the things that we look at very carefully in the report and call on the law to be changed to make sure that even if a state does have good laws, that they're not permitted to bypass state procedures and go to the Federal Government.

There's been horrible abuses of civil forfeiture laws where people's currency/cash is taken, without ever charging them with a crime and then, because the property amounts often times are small, people just kind of throw in the towel and don't even fight it. They feel like, 'I don't have the time and the effort to work my way through this system, hire a lawyer to try to fight for me, when they might only be seizing seven hundred dollars or fifteen hundred dollars or two thousand dollars. That's the way a lot of these forfeiture's play out. This isn't the taking of the big drug dealers mansion. This is taking a used car from somebody. It's taking fifteen hundred dollars or two thousand dollars in cash from folks. So it does disproportionately affect lower income people. Often times minority groups and it's one of the many ways that this power is abused.

DB: Can you give us an idea of the magnitude of the dollars involved?

SCOTT BULLOCK: It's exploded over the years and civil forfeiture was really kind of a backwater of the law, until the 1980's, when the federal government and a lot of state governments put this profit incentive into the law. Before that, if there was a forfeiture proceeding, the money went to typically the general revenue account of the state, where most fines and other fees that the Government charges go to, and then elected officials decide how the money is spent.

But once they took this 'Law enforcement can eat what they kill' approach, that is when you saw forfeiture skyrocket. It just gives you one example when the law was changed in 1986 at the federal level, the Assets Forfeiture Fund at the Department of Justice had seventy-eight million dollars in it. Today, even with some reforms passed in 2000, it did provide some greater protection for property owners. The property incentive wasn't changed at that time and now that same fund has over a billion dollars in it.

DB: I remember Karen Tandy was quoted as saying that the DEA, with the capture of two billion dollars during the time she was involved, had almost paid for itself.

SCOTT BULLOCK: Yeah. I think some people, who are involved in this business, don't really see any problems with it. They don't really see the fact that 'incentives matter' and that if you give people incentives to go out and take as much property as possible, they're going to respond accordingly. So it shouldn't be surprising then, that a lot of law enforcement effort is directed, not at capturing the bad guy, stopping violent crime.

But it goes toward, "How are we going to pay ourselves?" "How are we going to fund our agencies?" "How are we going to improve our work lives?" Or in some states, "How are we going to pay our salaries?" So that is really a perversion of law enforcement priorities. Away from what their goal should be. Which is 'The fair and impartial administration of justice'.

DB: Scott, as one of the coauthors of the book, *Policing for Profit: The Abuse of Civil Asset Forfeiture*, what was your focus?

SCOTT BULLOCK: What I really focused on was the analysis of the law itself. I'm a lawyer and I would not trust myself to do some of the pretty sophisticated statistical analysis that's in the report. So, I focused on the legal analysis and then we had three criminal justice researchers, all whom are professors and have PHD's, look at the numbers and really do an analysis that showed that not only can you see, almost on an intuitive basis as to why police might prosecute and do this for profit, but they actually demonstrate this through a very careful look at the data that's available.

What they really found was, that when laws make civil forfeiture easier and more profitable, law enforcement engages in more of it, and that's just not an assertion. This is the first study that puts some real numbers behind that and I think some really solid research. What we see this as, is really the inauguration of a campaign that we're going to have, that's going to manifest itself in a number of different ways. Through litigation. Through public awareness. Through further research. Through grassroots organizing. Hopefully through legislative change that will change the laws in a very significant way, throughout the country, to stop forfeiture abuse.

We're going to file lawsuits. As I said, we're going to work with folks to try to change the law in various jurisdictions, throughout the country. So we hope to use this really, as the launching pad for a nationwide campaign, to try to stop these abuses.

DB: This comes at a time when the nation, the states, the county, every municipality is hurting for money. They need that money, anyway they can and without your hopeful interference with their continuing this effort, it's bound to get worse. Right?

SCOTT BULLOCK: Right, and I think that's all the more reason to make sure protections for property owners are in place. Because the incentives to take property from folks are going to be even stronger and we don't have 'an end justifies the means' approach in this country. Or at least we should not have and people should not lose their property without being convicted of a crime and law enforcement shouldn't be able to profit from other people's property.

We're not talking about criminal forfeiture here. If somebody's convicted of a crime and you show, for instance, that someone defrauded investors and used that money to buy mansions and yachts and things like that, then sure. Nobody's going to be opposed to the use of criminal forfeiture.But that's where forfeiture should be confined to. It should be confined to people who are convicted of crime, in a court of law. It should not be used as a civil action against folks who may never even be charged with any type of wrongdoing.

EAPEN THAMPY

A young man with the very ambitious goal of ending the forfeiture of American citizens' bank accounts, homes and automobiles is Mr. Eapen Thampy the Director of Americans for Foreiture Reform. Cultural Baggage / June 27, 2011.

EAPEN THAMPY: My organization is Americans for Forfeiture Reform. We are young. We founded last year in Kansas City- myself and Sam Burnett, he just graduated from law school. Our objective is to reform America's civil and criminal forfeiture laws with an emphasis on federal reform which is important because state reforms are inevitably circumvented by federal law and federal agencies.

DB: Yeah, you know the former Drug Czar Assistant, Andrea Bartwell, She was quoted a couple years back as saying that the amount of funds that the DEA and the federal officials derive from forfeitures almost made up the billion dollars plus that they spend each year trying to stop these drugs. Your response to that.

EAPEN THAMPY: Well, I would tell you that the justice system has turned from a justice system into a giant money-making machine. And I estimate that fines, forfeitures, and other derivative proceeds that pertain to directly to law enforcement projects comprise between a quarter and one-third of drug war funding proper. Although, of course, no one has ever been able to track the whole extent of fines, forfeitures, and other revenue sources that law enforcement controls because we got 30 different federal agencies that use them. (chuckles)

DB: They're not going to give up that gravy train without a big fight are they?

EAPEN THAMPY: Oh no, absolutely not. You may be interested...I just got...I was in Boston this past Monday for congressional subcommittee hearings on the abuse of forfeiture funds and law enforcement misconduct at the National Oceanic and Atmospheric Administration. They have forfeiture funds too and in the last five years they pulled in over $100 million and still can't account for half of it.

DB: I think it's 80,000 raids happen across America each year, something like that. What's your response to that?

EAPEN THAMPY: These raids were happening at something like 300 a year in the 1980s. To hear that they are now happening at the rate of 80,000 a year in the United States of America is to conclude that something is seriously wrong. We are living in a world of, some would say, Soviet law enforcement. I think a fair parallel might be the Colonial law enforcement over Americans by the British. This kind of enforcement rates by, you know, by the military essentially for revenue purposes, revenue that is both taken by the government and pertains directly to the law enforcement is exactly what the King of England was doing to this country 300 odd years ago.

Cultural Baggage, November 17, 2013

DB: It seems to be like a plague almost that these various law enforcement agencies around the country are looking for and finding ways of taking our stuff.

EAPEN THAMPY: Yeah, asset forfeiture is something that congress introduced in the 70s and 80s as a tool for drug law enforcement. The problem with asset forfeiture is that it gives law enforcement a direct financial incentive in specific laws. Over the last 20, 30 years the law enforcement agencies have asked congress to expand these laws and they've gotten those expansions.

Forfeiture is a revenue tool that ...there are over 400 federal laws that allow for the forfeiture of property for a variety of things – not a lot which necessarily have to do with drugs. All the money goes to law enforcement either through the Treasury of the Department of Justice.

DB: In essence the U.S. government acts as a money launderer for these local agencies, correct?

EAPEN THAMPY: You know that's a funny way to put it but I'll say that the 5th circuit in 1992 said exactly the same thing. The situation was this man in Louisiana had money seized by a sheriff. The sheriff knew he could keep the money under asset forfeiture but then the man filed a claim against him in court. The sheriff took the money and said, "We're giving this to the DEA. They're going to accomplish the forfeiture instead of me so your claim goes away."

He gives it to the DEA. The man sued and the 5th circuit, a panel of federal judges said in their decision that this action by the federal government in conjunction with the Louisiana sheriff was essentially money laundering. It would have been money laundering if it had been done by a private entity.

DB: We're here at the DPA conference. A thousand people with I think a brand new mindset.

EAPEN THAMPY: This is one of the best conferences that you could imagine where drug policy reformers come together and discuss not only past victories but how to expand that.

Since Colorado and Washington legalized marijuana last year we definitely know that the tides have turned. We are beginning to unravel the drug war machine. One of the things I'm trying to talk to people about at this event is don't forget about asset forfeiture. It was one of the foundational tools of drug enforcement.

We can't legalize marijuana and walk away from the whole game. When law enforcement has financial incentives for drug prohibition and to enforce the law then that skews their behavior, how they act politically. Our biggest opponent in any project of drug policy reform is law enforcement.

One of their fundamental incentives is that monetary incentive that they get from the forfeiture revenue that comes in. If we can disconnect that we can roll back a lot of the structural features of drug prohibition.

DRUG REFORM ADVOCACY

"Many people, especially ignorant people, want to punish
you for speaking the truth, for being correct, for being you.
Never apologize for being correct, or for being years ahead
of your time. If you're right and you know it, speak your
mind. Speak your mind. Even if you are a minority of one,
the truth is still the truth."—Mahatma Gandhi

In this chapter we will showcase a few of the best interviews I have conducted with some major players in the drug reform community. My radio and TV programs have served as a springboard for many advocates over the years who seek to change the drug laws. My 100-plus published letters to the editor and a couple of powerful OpEds have also served to show my "allegiance" and to motivate perhaps a thousand, often leery, drug reformers to join us on the airwaves.

Each year, I attend three to five national drug reform conferences in the US and report from a dozen or more regional gatherings. Because I am most often found in the hallways or in my hotel "studio" grabbing interviews, I am seldom able to attend the sessions in person. Over the years I have managed to acquire lots of audio recorders which I use to "attend" these sessions for me and my radio audience. My YouTube site (FDeanBecker) has also grown over the years to include more than 100 videos featuring judges, scientists, doctors and especially drug reform advocates.

Most of what I do would be considered advocacy by those who disagree with my stance taken. However, this interpretation is itself subject to interpretation and reevaluation as is obvious per the following example. From 2003 to 2009 I spent many hours each week speaking with General Managers and Program Directors at radio stations in the US and Canada, seeking their approval to air one or more of my radio programs. We had great success in recruiting stations because programmers back then were afraid to produce their own, in-house challenges to the drug war which might incur the wrath of their local constabulary. In this same time frame, I called more than 30 NPR stations and the typical response from the GM or PD was to say they thought I was "biased." Thankfully, now years later, NPR has begun to take a more critical look at prohibition and has produced numerous truthful and quite powerful reports challenging drug war logic. Turns out the "bias" belonged to NPR, not yours truly.

My father and I had a long time in sorting out our differences and perceptions on the drug war. I am proud to say that in the last 5 years of his life he worked in prison ministry. He developed a new understanding of the mechanism of drug war and through this new advocacy, we became allies, calling for the end of drug war.

Do you ever get one of those deep-seated, emotions-stirring, long-term dreams of changing the world? Seems that's what happens to nearly every drug reformer. Some get a minimal paycheck, but they work in this arena because to do anything but accomplish their goal would seem worse than dying.

My advocacy began to form on a spring morning in 1971 when Ed, a 17 year old busted for a marijuana cigarette, climbed into his tree house and blew his brains out with a .22 rifle. My friend Ed was slight of build, perhaps 135 pounds. He had been caught in a scam a few months before by a snitch to whom Ed had given a joint as a sign of friendship. This was in Texas, the year was 1971, and the prosecutor had already told Ed he was going to prison for at least 5 years. Back then, each prison was run by the biggest, baddest son of a bitch inside. The guards seldom stepped inside the prison, and rape was deemed to be insufficient to bother with. Knowing the next several years if not a decade behind bars would mean daily humiliation, abuse and pain Ed chose to leave the planet with some dignity intact.

It was almost 30 years after Ed's death before I began my public drug reform efforts. Living in Texas and not knowing the full history of the drug war, all I could do was share Ed's story with all who would listen. In 1998 with my 50th birthday fast approaching, I realized that I had no legacy, had nothing of merit to leave to my children or to civilization. Once informed via DrugLibrary.org as to the deception and lies utilized to craft this eternal drug war I had found my new calling.

TOM ANGELL

Tom Angell is the founder and chairman of Marijuana Majority and served as media relations director of Law Enforcement Against Prohibition, an organization of police, prosecutors, judges and other criminal justice professionals who have seen the harms of the "war on drugs" up close. Previously, Tom worked for six years with Students for Sensible Drug Policy, first as a student chapter leader and then as a national staffer handling the organization's media outreach and congressional lobbying efforts. Century of Lies / July 21, 2013.

TOM ANGELL: The organization formerly known as the Partnership for a Drug-Free America this week released some new polling results. I guess they are tired of polling the population in general and specifically parents about their thoughts on marijuana policy. It's a real gift for legalizers which is surprising coming from an organization like that. They found majority support across the board for many of the marijuana policy reforms that our movement has been pushing. It really seems like this is part of a strategic shift on the part of the prohibitionists away from trying to stand in the way of legalization. I think they have recognized that they have lost that argument with the American people and are now trying to shape what legalization looks like and trying to make sure it is as least objectionable as possible to them and to their concerns.

DB: So your latest organization, Marijuana Majority is finding more allies, more supporters aligned with that need for change?

TOM ANGELL: That's correct. Marijuana Majority exists to help people understand the very simple fact that marijuana reform is a mainstream, majority supported issue. For too long many people (including those in our movement) have viewed our movement as marginalized, as radical and not necessarily representing the mainstream of America but the polls show that we do have majority support for the policy proposals we're trying to enact and that some of the most prominent people from across the political spectrum—from the left to the right and everyone in between—are on board with what we are trying to do and are becoming less and less afraid to say that publically. What we are trying to do is spotlight some of these voices to encourage even more people who agree with us currently only behind closed doors to feel emboldened and empowered to say it publically.

DB: Is the government trying to influence the change from our draconian policy by trying to confine and minimize the use of cannabis through new constraints, through new interpretations?

TOM ANGELL: I think it's part of a strategic retreat on behalf of the prohibitionists. They recognize that they can no longer prevent marijuana legalization from happening and now they simply want to shape what legalization looks like. While I think many on our side will be prepared to quibble and fight with some of the restrictions that Partnership for Drug-Free America and other organizations want to enact and will rightfully so fight against some of the most extreme and limiting of these measures I think it's a really good place for us to be in.

I, for one, welcome these folks to the table and look forward to the discussion about shaping what marijuana legalization looks like. It's no longer a question of whether marijuana will be legal it's a question of how and when that will happen. In the Partnership survey that I mentioned it seems like their main focus is trying to make the case that parents are very concerned with youth access to marijuana under legalization. They are talking about things like preventing people from using marijuana in public in places where cigarette smoking is currently banned and enacting some types of restrictions on advertising of marijuana in the new legal industry. To be honest with you I don't have much of a problem with those things. I'm not sure I would favor an outright ban on advertising, but certainly I and some groups have been working for a decade to change the marijuana laws are not that excited about the notion of huge marijuana billboards on the side of the road.This discussion is something that I think is important for us to have. Now that we're talking about what marijuana legalization will look like rather than whether marijuana should be legal, I think that's quite significant. Let's have the discussion. Let's hear from even the folks on the other side, and let's make our case in front of regulators and lawmakers. The fact is, very few people in society are now doubting that marijuana legalization is on the way and at this time our side is winning.

RUSS BELVILLE

Russ Belville is the Director of Media for the National Cannabis Coalition, where his duties include production of the world's only 24-hour source for cannabis news and entertainment broadcasts, National Cannabis Radio "Radical" Russ, as he is known on-air, hosts The Russ Belville Show, a two-hour news and talk radio program for the cannabis community, weekdays at 3pm Pacific on National Cannabis Radio. Cultural Baggage / November 10, 2013.

DB: Russ, we're here at the Drug Policy Alliance conference, 1000+ people mostly from the U.S. but from around the world. A lot of Central American folks are here. It just seems more cohesive, more powerful, more ready for change doesn't it?

RUSS BELVILLE: Well legalization is a reality now. We don't have to dream. We don't have to imagine. It's not an abstract concept. It actually exists in 2 states. Now, not as much as I'd like. Not as legal as it should be but we've gone over the precipice now. We've gotten into how rather than if. We've seen the massive jump in the Gallup Poll. We've seen a poll out of Texas at 58%. I mean, come on. This has changed the world. Uruguay is set to legalize marijuana and not just possession but the market of marijuana which we all know that's the big problem is the illegal market not the illegal possession. So, yeah, it feels good to be in the majority. It feels good to see the rest of America getting on the bandwagon and the rest of the world too.

DB: So we have here in Colorado a situation where it's quasi-legal, nearly legal—however you want to say it—and there are still those who are nay-sayers, still those who want to maintain through their efforts maybe without realizing it, the black market. Your thoughts on that.

RUSS BELVILLE: For me it's always been about stopping the imprisonment and the ruining of people's lives over marijuana. So first and foremost if something occurs that leads to that end I am for it and certainly that has happened in both Colorado and Washington. People whose lives would have been ruined for a marijuana possession charge or even if not ruined affected in any sort of negative way is no longer happening.

To the people who would say that's not "real" legalization or "true" legalization I would say real legalization is that which makes the ballot and passes and keeps people out of cages. Now, it makes me question for some people what has this been about for you—the ending of the criminality or the maintaining of the profits. If it's all been about business and maintaining the profits, well, welcome to the 21st century—that's going to change. Marijuana is going to become an industry like any other that's going to require business acumen and smart production and good marketing and competition. It's not going to be an easy "grow in your closet make a bunch of extra money" gig anymore.

Now we should work to include those people. When they passed these laws that say if you got a previous criminal record for growing you can't grow, well, some of these people that are growing medical marijuana we could use their expertise. It makes no sense to keep them out just because what they were doing to help someone who was sick before it was legal. They can't do it now that it is legal? That doesn't make a whole lot of sense to me.

A lot of folks are just going to have to accept that things are going to change in a radical way—not just for the mainstream that's not used to weed being legal but also for our side that's not used to weed being legal. There's going to be a lot of differences.

DB: Let me kind of extrapolate on the question, and that is by virtue of recreational pot being made legal here in Colorado they're setting up layers of taxing which will increase the price well beyond that available to medical users. I guess the thought there is that that will help perpetuate the black market. Your thought?

RUSS BELVILLE: Well, you know, nothing is going to help perpetuate the black market more than prohibition did. The black market is not going to get any bigger than it was. Will there still be a black market? Well, yeah. There's a black market in cigarettes. A pack of cigarettes in Manhattan is like $12. There's people who go down to Virginia where the taxes are nothing or North Carolina, a tobacco state, where they are almost nothing and load up a van full of cartons of smokes, take them to Manhattan and sell them in the alleys and make $50,000 a van load.

So, yeah, you can over tax something but when that happens—and it is happening, I think these taxes in both states are probably too high to start with—but when that happens and people aren't buying the overtaxed weed if the government wants to make some money they're going to have to do what any other business does. It's going to have to cut overhead or lower taxes or do something to get more customers in.

The fact that it might not get rid of the black market is actually our leverage. When people say black market there is an aspect of the Mexican cartels and that but for me it was always the guy that was a grower. He was an old Viet Nam friend of mine who grew weed. He was no black market. He was no sinister force.

Part of this black market that they so fear is going to still work is our friends that have been growing all this time. If that stays alive and provides the leverage to force those taxes lower—hey, great—let's see those taxes go lower.

JERRY EPSTEIN

After I spent 6 months in 1999/2000 drilling down into the website DrugLibrary.org, finding the original proceedings, the lies that comprise the foundation of the drug war I was mad as hell and seeking a way to inform the public; which led to my involvement with the New York Times, Pacifica radio, television scripts and productions as well as this book. One of the first people I ran into that understood my concerns was Mr. Jerry Epstein, a retired Marine Corp officer who was one of the co-founders of the Drug Policy Forum of Texas and who now serves as president of DPFT. Cultural Baggage / February 5, 2012.

DB: What got you motivated to help start up that drug policy forum?

JERRY EPSTEIN: Basically I got a phone call from someone who had read a piece I wrote and it turned out he was one of the biggest experts on drugs in the country—Dr. G. Alan Robinson, National Academy of Sciences award winner and so forth. He said, "I like what you wrote. Let's see if we can do something about it." We wanted to try to reach a situation where at least there was scientific accuracy in the debate and where we could open the doors and actually discuss it in public without people getting so upset because you had different ideas about what was going on.

Of course maybe the real background was the fact that I'm old enough now that my parents were born when all drugs were legal. So my grandparents lived for decades when heroin, cocaine were advertised in all the newspapers and so forth and so on and it was a lot better then than it is now. I can tell you that much.

DB: One of the people I was privileged to talk to while he was still alive was Professor Milton Friedman and he was old enough to have been alive when drugs were legal. He spoke very forthrightly, very boldly about the need to change our laws, our perspective and the way we go about all this. He knew there was a better way.

JERRY EPSTEIN: He's been a model for a lot of my thinking. I think he had the right ethical concepts. As a Nobel Prize winning economist he keeps reminding you that supply equals demand. If there's a demand for the drug, it's going to be there. So you start your thinking with the premise that drugs are always going to be with us. Now the question that always faces the public then is do you want them with cartels and drug dealers or do you want them without cartels and drug dealers. It just seems kind of bizarre to me to think that we would think our children, our communities and our country would be safer if only we would trust the drug dealers rather than the doctors, which is what the current system suggests.

They would like to make the case that because they make a given number of arrests or given number of seizures or they arrest a cartel person that that contributed to something significant. Two different threads of thought here. One is just about getting cartel people. We have found many instances in which the information that allowed them to get the cartel comes from another cartel. We've seen it even in the city at local levels like the big scandal out in L.A. Most of the time you will never know that is the circumstance. Even if he's an honest policeman the fact is if he takes some gang, cartel off the street—somebody's going to fill the gap because Milton Friedman has told us that the supply is equal to demand and they will find a way.

The other thing is that we have a measure for our ability to stop supply, in my opinion. It is the government research that has been done since 1975. Nearly everyone is concerned about what would be the level of drugs in our schools. These particular studies have gone on every year. We talked to teenagers from 8th, 10th and 12th grades. The two sentence summary from that information is that any kid has been able to get any drug that they wanted if they just asked a few of their classmates.

But we also have a situation where when we compare the kids who tell us these drugs are easy to get we find out that the number of kids who know the drug is easy to get is hugely greater than the number that actually use the drugs. So we have been flooded with available drugs for our kids and we not only get the drugs but now we have roughly one million teenage drug sellers. That's almost one for every classroom in America. They in turn want to protect it so we have a similar number that carry guns from time to time so you get that atmosphere. Now a kid can protect himself from drugs if he just chooses to say no but how do you protect yourself from accidental or deliberate hostility in an atmosphere of crime and violence with guns present?

Nixon commissioned a national commission in 1972, our only national commission on our overall drug policy, and one of the things they said was that there was so much money being carved up by legitimate interests that they were afraid that we would never solve the problem. The amount of money that so scared them back in 1973 when the report came out is maybe a fiftieth or a hundredth of what is involved now.

Finally, what we know is that drug abuse comes in small, medium and large—mild, moderate and severe. The most severe cases, the type of cases that you read about are about 7% of the total involvement of the population—we know that the roots of that are frequently there at birth. We know that we can see the signs and symbols of it and the actions before any drug is ever used. If we could do it, a very difficult thing, but if we can—the best times to interfere start with good prenatal care for everyone. It continues in trying to locate the children who have been abused before they're even five years old.

We have to try and do a better job of protecting kids who can't protect themselves: 2-, 3-, 4- and 5-year-olds. If we do that extremely difficult job better and we have more resources put into that rather than building more prisons, the payoff later in life will be enormous.

AMANDA FEILDING, LADY NEIDPATH

Amanda Feilding, Countess of Wemyss and March, is a British artist, scientist and drug policy reformer. In 1998, she founded the Beckley Foundation, a charitable trust that promotes a rational, evidence-based approach to global drug policy; initiates, designs and conducts pioneering neuroscientific and clinical research into the effects of psychoactive substances and investigates new avenues of treatment for mental and physical conditions as well as the enhancement of creativity and well-being. Cultural Baggage / October 29, 2008.

DB: I've seen several of your reports over the last few years dealing with various aspects in regards to drug policy and I think the most recent was a commission release of a study done and some recommendation towards cannabis controls, right?

AMANDA FEILDING: Yes, it's a very interesting report done by five of the leading drug policy analysts in the world. What I noticed was that at international drug policy debates; meetings, strangely cannabis was never really talked about. It was always about the cocaine and opium market and amphetamines. I couldn't quite make out why cannabis was always left out and so I decided to convene a report which would cover all the major issues to do with cannabis and it's regulations.

So the latest evidence on the health harms of cannabis and how different countries set about controlling it's use and; what are the results of the different techniques of controlling use and; what are the international regulations and how they affect how different countries work and indeed at the end, how one might act; change the international regulations so that individual countries are freer to create controls of cannabis, which better reflect the individual country.

DB: I noticed there were several issues dealing with the U.N. Convention on Narcotics and how it would impact or require nuances within the various countries and how they would treat cannabis, right?

AMANDA FEILDING: Absolutely. Because at the moment the international conventions limit, very strongly, how countries can deal with cannabis. Particularly at the level of producing and supplying. There've been many different ways countries have approached dealing with the cannabis issue but they've always been constrained by the fact that supply is illegal. I mean, in the Dutch coffee shops people can buy, legally, small quantities of cannabis to use. So use and supply is legal. But the back door that supplies the cannabis, is illegal. Which therefore put the police in a very difficult position.

Really, the overriding fact is that the war on drugs happen to have been a success, the forty years that the billions and billions of dollars spent on it. Drugs are cheaper, purer and more available than they have ever been before and indeed over the last fifty years, the use of cannabis has gone up from small pockets of use and traditional use, in certain countries, to really say that it's kind of normative among large proportions of the youth culture across the developed world.

So, quite obviously the war on drugs is not working and we need to really re-look at the whole situation and to think, 'How can we best regulate the use and supply of these substances, particularly cannabis is this case, which best to serve the individual and society?'

The report is laying out different ways that countries could set about reviewing how they regulate the use of cannabis in order to cut down the harms. Because it goes into, 'What are the harms of cannabis itself?' But also, there are very sub-stantial harms from the prohibition of cannabis and these are largely due to arrests of users. A very interesting fact is it has been shown that the drug policy control-ling cannabis really doesn't make any difference to the prevalence of its use. I mean while the control system is liberal or draconian doesn't seem to affect how many people use cannabis. Which really rather kind of makes it rather a waste of time to have these vast criminalization systems in place.

Prohibition causes more harms than it avoids. So it's a system which isn't working in particular regards with cannabis. Which is a very special issue because it's the most widely used drug, illegal drug, by a very long way. Interestingly, if it was withdrawn from the international prohibition system, the whole system would collapse. Because without cannabis, really the number of people using il-legal substances is too small, one to two percent, to warrant the vast expenditure, in both finances and human suffering, that the war on drugs involve.

DB: I have become aware in the last, I say the last five or six years, of the pos-sibility that drugs like LSD could be used to help those that are grieving or having other mental problems and that I've heard that MDMA; ecstasy, could perhaps be useful for our thousands of soldiers that are coming back from these horrible wars with Post Traumatic Stress Disorder and yet the government scientific com-munity seems unwilling to do those types of studies. Can we talk about that?

AMANDA FEILDING: When LSD was discovered, by Albert Hoffman in 1943, in the years that followed, the 40's and 50's and indeed the beginning of the 60's, it was hailed as a wonder drug by psychiatrists and psychotherapists and there were the thousands of scientific papers written about the wonderful, possible root to healing illness that these substances made possible.

Then with the escalation of the youth culture using these substances, the es-tablishment got into kind of a panic and as we all know they became prohibited to such a degree that one couldn't even do scientific research with them. I mean, that is an amazingly high level of restriction that one couldn't even get permission to use them in science.

I was very conscious of both the potential benefits and how much society is impoverishing itself by not opening up the possible ways to use these substances to the benefit of mankind. So a very major aim of the Beckley Foundation was to open the doors of scientific research to this category of substances, the psy-chedelics, including MDMA, which had been closed off since the middle 60's or 70's.

There're many, many different areas of potential use where they can be, as you said, to help alleviate suffering and the dying and people with terrible traumas that they can't reach by normal techniques of psychotherapy and also for transformational religious, spiritual experiences. There's a whole wealth of different uses and possibly even things like age related declining cerebral circulation.

Socrates and Plato and all of the great stars of the classical world all went to the ceremony of the great mystery at Eleusis, where they took the sacred potion, which was based on psychoactive substances. So the whole of the classical world, which our society is based on, had as their central sacrifice, the experience of altered states of consciousness.

In some way, down the century, thru Christianity and then these substances have got relegated into the world of criminality and the kind of underbelly of society and I think that's the great tragedy. We need to re-look at this. Hopefully society will realize the potential benefits that can be got for both the individual and society by a more rational attitude to altered states of consciousness.

Potentially valuable insights can be got from them and we need to balance attitudes and hopefully in the coming shift in consciousness we will get a better grasp on the true dangers and potential benefits this category of chemicals can bring to humanity.

ROB KAMPIA

Rob Kampia is co-founder and executive director of the Marijuana Policy Project, the largest nonprofit organization in the U.S. that is solely dedicated to ending cannabis prohibition. Century of Lies / June 30, 2013.

DB: Progress in regards to the understanding about marijuana, cannabis is really expanding on a daily basis isn't it?

ROB KAMPIA: Yes, the American people are understanding more and more that marijuana is safer than alcohol, for example, and no one's ever overdosed on it. It was really clear to me when I testified before the Texas Legislature a couple months ago that there were legislators who wanted to do more but they felt constrained because they were worried that their constituents were going to be angry with them. In fact it's the first time that I've ever testified anywhere where the legislators said right at the hearing in front of the TV cameras that he wanted to know how he could sell this to his constituents. He's asking me for advice to take home with him so he could not get his butt kicked by constituents at the town hall forums that he'll be having during the next year and one-half.

DB: I think he might be surprised at the support that he would actually gather here in Texas. A Scripps-Howard poll was conducted on Texas residents and I think it was 75 perhaps 76% were in favor of medical marijuana.

ROB KAMPIA: That number that came out about 10 years ago; there's also been other polling that has shown that the support for medical marijuana is always in the 70s in Texas specifically. Also there's a higher level of support for legalization and decriminalization in Texas than what I think a lot of people would guess. I think we have a shot at really moving legislation in a big way in the 2015 session.

DB: Now the Marijuana Policy Project is not just focused in Texas. You guys have a national organization. You have been instrumental in helping bring about changes in many of the United States. Let's talk about some of those efforts.

ROB KAMPIA: We've had 4 huge victories recently. The biggest one was legalizing marijuana in Colorado in November. That's the first time that anyone had done that in the history of the world. That was obviously a huge one. Then we've just had 3 victories in 3 state legislatures. One was passing a medical marijuana bill in Illinois. Another was passing a medical marijuana bill in New Hampshire and the third was decriminalizing marijuana possession in Vermont. The governor of Vermont just signed the bill right as this conference was starting. That was a nice little shot in the arm.

DB: I've been wondering and wasn't it just yesterday that Maine considered legalization outright? Didn't make it but it was voted on.

ROB KAMPIA: Right, the Maine House of Representatives fell 3 votes short of legalizing marijuana. The vote was something like 71—67. That was with us not even having a lobbying firm there. We had a legislator who is deeply committed to the cause and was serving as the lobbyist essentially and my organization has one full-time employee who has been roaming the halls in Augusta. Without spending any money on TV ads or radio ads or lobbying firms or pressure tactics, the thing almost passed, and that gives us the feeling that if we could almost get it through the legislature with almost no money then we can actually pass a ballot initiative in Maine. So Maine is on the docket for legalization.

RICHARD LEE

After leaving his hometown of Houston, Texas for Oakland, California, Richard Lee, a paraplegic confined to a wheelchair, founded a medical cannabis dispensary and Oaksterdam University, where people receive professional training for the medical cannabis industry. He invested more than one million dollars in the effort to legalize cannabis in California. As noted in his mother Ann's transcript, Richard's activism has influenced thousands of people to work for drug reform. Cultural Baggage / July 21, 2013.

DB: Tell us about the differences you perceive between Oakland and Houston.

RICHARD LEE: Oh, completely different. The attitude up here in northern California as compared to Texas much more open to medical marijuana and to cannabis utilization so it's hard to compare but there is a strong Libertarian bend to the Houston area and I think that gives a lot of hope to things changing here in Texas.

My parents are long-time Republicans and are big proponents of ending cannabis prohibition. They've come around and seen that this really is a Republican issue. If you believe in smaller government and more personal responsibility you should be for taxing and regulating cannabis to adults similar to the way we treat alcohol.

Nobody looks back at alcohol prohibition and says that it was a success. We all know that it just created more crime and didn't stop people from drinking. The same thing is happening with cannabis prohibition. The Republicans are ... more and more Republicans, at least, not all of them by any means but more and more are starting to wake up to that.

DB: A few weeks back I interviewed the Police Chief of Houston, Charles McClelland, and he talked about the racial disparity and the implementation of the drug laws in regards to marijuana use and he was calling for our elected officials to reexamine and redirect this policy.

RICHARD LEE: The one big opponent we have is law enforcement. In general we see the Sheriff's associations and the Police Chief associations who are against ending cannabis prohibition but we also see more and more law enforcement coming out and seeing the futility of it. They realize that it's not working.

We saw law enforcement in Washington State being in favor of I-502—their legalization referendum that passed last year. We have LEAP—Law Enforcement Against Prohibition. Your listeners can look them up and support them. They are a group of law enforcement that realizes that prohibition needs to end.

DB: Back in the election in the 2010 season you invested over one million dollars trying to get marijuana legalized in the state of California.

I've interviewed dozens of people since that effort and nearly all of them say that it was your sparking the fire that led to the legalization in Colorado and Washington State.

RICHARD LEE: That's very gratifying to hear. I have seen other quotes from other people who say they got started during the Prop 19 campaign. That's what we really hope to achieve with Prop 19—to get the message out there, the issue on the table and to encourage lots of other people to get involved.

ANN LEE

Ann and Bob Lee are the proud parents of several children; amongst them is Richard Lee, the founder of Oaksterdam University in Oakland, California. Ann is the founder of a new organization: Republicans Against Marijuana Prohibition. Cultural Baggage / May 19, 2013.

DB: Ann, tell us about that new organization.

ANN LEE: It got started at a NORML convention last year in October. I know the exact date because we were there at the time of Richard's 50th birthday which was October 7 th of last year. In talking to different people and while I was on a panel, it turned out that three of the five of us were Republicans, and we all deplored the drug war and think that the drug war goes against every Republican philosophy of principle in which we believe—smaller government, fiscal responsibility and less intrusion in your private life. The drug war flouts all of that. We now have a webpage http://republicansagainstmarijuanaprohibition.org

I think there are some things that need to be publicized. Certainly a myth needs to be dispelled that by supporting the drug war you are supporting law and order when, in truth, nothing could be further from the truth. The drug war supports bad law, much disorder and great, great injustice. There is so much injustice that we now have the documents that show we now have the new "Jim Crow." Michelle Alexander documents everything. She does not whitewash anybody. No president since Nixon cannot be blamed in some way—some more than others.

DB: I want to come back to the thought that politicians have been reluctant to speak.

ANN LEE: I'm so angry with that. I'm very angry with what we were not able to do with the legislature. I am really angry. You can't even tell the judge or jury why you are using marijuana. This was the bill that we tried to get through. If you had been there and heard 30 to 40 people speak in favor of the bill—not one person spoke against it. If you had sat there and heard our veterans—one from Viet Nam but most of them from Iraq or Afghanistan—who have suffered so much, who have had such injuries from service to our country, and it turns out that the best relief that they can get is from marijuana. Now the sad part or ironic part is that for them if they lived in a state that supported a person's right to use marijuana medically they could use marijuana with the approval of the VA but what a price they have to pay for living in Texas.

It is strange that people do not want to face the truth because they have had these long-held beliefs. I can relate to that because until 1990 I had believed all the lies and propaganda that my government had put out about marijuana. In fact, I've been quoted many times as saying, "It's the weed of the devil."

But even if that were true, even if marijuana was harmful why was I not smart enough to know that prohibiting it is not the answer?! They found that out with alcohol prohibition.

ETHAN NADELMANN

Ethan Nadelmann is the founder and executive director of the Drug Policy Alliance, a New York City-based non-profit organization working to end the War on Drugs. Described by Rolling Stone as, "The driving force for the legalization of marijuana in America," Ethan Nadelmann is known as a high profile critic and commentator on U.S. and international drug control policies. Ethan has been our guest more than 70 times on DTN. Below are excerpts from a few of those interviews. First up Century of Lies / December 10, 2008.

DB: Last week on the op-ed page of *The Wall Street Journal*, Mr. Ethan Nadelmann went mano a mano with the drug czar John Walters. At times I'm going to try to play the part of John Walters and let you respond to some of the things he said in his, I'll just say it, ridiculous posturing. Let's talk about what you put forward there, just last week.

ETHAN NADELMANN: One of the key points I made in that piece was that Americans back in the late 20's and early 30's made a fundamental distinction, and that distinction was between the problems associated with the misuse of alcohol and the problems that stemmed from alcohol prohibition. You can see cirrhosis and drunkenness and all the accidents are all about the alcohol itself, but Al Capone and organized crime and violence and corruption and overflowing jail cells and prison cells and courthouses packed to the gills and widening disrespect for the law and even many of the overdoses and the fatalities from people drinking industrial alcohol.

All of that stuff, people understood was not just about booze. In fact, it was really about a failed prohibitionist policy. Now, jump forward to today. Same thing is true today. Look at the half million people behind bars tonight, for drug law violation. Look at the almost two million drug arrests, each year. Look at, although the violence is not what it was in the late 80's, still significant drug related violation in this country and dramatically, when you look abroad in places like Mexico or Central America or Afghanistan or Columbia.

Then you look at what's going on, in terms of corruption and you look what's going on in terms of disrespect for the law and you look in terms of what's going on in diversion of judicial resources and you look at the overdose fatalities, from people using drugs in conditions which are more dangerous, because they're illegal. So, the analogy is very powerful.

DB: Ethan, as I said, I'm reading from Walters post in The Wall Street Journal, "Our policy has been a success. Although that success is one of Washington's best kept secrets." Your thoughts?

ETHAN NADELMANN: There's normally this game that goes on whereby, whoever's the drug czar, points to whatever indicators of adolescent drug use are declining and says, 'Look, we're winning, we're winning.' So if marijuana use has gone down the last few years or if methamphetamine use peaked a couple of years ago, they'll say, 'Look, we're winning right now.' Of course, the thing Walter's didn't want to talk about is that the biggest, fastest growing drug problem in America and many other countries today has to do with pharmaceutical drugs—drugs that are being prescribed appropriately and then used inappropriately or prescribed inappropriately or what have you, and that's an issue.

DB: OK now, here again, quoting John Walters, "The number of work place

tests that are positive for cocaine is down, sharply, to the lowest levels on record."
Why do you think that is, Ethan?

ETHAN NADELMANN: Well, cocaine had its heyday, back in the 80's. So
we're not seeing a hell of a lot of use of cocaine, in the workplace. I think people
have gotten savvier, if they're going to use this stuff. I've seen reports that cocaine
has actually been increasing in the last few years. But people are getting savvier.
They know if you use cocaine on a Friday night, you're not going to test positive
on a Monday. I think also that there's a greater variety of stimulants being used
in our society. Cocaine has lost its special place in the echelon of stimulants being
used by Americans. I think we see a reduction in cocaine use but keep in mind,
the use of cocaine in the workplace and by the middle and upper-middle class
was never the really a major problem. There were obviously people who got hurt
and people who did stupid things and got addicted. But overwhelmingly, probably
at least 90% of the people using cocaine at that echelon of society, were not creating problems. In fact, for many people working in the financial sector or in
sales, cocaine was actually the thing they saw as making them if not more effective, keeping their energy levels up. Now people age out of that and the fad and
the fashion changes. But when you look at the bigger drug problem, when you
look at rising overdose fatalities each year, when you look at incarceration, I
think his claims are a bit of a joke.

DB: Let's talk about marijuana, and here I have the words of John Walters
recorded here at the James A. Baker Institute just about a month ago.

DRUG CZAR WALTERS: "What's the effect of marijuana allegedly? Well,
it's kind of a nebulous and people say, 'When I smoke marijuana, if I'm depressed, if I have a headache, if I have pain, if I have writers block, I feel better.'
Well, of course you do, it's an intoxicant. You'd feel better if you smoked crack.
You'd feel better if you took meth. You'd feel better if you took heroin. You'd
feel better if you drank Jack Daniels is sufficient quantities. That doesn't make
any of those medicines and it's a ludicrous argument that's been made here."

ETHAN NADELMANN: The interesting thing about John Walters, I've
known him for a very long time, and he has been the single greatest failure as a
drug czar. I mean, almost nobody in America knows his name. He will not engage
in debate, because I think he knows the claims he's making cannot be defended.
But the bottom line is, marijuana is broadly used and accepted as a medicine.
That's been true for many hundreds of years.

In fact, most of the drugs that are illegal; I mean, cocaine has it's medicinal
uses, the stimulants, the amphetamines have substantial medicinal uses. All
the opioids, everything from morphine, Dilaudid, Demerol, Fentanyl, to Di-
amorphine, the name of heroin. These all can be used recreationally. They all
can create horrible problems of addiction, and they all are used and recommended and prescribed medicinally. So the distinction that Walter's making
is truly, truly absurd.

Cultural Baggage / August 30, 2009

DB: The situation in California with the major fire out in Santa Cruz started by some immigrants growing marijuana, your thoughts on that?

ETHAN NADELMANN: When people are growing drugs illegally sometimes some of them are less likely to be respectful of the environment and take proper precautions. So the fire that was presumably started by some Mexican drug growers in the California hills, I mean that is not the first time that something like that has happened. It is not something that only involves Mexicans growing marijuana in the United States. It has undoubtedly happened with other people as well. So that is just one of the costs of a prohibitionist policy. Same thing with all the illegal meth labs blowing up in peoples back yards and people getting hurt, both people living there and their children and law enforcement raiding these places. That is once again a consequence of prohibition.

If you look at the people growing coca down in Bolivia, the ones doing it legally for domestic production, are doing it in ways that are environmentally responsible. The land is properly terraced. They are using the proper sorts of fertilizers, what have you. There are no negative environmental consequences. In fact growing coca is probably the next best thing for the environment after leaving the jungle in place.

On the other hand when you look where coca is being produced illegally, you have people who are working often times for criminal enterprises. They are dumping the chemicals in rivers. They are not being attentive to the environment. Their number one priority is not being exposed, not being seen. And so you know these are all arguments for moving in the direction of having a sensible regulatory policy rather than continuing with the failed prohibitionist policy.

Now with respect to if there was a really intensive crackdown on the border as we had under Nixon with something called Operation Intercept and as we had under I think it was Ronald Reagan Commissioner William von Rob, the customs commissioner. What tends to happen when those sort of things happen is that you get a brief reduction in the flow of drugs from Mexico to the US. But the best study on the impact of Operation Intercept in the early 1970s which shut down the border for a few weeks, I think it was by a guy named Lawrence Guberman was that the export of marijuana to the United States dropped but that the export of heroin increased. That essentially traffickers who had the ability to switch from marijuana to heroin did so because that was going to be easier to smuggle and more lucrative.

DB: There are reforms being mandated out in California. The feds are demanding they reduce their prison population by some forty thousand I think it is. And here in Houston; the feds just did an inspection of our jail so totally overcrowded and gave it a D- for lack of security and medical services and so forth.

ETHAN NADELMANN: Well you know most law enforcement leaders give lip service to the need for more prevention and treatment. But when push comes to shove and when it is about resources and when it is about changing old ways and doing things that's not easy. I mean it is not as if, you know there are some very intelligent and thoughtful people in law enforcement but my impression often times is that there is not a huge number of them and that to the extent that they are, they are often times not thinking systemically. They are not thinking about the bigger issues.

Century of Lies / February 20, 2011

ETHAN NADELMANN: I think what you see is that Mexico is dealing with the sort of problems that Chicago dealt with during alcohol prohibition times fifty. I mean, the levels of corruption, violence and power of organized crime, fear, you name it and so much of that being fueled by a failed prohibitionist policy. I think that's why if you look and see the last three Mexican presidents, you see Ernesto Zedillo joining, firstly, the Latin American Commission and now in this new Global Commission that is pushing to break the taboo on discussing all drug policy options, including legalization.

Its why we you see the former President Vicente Fox has evolved for saying, "Let's put this on the table" to becoming a fairly strong advocate of legalization and you see even Calderón the current President who seems to have his own personal, moral reservations about the issue of drugs, nonetheless acknowledging that this needs to be part of the dialog, as well.

So what you have is the elite in Mexico, is a willingness and even a desire to put this really on the table. Then you look over at Columbia and you see President Santos who, you know, right now is maybe the most popular leader in his own country of any president in the world. He has 80-90% approval ratings and he's very openly saying, "You know, if legalization is the best way to reduce the crime and violence then maybe that's the way to go and we need a debate about this. We need to open this up." So, I think that the continuing problems of prohibition related crime, violence and corruption are actually providing additional momentum for opening up the debate more broadly in the US.

WILLIE NELSON

In 2010, the Marijuana Policy Project sponsored a major fundraiser in Austin, Texas. The headliner was Mr. Willie Nelson along with Asleep At the Wheel. I managed to wrangle a 15 minute discussion "on the bus"with Willie and Ray from "the Wheel." Not sure why it took me so long (best pot ever?) to turn on the recorder, but here is the transcript of what I recorded and broadcast on two 4:20 Drug War NEWS Reports.

4:20 Drug War News / August 17, 2007

DB: Last week Willie Nelson, Asleep at the Wheel, adn Carolyn Wonderland all played up in Austin at the Austin Freedom Fest to raise money for the Marijuana Policy Project, NORML and for the Wo/Mens Alliance for Medical Marijuana out in Santa Cruz, California. I got a chance to speak with Willie about marijuana and here's a little bit about that discussion. I'm telling Willie about Law Enforcement Against Prohibition and how we fight for the legalization for all drugs and, in particular, for medical marijuana patients.

DB: We work very much to fight for those patients who need medical marijuana. Valerie Corral, one of your beneficiaries...we work with MPP, with NORML...we try to bring the truth forward and I applaud you for your efforts, sir. What would you like to say to my audience out there...those that are having to fight for the right for marijuana?

WILLIE NELSON: First of all thank you for fighting and thank you for standing up for your rights. I was just telling some folks today Kinky Freeman now has a cigar out with my name on it somewhere and someone was asking what I thought all about that. I don't have any problem with it at all. I remember my friend Billy Cooper...somebody said something to him about his drinking and his smoking and he said, "It's my mouth. I'll haul coal in it if I want to."

DB: That's the point. They talk about the danger of marijuana and yet alcohol and tobacco are killing hundreds of thousands and I don't think they've found the first marijuana casualty yet.

WILLIE NELSON: No, they haven't. Once they realize how much money they are missing, once they realize how many millions and billions that the illegal drug dealers are making then they can step in there. It'll help the farmers. It'll help everybody. Once they start saying, "Wait a minute. We should tax it and regulate it like we do tobacco and alcohol."

DB: I want to thank you for the great groups you've brought together at the Austin Fest and the fact that it gives us the chance to bring that truth forward. The news media, the corporate media is gathering around. They're giving it some attention. Don't we all need to do more to bring this truth forward, to speak up?

WILLIE NELSON: Absolutely—whatever you're talking about...whether it's this or whatever. If you have something on issue that you'd like to see changed you gotta get out there and do something about it. You can't just sit still and not talk about it and, you know, you're the one that can start it.

DB: Over the years I've admired your music. I think I remember a High Time's article talking about your younger days when your house burned down and one of the things you salvaged from the house was Panama Red...

WILLIE NELSON: [laughing[Yeah, I knew there were going to be difficult times ahead so I salvaged what I thought was important. Plus it was in my guitar case with my guitar so I didn't want to lose that either.

4:20 Drug War News August 18, 2007

WILLIE NELSON: Let me ask you a question. Why should we legalize drugs?

DB: Basically because we're funding the cartels, the terrorists...it's the reason most of these violent street gangs exist, sir.

WILLIE NELSON: That's a great answer and I got the question off your shirt there. It was a great opening.

DB: If you would consider the brochure from LEAP. You don't have to be a cop or former cop to join. We would consider it an honor if you would just think about it.

WILLIE NELSON: Well, count me in. What do I do?

DB: Well, I think you just did it right there.

WILLIE NELSON: Well, alright...count me in there.

What you guys are doing takes more balls and guts and nerves than what I'm doing. I'm just a guitar player. You guys are policemen and you ride a lot of heat for what you do and say—a lot more than I do so I applaud you for doing it and God bless all of you.

STEPH SHERER

Steph Sherer is the founder and Executive Director of Americans for Safe Access. She has become the foremost international leader and expert on medical cannabis patient advocacy. Her highly acclaimed strategic skill in keeping patients needs at the forefront of the medical marijuana debate has brought safe and legal access to medical cannabis to millions of Americans. Steph is a medical cannabis patient with over fourteen years of experience servicing and managing non-profit businesses and community organizations. Cultural Baggage / February 17, 2013.

DB: One of my oldest friends in drug reform is Steph Sherer. I met her about 10 years ago. She was then helping to form a new organization to bring respect and common sense to the subject of cannabis and its use. I've seen the organization grow. I've even been there for a couple of the counter-DEA demonstrations that ASA helps put together. I've seen the growth and the respect for your organization over those same 10 years. It's amazing the progress isn't it?

STEPH SHERER: Thank you. When you're in the trenches day to day you don't always get to appreciate how far we've come. Having the 10 year anniversary this year gave me some time to pause and really remember what things were like 10 years ago. Yet we're still trying to end this federal conflict. It seems like there's so many raids and people going to prison.

I think if you put that in perspective of when we started ASA there were only about 30,000 Americans that were legal medical marijuana patients. There were only 11 distribution centers in the entire country and they were all in the Bay Area of California. Move forward 10 years and a bunch of grey hairs and we have 18 states with medical marijuana laws. You've got the District of Colombia with medical cannabis. There are over 1 million Americans that are using legal medical cannabis at the state level. Every day we hear more and more great news. We're turning a corner of mainstream America. We also have a lot of work to do.

DB: Yes we do, but you mentioned 11 distribution centers in the Bay Area and now we're up to thousands across America.

STEPH SHERER: That's right.

DB: You said we have a lot of work to do and indeed we do. There are still those few recalcitrant bastards saying we need to lock them up and all of this madness over a plant that's never killed anybody. Those people are fewer and fewer as time passes right?

STEPH SHERER: Something that I think that medical cannabis advocates forget about is how much an individual can do to change these laws. Often we sit around and we think about these big conspiracy theories against us. I'm not saying that we don't—we definitely do. I think that our biggest enemy is that individuals don't get involved.

When I first opened our office here in D.C. in 2006 I spent some time going around to all of the offices of members of congress that represented medical marijuana states and something I heard time and time again was, "We're just not hearing about this from our constituents."

My first reaction was that they were lying to me but then I started incorporating into my public speaking to ask people if they've met with their members of congress or their senators or if they've even reached out to them and I am always shocked to find that about 1% of the room raises their hands. These are people that …if they're coming to hear me speak they're obviously pretty committed to medical cannabis.

I think that our message of Americans for Safe Access is—here I'm leaving for this conference next weekend—it's up to us. Our representatives aren't elected to represent the laws of the land. If that were true all of the congressmen of Rhode Island would be protecting laws about not having ice cream cones in your back pocket.

The reality is the elected officials are in Washington and they're representing their constituents. If you think about everything that's happening in this country right now and all of the people that they are hearing from they're not going to just jump on medical cannabis unless their constituents ask them to.

DB: In tandem with that thought is when these laws are up for review or the discussion comes about one of the main players that steps forward and thinks it's their business to put forward their opinion is law enforcement and prosecutors. They're just supposed to represent the law not craft the law. Your response?

STEPH SHERER: We definitely see law enforcement lining up for opposition against medical cannabis and I think the thing that we need to remember is yes, law enforcement and everyone involved in the prison industrial complex is there to carry out the laws of the land. It isn't their job to create policy. I'm definitely always frustrated to see how active they are but the truth is if an elected official heard from a patient as often as they heard from law enforcement they would be hearing another side of the story.

It's easy for us (especially those of us who aren't in Washington, D. C.) to think that the DEA, law enforcement and Partnership for Drug Free America are constantly walking the halls of congress lobbying against us. Someone who has been in D.C. for over 6 years now it's just not the case.

What's really happening on the 101 basis is that these agencies are meeting with our elected officials on a regular basis and when medical cannabis comes up they definitely say their opinions to the elected officials. The optimism I have after 10 years of trying to push a compromise between the feds and the states is that we haven't all done our part.

If just a percentage of the 80% of Americans that believe that patients should have access to medical cannabis called their members of congress and told them that they wanted them to change the federal laws we would be having a much different dialogue with the federal government.

I know that there is definitely an opposition mounted against us and I know that there is often severe discrimination for those of us who use medical cannabis but no one else is going to do this for us. There may be a couple billionaires that will help pass a law but in each one of these states where the laws have changed it's patient advocates that are implementing these laws, that are making sure that regulations get passed and working with city government.

I would just encourage anyone that's listening that cares about medical cannabis and wants to see safe access for every American to really think about what they can do to help that change happen. For me I always say I can complain as much as I do.

If I'm out there I get some latitude to be able to complain about things not changing. If you're just sitting around with friends and talking about how things aren't changing, know that part of that is because you are not being active and being a part of that change.

ERIC STERLING

Since 1989, Eric E. Sterling has been the President of The Criminal Justice Policy Foundation, a private non-profit educational organization that helps educate the nation about criminal justice issues and failed global drug policy. Mr. Sterling frequently lectures at colleges, universities, and professional societies throughout the nation and is regularly interviewed by the national news media. Mr. Sterling was Counsel to the U.S. House of Representatives Committee on the Judiciary from 1979 until 1989. On the staff of the Subcommittee on Crime, (Rep. William J. Hughes (D-NJ), Chairman), he was responsible for drug enforcement, gun control, money laundering, organized crime, pornography, terrorism, corrections, and military assistance to law enforcement, among many issues. He was a principal aide in developing the Comprehensive Crime Control Act of 1984, the Anti-Drug Abuse Acts of 1986 and 1988, and other laws. He has traveled to South America, Europe and many parts of the United States to examine the crime and drug problems first hand. In the 96th Congress, he worked on comprehensively rewriting the Federal Criminal Code. Mr. Sterling was honored by the U.S. Bureau of Alcohol, Tobacco and Firearms, and the U.S. Postal Service. Cultural Baggage / November 20, 2011.

DB: It's been a while since I've been in the studio and I had a couple of letters arrive from some prisoners in the Estelle unit. One of them, 68-years-old, got caught with some heroin. He's now behind bars, locked up. He's on dialysis, got heart problems, Hep-C and cancer. He is, needless to say, a significant burden on the state of Texas.

ERIC STERLING: Certainly it's expensive to treat…to house prisoners who have medical conditions and the cost of imprisonment have grown dramatically as both the populations have grown, as the length of sentences have grown many times longer and every state and the federal government that are struggling to figure out how best to use taxpayers' resources, our taxes, have to be aware that keeping people locked up is a very, very expensive proposition.

DB: Yes sir and then, if we can, talk about the other gentleman. He was caught 17 years ago with 2 rocks of crack. Now this was his third offense. He got life. And, again, that's hardly a good investment of our tax dollars.

ERIC STERLING: It's important to sort of recognize that congress and legislatures in 1985, 86, 87, 88 reacted with a degree of hysteria about the crack cocaine epidemic. There's no question that crack cocaine use and trafficking were serious problems in many communities and people who have compulsive cocaine habits are buying cocaine on the order of perhaps 10 times a day.

Also that requires a crime that gets committed to get the money before you can buy the crack—whether it's prostitution, breaking into a car, shoplifting. This crime disorder was a very serious problem but this was not a problem that could be solved by locking people up for the kinds of sentences that used to be reserved for the most heinous of all criminals. Yet those sentences were imposed and there are tens of thousands of people who are serving sentences that everyone in criminal justice recognizes is excessively long.

What's so depressing to people like me is that President Obama has completely failed to use his constitutional power of pardon and reprieve to begin to let out of federal prison after 10 or 15 years people who are still serving life sentences. This power was created by the framers of the constitution—it's in the same sentence of the constitution that says the President is the Commander in Chief—a power that all the presidents used. And this power of pardon and reprieve was used by all the presidents up until the last few. President Obama has used it the least of any president in our history.

Yet at the same time the President's asking for hundreds of millions of dollars to build new federal prisons when by simply letting out men and women who have served 20 years already for what we recognize as a low-level drug offence could free up the prison space that they feel is necessary. A few rocks of cocaine is in the global drug trade a tiny amount.

What happened, in part, is that many people failed to sort of understand the difference between being a low-level drug offender and a major drug offender. What got lost...we had congressman like Bill McCullum from Florida who would say, "So you want to reduce the sentence so you really want to legalize these?!" We're saying that these are not serious crimes. Before these mandatory minimums you still could get sentenced up to 20 years for trafficking in cocaine. That's a very long sentence. The mandatory minimums and the sentencing guidelines together then meant that people got mandatory life sentences because of the way those laws work together.

When you think about congress wanting to go after high-level traffickers... An organization, like a Mexican cartel, that brings in, over the course of a month, a ton of cocaine into the country—that's one million grams. And yet the mandatory sentences get started at 5,000 grams of powder cocaine. That gets you 10 years to life imprisonment. That's 11 pounds. That fits into an oil riggers lunch pail or a school kid's backpack. That's not major trafficking—that 12 pounds.

And so what has happened is when you look at the data from the justice department overwhelmingly they focused on low-level offenders and they're not focusing on the high-level offenders. At least if you believed that drug enforcement made sense the federal government should be focused on the highest level of trafficker not the lowest level of traffickers that could be prosecuted in state courts around the country. So there's been a very serious misuse of these laws. People served incredibly long sentences. We're not getting any public safety benefit from this enormous expense.

DB: The expenditure involved in maintaining or continuing these long sentences is becoming obvious to more and more politicians, but sadly not enough of them. They did change the structure of the crack versus powder sentences to where you can have little bit more crack without having...

ERIC STERLING: What happened is that in August 2010 congress sent to President Obama the Fair Sentencing Act of 2010 and President Obama signed it on August 04. What that did is that it raised the quantity of crack cocaine that triggered the mandatory minimums. The old law was 5 grams. 1 gram is like a Sweet and Low packet. It's a couple of sugar packets. And it raised it from 5 grams to 28 grams which is an ounce.

The other quantity, 50 grams of crack cocaine which is the weight of an ordinary candy bar, that got you 10 years to life—that was raised to 280 grams. That's 10 ounces—slightly more than one-half of a pound. It's not that much cocaine. The thing to remember about crack cocaine is that it's made very close to where it's sold. It's made locally. The crack that is sold from a crack house in Houston is made in Houston. It's not made in Mexico. It's not made in Colombia.

The powder cocaine is. The powder cocaine comes in in very large quantities. The federal government should not be prosecuting low-level local offenders.

There are only 25,000 federal drug cases a year and yet the states do over one million drug cases in a year. So the federal cases should be reserved for the highest level traffickers.

So the Fair Sentencing Act of 2010, by raising crack quantities to 28 grams or 280 grams, made only a very tiny little change in the trigger quantities for the mandatory minimums. What we have yet to see is will any major change in the department of justice occur. What we know is in the most recent data overwhelmingly the offenders are still low-level offenders. They're overwhelmingly people of color. They remain overwhelmingly unjust. So it was a minor fix after many years of struggling. Nothing to get particularly excited about unfortunately.

DB: No sir. Just 1500 or so prisoners will get out early, if I remember right.

ERIC STERLING: That's correct. The U.S. Sentencing Commission over the objection of the Justice Department ruled that the sentencing guidelines that they changed for people who had sentences between 5 grams and 28 grams or between 50 grams and 280 grams of crack could seek retroactive application of the new sentencing guidelines. This is going to affect a tiny number of prisoners. There are over 100,000 federal drug prisoners. 1,600, 1.6% is a very small fraction and the average sentence reduction is about 2 years for those who are getting their sentences reduced. It's a tiny, tiny change.

DB: Now, Eric, at the reform conference out there in Los Angeles as usual I didn't get to attend too many of the individual speaker's groups but you spoke at one. Why don't you tell us what it was about, what you brought to that conference and, perhaps, what you are taking away.

ERIC STERLING: What I brought to the conference probably is not of great interest to your listeners. The point of the program that I was on was that people who are concerned about drug policy reform need to work with people who are recovering from drug addiction. People who are recovering from drug addiction are people who very often understand what's been wrong with our current system of drug control.

In many cases they've been victimized by that system. They understand that the system didn't protect them or their family members. The other thing, of course, is that these folks in addition to perhaps being potential allies have a very high degree of credibility with policymakers and the general public. People who have successfully fought their addictions and can say, "I'm abstinent now. I've got my life in order. I recognize the problem that drug addiction had with me. I speak as someone with that experience." They have a great deal of credibility to speak about the problems of drugs if they're not trying to get drug law changed so they can go back to using the drugs that so badly messed up their lives.

To the extent that the drug policy reform movement focuses intensely on the liberty interest, the liberty to use drugs there is a serious disconnect between the reform community and the recovery community. I wanted to make the point to the people working in drug policy reform that if we want to build alliances with people who are in recovery then our language, our conferences, our activities must make them feel comfortable and safe.

If I were a person in recovery and I felt that my recovery was in danger by going to a reform conference—that I would find triggers or stimuli that might jeopardize my recovery—it would be a dangerous place for me and I wouldn't come and I wouldn't participate and so that was essentially the message I was trying to make. The drug policy reform movement needs to think about how it functions, what its language is in order to continue to expand the alliances that are important for its ultimate success. That was the point that I was trying to make.

DB: Your discussion there brought me back to what kind of aggravates me sometimes is that the Drug Czar will hold a conference and he'll have people who will come forward and talk about the day they got busted was the best day of their life. I see that as confessing their sins—as somehow jumping through hoops in order to go out the exit door. Your response to that.

ERIC STERLING: Remember those people who are saying that the day that they were busted was the best day of their life are people who are at that time free and on the street. These are not the people who are sitting in prison now with 5 or 10 or 20 or lifetime sentences.

There isn't any question that there are people who found that their getting arrested led to a self-examination that got them into treatment. But it is wrong to think then that using the justice system and penalizing millions of people is a good social policy because some people found it helped them get into recovery. Those people may not be dead from drug overdoses but it may be very hard for them to get a job because of the lifetime collateral consequences that drug arrests create for millions of people.

It's important to realize that you have to look not at single anecdotes, one person who says, you know, "Oh, it was so great that I got arrested because then I got the treatment I needed." When there are hundreds of thousands or millions for whom it didn't help at all.

RICK STEVES

Richard "Rick" Steves is an American author and television personality focusing on European travel. He is the host of the American Public Television series Rick Steves' Europe, has a public radio travel show, Travel with Rick Steves, and has authored various location-specific travel guides. Unvarnished Truth TV, October 19, 2007.

DB: I heard during your speech today at the NORML conference, you talked about certain nation's police forces taking a new look at this, a new approach. Do you want to talk about that?

RICK STEVES: Law enforcement wants to help reduce the harm that drug abuse causes a society. I would imagine that motivates a policeman. They care, and there is harm caused to society by drug abuse. I would think it's demoralizing for a policeman who wants to contribute in this area to have to do something that he doesn't believe in.

I think a lot of police officers don't believe that the responsible adult use of marijuana is causing harm to anybody. If you get that out of the way then police officers are free to really tackle the serious problems and make a difference. I would feel better if I was a policeman knowing that I could actually help a society rather than criminalize people who are just exercising what I think is a civil liberty.

DB: Yes, my thought on that is to judge people by their actions not the contents of their pocket.

RICK STEVES: Nobody is saying drug use is good. Nobody is saying kids should smoke pot. All we're saying is let's consider the problem a health issue rather than a criminal issue. Let's be pragmatic about it. Let's learn from Europe from their track record of not arresting adult pot smokers that it is a constructive way to deal with this problem. What's a curious thing to me is that in Europe law enforcement people who are not retired can say this makes sense. Here, in America, I would think most members of LEAP (Law Enforcement Against Prohibition) are retired law enforcement officers.

DB: Exactly, we've had a few...a working Texas warden actually spoke a few years back.

RICK STEVES: That's a sad, sad situation when you can't speak the truth until you are retired.

DB: You also had a phrase that caught my attention dealing with the fact, as you stated, that you are child-rearing, church going pot smoker. We're not the ones kicking in doors, destroying people's lives and futures. I think it's time to claim the moral high ground. Your thoughts?

RICK STEVES: First of all you can't legislate moralities. I don't think the morality of it is an issue. You can't lock up people for watching Playboy. You can say that's moral or immoral. You can't lock up people for being obese. Some people can say that's not good.

I think that the morality issue is not that big of a deal. On the other hand I think that ...I guess I just don't care about the morality issue of it. I don't see any incongruity at all if I am going to enjoy relaxing with a joint and going to the church the next morning, going to work, paying my taxes—I just don't see the connection.

The real bottom line is am I hurting anybody? Am I driving while impaired? I mean, throw the book at them. I wouldn't give those people any sort of slack. I'm talking about people who want to listen to the Beatles and actually hear everything that's in there. There's something to that. That's a beautiful thing.

I'm talking about people who can enjoy a little nuance in what they're eating because they just enjoyed a little bit of marijuana. How can that be evil? It's just not. I try to stay out of the medical marijuana thing because I'm not passionate about it. I think it's an important cause and I understand why people are passionate about it. I'm involved in NORML and drug policy issues because I think it's a civil right for adult, responsible users to enjoy a joint. I think that it's a little bit disingenuous and I think it hurts the credibility of the movement, frankly, to say that we should just do the medical stuff first and then we can get to the issue that we care about after that.

I think from a law enforcement point of view there's a lot of abuse in the medical...sort of a "wink, wink" and "this is a way to get our pot because we've all got our cards" or whatever.

So, I'm not a good defendant of the whole medical marijuana thing. I think it's a distraction and the reality is 50 million Americans smoke pot. They're not criminals and if we arrested them all tomorrow like they'd like to. If they implemented this prohibition thoroughly and effectively this country would be a much less interesting place to live in.

JOY STRICKLAND

Joy Strickland is the founding CEO of Mothers Against Teen Violence in Dallas where we are rethinking drug policy in Texas. The organization's mission is public information, education and advocacy for drug policy reform. It began 17 years ago as a community-based social services organization to fight teen violence, but in 2008 its focus changed to drug policy reform. Recorded in Denver at a Drug Policy Alliance conference. Cultural Baggage / May 8, 2011.

JOY STRICKLAND: I'm not sure about the intent of the drug war, but without dealing with intent, I think we just need to look at the actual impact. What is the reality here today? We are 25% of the world's prison population, and African Americans are being incarcerated a rate 7 times the rate that black men were incarcerated in South Africa under Apartheid . And that, to me, is a jaw-dropping statistic.

DB: Politicians are very adverse to change or at least to changing their ways, are they not?

JOY STRICKLAND: Politicians, as you may know, are not activists. They are not going to lead change. What they're going to do is wait until there is a critical mass for change, groundswell for change, but they're not going to jump out in front of it. So that is, as I see it, the job of the activist. To inform the public, to get the public motivated for change, to help them to see the impact. That's one of the things we are doing with our drug policy forums; we're helping community people see how the drug war impacts those issues that they care about.

Most people care about education but they're not aware of how drug policy impacts education. Most people care about gang violence, but amazingly do not make the connection between gang violence and drug prohibition and how that creates an opportunity for gang violence. And I could go on and on and on down the list, so that's what we have to do. We have to help people, as activists, we've got to craft this message in a way so people can hear it. And because it's such a complex issue and touches in so many areas, it touches so many sectors, you can just see their eyes kind of glaze over if you start trying to explain to them what this is about. So our challenge, I think, is to craft a message in a way that is simple and understandable and will resonate with the community.

It's a part of our foreign policy, the Drug War. It's a dimension of our national policy, and a dimension of our state policy. I'm not an expert in any of them. I'm just a mother who wants a community that is safe, where children can grow and thrive and reach their human potential. And I think when we lock people up for what they choose to put in their bodies, when we lock people up who are in the throes of addiction, I think it's barbaric. It's not only a human rights issue, it's a civil rights issue.

One of the challenges is that the people who are most impacted by drug war policies are the people who are least able to do something about it, right?! Because arresting people and putting them in prison, that only happens to poor people. It does not happen to affluent people. And so the people who are in the middle-class or upper-middle-class, educated, doing well—they don't really see how this impacts them. And that's really a huge quandary. That keeps me up at night, as they say.

DB: I hear of "two steps forward, one step back" going on all across this country, and politicians are still rabid about marijuana for some reason. And yet we are in a city and state (Denver) where much of that hysteria, that paranoia, has gone away. It can be done, do you think, even in Texas?

JOY STRICKLAND: Oh, I believe it can be done in Texas. If I didn't believe it, I would pack up and go home. I'm an optimistic person, a woman of faith. I believe there's hope. I believe in redemption, and I certainly believe it can happen. But I tell you, when you come to a state like Colorado where they have a more progressive take on their drug policy, it's sort of like you're in another world. It could depress you, in some sense, because you realize you have to go back! Where people are still saying, 'They have to lock 'em up if they're using marijuana" or "They're addicted to marijuana, they need to be locked up." But it gives me hope. Being in the room with the people who are on the ground working with hope—that's inspiring to me.

DB: I can taste it, I can feel it, I know it's on that horizon. I know we're approaching a day of reckoning, so to speak. When these politicians can no longer stand forth in their senate or congressional chambers proclaiming their lies again and again. It's up to good folks like us to get this information out, to share it, to motivate, to move people to do something about it. "Morals are on our side," if the discussion can just be had.

JOY STRICKLAND: That's one of the things we do at Mothers Against Teen Violence; we have a monthly drug policy discussion group. It's led by Dr. Martin Delaney from the University of Texas at Arlington. He's a history professor. And it's so important for this discussion to take place in an area, in an atmosphere, were it's not threatening, where people can ask questions, where people can disagree. That is absolutely critical. So that's one of the things that we do every month. Our drug policy forums, those community forums, are another opportunity to have this conversation.

I don't worry so much. I believe it's going to happen. I certainly don't know when it's going to happen, when Texas takes a more progressive stand in terms of drug policy. But I think that if people like us work with a sense of urgency and we are faithful and keep our nose to the grindstone and continue to do it and continue to do it—it's going to happen. Now, I don't know if it's going to be next year or the next decade but it will happen. And when it does, we'll look back and say, "How in the heck did it go on this long?!"

KEITH STROUP

Keith Stroup is an attorney and founder of the National Organization for the Reform of Marijuana Laws. He's the author of It's NORML to Smoke Pot: The 40 Year Fight for Marijuana Smokers' Rights. Century of Lies / June 16, 2013.

DB: We're here in Fort Worth, Texas at the DFW NORML gathering and we have the former head of the National Organization for the Reform of Marijuana Laws.

KEITH STROUP: It's great to be back in Texas. This is where we started 42, 43 years ago. The very first state we went in to was Texas. Back then because you were the worst state. You were locking the most people up for the longest period of time. You've got a lot of rural areas in this state. Traditionally, not just in Texas, the rural areas of most states have been slower to change on this. You're going to have to be patient but I heard somebody this morning make the point— they were determined that Texas will not be last. I guarantee you won't be near last. I think Texas will be in the middle group of states to finally legalize marijuana. You won't be one of the first. We'll have Massachusetts and Oregon and California and probably a couple other New England states by 2016. I don't think Texas will legalize by then, but I am hopeful that you will have stopped arresting smokers by 2016. I think that's a realistic goal.

DB: There was a report issued just last week that talked about 3.7 blacks being arrested for every one white marijuana user, which showed the racial disparity. One of the things I noticed it talked about was my city, my county (Houston, Harris County) being the second leading in that number of arrests.

KEITH STROUP: By the way there were some parts of this country where it was 8:1. 4:1 it is outrageous, of course. The rates of marijuana smoking—for people who might not know—it's consistent across Hispanics, blacks and white. It's about 13%. In a few states in the west and east coast it might go up a couple points, maybe down a little bit in some other areas, but essentially the same percentage of people smoke, regardless of race, but you have places where anywhere from 4 to 8 times as many blacks and Hispanics are being arrested on marijuana charges as whites?! There is only one possible answer—it's racism.

DB: And it started as racism.

KEITH STROUP: Of course, of course. In some ways it's full circle. We are finally coming to grips of the fact that marijuana would have never become illegal if whites were smoking it. If only white people would have been smoking marijuana in the 1930s, it would never have become illegal, but the only people smoking it at those points were Mexican migrant workers and black jazz musicians predominantly, and neither one were held in very high regard. They didn't have much political power at the time.

ACLU really deserves special credit. Harry Levine, who is a professor at the City University of New York, has been working on some of this racial analysis. He started with New York City and then he did 10 other cities. ACLU has embraced that and taken it nationwide. It's a marvelous report. I think it will have incredibly positive benefits to help the movement among people who don't have the slightest sympathy about smoking marijuana but who understand that we cannot have a criminal justice system that has one standard for minorities and one for whites. Major editorials around the country ran during the past week on this subject. Insiders, those of us who work on the issue, have been aware of this for years. What's important is the average American be aware of it and especially elected officials because, I'm serious here, sometimes those of us who smoke marijuana forget that we are in a minority—we are roughly 13%—so for us to have the ability to pass good marijuana laws we have to make arguments that appeal to the 87% of the country who do not smoke.

For example, if it were only smokers, we'd probably all say let's have a tomato model—you can have as much as you want, the government is not involved, you can sell it, give it away, whatever you want to do because, frankly, it's an essentially harmless drug. But it's been 75 years, and you will never get such a system. In order to eliminate three-quarter of one million marijuana arrests a year, you have to make appeals to the 87% who don't smoke. They are now with us for the first time.

During the last couple years we now have majority support, but there are two things that still bother a lot of non-smokers. They want to make sure that if they legalize marijuana they won't have a huge new influx of marijuana-using drivers on the road. That's a reasonable concern. By the way, it's not a real problem because we already drive—the 30 million of us that smoke drive already—so it's not like some new people on the road, but nonetheless we have to be able to answer that question. One thing is we need to develop an effective test for impairment so we don't have to rely on some silly 5 nanogram THC test that measures THC but doesn't measure impairment. It's not like alcohol. So that's important.

The other thing is that we need to demonstrate that there is no significant increase in adolescent use once a state legalizes. We have that chance now with Colorado and Washington. We know that it's harder for kids to get marijuana when it's legalized and regulated because you have an age control, so I think the rates will actually go down, but that is a legitimate concern.

So, again, I think sometimes that those of us who work on the issue forget that we talk to each other and we talk to other smokers and we think that these laws aren't good enough that maybe we can get passed. We're never going to have the perfect law, but let me tell you, Washington State, for example, they've been having 12,000 marijuana arrests per year—they just passed an initiative where that will probably go down to not more than a couple thousand arrests per year. That's worth a hell of a lot, even though they didn't allow home cultivation. I very much favor home cultivation and so does NORML, and even though they included a 5 nanogram "per say" DUID provision…it's not a perfect law but, for God sake, the importance of a few states breaking through, thumbing their nose at the federal government is so important that we can put up with imperfections. We'll be back and fix those laws.

DB: I have talked in the past about the fact (and don't take this wrong) but pot stinks. If it did not have that lingering aroma in the cars, on your clothes, on your breath, police would have a very difficult time determining who smokes marijuana, because other than that lingering smell there's really no reason to search that car.

KEITH STROUP: That's right. Right now the law in 48 states is if a police officer pulls you over for any legitimate traffic offense—it can be a light out on the license plate, they can claim you didn't signal when you switched lanes (a lot of times they make that up) but either way—when it happens they pull you over, you roll down the window, and they ask for your driver's license and insurance. If they say they smell marijuana, every state in the country (other than the two legal states now) say that gives them the right to search the passenger compartment without a search warrant. Your 4th amendment rights are waived.

Now the importance of Washington and Colorado, which people didn't realize at first, is that it is no longer contraband, so it's no longer probable cause to do anything. You can have up to an ounce of marijuana on your front seat in both of those states, and if the cops pull you over and see it, they can't even search the goddamn car. It is not contraband.

So, you see, in terms of getting our rights back, it really is an important first step. It will no longer allow cops to make up, "I smell marijuana." Because if you smell marijuana, that doesn't provide any probable cause that there is more than one ounce in the car, so they have no probable cause to believe that you've committed a crime. It is the beginning of the end of prohibition I assure you. The laws will get better, but this is a beginning of the end.

SANHO TREE

Sanho Tree is a fellow at the Institute for Policy Studies in Washington D.C. Sanho is director of the Drug Policy Project, which works to end the domestic and international "War on Drugs" and replace it with policies that promote public health and safety, as well as economic alternatives to the prohibition drug economy. The intersection of race and poverty in the drug war is at the heart of the project's work. In recent years the project has focused on the attendant "collateral damage" caused by the United States exporting its drug war to Colombia and Afghanistan. Cultural Baggage / February 12, 2012.

SANHO TREE: As we see in Mexico, as we knock off the kingpins, for instance, the veteran leaders of these cartels or trafficking organizations, the ones that take over, their lieutenants, may not be as experienced or as wise so they often think with their testosterone. They have fights when they ought to be smoothing things over so they can make more money but their egos and their testosterone gets in the way. Their own violence sometimes becomes their own downfall.

It's not in the interest of a drug trafficker to wage these incessant turf wars that they've been waging for so long now. It's bad for business—not good for making money—which is the bottom line for drug trafficking.

DB: The guy I least thought would call for legalizing drugs stood up last night and said as much at a Clive Davis concert, Mr. Tony Bennett. What's your thought to that?

SANHO TREE: I think it's terrific. He's going to reach a whole new generation and new demographic that wouldn't necessarily hear this message otherwise. Also, again, it's counter-intuitive that because he's of that generation he must be more conservative but he's also been around the block for quite a few decades. He's been told the drug war promises of victory around the corner for decades. In that sense there's something new under the sun in his position to reach those conclusions. It is wonderful that he's come out and said this so publically at a moment when the country really needed to hear this.

DB: Yeah, I would agree. Here, again, he's not alone. There's 12 heads of state from Central and South America who got together and came to a conclusion that it's time to regulate. They didn't use the word legalize. It didn't get much splash because I guess there are just so many people talking about it these days.

SANHO TREE: Yes. This is the 13th regional meeting they've had. It's called the Tuchala Mechanism for Coordination. It's a very welcome step forward. It's not a decisive statement in that they say the U.S. ought to reduce demand severely, dramatically, and, if not, we should consider market alternatives, which is a diplomatic way of talking about legalization, regulation. Taking the profits out of this economy.

I think we also need to consider their own domestic politics. It is very difficult to sell a counter-intuitive argument to voters, which is why we've had this problem in the U.S. for so long as well. The easy, knee-jerk solutions are the ones that are easiest to sell.

If you think the Rupert-Murdoch media is right wing and opportunistic and simplistic, think what some of the Central American media are. So if you think drugs are bad then why not have a War on Drugs? There are a lot of people who are calling for the iron-fist approach to clamping down on these things because it's the easy option, it seems, to a lot of people who haven't thought this through necessarily. There are an awful lot of people, as well, who have seen this go on for so long, and they're sick of it. They've done some reading and thought this through and think that ending prohibition is the best option, which I would agree with.

It's a very interesting moment in drug policy right now. With regards to Guatemalan president, former General Otto Perez Molina—it's a very early stage. He just came out with the statement yesterday and we need to hear more from him as to what his real thoughts are. The prohibitionists are very much panicked right now. With states like Colorado and Washington State and possibly Oregon and other states with ballot initiatives to tax and regulate recreational marijuana use this fall. This is a sea change.

The drug war overall, from my perspective, is really about turf. Turf is really about funding. The way you secure and maintain funding whether you're part of the government drug war complex or Sue Rush's type group (the so-called non-governmental pro drug war groups) it becomes an existential crisis. The way you protect your budgets is through controlled doctrine, which is why ONDCP and the DEA will never admit that they've made a mistake. Once you open up that can of worms, you start second-guessing their other decisions, so they want to portray this sense of infallibility. Otherwise, where does it stop? And it can start affecting your budgets after a while.

I think people really need to understand the importance of budgets in Washington with these federal bureaucracies. It is an existential crisis. If you're a non-profit organization and I threaten your funding through your foundation, you would move heaven and earth to make sure that didn't happen. These bureaucrats are no different, and they know how to play these games. They know who to run to in congress or their allies and FOX News and the places to scream "bloody murder." "If you dare touch my funding there'll be hell to pay."

So there are lots of different interests involved and they play lots of different games.

MASON TVERT

Mason Tvert is a founder and executive director of Safer Alternative For Enjoyable Recreation (SAFER), and current communications director for the Marijuana Policy Project in Colorado. He co-directed the campaign in support of Amendment 64, the initiative to regulate marijuana like alcohol, which Colorado voters approved 55-45. He is co-author of Marijuana is Safer: So Why Are We Driving People to Drink? This was recorded before Washington state and Colorado legalized cannabis for adults, but it should serve to educate and motivate the listeners living in other states. Cultural Baggage, December 6, 2009.

DB: The analysis and the determinations are being made in various legislatures. Governors are considering it. Medical associations are delving into this. It's getting a lot of attention now, right?

MASON TVERT: Yeah, absolutely. As more and more people are coming to hear about marijuana in the news and discuss it with their friends and colleagues and family members and really get to understand that it's just another substance, much like alcohol, that millions of people use and enjoy and it's relatively benign. We're starting to see some strong consideration as to whether we should change the way we're going about handling it.

DB: Colorado has its own changes underway. It's been some years in the making. But give us a snapshot of what the medical cannabis situation is like in Colorado.

MASON TVERT: Well, voters approved the medical marijuana law here in Colorado in 2000, and at this point, over the last year, we've seen a huge boom in the number of patients in the state, as well as the number of dispensaries. Many are storefronts and very out front in public. Some are in office complexes and really kept relatively private. But all in all, we have about two hundred medical marijuana dispensaries here in the state, and we really don't seem to be having too many serious problems, although there's a whole lot of discussion about starting to put some regulations in place, and we will see how that goes over the course of this next legislative session.

DB: In Oregon, they were saying they had the first cannabis café, if you will, in America. But that's not actually true. It depends on how you define it, I suppose. But other states have been, kind of following in the footsteps. Using some of the same information you guys at SAFER have been putting forward, right?

MASON TVERT: There are certainly some dispensaries here in the state that do allow on-site use in smaller little café areas, within their properties. But by and large, what we're seeing are people setting up businesses, following the regulations and rules. Really going a great length to try to remain as legal and upfront as possible and I think that it's setting an example for what we are going to see at a broader level, in the near future.

DB: There's been a lot of discussion of late about the alcohol vs. cannabis switch-a-roo, if you will, that some people find it easy to quit using alcohol or even 'hard drugs' by substituting the use of cannabis. Let's talk about that safety factor.

MASON TVERT: We recently saw a study out of the University of California, Berkeley in which the researchers ended up finding that marijuana use could be a treatment for alcohol abuse insofar as it being substituted, as you mentioned, and obviously, for any of your listeners that don't know, marijuana's a far safer substance than alcohol. It's less toxic, it's less addictive, it poses less harm to the body and far fewer problems to society. Millions of people have problems with substances, and many of them are with alcohol. But, we really don't see a whole lot of people with serious problems associated solely with their marijuana use, and we have to ask ourselves, 'Well, if some people would prefer to use marijuana instead of drinking, or if they had a problem with drinking and they're still looking for that form of stress relief, or recreation, or simply looking to party and have fun with their friends, there's no reason why they shouldn't be allowed to make the safer choice to use marijuana instead of alcohol, if that's what they prefer.

DB: You mentioned the severity of problems with use of marijuana are not as severe as, say, with other drugs, and yet officials of the Office of National Drug Control Policy tour the nation saying, 'Marijuana is the leading cause of being sent to treatment centers.' Let's talk about the fallacy of that thought.

MASON TVERT: Yeah. That's a really disingenuous argument that they have been making. What we see are more marijuana arrests, or citations, these days than ever before. We're also seeing more people being diverted to treatment as a way to avoid harsher penalties, and that's largely the result of our courts and prison systems no longer being able to handle so many drug cases. Obviously marijuana cases being the least problematic of any drug cases.

So, we're forcing more people into treatment than we've ever done before, and as a result, we're seeing more people in treatment for marijuana. Yet, many of them, I think what we find are about sixty/seventy percent of these are for criminal justice referral. But most people feel they don't need treatment, and they probably don't.

Ah, but then we have the government obviously holding up this number of people in drug treatment, as if it's indicative of the harm of marijuana somehow. When in fact, it's only indicative of how stupidly we handle it.

KEVIN ZEESE

Kevin Zeese is President of Common Sense for Drug Policy. He also works on anti-war issues though a group called votersforpeace.us, as well as comehome-america.us, and on economic issues through prosperityagenda.us. He was on the ballot as the nominee of the Maryland Green Party for a U.S. Senate seat during the 2006 election. Century of Lies / March 13, 2011.

DB: Here in Texas you were the attorney and advisor, I suppose, for a group of activists who were touring across Texas trying to change our perspectives, trying to change our marijuana laws, correct?

KEVIN ZEESE: That's right, Journey for Justice.

DB: Tell us a little bit about how that came about and how it ties into the recent presentation you gave about replacing the rule of force with the rule of law, which has been kind of the undoing of our Democracy, hasn't it?

KEVIN ZEESE: I think it's a critical lynchpin that's been undone, that's been pulled out and is helping our Democracy to fail. Journey for Justice was organized by a group of activists lead by Jodi James in Florida. It was a project that had us going from prison town to prison town and from prison to prison across the state of Texas to highlight the mass incarceration of people for nonviolent drug offenses in Texas. We ended up in Austin, and this was in the midst, by the way, of the Bush/Gore election year. In Austin, we not only protested at the Bush mansion, the Governor's house, but also at the Gore headquarters, because while we were on the road, Vice President Gore had come out against the medical use of marijuana. So, we didn't support his comments on that. So, we were nonpartisan and critical of the prison industrial complex.

There's a talk I gave on replacing the rule of force with the rule of law that looked at the discrepancy on how economic and political elites are treated in this country versus how most Americans are treated. We know we have one of the largest prison populations on the planet, probably the largest prison population in world history. It's more than 2,000,000 people behind bars, 25% of the world's prisoners in the land of the free, even though we only have 5% of the world's population. In fact, it's worse than that, in that we have even more on probation or on parole, so we have a very strong law enforcement. So, there is a rule of law, but it's a rule of abusive law. A lot of those offenders are people who shouldn't be in jail or should never have been arrested and should not be under government supervision. It's really a racist and a classist impact, the way the laws are enforced.

On the other hand, we see people like the Supreme Court of the United States Member Justice Clarence Thomas, who for twenty years has filed false financial reports hiding his wife's income from conservative groups, so litigants don't know he might have a conflict of interest, since his family gets money for supporting conservative causes that are before the court.

She was getting almost $750,000 over that time period from the Heritage Foundation and among other organizations. In addition, one of the most important decisions in the last few years was the Citizen's United decision, which opened the floodgates of corporate money into political campaigns by allowing corporations to spend as much money as they want on elections. Independently from the candidates, they can just run their own advertising campaigns.

What makes that decision despicable in the light of Clarence Thomas is that during his nomination battle, which was quite a battle as you recall, it was a very intense debate as to whether he should be put on the Court. He received support from the Citizen's United Foundation and a mass advertising campaign attacking Senators who opposed his nomination. So essentially, Citizen's United helped to put him on the court, and then when he got on the court, he voted in their favor. That is a blatantly unethical activity on his part. He should have recused himself from that case, but he failed to do so, and that is one example of many of the elites not submitting to the rule of law.

I'll give you one last example then and we can answer your questions. One of our projects is called stopthechamber,com. It's a focus on the National Chamber of Commerce, which has become a very rightwing corporate bully and the largest spender on lobbying in Washington DC, by far.

So, we're seeing the rule of law abused. We're seeing people who expose crimes, people like Bradley Manning, the private who is accused of leaking the documents to Wikileaks, being treated in solitary confinement and forced nudity and all sorts of abuse pretrial, while the war criminals get off free. So, we are a country that has it mixed up and need to get it back on track for the rule of law.

DB: All these government officials, as you have said, tend to absolve one another, to find a way to avoid the prison or even the trial. I'd like to think that it began in the early part of last century with what I tend to think of as the "little lie" that marijuana was dangerous and people said, "Well, to protect the children perhaps I'll go along with the lie," and that has morphed, expanded and become a much bigger lie and that many lies are told and winked at and allowed to continue "for the public good." Your response, please.

KEVIN ZEESE: I don't know if the problems began with the Marijuana War, but there's no question that the war on marijuana and the war on drugs has added those problems. The enforcement of the drug laws and the marijuana laws requires police to get very close to people, violate their privacy, do undercover operations, have informants work with them, and do all sorts of activities that really erode the Bill of Rights. When I was working, focused on the Drug War in the eighties, we called it the Drug Exception to the Bill of Rights because it was leading to such massive erosion of the Bill of Rights.

When I started law school in 1977 and when I ended it in 1980, we started to see the radical shift in civil liberties in the United States because of the war on drugs. That continued during through the Clinton Administration, of course, President Clinton added lots and lots of police, hundreds of thousands of police to the streets to increase enforcement of the drug laws. He put a General in charge of the health problem of drug abuse in order to convince—to outflank the Republicans on the right, putting a General who knew nothing about drugs in charge of drug abuse. It's gone badly, and then since 9/11, of course, the war on terrorism has turned that erosion into an avalanche where we're seeing the Patriot Act, we're seeing domestic spying, we're seeing people held without charges, we're seeing more torture and all sorts of things.

Now, President Obama, he's taken it on himself that he has the right to kill Americans without any kind of trial. So, it's a very strange situation that these wars on drugs and wars on terrorism, these wars on concepts and substances, these are really wars on people, and they have tremendous adverse effect on the rule of law and in turn to the abusive rule of man.

DB: This thought that we have two wars, two eternal wars; the first ever declared for the history of mankind, what does that tell us about America?

KEVIN ZEESE: Well, we've have too often relied on force rather than reason, and we are not people who honestly look at the history of the United States going back from the ethnic cleansing of the native American Indians who were here, to the slavery of African Americans, to denying women the right to vote for two hundred years, to segregation. All these problems are in our history, and we haven't had an empire, a world empire really. Now, we're the largest empire in world history. At its peak, the British Empire had 37 military bases around the world. The United States today has more than 1100 military bases and outposts around the world.

So, we are the largest empire in world history and we spend more than the rest of the world combined on weapons and war. The military budget makes up more than half of US federal discretionary spending.

If you add the security budget, homeland security, and intelligence budget, 66% of the discretionary spending in the United States is spent on militarism. We allow this military budget to expand at the expense of mass transit, healthcare for all, high quality education, building new industries, a sustainable economy— we could be the leader in that but instead we are a follower.

On all of these issues and so many others, we could be doing so much more if we weren't spending 66% of our resources on bloated bureaucracy that we call the "security budget." So, we have become the security state.

When I look at Egypt and the revolution there, they had a security state, as well, but ours is pretty powerful—our security state. We live in a security state where 1 out of 32 Americans are under court supervision, prison, probation or parole, mass incarceration. Video cameras, even in small towns, protect us from imagined terrorists. We have this massive security budget that includes domestic security, people infiltrating into anti-war groups and anti-death penalty groups, and all sorts of advocacy groups. We see infiltration now.

The Wall Street bankers who sold fraudulent mortgages, they got off—not only got off free, they got a massive government bailout. So, they got rewarded for their crimes. We see crony capitalism in the United States because of essentially legalized bribery where President Obama takes $20 million from the insurance industries and rather than reforming health care, he entrenches those insurance industries further, giving them $400 million a year in taxpayer subsides. On issue after issue, we see that kind of tradeoff. In fact, then there are $400 billion a year in the United States in corporate welfare, payoffs, you know, are paybacks for the payoffs. They give money to the politicians, the politicians give them corporate welfare, the corporate welfare gives the money back to the politicians, politicians give them even more corporate welfare. It's a corrupt system.

That's why we've gotten to the point where 1% of the public now, the richest 1%, has wealth equal the bottom 95% of us. That's not because they work harder or smarter. It's because they are part of a politically corrupt system. It's because they are part of the politically corrupt system where the rule of law no longer matters.

When you look at the corporate media, the traditional media, you have to do it with a filter and recognize this is the message that a very sophisticated propaganda arm of the government is using. The corporate government media has a sophisticated method of misleading us. So, once you see that, once you're aware of that you can see the lies but until you see that you are going to be fooled.

DB: Whistleblowers who report on corruption, corporate corruption and the shenanigans of government, are demonized; they are destroyed; but there's one area where there's a modicum of respect for whistleblowers and that is those snitches and informants.

KEVIN ZEESE: (Laughs) Good point. I like that. That's similar to the rule of law. We have this disparity where the informants who help to propel the war against Americans who use some drugs are respected and the abuse of informants in those situations—we saw it in the Delorean case, and we see it very often now in the terrorism cases—which is they essentially take a patsy and surround him with DEA agents and informants who provide the drugs and the money and then arrest him for a drug and money conspiracy.

We see that now in the post-9/11 terrorism cases. Very few— only one I think, a recent case in Texas—otherwise, all the other cases have been a patsy surrounded by the FBI and Homeland Security people setting them up. Patsies have no ability to actually conduct any kind of terrorist activity or any intent to conduct it, unless the FBI made it easy. So, that kind of informant is rewarded.

The Drug War is maybe the biggest example of lives ruined in a country that misuses the rule of law. We should not even be prohibiting these substances. Marijuana in particular, but all these drugs really, would be much better handled in a public health system without criminality getting in the middle of it. When you bring the law in, you create corruption, you create violence, and you create destruction of people being put in prison for something that shouldn't even be illegal. It's a big part of the development of the security state and the ability of the government to spy on people, to gather intelligence about people, and it's a very destructive policy that needs rapidly to change, but it's very entrenched, and like so many of the status quo that's harmful to our environment, to workers, and to our justice system, breaking that entrenchment is difficult because the status quo is where the money is, and unfortunately all politicians are corrupted by that kind of money.

JOURNALISM OR JINGOISM

"To whom should propaganda be addressed? It must be addressed always and solely to the masses. What the intelligentsia need is not propaganda, but scientific instruction. The receptive ability of the masses is very limited, their intelligence is small, their forgetfulness enormous. Therefore, all propaganda has to limit itself to a very few points and repeat them like slogans until even the very last man is able to understand what you want him to understand."
—Adolph Hitler, *Mein Kampf.*

When I first began reporting on the drug war, there were occasional radio or TV programs dealing with "crack babies" or increased production of coca in Colombia and then later in Bolivia. My first show, Cultural Baggage, was the first weekly one hour broadcast of nothing but the "unvarnished truth about the drug war." I am thrilled that today there are dozens of broadcast radio and TV programs dealing with many aspects and failures of drug prohibition. Mainstream media seems to have awakened from their propaganda-induced slumber.

For decades, we have been living a new reality, one where the citizens of this country have been put into boxes, assigned a rating, given a number, categorized, and told to await orders. Our intelligentsia has their scientific instruction, and the lifetime of propaganda has certainly led the American masses to believe what the government wants them to believe about the drug war. The leaders of this nation, now more so than ever before, rely on fear to accomplish their bidding. They want your attention, your tax dollars, your vote, and they want your unyielding obedience.

The drug war is not just the sham I have described heretofore; this sham is the "new reality," highly desired, designed, and implemented by the drug warriors.

Certainly this war benefits law enforcement and growers, prison builders and smugglers, politicians and distributors, street corner crack sellers and corrupt cops, and it helps prevent unwanted competition for alcohol, tobacco, and pharmaceutical houses, and additionally supports millions of "legitimate" jobs worldwide. We must examine the possibility that the drug lords run both sides of this equation.

It is time to stand up to the drug warriors, on both sides of this equation; their lies and hypocrisy have for too long been responsible for the vast majority of death and destruction they ascribe to drug use. Prohibitionists carry their "beliefs" about drug war around like a shield they use to deflect any pronouncements that might cause them to change their beliefs. This belief system is akin to belief in certain Bible passages, a select few, which for these drug warriors of influence means a fat paycheck and prestige TV time.

There never will be another real debate over drug legalization. In any knock down fight over drug legalization in an open public venue, any of the top echelon of LEAP would end the fight in the first round. Bring on the best of DEA, HHS, the whole damned alphabet and they will get their asses handed to them, pronto. None of the feted ministers of drug war want to be the one on stage, taking it on the chin for the sins of their forces, their ministration of madness.

Sadly I feel the producers of most TV discussions seem always constrained by short segment time slots and are seldom allowed to present anything like a real debate. I feel they also seek to constrain the discussion to what splashed on the page this week and nothing beyond. Each time I am pre-called for a TV interview or debate, I tell the producers of my desire to broaden the discussion, that if we were only to look at the whole of the drug war, the problem surrounding (usually) weed would become whatever is less than moot. I feel the producer's dilemma is like any worker's—they need to please those they work for and work with. They work with these DEA agents, cops and prosecutors on a regular basis, so they don't dare piss them off by setting up an on-camera showdown with the likes of yours truly.

RADLEY BALKO

Radley Balko is a senior writer and investigative reporter for the Huffington Post, where he covers civil liberties and the criminal justice system. His work has been published in the *Wall Street Journal, Forbes, Playboy, TIME* magazine, the *Washington Post, Los Angeles Times* and many others. He is the author of the book *Rise of the Warrior Cop: The Militarization of America's Police Forces.*

DB: Back in the late 60s I was a cop. I pinned on that badge, strapped on that gun and swore to uphold the Constitution. It was a whole different world than what we have created now through this methodology of eternal drug war.

RADLEY BALKO: Yeah, I think the world of policing has changed dramatically through a number of evolutions over the years but I think what we have today are police officers who are armed like soldiers, uniformed like soldiers, trained like soldiers and told that they are fighting a war. It is having a very real effect on the way cops approach their job and having a real effect on the relationship between cops and the communities that they serve.

DB: It's enormous overkill, right?

RADLEY BALKO: Absolutely. There is an appropriate use for these SWAT teams and that's when you're using violence to defuse an already violent situation—where somebody presents an immediate threat to the safety to other people. You think bank robbers, terrorists or active shooters. The problem is the vast, vast majority of these raids are to serve search warrants. When you are serving a search warrant on someone at that point they're merely a suspect of a crime and you're visiting violence upon them before they are even charged. On top of that you're creating this violence. You are not using violence to defuse violence. You are creating violence where there was none before. I think that's really the rub of the problem.

DB: The book also talks about militarization and how it's for officer safety, but the number of police deaths has been going down, the level of violence conflicted against them has been going down.

RADLEY BALKO: Last year was the second safest year for police officers since the early 1960s. The number of officers actually murdered on the job was tiny. You are actually more likely to be murdered just by living in a city like Chicago or Philadelphia or Miami than you are to be murdered on the job as a police officer. This isn't to say that some police officers don't have more dangerous jobs than others. I'm sure every officer's job is more dangerous than a journalist who writes about police issues. The problem is cops are constantly told how dangerous their job is and that every day could be their last and that every interaction could be their last and if you are told that over and over again you are going to start to view those...if you are told over and over again that every interaction with a citizen could be your last you are going to start looking at citizens (the people you are serving) as potential threats. That's going to affect the way you interact with them. It's going to affect the way you approach your job and the relationship you have with the community that you patrol. It's the classic, "When you have a hammer every problem looks like a nail" situation and this is what we are seeing. Even beyond the drug war we're seeing SWAT tactics used to serve warrants on people suspected of gambling and poker games and even on regulatory law. SWAT teams are sent to bars where the police thought there was underage drinking going on. It's gotten to the point where this is not force that is reserved for threats that are comparable to the force. It is force that basically being used as a first option.

Yesterday I actually debated a police officer on cable news who said he knew of police departments that serve every single warrant with a SWAT team. There was a time when you reserved the SWAT teams for these once a year, once every 5 years, once every 10 year situations. Now this is the first option for serving search warrants. There hasn't really been a good public discussion or public debate about this.

DB: I think it important to note that through our actions we have empowered the drug war even further.

RADLEY BALKO: I think this is an important point that I try to emphasize in the book which this is not about hating cops. This is not about directing all of your anger at cops. These are policies that created the situation that we're in today, bad policies. A lot of them had effects that the lawmakers passed and never intended. Congress never voted to militarize the country's police forces. There was never a debate about that. This is a result of a lot of laws taken together that have got us here. If we want to roll this back, if we want to make sure that the police are using the force that is proportional going forward it's really the politicians that we are going to have to move to act and to start taking this issue seriously.

DB: Another component of the book is you reach back all the way to Old English history and follow the Castle Doctrine. It kind of touches on what you were just saying—how it has evolved or devolved over the decades.

RADLEY BALKO: The Castle Doctrine is this age old notion that the home should be a place of peace and sanctuary. It should be a place you can go and expect not to be attacked or confronted. Even going back to Old English law, common law in England there was this idea of Castle Doctrine and the policies that went with it like "knock and announce" which said that if the king was going to send someone to your home he had to knock and announce his name, his presence and purpose and give you the chance to come to the door and let him in peacefully and avoid the violence and destruction of property of forced entry. Only then could they force their way inside if you refuse them entry and even then it should only be for the most severe crimes or most severe reasons. That carried over into the founding of the United States. The founders all cherished the idea that the home is a place of peace and sanctuary. It's really just been in the last 40 years or so with the drug war that we've seen the Castle Doctrine slowly evaporate.

One of the Supreme Court cases I cite in the book in the early 2000s was a unanimous decision in a case where the police had knocked and announced themselves and then waited 15 to 20 seconds before forcing themselves inside. The suspect argued that wasn't enough time because he was taking a shower and it wasn't enough time to get to the door. Whether or not you agree that that's enough time is beside the point. The problem was the Supreme Court came to its decision and it calculated what it thought was an acceptable time for police to wait not by how long it would take the average person to get to the door to let them in—which is the whole point of the Castle Doctrine—instead the Court said that the police should not have to wait so long that somebody inside would have the opportunity to destroy evidence—basically flush drugs down the toilet. At that point the Castle Doctrine turned from this policy that was supposed to give homeowners a chance to protect their home from violence and destruction to a policy that assumes people are guilty and the police should be able to enter before you can destroy any evidence. That case didn't really make a lot of headlines when that decision came down, but I think it was really a kind of a turning point.

Before you can fight a war against an enemy you have to dehumanize the enemy. I think for a generation now politicians have succeeded in dehumanizing drug offenders—making them into these existential threats to our children and society and everything we hold dear. It's only once you do that we become sort of complacent and OK with the idea that, again, sending 10 heavily-armed police officers, dressed and trained as soldiers to force their way into somebody's house in the middle of the night over basically a few plants. You can't just start doing that overnight. You have to condition the public to become OK with it.

I think a lot of people today don't realize that there was a time when drug warrants were served by police—uniformed cops coming up, knocking on the door and waiting for somebody to answer. It hasn't always been the case that you have these battering rams, flash grenades, heavily-armed police officers dressed like Robocop. It hasn't always been this way. I interviewed a lot of older cops who talked about even with the Hell's Angels you knocked on the door. They made it clear that they were police and they let them in.

The justification for these raids is that these people want to kill cops. I just don't think that's true. Most people, even drug dealers and criminals know that if you kill a cop you are going to be lucky to last the next 5 seconds. If you last those seconds you're going to be in prison for the rest of your life. If you're in a death penalty state you're probably going to be executed. I think that most of the time even when drug dealers are shooting at cops during these raids it's because they think they are rival drug dealers breaking in in the middle of the night and not announcing themselves.

FRED GARDNER

Fred Gardner is a journalist who has been covering the medical marijuana movement in California since 1996. Since 2003 he has been managing editor of *O'Shaughnessy's*, a journal he co founded with the late Dr. Todd Mikuriya. In 2010 he began work with Martin A. Lee on Project CBD to expedite production of cannabidiol rich strains of cannabis. Cultural Baggage / August 23, 2009

FRED GARDNER: O'Shaughnessy's is a journal that pro-cannabis doctors share among themselves. It's a specialty journal for the growing group of specialists who have focused their practices on Cannabis Therapeutics.

They are learning more and more about how different strains seem to affect different symptoms and different conditions, and they're learning more about the body's own cannabinoid system, which most doctors never learn about because they don't teach it in pharmacy classes and medical school, and the drug company reps who come around and continue their medical education of course don't say that there's an herb with these medical properties. It would make a big dent in pharmaceutical drug sales.

DB: The contributions pharmaceutical companies make to these elected officials, that keeps this topic from being given proper focus.

FRED GARDNER: You're being very polite by saying 'contributions.' They own these politicians. The drug companies, they're as powerful as the oil companies. They're interlocked with the oil companies, through the chemical companies, food companies, agro business. They combine through their banks and through their interlocking directorates. It's the 'Big Corporate' structure of America that we're up against.

DB: Last time I was out in California I learned some gentlemen had started a scientific analysis of Cannabis that was being put into the marketplace, and many of the dispensaries are now making use of their services...

FRED GARDNER: You're referring to the Analytic Test Lab that started in California? Two young entrepreneurs, they had both been growing medical marijuana and had gotten busted. They were growing for medical collectives so they had a valid defense. But they were both young dads and they realized they wanted a different niche for themselves within the industry. One of them was scientifically inclined, and he spent a little over a year leaning Analytical Chemistry and learning how to operate the very sophisticated Gas Chromatograph and Mass Spectrometer—the gear that they use to identify what substances are in the given samples that the dispensaries send them. They are testing for safety purposes to make sure that there are no pathogenic molds on these products that the people are going to then ingest and inhale and they're also testing for potency. For the prevalence of certain cannabinoids, in the plant.

THC, which is often called the active ingredient in marijuana, is not the only active ingredient. It's the predominant ingredient, because it's been bred for the plants for generations. It's been breed to maximize psycho-activity. But there's another cannabinoid called Cannabidiol that has many of the same anti-spasm, anti-pain, anti-nausea effects, without any psychoactive effect. In fact, it cancels out the THC effects. So we may soon develop a strain in California that has many of the medical effects, without any of the psychoactive effects.

DB: Fred, I'm looking at the latest edition of O'Shaughnessy's and I see one here that catches my attention. Cannabis for Autism Spectrum Disorder by Dr. Philip A. Denney. Tell us about that?

FRED GARDNER: Well, Dr. Denney has written up two case notes. In both cases, it was the parents who came to him and said that they had problem children who were acting out and nothing seemed to work. They tried every drug known to Western medicine, from Ritalin to the SSRI's to Risperdal, Seroquel, these anti-psychotics and atypical anti-psychotics, and the parents knew enough from their own experience to think that marijuana might have a calming effect.

Both these cases that Dr. Denney wrote up, have had a miraculous effect. This is really violent autism, kids who had to be restrained, many hours of the day, and it was a night and day transformation, when they were using Cannabis—

which the parents provided for them in cookies and in controlled situations.

DB: Tell us about Dr. Donald Tashkin.

FRED GARDNER: Well, Donald Tashkin is the UCLA Pulmonologist who's work in… The Drug Czars and the prohibitionists use his work, his experiments from the seventies, eighties and nineties, to claim that marijuana smoking caused cancer and Tashkin himself, assumed that it did. Cause here's what he found.

When he took micro-photo micrographs of lung tissue, he saw cells that were damaged; that were disorganized; that were obviously abnormal cells. So he thought that indicated that they were pre-cancerous. Secondly, when he analyzed the components of marijuana smoke, he found known carcinogens—including Benzpyrene, predominant among them.

So with seeing the damage that it did to the cells and knowing the contents of the smoke, he assumed that marijuana smoking caused cancer. But there were some contradictory studies. There was a study of fifteen thousand Kaiser patients that indicated that the marijuana smokers did not have a higher incidence of lung cancer.

So Tashkin decided to do his own study, with the backing of NIDA and UCLA and it was a gold standard study with eleven hundred cancer victims and eleven hundred controls who were matched for age, sex, income, race, so that you knew that the two groups had similar experience in life and exposure to possible causes.

When he looked at the data he found, to his surprise, that the group of pot smokers had a slightly lower cancer rate and cancer of the lungs and head and neck. As I say, he is the Pulmonologist; he's the establishment and it was when he concluded that smoking Cannabis does not cause lung cancer, this was a huge story. It was NIDA, which had sponsored his work for decades, buried this study in their own PR journal, which is called NIDA Notes.

MIKE GRAY

Mike Gray was the chairman of the Common Sense for Drug Policy Organization, an accomplished screenwriter (*The China Syndrome*) and the author of *Drug Crazy: How we Got in to this Mess and How we Can Get Out*. Mike passed away in 2013, but his book remains to inform and enlighten us to the horrors of drug war. Century of Lies / March 19, 2009.

DB: Mike Gray, you just had a major op ed published in the *Washington Post*. If an op ed can be a trailer for a movie, this is it.

MIKE GRAY: Well it's very interesting that you should say that. I just got an offer from a major Hollywood director who is interested in turning this op ed in to a documentary. So apparently it struck a nerve. I think and I got a lot of comments from people all over the country, many of them former law enforcement officers. One was a senior DEA agent in Virginia who said, thank god somebody's finally telling the truth about the failure of the drug war.

So it did provoke a response but let me just quote the first sentence. I think this is what caught everybody's eye. In 1932 Alphonse Capone, an influential business man then living in Chicago, used to drive through the city in a caravan of armor plated limos built to his specifications by General Motors. Submachine gun toting associates led the motorcade and brought up the rear. It is a measure of how thoroughly the mob mentality had permeated everyday life that this was considered normal.

And this was just two weeks before the famous St. Valentine's Day Massacre in Chicago. And I was struck by the similarity between the end of alcohol prohibition—which was brought about by two things, violence and unbridled criminality—and the present moment where we are going through an economic time not unlike the 1930s where the money ran out.

One of the things that ended alcohol prohibition was the fact that it snapped everybody in to focus. The mobsters were cultural icons. They they were looked up to. They provided free soup kitchens in Chicago, to the poor during the depression. Capone was a sort of folk hero to a lot of people, and we see that now going on in Mexico, exactly the same thing.

The violence is totally out of control. The government doesn't have a handle on anything that the everybody down there is seems to be either too terrified to face down the narcos or they're on the payroll. So it just seemed to me that this was a repeat of what we went through in 1933. And that in fact we may be witnessing the end of the drug war.

A lot of US officials have been agonizing over the fact that this violence in Mexico may spill over the border and that these guys may be headed in this direction. Well that's nonsense. They're already here.

The DEA just staged a big raid here throughout the United States. They arrested something like seven hundred people, and it turns out that the Mexican cartels are already operating in two hundred and thirty US cities. That's the DEA telling us that. So how can that be a success? I don't care how many people they've arrested. You know if the Mexican cartels are already operating in two hundred and thirty cities inside the US, we're in deep, deep trouble already.

This whole drug war was able to stagger on despite the fact that it's pointless and has consistently made everything worse. Drugs are more available, cheaper, and higher quality than ever before. And this is after we've spent a trillion dollars in the last forty years on trying to stop the flow of this stuff. It's only made it worse.

I think people basically didn't pay much attention to the whole thing. People said, well the drug war isn't working, but it doesn't bother me. Personally, I am not involved. Now that the money had run out, I think everybody understands we are all involved, because the war on drugs is costing us, according to LEAP, sixty-nine billion dollars a year. That includes all the criminal costs, courts, incarceration and prosecution and law enforcement and so forth. Sixty-nine billion dollars, oh my god. We can't afford that.

It was just like alcohol prohibition. It was a lot of fun while it lasted. It made for good movies and, and it was a lot of laughs as long as you weren't actually one of the ones that was being gunned down. But once the prohibition, the full force of the depression hit, people realized that we didn't have any loose change to throw around on something like this. And I think that's what we're seeing now.

GLENN GREENWAY

One of tbe first DTN reporters was Glenn Greenway. I invited Glenn to cover the situation in Afghanistan where our troops were guarding the opium poppies for the farmers aligned with the Taliban. Following are two of Glenn's "Poppygate Reports." Poppygate / July 16, 2008.

Glenn Greenway: According to the 2008 World Drug Report recently issued by the United Nations, Afghanistan's opium harvest last year was equal to nearly 2 million pounds of pure heroin, up 45 fold since the U.S. invasion nearly seven years ago. The trade of Afghan narcotics, which has been tolerated, even protected by the U.S. and its allies, is now responsible for over half of the war-ravaged country's economy. Ninety-three percent of the world's heroin supply is now believed to originate in the so-called fledgling democracy.

The level of violence in the country is exploding. Suicide bombings and IED attacks are now daily occurrences. Last week, a suicide bomber rammed an explosives-filled car into the gates of the Indian embassy in Afghanistan, killing more than 40 people. Yesterday, at a remote outpost in North-Eastern Afghanistan, nine U.S. soldiers were killed in a close-range battle with insurgents. This, the deadliest attack on U.S. troops stationed in Afghanistan since 2003, followed a separate incident last week when the United State dropped three bombs on a group of women and children accompanying a young bride en route to her wedding. Fifty people, including the bride, were killed in the incident. My humble and heartfelt sympathies to all the grieving families and bereft loved ones.

Even though the latest figures from the U.N. estimate that the Afghan heroin business provides as much as $400 million per year to the insurgency, the U.S. and its allies have largely refused to address the issue. U.S. Marines are ordered to carefully avoid so-much-as injuring the poppy plants which provide their enemies with weapons with which to kill them. U.S. led international drug control efforts very effectively subsidize the illegal opium harvest, with black market prices at point of origin about three times that of legal opium grown elsewhere.

Afghanistan perfectly illustrates the nightmare symbiosis between illegal drugs and terror. The War on Terror means more drugs. The War on Drugs means more terror. Drugs feed terror, terror feeds drugs. It's long past time to stop this macabre merry-go-round. Rest assured that the guns and explosives which are killing us, our allies and Afghan civilians are paid for by international drugs prohibition.

It's one or the other: War on Drugs or War on Terror. Your choice.

Cultural Baggage / December 8, 2008.

Glenn Greenway: This week the UN Drug Czar announced that Afghan narcotics have completely saturated the world's underground market place. In Afghanistan, the farm gate price for fresh opium has fallen 20% this year and it is believed that major stockpiling is now underway in an attempt to preserve prices. The UN furthermore claims that the Taliban earned as much as $300 million from the opium trade last year alone.

Fairfax County, Virginia is perhaps best known as the home of the CIA. Last week, authorities in the wealthy, Washington suburb arrested ten people, most aged either 19 or 20 for their role in a heroin ring, which was allegedly responsible for the fatal overdoses of 18 area young people so far this year. The group of friends frequented a local Starbucks and included members with names such as Tayler, Ashleigh and Skylar.

This week as heroin ravaged Pittsburgh, Pennsylvania, US Attorney Mary Beth Buchanan took a bite out of crime with her successful prosecution of plastic penis manufacturers. The two California businessmen, who marketed the 'Wizzinator' as an aid to subverting drug testing, were found guilty of conspiracy in federal court and face sentencing of up to 8 years in prison, a half million dollar fine or both. Attorney Buchanan is best remembered for her prosecution of comedian Tommy Chong on drug paraphernalia charges. $20 Trillion of 'Bush White' later, Mary Beth has now moved from bongs to dongs.

JIM HIGHTOWER

James Allen "Jim" Hightower is an American syndicated columnist, progressive, political activist, and author who served from 1983 to 1991 as the elected commissioner of the Texas Department of Agriculture. He is the author of *Swim against the Current: Even a Dead Fish Can Go With the Flow*.

DB: In the last couple of weeks they've reported that more than one out of one hundred of us are behind bars and predominately because of this drug war.

JIM HIGHTOWER: That's a cultural statement, isn't it? We're number one, number one in the world, we outdo China, we outdo repressive regimes all around the world. We have more people in prison and therefore more people guarding people in prison and more expenditure of funds and mostly, as you indicate Dean, off on absurd things like our so-called 'drug war' that really is a war against the people and war against common sense. So many people in our prisons and, you've got all the numbers, who are there for nothing more than a toke of marijuana and this is a, not only a humungous waste of billions and billions of dollars that we spend trying to get these people each year but also leading to total cynicism, distrust, disgust with the legal system and that's not healthy for any sort of democracy.

DB: I think for generations people have been fed this bag of lies about the drug war and have just kind of gone along to get along with the situation, unwilling to speak up, and yet the truth about this matter is becoming more and more evident and I see signs that people are working together to expose this fraud for what it is. That's happening across America, is it not?

JIM HIGHTOWER: It is and the early progress has been achieved through the medical marijuana movement. This is a medicine that people need, that the doctors and the scientists now agree is enormously beneficial to cancer patients and people with chronic illnesses, especially illnesses involving great pain, that marijuana is of medicinal value to these folks.

And of course the idiots who run the drug war out of Washington D.C. trying to score political points and also to keep the billions of dollars flowing into this absurd process, they try to do 'reefer madness' type scare-tactics, and even worse, to engage in thuggish, repressive police actions, literally kicking in the doors of ill people and ripping out their marijuana plants in the case of California and a couple of other places, that are perfectly legitimate, had been authorized by State law under the supervision of doctors, so this insanity has caused people to say 'It is insane' and there's got to be a better way and so there has been State after State legalizing the medical use of marijuana and I don't mean Massachusetts and Greenwich Village and Berkeley, California, I'm talking about Arizona and Montana and Alaska and very supposedly 'red' states. Just 'cause you're conservative doesn't mean you're nuts. And these people are making sense and are rebelling against this repressive nature of the drug war and now we have efforts in Colorado and elsewhere for people who are pushing the decriminalization of marijuana.

DB: Jim, you have become more focused on the marijuana situation. But we've been duped insofar as these other drugs, I think, as well. We have truly been duped, have we not?

JIM HIGHTOWER: Well, we have and we've been sold into a police state mentality. I don't want to overstate that, but also it's fair I think because there's money in this drug war for police organizations, there's political gain for politicians to be able to look like they're 'tough', when in fact they're making something of a mess, spending billions of dollars that's doing no good, and creating a level of cynicism among the public about the legitimacy of our legal and police organizations in the country.

DB: People have to become citizens. I mean the 80s and 90s were such a financial windfall to most everybody and they just trusted that these politicians were doing the right thing and that everything was going to work out fine but it's having enormous blowback, is it not?

JIM HIGHTOWER: Yeah. Democracy is not a quick fix. Democracy takes effort. And we have, oh, over the last thirty years and then accelerated under the Bush/Cheney regime, we have moved away from our principles of democracy toward plutocracy, autocracy, theocracy and ultimately kleptocracy, a government of thieves, in this country and that's not going to change because somebody's running for president. It's going to change because the citizens themselves stand up and say 'We have values in this country. We have principles. We have the rule of law. We have the balance of power, checks and balances, and we're going to insist on those.'

BILL KING

Bill King is a columnist with the *Houston Chronicle*. Cultural Baggage / June 10, 2012

DB: Your columns in the last few months have been talking about the need for a reexamination of our drug policies.

BILL KING: I start with the proposition that I think drug addiction is one of the great banes of human existence. I've got a lot of my friends who have struggled with that, with their children so my goal is to reduce addiction. It doesn't appear to me that the War on Drugs that we've been fighting for the past 40 years is really accomplishing that.

DB: I guess what comes to mind is we have spent half a trillion, some say over a trillion dollars on this drug war, money that, perhaps, could have been used to provide for this same community. What is your thought as to money being squandered?

BILL KING: My career was really as a businessman not as a journalist and so I tend to view things as a businessman would look at it. In any business you're in you look at the investment and the return and how cost-effective are your expenditures. There's really no way to estimate how much we've spent on the drug war. There's no real accounting for that but certainly it would be something approaching a trillion dollars.

There are all sorts of ancillary costs to families that have costs as well. There's been no real meaningful decline in accidental drug deaths, in addiction rates. We haven't really gotten anything for that money. So just as a pure, cost effective analysis to me this is not money well invested.

Among the people that I talk to about this there's sort of an interesting divide. You have people that have a vested interest in the law enforcement tend to promote interdiction and enforcement but when you talk to the doctors that deal with medicine of addiction day in and day out they clearly believe that prevention and treatment is a better expenditure.

Our society has fundamentally made a decision that we're going to deal with the problem of addiction through the criminal justice system. I think that's the premise that we need to stop and analyze because number 1 (as I previously said) it's not effective. But also any doctor will tell you that once a person becomes addicted they really no longer have free will to use or not use the drug.

Our entire criminal justice system is based on the concept of free will that, "I've got the ability to make a decision to go down one of two paths." The criminal justice system is designed to punish you for going down the wrong path and to encourage you to go down the right path. But if that free will has been taken away from you because you are addicted to a drug then the whole paradigm with the criminal justice system doesn't make any sense anymore.

We have to stop and examine: is the criminal justice system really the way we want to approach this or do we want to make this more of a medical issue? I think it's also important to note what the doctors will tell you also is that most people become addicted in their teenage years. So if you can get to about age 25 without having an addiction very few people become addicted after that age. We really need to be thinking a lot about how do we keep our young people from making those decisions in the first place. Again, I'm not sure the criminal justice system is the way to do that.

I think we've got to separate how you feel about the drug war from how you feel about drugs because, like I've said here several times, I'm not an advocate for using drugs, don't like them, don't use them, never have used them other than an occasional glass of wine. I wish they'd all go away tomorrow.

I've got a lot of friends of mine that have suffered through especially their children becoming addicted. I know what a heartbreak that is. You see these young people's lives that are completely ruined and wasted. But the fact of the matter is that the war on drugs and the criminalization of drugs makes those families lives more difficult. The less likely, frankly, that their kids are ever going to recover from that. Let's do something that's effective and something that's humane at the same time.

MARTIN LEE

Martin A. Lee is the author most recently of *Smoke Signals: A Social History of Marijuana*. Lee's first book, *Acid Dreams: The CIA, LSD and the Sixties Rebellion* (co-authored with Bruce Shlain), covers LSD's use by both the counterculture of the 1960s and by the CIA. In 1994 he was given the Pope Foundation Award for Investigative Journalism.

MARTIN LEE: *Smoke Signals* is a social history of marijuana, meaning it's a character-driven history which focuses on individuals. It talks about how the plant first came over to the Americas which was really through the slave trade. Seeds were brought over by African slaves to the Western hemisphere. How it worked its way up through the South America to North America. What happened to make it become illegal and how, most importantly, citizens banded together, starting in the 1960s, to oppose the prohibition of marijuana. That movement that started in the 1960s has branched out in manifold ways and is now a mass movement today still fighting that same battle. Hopefully we're at a threshold and something is about to change.

DB: I would think you're right. It's like how much snow can the mountain side hold before the avalanche happens?

MARTIN LEE: Yeah. It could happen all of the sudden, very quickly. Yes, given what we know about the history of prohibition and the history of marijuana in the United States, it might take a lot longer. I'm reminded of what happened in Eastern Europe and the Soviet Union when the Berlin Wall all of a sudden came tumbling down. When I was growing up, the Berlin Wall seemed like a fixture. It just seemed like a given. It would never change. All of a sudden, practically overnight, such dramatic changes. I think it could happen that way for marijuana prohibition in the United States, and as the United States goes on issues, so goes the world.

DB: One of the earlier chapters talked about one of my favorites as a kid—Louie Armstrong. He was such a talent with his trumpet and with his voice and he had his troubles with cannabis along the way but he never gave up on it, so to speak. Let's talk about him.

MARTIN LEE: Well he was arrested in 1930 in Los Angeles while playing jazz at a club—during a break actually. That arrest stayed with him as a stigma but he never would waver from his love for cannabis. He called it "Mary Warner". It went by many names in the jazz community—gage, muggles, so forth and so on. Armstrong is really the first character I introduce in the story. Not because chronologically he comes first. He was born about 1900 and lived until 1970. The story starts actually much earlier but he embodies such important elements of the marijuana story. He said he used it as a medicine. He didn't have a recommendation from a doctor. It didn't happen like that in those days when he was alive. That was the Jim Crow era until the Civil Rights movement changed things.

When he talked about marijuana as being medicine he actually referred to how it helped him as a black man in the United States cope with the stress of living in Jim Crow's society—the unequal society between whites and blacks. It helped him ease the chronic pain of racism.He talked about it that way as well. Not exactly in those terms but very explicitly as something that helped him cope as a genius, an artistic powerhouse living in a society that belittled him every day simply because of the color of his skin.

DB: You mention in your book a gentleman who's infamous here in Houston, a black militant sentenced to a 30 year jail term for sharing a joint with a narc.

MARTIN LEE: In the late 60's it was very clear that police were using marijuana and the marijuana laws to target political radicals, to target segments in society that the established did not approve of. So you had black militants like you referred to in Houston who were busted and given ridiculously long sentences. For just a tiny bit of marijuana they would be sentenced to 30 years. John Sinclair, who was a white cultural activist in Detroit although very close with the black community, was also sentenced to 30 years for two joints. Oh, actually, it was 10 years for two roaches—that was the specifics.

John Lennon actually played a benefit concert for John Sinclair at an Ann Arbor stadium. I happened to be a student in Ann Arbor at the University of Michigan at the time in 1970 and as a result of that rock concert John Sinclair was freed. That was John Lennon's first public concert after the breakup of the Beatles. So it was an important moment. It actually changed the law in Michigan. It was ruled unconstitutional that John Sinclair should be put in jail for such a long time for such a meaningless "crime"—if you can even call it that. But it was on the books as marijuana is still on the books today. But this is part of the story how John Lennon and The Beatles were very active politically agitating for the legalization of marijuana.

DB: It occurs to me that there's just this linkage between pot smokers in general, if you will. I remember the first time I got high I had to go to Mexico to buy it because I just didn't know anybody that smoked pot. But when I came back suddenly I recognized those people. What's your thought on that?

MARTIN LEE: It's interesting that in the 1960s there was such dramatic changes within American society with respect to attitudes towards cannabis. In the beginning of 1960s the Federal Bureau of Narcotics Chief Harry Anslinger's "reefer madness" mentality still really held sway in society. That's how the media looked at it: that marijuana is something that was very dangerous, it should be kept illegal, we shouldn't even consider changing the law. That "reefer madness" theme still held sway.

But that changed, in part, because of the cultural revolution that occurred in the 1960s that marijuana symbolically became mixed up in it. When young people "turned on" and tried marijuana, they realized that it was nothing like the government was saying. I think that helped to spur kind of a cognitive dissonance—a mistrust of authority in general. Not because marijuana was necessarily the most important issue in society at the time…I mean, heaven knows there was the anti-Vietnam War movement at the time, the Civil Rights movement, there were so many things happening in the culture, but cannabis was an important part of the mix, both symbolically and because it promoted a cognitive dissonance of mistrust of authority.

The reasons why so many millions of people "turned on" to marijuana for the first time during the 1960s is a very interesting issue, an interesting question. It's something that I engage in and analyze in *Smoke Signals*, and I suggest that it had to do with the overall stresses in American society.

DB: One of the maladies for which many of the medical marijuana states allow for is PTSD. When I was a kid I remember the drills—hiding under your desk, cowering the in hallways—getting ready for the H-bomb. I think there's a lot of truth in what you just said. You talk about how the Netherlands took seeds and enhanced them and came up with all these wild strains. You talk about the Schafer Commission which was Nixon's call for a new position on marijuana.

He didn't like it and threw it in the trash. A large part of your book deals with what's happened to what I call heroes here in the United States—people who stood up and spoke the truth and got knocked down but not out for their positions. Your thoughts there about all these medical patients and groups.

MARTIN LEE: If I step back and look at the history of marijuana in America in some ways it's almost constructed like a screenplay of a great movie. Typically in a film you have two points in the film. About 30 minutes into it something happens which sends the whole plot and narrative of the film spinning off in a different direction. Then about 30 minutes before the end there's a second plot point that sends the story off again spinning into a new direction.

Looking back on the history of marijuana the 1960s is that first plot point—the drug is illegal, the herb is illegal and then all of the sudden the 60s happens and the whole story gets spun off in a different direction. That second plot point, that second key turning point in the marijuana story I believe is Proposition 215 in California—the first medical marijuana initiative which passed by a popular vote. It really is a revolution in a way and it paved the way for subsequent states. Now we have 16 others and the District of Columbia who have legalized medical marijuana to one degree or another.

It's very, very important what has happened. I describe the events leading up to Proposition 215 in California and what happened afterward when the police agencies and the federal, local and state government illegally conspired to subvert Proposition 215 in California and other medical marijuana laws.

The law enforcement story is really what initially drew me into writing about marijuana and this book. I had no idea what was going on with the science and the research that was going on in academic and even in corporate laboratories that was documenting how medical marijuana actually worked.

The irony here is the U.S. government funded many different studies, pre-clinical studies meaning studies involving animals, studies involving test tubes and petri dishes not so much on human subjects themselves. A lot of this research ended up validating what medical marijuana patients were saying. The irony is the U.S. government funded this research in order to explain how marijuana harmed the human brain and body and, instead, they ended up explaining how medical marijuana helped heal the brain and body. It's a great irony and the science really blew me away. I had no idea about this when I started researching this book and it ended up opening up a whole new world for me and I got really involved with that. A good bit of the book talks about the science because it's my belief that when that is explained to people—even public officials who are unaware of the hard documentation that shows why medical marijuana and why marijuana is so effective as a therapeutic—then prohibition can no longer stand.

We are still confronted with the myth that somehow there's not enough research that's been done yet on marijuana. We don't know if it really works or not. There's claims made for it. There's claims made against it. The news media tends to throw up its hands and say, "Well, we just don't know either way yet."

That's a little bit different from the old days when they just said marijuana is bad. No debate. Nothing to say about it afterwards. Really, when you look at the science that's been done—there's been extensive pre-clinical research—it is astonishing what they've come up with. Explaining how the receptors in the brain and body respond pharmacologically to compounds in cannabis—how that works and how they interact in the body and what that actually means.

It's devastating. It's such a powerful refutation of the premises of marijuana prohibition. It's something I wanted to emphasize in the book and try to explain as best I could so that this rather obscure science which is full of jargon and these academic papers that are being written could be explained and understood by the general public, by doctors, by patients, by public officials. That's one thing that I hope "Smoke Signals" can contribute to the debate over marijuana and shed some light on very important facts that generally we don't know about.

DOUG McVAY

Doug is the longest serving reporter for the Drug Truth Network with well over 130 appearances on our programs. For many years he has produced a weekly segment in support of his work with Common Sense for Drug Policy (csdp.org). Cultural Baggage / August 4, 2013.

DOUG McVAY: Recently, I reported on Sweden's annual national drug report to the European Union. All the new national reports by EU member nations were released in late June of this year. These new annual national drug reports are great sources of material for reformers. Two EU nations in particular, Portugal and The Netherlands, are frequently referred to in drug policy debates as examples of the success of reforms, so their reports are of course of great interest to reformers, though it must be said, the news isn't all that great.

Portugal essentially decriminalized their approach to drug use in 2000. They did not legalize. Some have argued that it's not like US-style decriminalization. That's true. In US-style marijuana decrim, sanctions are typically a fine of one hundred up to possibly one thousand dollars. Interestingly in most of the decrim states in the US, a marijuana possession citation counts as a real criminal arrest. California changed that only a couple of years ago under Governor Schwartzenegger. In fact it's arguable that even US decrim isn't really decriminalization, rather it is simply penalty reduction.

But that's a discussion for another time.

In Portugal, people who are arrested and prosecuted for drug possession may be given a range of sanctions. The charges could be dismissed with the people sent on their way, they could be given an order excluding them from certain places, they could be forced into drug treatment.

The Portuguese model has worked quite well. Now the bad news: the global economic crisis and the Euro-zone meltdown in recent years has created problems. Social services, like drug treatment, are low priorities for budget officials, and austerity measures mean that Portugal's success may be short-lived. The question, ultimately for the whole EU not only Portugal, is whether human beings will take priority over banks and corporate bailouts.

Now to the Netherlands. The Dutch divide drugs into two categories, hard and soft. They deal with these drugs differently depending on the dangers they present. For a long time, simple possession of cannabis was treated as no offense at all. That has now changed, officially. The Opium Act has been amended and according to this year's Netherlands report:

> Instead of decreeing that a police dismissal should follow if a cannabis user is caught with less than 5 grams of cannabis, it says now that in principle a police dismissal will follow in these cases. This opens the way to arrest and prosecute persons who possess less than 5 grams of cannabis (for instance: drug dealers who could not be prosecuted before because they carried only a small amount of cannabis).

Their coffee shops have been an international symbol of tolerance for decades, yet they have also been a source of contention as some, including some local officials, have complained about the growth of drug tourism. The coffee shop laws have changed dramatically in the past few years, and are still evolving. This Netherlands report outlines those changes, and provides vital information for anyone planning a trip overseas.

The bottom line is, times are changing. It's important in the policy debate to keep up with those changes. My website at drug war facts dot org is a terrific resource. We give you the pertinent data and quotes, along with full citations and links whenever possible to the original source material so you can do additional research. Reporting for the Drug Truth Network, this is Doug McVay with Common Sense for Drug Policy and Drug War Facts.

Doug's last report before this book
went to press was December 26, 2013.

Doug McVay: It's the 420 Drug War News. Some good news for a change. Preliminary data for the new Monitoring The Future Survey was released this week. The MTF survey has been carried out for decades and looks at substance use and attitudes among 8th, 10th, and 12th graders in the United States. This is the twenty fifth anniversary of the Office of National Drug Control Policy as well as being the first full year since cannabis was legalized in two states, so the results of this year's MTF are of particular interest.

First, regarding attitudes toward marijuana use, the lead author of the survey, Dr. Lloyd Johnston, is quoted in the MTF news release saying, quote: ""But more noteworthy is the fact that the proportion of adolescents seeing marijuana use as risky declined again sharply in all three grades. Perceived risk—namely the risk to the user that teenagers associate with a drug—has been a lead indicator of use, both for marijuana and other drugs, and it has continued its sharp decline in 2013 among teens. This could foretell further increases in use in the future." End quote.

Now, consider the actual numbers for current daily marijuana use, quote:

"Daily use of marijuana, which also has been rising in recent years for all three grades, remains essentially flat at relatively high levels between 2012 and 2013. The prior increases were substantial—up by a quarter to one-half compared to the low points reached between 2006 and 2008 for the three grades. Today, one in every 15 high school seniors (6.5 percent) is a daily or near-daily marijuana user. The comparable percentages among 8th and 10th graders are 1.1 percent and 4.0 percent, respectively. " End quote.

Changes in use rates—here's where it can get confusing for people. Prevalence of use is given in a percentage of the population. Increases by a quarter to one-half, 25 to 50 percent, certainly do sound substantial, yet the numbers were small to begin with: Prevalence of daily marijuana use among 12th graders was estimated at 5.0 percent in 2006, rising to 6.5 percent in 2013—up by 1.5 percent yet relatively speaking, it's a whopping 30 percent increase.

For fun let's compare use rates in 2013 with rates in the mid-late 1990s. They report the prevalence of daily cannabis use among 12th graders is estimated to be 6.5% in 2013, which is up from 5.8% in 1997. The number went up, obviously, by 0.7%, which is 12% of 5.8%—a 12% increase but in absolute numbers, the difference really represents 0.7% of the total 12th grade population.

I chose 1997 because looking at that year helps highlight the really big news in this year's MTF. We've seen major reductions in daily use of both tobacco and alcohol by 12th graders in 2013 compared with 1997 (8.5% and 2.2% down from 24.6% and 3.9%, respectively). The drop in daily alcohol use is big: 43.6% in relative terms, important though really that represents only 1.7% of the total 12th grade population, going from 3.9 to 2.2%. Most impressive is the change in tobacco use rates: prevalence of daily cigarette use among 12th graders dropped by 65.45% in relative terms from 1997 to 2013. In absolute numbers that change represents 16.1% of the total 12th grade population, any by anyone's measure that's huge, we've gone from almost a fourth of all 12th graders being daily cigarette smokers to fewer than one in ten. And the daily cigarette numbers have been dropping more or less steadily since 1997 (aside from a couple of hiccups). All that success without criminal sanctions against users.

NEAL PEIRCE

One of the first nationally syndicated journalists to visit the Drug Truth Network was Neal Peirce of the Washington Post Writers Group. Like many old timers, Neal was gradually awakened to the horrors inflicted by, and obviously not from, the drug war; sharing these thoughts in newspapers around the US. Century of Lies / May 27, 2008.

DB: Where do the Mexican cartels get their weapons of death?

NEAL PEIRCE: It appears that a high proportion, ninety to one hundred percent, of the weaponry used including assault rifles, AK-47s and so on, are being smuggled across from the United States. They're bought by shady characters, shall we say, at gun shows and so on that the loopholes in federal law permit. You can buy a gun without having a proper background check. Therefore it's easy for some of these characters to pick up these weapons and then, there's sort of an 'ant trail' it's called, of smuggling back across the border into Mexico where the cartels pay high amounts of money for these weapons. So it's a pretty unhappy scene. Of course, assault rifles are now easily purchased in the United States because Congress, which had banned them, stopped banning them, knuckled under to the gun lobby, with the acquiescence of the Bush Administration about four years ago.

DB: The Rand Corporation had done an investigation of drug treatment versus incarceration. Your outline of that please.

NEAL PEIRCE: They found that, dollar for dollar, drug treatment is about ten times more effective at reducing actual abuse than the attempt to prevent drugs from reaching a market in the first place.

DB: Now, you quote a man of great intellect and courage, Mr. Milton Friedman, the Nobel Laureate. Outline for us what you quoted from him.

NEAL PEIRCE: He had seen what alcohol prohibition accomplished when he was a young man, which was a huge amount of crime with all of the illegal rum-running triggered the really, the huge wave of gang wars, Al Capone is a name we all know out of that era. And his theory was that, and I think it's been proven pretty well again and again around the world, that the illegality creates the profits and therefore pulls the people, creates the criminal activity, and then you corrupt law enforcement officials in the process, so that you get the drugs being pushed and quite aggressively sold. That criminalizes the people who then use them, so you end with, as Milton Friedman put it, a 'tragedy.' It's a disaster for society, users and non-users alike.

LEONARD PITTS

Leonard Pitts Jr. is an American commentator, journalist and novelist. He is a nationally-syndicated columnist and winner of the 2004 Pulitzer Prize for Commentary. Century of Lies / January 22, 2012.

DB: You and I have had a couple discussions over the past few years. Most recently, I think it was Friday, here in Houston they printed one of your more recent columns. They titled it "Helping to spread the word about the new Jim Crow." You've had the chance to speak with the author of that book *The New Jim Crow*, Michelle Alexander. Tell us about this most recent column. What brought you to put it together?

LEONARD PITTS: I want people to read her book. I think that it would be impossible for most fair-minded people to read her book and come away without feeling that we need to do something about the Drug War. Having spent I believe the estimate now is one trillion dollars, 40 million arrests and seeing the drug use in this country go up 2800% over those years that maybe it's time we try something new. So I wrote a column offering to give away copies of her book. I bought 50 of them, asked her to autograph them, and I wrote a column telling my readers that we would have a drawing and give them away.

I wanted to do that first to put 50 books into people's hands, and I felt that buying the books and giving them away would impress upon people how important I feel it is that they read it, even if they don't win the drawing.

DB: The fact of the matter is that your example has led me to the point that now I'm going to buy a copy of it and give it to our District Attorney here in Harris County with the provision that she come back and we talk about it with her opponents running for that position.

LEONARD PITTS: I think it needs to be read by every law enforcement official in this country and if I had a way that I knew I could get it into their hands for sure I'd give copies to President Obama and Attorney General Holder because I think they need to read it.

DB: Let's talk about what's in that book. What compels you to do this.

LEONARD PITTS: It wasn't so much that she said anything that I did not know. Mainly that the "injustice system" funnels African-Americans in for drug crimes at a widely disproportionate rate. But what she did was sort of put it all together. Because you take that fact that African-Americans are being incarcerated at a disproportionate rate even though, as she points out, white Americans are far and away the nation's biggest users and dealers of drugs. You take that and combine it with the fact that we now have all these laws that prohibit people with drug felonies or drug arrests on their record from doing things most of us take for granted. They can't—a lot of them can't vote. Their voting rights are interdicted. They can be discriminated against in public housing, in loan applications, in work, in going to school. They can be legally discriminated against in all those things.

You combine those two things and she's right—you've got basically a system of racial control which is just like, say, the grandfather clauses or other things they used to use to keep African-Americans from voting once upon a time and that is officially race neutral.

There's nothing on it that says only arrest or effect the African-Americans but, in practice and for that matter in design, controls the African-Americans population, keeps African-Americans suppressed in terms of voting, in terms of getting ahead economically and a bunch of other ways. Ergo—the new Jim Crow.

DB: It was Nixon who officially declared the Drug War. He had this Southern Strategy which was a carefully disguised reimplementation of racism. Your response to that.

LEONARD PITTS: Yeah, again, what happened after the 1960s was it was no longer politically correct or politically safe to say, "I'm a racist or for segregation." So what happened is that you learned to speak in code and that's happened ever since.

That's what you get when you have the likes of Mr. Gingrich and Mr. Santorum casually conflating black with welfare or black with food stamps, etc. etc. It's sort of speaking in code, speaking in dog whistle for those who have ears to hear. That's what Nixon did and that's what the Drug War is about.

One of the most interesting stats in Michelle Alexander's book which just amazed me was a study that was done where they asked people to close their eyes and visualize a drug dealer and I think something like 90 to 95% of them (if I'm recalling correctly) when asked the race of the visualized drug dealer it was reported as black.

Well, as I just said, the average drug dealer or most drug dealers are not black. They are, in fact, white but this sort of tells you that the code has had its effect. Therefore when I'm running for office and I say, "We got to get these drug dealers off the street", you as the voter know what I mean. You know, "I'm going to be tough on these black folks in the inner city."

DB: Yeah. It plays out in the media, on television, movies, everywhere you go. That's the example that's most often given. Some young, black punk is …

LEONARD PITTS: Yeah, exactly. What bothers me about that, frankly, is not just that it effects law enforcement and white folks but black kids believe it as well. That becomes self-image and then it becomes a self-fulfilling prophecy.

DB: You have written about other aspects of the Drug War as well. It's not just racially implemented, so to speak, it's economically implemented as well. Those who can afford good attorneys usually don't spend much time behind bars, right?

LEONARD PITTS: Well, that's like the whole "injustice" system. I told people the story about O.J. Simpson as a story of race. The story of O.J. Simpson was a guy who could afford to hire 4 or 5 of the best lawyers in the country. That's the story of O.J. Simpson. People really don't want to deal with that. But, yeah, there's different "justice" in this country based on your economic standing.

DB: Going back to your idea. You're going to distribute 50 copies of Michelle Alexander's book, "The New Jim Crow: Mass incarceration in the age of color blindness," it is my hope that not only will those winners read it but that they'll share it with friends and family. As you and I were talking about—maybe pass it on to their state or federal rep, right?

LEONARD PITTS: I've had a lot of readers…I've been very, very gratified with the response from readers—like 15,000—which is way more than I ever expected. 15,000 for 50 books—yeah. But what is really interesting is that I've had a number of readers say, "Don't enter me in the contest. If you feel that strongly about it, I'll buy it and read it myself and pass it on." A number of the readers who entered the contest said, "I will read it and pass it on." I'm hoping that through this expedient we can get people talking about what she's talking about in this book because I think it's long overdue that there be a discussion over these issues.

DB: Too many Americans tend to think that the Drug War has been around since Adam and Eve I suppose, It just goes to show that prohibition is just a failed policy. You talked about it, 40 million arrests, one trillion dollars squandered and what have we got to show? Empowering terrorists, our enemies. We are enriching these barbaric Mexican gangs. We're giving reason for 30,000 violent gangs to be prowling American city streets selling drugs to our kids. It needs reassessment, doesn't it?

LEONARD PITTS: Yes it does. I wish that somebody…Part of the problem is as Americans we are historically illiterate a lot of times. I wish somebody, more people frankly, had bothered to look at the recent documentary that Ken Burns did on prohibition. Or the book that Daniel Okrent called "Last Call"—also about prohibition which goes into depth about how futile it is to try to legislate people out of wanting what they want. You're just not going to do that.

The best thing you can ever hope to do is to tax it and control it and treat it as a public health issue as opposed to this crazy response that we have now which, frankly, reads like something out of the Cold War era.

DB: Yeah, the fact of the matter is he (President Obama) like many other high echelon, CEOs and others as well as a lot of nobodies like me who experimented with drugs and went on to have very productive and useful lives despite that drug use. It should give some concern to these rabid prosecutors. Your response.

LEONARD PITTS: I would think it would because what we're talking about is something that could impact any of us or any of our children. It probably takes a different tone when it comes home.

There's an old Richard Pryor joke about a white couple that goes to the inner city, and they see people strung out on drug,s and they say, "Oh my God…tsk, tsk—looks what's happening here." Then they go home, and they find their son shooting up, and they say, "Oh my God, it's an epidemic."

The reason I raised that story is I think a lot of us find it easy to sort of dismiss this if it can be seen as something that's happening to other people "over there." We need to understand that this affects us here wherever "here" is defined and whoever "us" is defined. There's none of us that are really safe from this. We tried that via a Constitutional amendment for 13 years and it didn't work. Try something new.

JEREMY SCAHILL

Jeremy Scahill is the National Security Correspondent for The Nation magazine and author of the international bestseller *Blackwater: The Rise of the World's Most Powerful Mercenary Army*, which won the George Polk Book Award. His newest book is *Dirty Wars: The World Is a Battlefield*, published by Nation Books. On January 8, 2013, the documentary film of the same name was released. Scahill is a Fellow at The Nation Institute. He is also a producer and writer of the film Dirty Wars, which premiered at the 2013 Sundance Film Festival. Scahill learned the journalism trade and got his start as a journalist on the independently syndicated daily news show Democracy Now! Cultural Baggage / July 23, 2008.

DB: What's been the response to your book, *Blackwater: The Rise of the World's Most Powerful Mercenary Army*?

JEREMY SCAHILL: The initial response when it came out last year in hardback was that it was basically ignored by the corporate media completely, ignored by almost every congressional office and it really was a book that found its home in the grassroots movements, independent media outlets, community media outlets. I think a coalition of independent media outlets really built this as a story before most people in this country had ever heard of it. When Blackwater operatives gun 17 Iraqi civilians in September of 2007 this was a story that had already been thoroughly investigated and reported on by community media outlets. Only then really did we see major media outlets paying attention to this story, members of congress paying attention to it but it really had been pushed by independent media—stations like KPFT and others airing the reports under Democracy Now and elsewhere.

DB: Our programs deal primarily with the drug war and, as it turns out, Blackwater, Dyncore and others are just as involved in the drug war now as well, right?

JEREMY SCAHILL: First of all we have to understand that private companies have been involved with what's call the War on Drugs for a long time in the form of law enforcement training, training of foreign forces. Beginning in the 1990s we saw a real escalation of funding of private companies to insert inside of Latin American countries. This was something that was promoted by the Clinton administration. Dyncore which is a massive, publicly traded mercenary company has been the greatest recipient of so-called War on Drugs contracts in Latin America primarily in Colombia where the U.S. gives about 630 million dollars a year justified under the guise of the so-called War on Drugs.

Bogata is directed to turn around and spend about half of that hiring U.S. companies to deploy inside of Colombia to fight what they call the War on Drugs but it, in fact, is a counterinsurgency war that has been waged in Latin America for well over a century by the United States, by corporations. They've used the justification of War on Communism, War on Leftist, War on Populace Movements then it became the War on Drugs. Now it's War on Terrorists with drug trade ties.

The reason I throw that phrase out "Terrorists with drug trade ties" is right now Blackwater is bidding for a share of a massive Pentagon contract (15 billion dollars) to fight this so-called War on Drugs. The *Wall Street Journal* said it could be Blackwater's biggest job ever. This is clearly an area of the private security industry that's going to grow radically regardless of who is in office. Blackwater is positioning itself now to take advantage of this counterinsurgency war in Latin America under a Pentagon program that funnels money effectively into countries in Latin American like Bolivia and Colombia, as well as into Central Asia and Afghanistan. Blackwater already is working for the Drug Enforcement Agency in Afghanistan training the Afghan forces.

DB: Speaking of which the Afghans who I hear are some 3 million strong are growing opium on the mountainsides, some 400 million is going into the coffers of the Taliban—doesn't sound like they're having much success does it?

JEREMY SCAHILL: I think that the poppy production and heroin trafficking is at very high levels in Afghanistan right now and it's certainly worth investigating what exactly is that money going for that's being spent under the auspices of the Drug Enforcement Agency to have Blackwater operating in Afghanistan when we see for all practical purposes a steady flow of narcotics coming out of Afghanistan. It's yet more evidence that this really isn't a war on drugs. This is counterinsurgency. It's a backdoor military presence. It's a justification to use these politically connected war corporations in very sensitive regions around the world.

When you look at the situation in Latin America right now you've had over the past 10 years a growing tide of populist movements. You can draw a chart of the rise of these populist movements and put up against a chart of the escalation of funding under the guise of the so-called War on Drugs. The reason is clear. It's extremely easy to justify. The War on Drugs to most Americans sounds innocent, "Oh, of course we want to fight drugs."

But it's not about fighting drugs. We know from Gary Webb's reporting and other people's reporting that government agencies have been with the drug trade, deeply involved with the drug trade. So it's really a false flag operation in a sense because you're funding a program that would have a lot of support I imagine from people because they believe it's about the War on Drugs and it actually has very little to do with drugs. It's all about counterinsurgency and about having a U.S. military presence without having to send in the official military.

DB: One last question for you. The Drug Czar recently touted the fact that he said they had reduced the supply of cocaine when the UN came out more recently and said it's actually risen some 27% despite the spraying of the glutophosphates and all that on the plants—the work of Dyncore and Blackwater down there. It's escalating in Mexico. Very real and bloody war is going on. What can the average person do to refute these propaganda wars about drugs?

JEREMY SCAHILL: I was just down recently along the U.S./Mexico border and there's no question that there's a radical escalation of violence on the part of the drug cartels in Mexico that's spilling over into the United States. We're also seeing the involvement of Mexican forces, deep involvement of Mexican forces with these narco-cartels.

Police are finding when they raid some of these buildings that there are uniforms of Mexican law enforcement, flak jackets, weapons and other equipment. When you look at that and realize that there may be involvement of Mexican forces with the drug cartels and you look at the United States now pushing through Plan Mexico—1.5 billion dollar scheme—you have to ask the question: Is the United States aware of this reality along the border and doing nothing about it or is this part of the program?

The fact is if we don't decriminalize drugs in this country it's going to continue to be a justification for these kinds of belligerent policies that are being pushed through. It, in fact, benefits the war machine to have the perception that there is a war over drugs.

If you decriminalize drugs then you are going to take away the incentive for what they refer to as a war. These companies will lose their money. They will lose their business because it's not going to be a source of contention and violence the way that it is now.

DANE SCHILLER

Dane Schiller has been a professional journalist for more than 20 years. He's been based in Texas, California and Mexico. He graduated from The University of Texas at Austin, speaks fluent Spanish, and served in the U.S. Navy. Dane is currently a senior reporter on the *Houston Chronicle*'s investigative, projects and enterprise team. His column is Narco Confidential. Century of Lies / November 27, 2011.

DB: Now, the story that caught my attention and got me to phone you was "Zeta soldiers launched Mexico-style attack in Harris County." I don't know if it's the first such instance that's been so framed here in the United States but it's scary, isn't it?

DANE SCHILLER: Sure. It reads to me like something out of Mexico. Certainly it's not spilling into the United States to the degree that it's saturated Mexico but it's undeniable that they're here—meaning the cartels are here and they're doing business. They're doing it a little differently than Mexico but this latest attack, for example, when a convoy tried to hit the tanker trailer hauling dope through Houston, and the shoot-out and a hundred officers responding, and a guy getting "Bonnie and Clyde'd" in the truck cab…fascinating.

DB: And the fact of the matter is it wasn't an enormous amount of dope…not a very significant cost amount. It was 300 pounds which would make you $100, 000, maybe, but it's not going to swing the cat—so to speak.

DANE SCHILLER: Well that adds to the mystery. Why would they do something so bold for just 300 pounds?! Perhaps, within their organization, they thought there was going to be much more dope on this truck and somebody thought: "Something doesn't smell right. Let's send up a little less." These guys didn't get the word. Perhaps there's something else at play there. If they knew that something was up—why on earth would they attack a truck that was virtually being escorted by undercover law enforcement through Harris County?!

DB: I wonder about the origin of that shipment—about how this gentleman became a confidential informant…if he was busted at the border and swayed into delivering it in exchange for a better sentence or something.

DANE SCHILLER: We don't know a lot about him. I know that he's been working as a trucker for many years. I think he's been a confidential informant before. Had a decent repoire with law enforcement officers he was working for. But, I don't know that for sure. It could have been that they busted him and said, "Now you're going to work for us."

DB: Well you've been talking to folks here in Houston. The head of the DEA's Houston division said, "We're not going to tolerate these types of thugs out there using their weapons like the wild, wild west." Can they really make a difference?

DANE SCHILLER: I think they can make a difference. They can't stop drugs from coming through here, but they can tell these guys to crawl back under their rocks. I think it's interesting that they quickly charged four of them with capital murder. Others were arrested. We took photographs of them at the scene and those aren't the same gentlemen charged with capital murder. There's other people out there as well that are in the hands of authorities. I think there just squeezing, saying, "We're not going to tolerate this here."

DB: I think even the cartel bosses probably would object to what happened. Because the situation was too like Juarez and El Paso—the deadliest city in the world and one of the safest cities in the world. I think the cartels want to keep it that way where the U.S. authorities are not so enraged.

DANE SCHILLER: They don't want to put it in their face to where they have to do something. Home invasions and that sort of thing have been going on for quite a while and I think they've been able to get away with that. But when you start talking about a convoy of soldiers attacking a tanker truck in broad daylight rolling down the road—that's crossing the line, I think.

DB: Well you mentioned home invasions and that was one of your next stories in the *Houston Chronicle* was, "Tension follows home invasions by masked attackers." That was you and James Pinkerton there and that's not rare at all. That happens every week, does it not?

DANE SCHILLER: It happens all the time and we usually don't hear about it because nobody's going to call the cops. If you're a trafficker and you get busted and they take $200,000 of your money or they take 30 kilos from you—you're not going to call. The only way we find out is if somebody's shot.

And when you say, "Why are the cartels really in Houston?" This is how they're here. They have their stash houses—some for money, some for drugs, some for guns—and they're right here. And these often are not in your "bad neighborhoods".

DB: I would think, yeah, they'd prefer a better neighborhood just for the lack of incongruity or something, right?

DANE SCHILLER: Exactly.

DB: The situation here in Houston is, I guess, exemplary really, of Atlanta and other major hub cities, if you will, where the shipments are filtered through. I guess the question becomes, "What can we do? What should we do?" Your editorial board back in June of this year stood very much in support of the Global Commission on Drug Policy. They're recommending that we, at least, open this can of worms. That we delve into this issue. They're maybe not recommending outright legalization, but they think it's time to do something. Right?

DANE SCHILLER: I think anybody would agree that it's time to reevaluate what's going on—what's working, what's not. Clearly no drugs have been stopped from coming into this country and clearly the violence is increasing so what have you accomplished?

DB: My guest on the last show was talking about the easy availability of drugs in middle and high-school. As I understand, in prison it's relatively easy as well, so I guess the question becomes, if we can't stop drugs from entering our schools or our prisons, what have we actually done, right?!

DANE SCHILLER: Good question. A lot of people in prison, a lot of people making good money…I think that people in law enforcement will say that we've got to do something—we can't just surrender and say we're not going to enforce these laws. As long as the laws are there they're going to say, "We've got our badge. We've got our gun. We've taken our oath and we must enforce them."

But they might look up over their shoulder and say, "Hey, lawmakers, is this really what you want us doing?!" They know what's happening. They know absolutely what's happening. Some of them will say privately, "Well, I could perhaps live with them legalizing weed. The other stuff—no way."

But we've really got to think about what's happening. Is it really worth it? And I think you'll see, in some instances, they don't really pat themselves on the back or you don't get the medal when you're making a bust of a bunch of marijuana because it's kind of, well, is it that big of a deal anymore?!

DB: Right, and I think that's the case that it's kind of like rote—just doing what's been done before. It's one step after the other but the truth of the matter is very few people can stand forth…actually, I don't think there's anybody who can stand forth for this policy—only for the hope of what it might achieve but it has never managed to achieve any of its stated goals.

DANE SCHILLER: I know you talk about this all the time and I really wish we could jump forward in time—50 or 100 years—and look at what they're going to say about what we're doing now. Such as we look back to the Al Capone days and say, "Look at what they were doing!" I really wonder how this is going to get put into the history books.

DB: I think there's going to be a whole host of politicians that are going to look pretty silly and have egg about a mile thick on their face for having believed in this for so long.

DANE SCHILLER: I hope it will also include that people here and now were saying, "Is this what we really want to do?!" Are we looking behind the curtain here? Hopefully it will include all of that. But I just wonder, 50 years from now, what's going to be in the books.

DB: The *Houston Chronicle* has been very bold in their editorial boards and their reporting. The one thing I wish you guys might do is just leave out that drug-related and put in prohibition-related because I think it's a lot more pertinent but the Washington Post was talking about more than 20 bodies discovered Thursday in vehicles abandoned in the heart of Guadalajara and the folks I was talking to in El Paso said, "Yeah, in Ciudad Juarez it's calmed down a bit but it's moved to other cities…Guadalajara, Monterey, Mexico City and the resort cities as well."

DANE SCHILLER: Traveling circus of horrors. It goes one city, another city then, move over here, move over there. The brutality, what they're doing is far worse than what we've seen in Iraq and Afghanistan. I look at what's going on in Mexico and I say, "My god! 20 dead. 30 dead. 50 dead." You don't see those kind of numbers and you don't see that many bodies chopped up, quartered, beheaded, etc. in the "war zones."

DB: We've almost become immune to it and that's something I fear too is that the number of deaths mean nothing. We're approaching 50,000 dead in Mexico and it doesn't seem to mean anything to…I don't expect the pot smokers to quit smoking but I do expect these politicians to open their eyes.

DANE SCHILLER: I was talking to a man today from Veracruz, Mexico and I said, "What would you do? What would you do if you were in charge?"

He said, "Mexico needs to…" He'll be blunt. He says, "We need a revolution. We need communities to take the law into their own hands. We need for them to say, 'We can't trust our army. We can't trust our police.' Now we're going to be in charge. We know who belongs here and who doesn't and we need to tell the cartels and the gangsters to get out of here."

I know it sounds radical for us but our country is not going through Hell like their country. There's truly not a rule of law and nobody sees a way out.

DB: I understand that the murder rate there…the solution to those murders is miniscule…it's 1%, it's 5%…it's very few of these murders ever get solved.

DANE SCHILLER: Freebies. You can get away with it. Someone the other day, showing some gallows humor said that if you want to kill your mother-in-law just handcuff her, shoot her, and throw her in the street. It'll look like a gangland hit. I know it's horrible to say that, but the point is everything in Mexico is being written off as a gangland hit, therefore they don't solve it. I have no doubt that the overwhelming majority of those murders are gangland hits, but authorities have thrown in the towel. I guess the most bored person in Mexico is a homicide investigator, because they're not going to look into anything. Not if they want to live.

PHIL SMITH

One of our most frequent guest reporters on DTN is Mr. Phil Smith who reports weekly for the Drug War Chronicle and Stop the Drug War. Phil was honored in October 2013 for his journalistic efforts by the Drug Policy Alliance. Century of Lies / July 21, 2013.

PHIL SMITH: When I first started doing this 12 years ago I would have a hard time coming up with 10 or 12 stories to crank out every week. That situation has shifted dramatically especially in the past couple of years.

We are now inundated with drug policy news. We are also inundated with whole new media sources—bloggers, Twitterers as well as increased attention from the mainstream media especially in the wake of the elections last year where we had 2 states vote to legalize marijuana. It has just excited a whole new level of interest in drug policy reform and marijuana law reform, in particular.

DB: I was delayed in contacting you today because I was capturing a video out of Canada, CTV. It is a very well-produced video talking about the need for medical marijuana for children with epilepsy—just one of many such stories that are, as you say, hitting the broadcast media.

PHIL SMITH: It's a rapidly evolving situation. You noticed changes in the tone of the coverage over the past few years as well as the degree of coverage. Things are really moving in our direction. The biggest thing I've been watching this week is Mexico. The arrest of the leader of the Zetas is a big deal. The government there is treating it as a big deal. The government here is treating it as a big deal. This gentleman (if that's the right term to use), Miguel Morales , is probably responsible for thousands if not tens of thousands of murders in Mexico. He is also led the Zetas for the past year and one-half after his predecessor was killed by the Navy. In the last few years they have become arguably the second most powerful cartel in Mexico standing up only against the Sinaloa cartel. What's interesting to me is while the governments of both countries have portrayed this as a big deal the Mexican government has been fairly low-key especially when compared to Pena Nieto's predecessor, former President Calderon.

Calderon's strategy was to go head on against the cartel leaders, to bust them or kill them and they always took great pride in that whenever they accomplished that. They would do the big publicity "perp" walks…you know, have the guys in handcuffs in front of the guns and drugs. It was much more low-key this time under the new administration. I think that reflects a shift not only in public affairs but also a shift in strategy and one that may be a shift for the better. The new administration of Pena Nieto has downplayed the significance of going after top cartel leaders and, instead, seeking to emphasize public safety. That appears to be working for them.

It's hard to say for sure but it seems the number of prohibition-related murders is down a little bit in the first part of this year compared to the same time last year. Also the fear in Mexico is down. Part of that is due to the perceived reduction in violence. Part of that is due to the administration in Mexico City just not harping on the drug war all the time. It's been a real change from Mr. Calderon who was always wanting to talk about the War on Drugs. Mr. Pena Nieto doesn't want to talk about that very much. He would rather talk about other things particularly the economy. So it seems like things are a little calmer in Mexico even though the violence continues and even though the attention of Mr. Morales is unlikely to really change anything.

DB: You were talking about this guy killing thousands perhaps tens of thousands. We know the Zetas have been very much involved in the deaths of thousands if not tens of thousands of people and, as you mentioned, they're in second place to the Sinaloa cartel headed up by Forbe's listed billionaire, Chapo Guzman.

I see this as a chance to redirect the conversation not just for Mexico but for the United States that through measures other than intervention, arrests and going after these people with a vengeance perhaps there is a way to return to the days of yesteryear in Mexico where things ran much more smoothly. Things were just rubber stamped and "donations" made to the political officials.

PHIL SMITH: We may, indeed, be returning to the days of yesteryear but you have to understand what that implies. Prior to 2000 when there was the perfect dictatorship of the PRI in Mexico there was one party that controlled the Mexican state. That meant there was one party that you had to bribe somebody.

It has long been common knowledge that under the previous administration (previous to 2000) Mexico's role in the drug trade was not so much to repress it but to manage it. That is kind of sleazy. We're talking about widespread bribery and corruption.

On the other hand it was much more peaceful than what we had under Calderon. Yes, there were killings before and, yes, there were killings after 2000 but the levels of prohibition-related violence were much, much lower than they have been in recent years.

Whether it's politically possible for the Mexican government to go back to cutting deals with traffickers is one thing. Whether it will happen quietly is another thing. Whether it's going on already is something that a lot of Mexicans suspect. I think if you talk to anyone in Mexico most of them will tell you that they think the Sinaloa cartel is begin protected by somebody in the government and it doesn't seem to depend on which party is in power. Making deals with criminal drug cartels is bad politics so I don't know how that's going to work.

DB: You mentioned the ultra-violence and you and I are both in tune with the blog del Narco which features emails and horrible graphic pictures and video. Let's hope they do curtail the violence of the Zetas. One video I featured on my television program showed the Zetas holding hostages—5 wives of Gulf Cartel members—and then chopping off their heads and legs and building a big pile of body parts. It's a horrible situation down there.

PHIL SMITH: It's absolutely terrifying. I've seen some of those videos myself and I wish I never had. I don't think I will ever be able to un-see them. Since you're mentioning blog del Narco I want to mention the stuff that they do is now available in book form in a bilingual edition published in the U.S. by Feral House Press. It's called "Dying for the Truth." It's by the fugitive reporters of the bloggers of del Narco. They have now left Mexico.

The lead person behind del Narco identified only as a woman named "Lucy" fled to the United States several months ago after several of her collaborators were disemboweled and hung from a bridge and another one went missing. As I understand it "Lucy" has now left the United States and is in Spain trying to find a safe place to hide out. That book is available to English speakers and Spanish speakers in the U.S. Be forewarned it is extremely gruesome. You heard the kind of things that Dean and I were just talking about. That book is copiously illustrated with them.

We have managed to export a large degree of our drug prohibition-related violence to Mexico. We have people dying in the streets in our country but not to the extent that they are dying in Mexico. They are dying because of drug prohibition. These criminal gangs (so-called cartels) are the Frankenstein monsters of drug prohibition. We made them. We provide the oxygen that they breathe.

DB: And we insist that this last forever.

PHIL SMITH: That appears to be the policy. I don't see any real signs of significant change in Washington's policy towards Mexico or the drug cartels or drug prohibition, in general.

DB: No, but I think the time has come to shame them, to embarrass them, to force them to look at what they have wrought.

PHIL SMITH: I will say to the drug warriors in Washington and elsewhere are coming increasingly under pressure and isolated. You see movement all around the globe on this issue especially from Latin American countries who have suffered the brunt of the prohibition-related corruption and violence.

You have leaders like President Santos of Colombia speaking out about wanting a discussion about legalization. Likewise the leader of Guatemala and Costa Rica. Of course there have been the various Global Commissions and Latin American Commissions—the OAS (Organization of American States) is pushing ahead, looking at alternatives. The drug war continues but it is under increasing pressure.

DB: You mentioned Guatemala and Honduras for folks who don't realize that as bad as things are in Mexico they're several times worse in Guatemala and Honduras because it's such a narrow isthmus to bring those drugs through.

PHIL SMITH: They have higher murder rates than Mexico. That's absolutely correct. They also have huge street gang problems which ironically is sort of blowback from earlier U.S. ventures in Latin America and I'm speaking particularly about the Salvadorian gang bangers. Where do they come from? They came out of Los Angeles after hundreds of thousands of Salvadorians fled the civil war that we paid for in their country in the 1980s.

They went to L.A. The kids grew up on the streets of L.A. Not being part of the Mexican-American-based street gangs they formed their own gangs to protect themselves. Learned all the tricks of being an American-style gang banger. Then they get deported back to Central America and applied the lessons they learned—not to mention we have the Zetas and other Mexican cartels moving in force into Central America. You see lots of cartel-related deaths there, too.

DB: It's just a horrendous situation all around. No one can defend the policy. Who wants to continue funding terrorists, cartels? Who wants to create gangs in the United States? Politicians, I guess.

PHIL SMITH: Apparently our elected representatives because they keep on doing it. Even if they don't want to defend it out loud they keep voting for it.

JOHN STOSSEL

John Stossel is a journalist, author and libertarian columnist who was won 19 Emmy awards for his reporting. In October 2009, Stossel left his long-time home on ABC News to join the Fox Business Channel and Fox News Channel. He hosts a weekly news show on Fox Business. Century of Lies / July 8, 2008.

DB: You've delved into the subject of drug war for well over a decade now, and your latest article you had published in TownHall.com I think could earn you a place on the LEAP board of directors. Would you outline that piece for our listeners, please?

JOHN STOSSEL: I was in a marijuana celebration, from the Marijuana Policy Project, and they were all excited because the New York legislature, one house, had passed a medical marijuana bill. And I said 'How pathetic.' I mean, you're celebrating what should be just so obvious. That if someone is sick and medical marijuana helps shouldn't they be allowed to have that? But more importantly, in a free country, don't we own our own bodies? Once we're an adult shouldn't you have a right to poison yourself if that's your choice? What gives the government the right to boss us around like that? Everything should be legal. The only intellectually consistent position, if you're saying we own our own bodies and we are adults, is that crack and heroin, everything should be legal. These are not the demon drugs the DEA has made them out to be. Most people who experiment with them give up their drug or their addiction, depending on what you call it, on their own without a program to help them. And this hysteria is just doing vastly more damage than the drugs themselves.

DB: There are indications that the roadblock is being broken. That major newspapers—they're not going as far as your piece—but the New York Times just last week had one 'Not Winning the War on Drugs,' the L.A. Times had one featuring Judge Jim Gray talking about 'This is the U.S. on Drugs.' It's an issue whose time has come, is it not?

JOHN STOSSEL: I don't know. Jim Gray and I have been saying this for, I've been saying it at least ten years, Jim Gray at least, I think, eight years. If that makes it the time having come, I haven't heard Barack Obama say anything along those lines. The politicians still run from it.

DB: I speak to various groups in the Houston area as a former cop, member of Law Enforcement Against Prohibition, mostly Lions Clubs, people average age of about 75, and I've only found one person out of about fifty that I've talked to this past month that thought the drug war held any water whatsoever. I think it's a case of we're deceiving ourselves or believing in, I don't know what it is, sir, a tribal taboo. You just can't talk about changing these drug laws. Your thoughts on that?

JOHN STOSSEL: I agree. It's kind of like a tribal taboo and, look, because I defend free markets get invited to speak by conservative groups and for 25 years I've gone to rock-ribbed conservative groups and said 'Look, prohibition didn't work. Drug prohibition is worse. We forget that alcohol prohibition created Al Capone and the Mafia. Now this war is creating groups so rich they could afford nuclear weapons. Why are we doing this? To protect us from ourselves. Then we give the government the right to have exercise police come into our homes and tell us what to eat and make us run laps and do push-ups. Plus, what are we protecting ourselves from? The drug crime? Well, no, the drugs don't cause the crime, maybe the worst is meth, and cocaine sometimes makes people do nasty things, but 99% of the crime is because it's illegal. Nicotine, our governments says, is equally addictive as heroin, yet no one's knocking over 7-11s to get Marlboros. It's the law that causes the crime because the sellers can't rely on the police to protect their private property, so they arm themselves and form gangs and the buyers steal to pay the high prices.'

When I'm finished with that, even these conservative groups seem supportive. It's funny. There's been Bill Buckley, a lot of people on the right who are the ones who have spoken more strongly against the drug war. But I still don't see a movement. I see these pathetic little attempts to get medical marijuana legalized but everybody just accepts that it's right for America to bomb peasants in Colombia to stop the cocaine supply which it doesn't do anyway.

DB: There was a story, I guess a couple, three weeks back, they found a major stash of hash in Afghanistan. And it surprised me that rather than pouring gasoline on it they dropped a couple of five hundred pound bombs to destroy that hashish. What's your thoughts on that?

JOHN STOSSEL: I didn't know about that. Maybe that's just this righteousness that comes from 'I'm destroying something evil. I'm going to blast it to smithereens.' I don't know.

DB: We see the numerous stories in the newspapers and the TV all the time now, it really seems to be escalating, that deal with the blowback of our drug war policy. The international wars, the overdose deaths and so forth but nobody this respected—you were talking about this—not even Obama, nobody high in government ever seems to question this 'Groundhog Day' decades long repetitiousness of it all. And do you know why?

JOHN STOSSEL: They don't think it's a vote-getter. Politicians pander. That's why I like politicians less and less. They rarely lead, even on good things. And until you can convince your listeners and I can convince mine that the war does more harm than the drugs then the politicians won't come around. And it's tough. Normally on these things I say 'Look, the wonderful thing about America is we have fifty states. You can have an experiment and we could see what's better.' But the problem there is like what you get with Needle Park in Switzerland or to some extent in Amsterdam, that then all the drug trade goes to that one place and some of the people are unsavory folks who don't, aren't very socially responsible and it doesn't make a good impression and then the drug warriors can say, 'See all the evils of drugs?' and then repeal those laws.

DB: John, it seems that there are only a handful of reporters that openly discuss the subject of drug war. In Mexico, many of them will be killed if they do so. And I wanted to ask, why are so many reporters so silent here in the U.S.?

JOHN STOSSEL: Because reporters love the government and they think regulation is a good thing. Just about, no matter what it is. Even my colleagues who I know have used drugs, they say, 'Well, I could handle it but the government needs to protect us from other people.' And I'm not popular with my peers for my general anti-regulatory stance but my head turned around because I've been a consumer reporter for 35 years and I watched regulation fail on every front. Economic regulation, drug regulation, government sucks at doing almost everything. We need limited government to keep us safe but otherwise government should leave free people alone. That's why I'm a libertarian and the libertarians are right.

DB: I envy you John. You're able to get John Walters or one of his allies to come on your shows to discuss some aspects of the drug war. Now they realize I won't be kind so no one ever comes on my show to defend their policy. And I want to ask you, is it always necessary to give both sides of the story when one side is founded in ignorance and flourishes only because of propaganda and fear?

JOHN STOSSEL: Well, I would say 'Yes.' And I think your characterization is unfair because they're not just spreading propaganda and fear, they genuinely believe that the law will reduce the harm. They focus on the harm they've seen among some addicted family and they genuinely believe prohibition will stop that. I think it's important to give their arguments and then make yours.

DB: Well, OK. I'd love the opportunity, I'll be honest there, but...

JOHN STOSSEL: They don't talk to me that often either.

DB: Now, having discussed that thought, the politicians, the reporters, your friends and others that have never investigated the beginning of this drug war, have never looked at the reasons why it came into existence and perhaps don't look at the blowback, the international ramifications that create more death, disease, crime and addiction. It's a simple task to learn the truth of this matter. Why do you think most folks don't do it?

JOHN STOSSEL: They're intellectually lazy in some cases. I don't know that it's that convincing of an argument on any front. So there's a lot of racist laws and how they began is less important than what they're doing today.

DB: My city of Houston in many categories leads the world in it's incarceration rate. I used to open the show with 'Broadcasting from the Gulag filling station of planet earth.' And I wonder why those who are impacted, the families and the communities that are impacted by this do not speak up more, do not get more involved in helping overturn these laws. Your thoughts on that?

JOHN STOSSEL: They aren't politically connected people. But if you are—if you've just been raided by the cops you probably live in a poor neighborhood and they came in the wrong door, they knocked down the door, they terrorized your family—you just don't have the same political clout that the richer people have. Also, let me just say you're assuming that in those neighborhoods most people are against the drug war. But that's not been my experience. When I go into poor neighborhoods I find most of the people confuse the harm from the war with the drugs themselves and they are big gung-ho supporters of crackdown on drugs. They don't understand that if it were legal it wouldn't be in their face and there wouldn't be the crime.

DB: Going back to your piece, 'Legalize All Drugs,' there was a couple of paragraphs here kind of dealing with that subject. That your assistant had kind of ridiculed you, saying 'How could you say such a ridiculous thing that every drug should be legal?' And 'heroin and cocaine have a permanent effect' and so forth. It is that legacy, that tribal belief I guess, that keeps those neighborhoods from wanting to end it, right?

JOHN STOSSEL: Yeah. And if you see a junkie on your street, a woman prostituting herself to get the drug, it's hard to think that legalization would be better. You have to think through how, well, it would be as cheap as Marlboros and she wouldn't have to prostitute herself and she would be taking it in private and not hurting herself and a lot of people take this stuff and, in countries where it's legal, England for example, and hold down jobs. But it's hard to imagine what life would be like once government has already distorted the rules.

DB: Now, I see enormous blowback from the drug war on the international scale and more death, disease, crime and addiction but I think the average person out there who thinks 'Oh, it doesn't impact me, my kids aren't in jail, it's not something I want to bother with,' but it's starting to extend more and more into things like needless millions of urine tests, prison labor producing goods that undercut legitimate American businesses and, truth be told, it just seems to me we can no longer afford to lock up these people we're mad at, whose morals have offended our morals.

JOHN STOSSEL: I totally agree. We have a government that grows and grows and grows and people meekly put up with it. The Founders fought a war for liberty, and we are voluntarily giving it back. Bit by bit, the smokers rolled over on all the anti-smoking rules, all the car safety rules that force you to pay for more safety than you might choose for on your own. The regulators, if they're not regulating, they feel they're not doing their job.

So people say under Bush regulation was reduced, but the truth is that 50,000 pages were added to the federal register every year under Bush. The regulators don't stop. They feel they always have to do more. And until Americans say, 'Shut up. Get out of my life. None of your business,' it's going to keep going that way.

DB: John, you have astounded me over the years. You had a piece, how long ago, seven, eight years ago, was it called just 'The Drug War'?

JOHN STOSSEL: 'War on Drugs. War on Ourselves.'

DB: Yeah, and it was part of what awakened me.. that it was possible to speak the truth and not get blasted for it. When I first began doing these programs, I expected the front door to get kicked in every night by either the cops or the cartels because it's just a dangerous subject, or had been. For me, I feel free and liberated because I'm able to talk about it now.

JOHN STOSSEL: You also have a gun around your ankle. [laughter] But look. We live in America. They rarely kill people for what we say. So I don't think it's courageous to say this. People will disagree, and my drug special was one of my lower rated specials. The audience spoke by saying, 'Oh, I don't want to think about that.' But it's not like being in South America where you might get killed for disagreeing with the government.

DB: Well, I am in Houston, sir. [laughter] Put that in the equation. We have a criminal justice system here that's being investigated; the D.A. resigned because of his drug use, and it just goes on and on, the blowback. Our jails are so overcrowded we're shipping them to Louisiana, we're responsible for about fifty percent of the prisoners behind lockup now at the state level, and primarily for microscopic amounts of drugs. I even had the D.A. candidates on about a month ago and both of them were talking about the need to change our sanctions, I guess, to lessen the severity of the penalties.

JOHN STOSSEL: I've often heard them argue, 'Yeah, well, he's pled guilty to possession of a miniscule amount but in fact he was carrying a knife and he is a danger to society and that's only what he pled to.'

DB: Can you share your conviction, perhaps motivate some of the listeners out there to step up the plate, to do something about ending this 93-year-old fiasco?

JOHN STOSSEL: So much of what I learned in college and what I learned from my peers was wrong. It's the subtitle of my Myth book, "Everything You

Know is Wrong." And this was another example. It's so intuitive to want to have Big Mommy and Daddy protecting us, whether it's passing more safety rules or policing the food supply in more ways. It's harder to imagine that free people will work this out on their own and some have a right to hurt themselves, most won't, but freedom works better. A limited government that keeps us safe and otherwise leaves us alone is what's built America. For most of the history of our country, government was less than five percent of GDP. It's only since Lyndon Johnson and the so-called Great Society that it shot up to the forty percent of GDP it is now. And this is not a good thing on all fronts. Thomas Johnson said 'It's the natural progress of things for government to gain and liberty to yield.' And when it comes to the War on Poverty and the War on Drugs and the War in Iraq—I think we ought to have fewer wars.

PLATA O PLOMO

'Yes, there is propaganda that has been constructed and built generating fear—a fear that leads to violence and ultimately feeds into this war. It's terrible. Fear is the worst of vices." —Javier Sicilia, Mexican Poet

In the summer of 2012, I traveled more than 7,000 miles with the Caravan for Peace, Justice, and Dignity. Leading the Caravan was Mexican Poet Javier Sicilia, who lost his son to cartel violence. Traveling with Javier were 100 Mexican citizens who had also lost loved ones to Mexico's drug war violence. From San Diego, we traveled to Los Angeles for a march on city hall and a massive press conference. Sadly, the boisterous scrum of reporters and camera men did not translate into much national or even regional coverage.

From LA we traveled to Phoenix, Tucson, Las Cruces, Albuquerque, and Santa Fe. When we arrived in El Paso, Texas, the crowd waiting for the Caravan was well in excess of a thousand quite jubilant supporters carrying signs, banners, and shouting slogans. El Paso is one of the safest cities in the US, but just across the Rio Grande River, Ciudad Juarez is the deadliest city on the planet. There was little wonder as to why the citizens of El Paso were jubilant to hear the call for ending the drug war.

From El Paso we traveled to Laredo, McAllen, Brownsville, then Austin, the state capitol of Texas. Next was my hometown of Houston, where the Caravanero's were feted at the James A. Baker III Institute at Rice University. In Houston, at a local park, Javier used a metal saw to cut in half an AK-47 as a protest against the weapons being supplied from the US to the hands of bloody cartels.

Next we traveled to Dallas before heading to Ft. Benning, Georgia, to protest at the US School of the Americas, where the barbarous Zeta gang members were trained. The Caravan held a "die in" to protest the continuing education of bad actors from around the world that take place on US soil.   Leaving Ft. Benning we next traveled to Atlanta, Georgia, and Charlotte, North Carolina. The next leg was the longest, taking us to Chicago, where the Caravan held a massive march with hundreds of locals joining in the demand to end the drug war. The last leg of the Caravan took us to New York City, the "Wire'y" streets of Baltimore and then on to Washington DC.

Whether they acknowledge the facts or are even aware of their collusion or their silence in regard to the methods used to wage this eternal war, the "drug warriors" stand in support of ever escalating drug war and thus continuing support of the barbarous cartels that are decimating communities south of our borders. Worldwide, criminals are able, because of prohibition, to profit enormously from the sale of flowers and plant extracts.

Violent enforcers of the drug cartels are rampaging on both sides of the Mexico-US border, killing cops, journalists, and innocent civilians. The truth is that the drug lords run both sides of this equation and that those who support the drug war are, whether by choice or ignorance, the best friends the drug lords could ever hope for. In other words, without the death, disease, international complications, and violence on American streets, the drug war would not last a week, and yet it continues because we fear drug-related death when in reality, they are all prohibition related.

The drug war ensures vicious attacks on government, massacres of whole villages, and continuous war in central and south America. In the US, we all love to watch "Who Wants to be A Millionaire?" In the drug-supply countries of Latin America, they play "Who Wants to be a Billionaire?" The game pieces are corruption, deception, weapons, and violence galore. You must kill enough of your enemies and friends to rise to the top of this empire.

CHARLES BOWDEN

Charles Bowden is a non-fiction author, journalist, and essayist based in Las Cruces, New Mexico whose work has appeared in *Harper's Magazine, New York Times Book Review, Esquire*, and *Aperture*. He is a contributing editor of *GQ* and *Mother Jones*. Century of Lies / June 27, 2010.

DB: Tell us about your book *Murder City: Ciudad Juarez and the Global Economy's New Killing Fields*.

CHARLES BOWDEN: Juarez is now the most violent city in the world. I'll give you an example, in 2007 we had 307 murders, in 2008 it went to 1650, in 2009 it was over 2700. So far, this year the murders are up 60% on 2009. There's a lot of causes for the murders but certainly our drug laws and our official War on Drugs and our giving Mexico half a billion a year for their army, for the War on Drugs has killed a lot of people.

Since January 1st in 2007, about 25,000 people have been slaughtered in Mexico by this drug initiative of the Mexican army. The government of Mexico, the government of the United States, insists these people were all dirty. Meaning that they are somehow criminals. When in fact, by the Mexican army's own admissions, less than 5% of these people murdered, have their killings even investigated. What you're seeing is a kind of slaughterhouse growing in Mexico. One of the triggers is the drug laws, another trigger is corruption and a big trigger is poverty, part way induced by trade, fostered by the North American Free Trade Agreement. So we have hell at our doorstep and we refuse to acknowledge why it is happening and what's happening.

Our secretary of State, Hillary Clinton, and other officials in our government keep insisting that the violence in Mexico is caused by American drug users. A statement I find preposterous, because I don't know anybody in Kansas, smoking a joint, trying to kill Mexicans. The violence in Mexico, the reason it comes from drugs is because of drug prohibition. As I am sure your listeners know, drugs would not be very expensive or worth all the violence if it were legal. So, yes, we live in an illusion.

The other illusion is our government now, since President Bush initiated it, we are committed under Plan Merida to finance the Mexican army. Which has about 250,000 members. The Mexican Army is the largest criminal organization in the country. It kills people. Now we are paying it to kill people. While we've been paying it to kill people, while this violence has exploded, it's had essentially no affect on what you'd call the drug industry. It's not like the drugs have disappeared from the United States. It's just a slaughterhouse that's killing Mexicans and our government keeps saying, "Let's do more". Secretary Clinton, in March, when three people associated with the Mexican consulate in Juarez were killed, flew to Mexico City and reaffirmed our support of all the current policies.

Out of everything, I'm sure, I doubt your listeners know, that this is a war by the Mexican army against people in the drug industry. If the 25,000 people have been killed are all actually criminals, then how come no one in the Mexican Army dies? As far as I can tell, less than a hundred people, in the last three years, in the Mexican army have been killed. This is a strange war where your adversary never tries to hurt you but you kill 25,000 of them. What's really going on under disguise of a Drug War is a grab for power and drug money. It's happening all over Mexico, and a lot of Mexicans get killed.

I don't want to belabor this, but if you look into the dead in Juarez, which in three years are now 5,300 corpses in a city of a million, you'll find that almost all the people that are killed are extremely poor. They don't have gold chains. They aren't big people. They're just starving people trying to make a living. You'll find that at least eight drug clinics have had people suddenly descend with machine guns and kill the people in them, in the last three years. You'll find that the army's been present according to everybody in these neighborhoods when these killings went down and has done nothing. What you'll finally think when you smell the coffee, is under the disguise of our drug war there's a kind of social cleansing going on in Mexico. It's a war of the government on the poor.

DB: This book was dedicated to Armando Rodriguez. Tell us about him.

CHARLES BOWDEN: Armando Rodriguez covered crime in Juarez. He was executed November 13, 2008 at 8:30 in the morning. He was in front of his little house, warming up his car to take his eight-year-old daughter to class, when some guys walked up and machine-gunned him.

Now Armando, as of November 13th of that calendar year, had filed 907 murder stories in that city. So, I dedicated the book to him because he's what a reporter should be, somebody that reports the news and he's a casualty as someone who tries to report the news.

Of course, his murder's never been solved, but I think it is 2,753 people executed in Juarez in 2009. There were no convictions. There were thirty arrests, almost all those were tossed out. So you have a city, where you can kill and nothing's ever going to happen to you, legally or though the justice system. It's just a feral city. This is a city now with 500-900 street gangs. This is a city with professional criminals in the drug industry. This is a city with 10,000-11,000 soldiers and federal agents. This is a city where average working people trying to make a decent living are defenseless.

A lot of what's fueling this violence is obviously the American laws on drugs. They've created an enormous capital wealth, estimated by the DEA, they vary from 30-50 billion dollars a year in foreign currency for the drug industry. That's more than Mexico earns in its official largest source of money, oil. That's more than it earns from remittances from people who have come here illegally and are sending money home to help their families, which is twenty-odd billion.

This is a huge part of Mexico. One of the preposterous things about OUR support of the War on Drugs or the claim of a war on drugs, is that if Mexico actually obliterated the drug industry, it would commit suicide. It's solely dependent on the money to keep its society on life support now. Why this charade goes on is beyond me. Why people don't look at the numbers is beyond me. Why I see officials and reporters constantly talking about the Mexican army fighting drugs, when in fact the Mexican army hardly ever gets work is beyond me. You almost have to use drugs to understand the reporting on this war.

DB: I hear you, Charles. Now, again, reading from you book, "four years ago the Chihuahua State police were doing contract murders. They supplied their own guns and bullets with a full knowledge of the US Department of Homeland Security".

CHARLES BOWDEN: That's right. There was a House of Death, as they call them, a place where you're kidnapped. You're taken there. You're tortured. You're murdered and you're buried in the backyard. The state police are the official executioners being hired by the people in the drug industry but in this instance, the guy running the death house was an ICE informer for Homeland Security. On the first killing, he left his cell phone on so it was broadcast, so ICE was fully aware. That happened, in August, the death house ran until January; twelve, fourteen people were killed eventually. Twelve were buried and two they didn't have time to put in the ground. ICE never intervened, never did anything. They didn't care because it was dead Mexicans as far as they were concerned. They screwed up a little when one or two Americans went into holes in the ground. Well, this is typical at the border.

Usually it's never revealed. The reason it's documented and public is these people running this death house in Juarez went to the wrong address to kill a family because they thought it was a stash house and they hit the house of a DEA agent that was living in Juarez, of course. Then the proverbial stuff hit the fan and that's why we have documentation.

DB: You referenced the fact that it was a city of poverty and again, reading from your book here, "There are no jobs. The young faces, blank futures, the poor are crushed by sinking fortunes. The state has always violated human rights and now in the general mayhem, this fact becomes more and more obvious".

CHARLES BOWDEN: Let me give you an example. El Paso, Texas and Juarez, face each other, you know, they're twin cities. This year, there's been about 1300 murders in Juarez. There have been two in El Paso. Both cities are overwhelmingly Mexican American or Mexican. Many of the families are related. In Juarez, you can get a job in an American factory and make about $45 a week. Your cost of living will be about 90% as if they were living in the United States. In El Paso, there's decent wages. The cops aren't corrupt. The water works. The electricity works and I think so far this year, as I said, there's been two homicides. So, you can't explain this simply culturally. It's how you treat human beings. There's 400 factories in Juarez. They pay wages nobody can live on. They're mainly owned by American corporations. The turnover in these factories, in a city of poverty, where people need jobs, is a 100-150% a year because people leave because the work is killing them. They work five and half days a week for $45-50 a week and you never get ahead. This is part of what fuels the violence, as I said, the War on Drugs was a trigger for a city getting to the breaking point and I mean, breaking point.

Twenty-five percent of the houses now in Juarez have been abandoned. Forty percent of the businesses on the commercial strip have closed. Thirty to sixty thousand of the rich in Juarez, essentially all the rich, have moved to El Paso. The city is just breaking down and disintegrating and it's all been denied because we're busy with our War on Drugs. What really stuns me is that I now live in a country where American politicians are willing to talk about gay marriage but they won't talk about legalizing drugs. This is preposterous.

We've created the largest prison population per capita on Earth. We've got a NARC industry that consumes tens of billions and every drug is more available and of higher quality then when Richard Nixon officially started the Drug War forty years ago. I don't know how anybody can support this war. Even if you want to say drugs are terrible. Let's say they're like Big Macs or some damn thing, what we've done is taken what is at most a public health problem and made it a criminal problem, and we have failed. No one looks at these things and could possibly think this war is a success.

We have criminalized human behavior that's private, essentially. One thing that drives me nuts about this, among other things, is when people talk about all the crime created by drug addicts. Well, the only reason that people have ever become criminals because they consume drugs is that the drugs are illegal and they've stole to buy them. The actual stuff would be relatively cheap without the intervention of government. It just seems to me a false argument. Well, I'm waiting for the day where any American politician will finally speak up. As it happens, there's a city councilman in El Paso Texas, Beto O'Rourke. This guy got in trouble for simply saying that we should talk about legalizing marijuana, like we should have a public discussion. The federal government fell on him and the rest of his council members like a ton of bricks. The reason I bring him up is that he's about the only politician I know that's willing to raise the question.

DB: They say a suspect of 62 homicides has been arrested there in Juarez. Let's talk about the big time killers. Who are they? Where do they come from?

CHARLES BOWDEN: The term they use is "Sicario." Normally, they were contract killers in the drug business and they were paid. There's a guy in the book, I interviewed at length, who's killed hundreds of people under contract. Now, because the violence has spread, there are a lot of freelancers. This guy used to get several thousand dollars for a killing. Now you can get murdered in Juarez for fifty bucks, a hundred bucks, a hundred and fifty bucks. One thing I should point out, not to get too much into detail, is that the Mexican government has a way of arresting alleged "Sicarios." saying they killed fifty or a hundred people, parading them—the perp walk—and having them confess. Then if you check the records, two weeks later, they've been released. In other words, it's a charade.

You really have to get down to what the Drug War really is though. The tunnel is more interesting. What the Drug War—what the prohibition on drugs does is corrupt decent people. It's corrupting the agencies on this side. Anyone who deals with them knows that. That particular tunnel went under the Rio Grande but where it popped up in Mexico, where the entry point was, was at the Mexican Customs House. (laughs) Which is kind of poetic. You can't tell me they didn't know it was there. There was a big tunnel right in the middle of the customs house.

The drug industry in Mexico is part of the State. The State's dependent on the money and the drug industry cooperates with the State because it wants to function. What's going on now, the only way to explain what killing in Mexico is, it's a war for drugs. The various entities that the State erodes in Mexico, are fighting for the turf and the money and the industry, including the Mexican army. That's what a lot of the killing is. There's no question, in Juarez, that some, I think a lot of the killing is done by the Mexican army. You just talk to the people and that have been there when guys come with machine guns and kill everyone and leave. They'll tell you it was army. Trust me, there's nothing in it for them to say that. It's dangerous to say that. There have been thousands of complaints against the Mexican army for rape, torture and murder for the last two or three years, since they've been unleashed.

On this side, what you're seeing in the agencies—and this isn't publicized—but you find if you trawl the press, which you apparently do, is a steady corruption of the people in these border agencies, like in border control and customs. That's because of the money. They're basically taking guys and gals from small town sheriff departments and they get a bump up with a federal job and a decent salary, pension and health benefits. Then they realize they're involved in something that's hopeless, it's like an endless tide of people and drugs, and they start taking money. Then, we say they are criminals but we're creating criminals by the laws, in my opinion.

DB: I went down to Ciudad Juarez just briefly for an evening last year, as part of a conference, and I saw on every major street corner, police, multiple numbers of police on each street corner with machine guns strapped across their chests or just holding them out towards the sidewalk. The little parks had a machine gun nests in the middle of it. It's serious there, isn't it?

CHARLES BOWDEN: You have to realize that the heavy presence of police, police roadblocks, and military roadblocks, since March 13th when the three people affiliated with US consulate were killed and executed. They were pursued in broad daylight on a Saturday afternoon for miles down major streets in Juarez and under these police and roadblocks. It didn't have any affect. What I'm saying is, whoever did the killing, for whatever reason, it was sanctioned. Two other people were killed and finally at City Hall of Juarez, right at the foot of the bridge where you cross into the US, in plain view and nobody did anything. What you see in Juarez, I think, is a new kind of city where no one is in control. It's like violence has become general and a fact of life. What bothers me is that we aren't going to put the genie back in the bottle that easily.

We've created with our drug laws and our factories that don't pay wages, a couple of generations of poverty. We've created a city where 50% of the adolescents in Juarez neither have a job or they are not in school because you have to pay to go past the ninth grade there. They're all wandering around and it's become a feral city. We can't have all these murders and all these gangs and then suddenly wave a wand and it all goes away. We've created kind of a monstrous environment and we'll never fix it until we face it and admit it. It's just like with the drug laws in our country. Somebody who is in favor of the drug laws should finally sit down and smell the coffee and realize that things aren't working.

GRETCHEN BURNS-BERGMAN

The Caravan for Peace and Justice, in support of ending the drug war in Latin America made a 7,000 mile journey across the US in July and August of 2013. One of those who participated was Gretchen Burns Bergman. Century of Lies / August 19, 2012.

GRETCHEN BURNS BERGMAN: I'm Gretchen Burns Bergman and I'm

the co-founder and Executive Director of A New PATH and that stands for Parents for Addiction, Treatment and Healing. I'm a lead organizer of our national campaign called Moms United to End the War on Drugs. We're collaborating with partners from across the United States—mothers and family members speaking out against this disastrous War on Drugs that has really become a war waged against our own families. It's time, as mothers, to stand together and speak out.

That's why it's so particularly poignant that we're joining forces with the caravan right now because of the destruction happening to families in Mexico. But it's happening in the United States too. We're losing our children to mass incarceration. We're losing our kids to overdose deaths because they're afraid to call when there is an overdose for fear that they'll get caught up in the system.

We're sharing those issues with people in Mexico. There's so much pain on both sides of the border and I think we're all saying, "Enough is enough." As Javier would say, "Enough words."

It's time for action. It's time to end these punitive, prohibitionist policies that criminalized people who use drugs, criminalize people like my son who have a problem with drugs. My son spent ten years of his life cycling through the prison system because he was arrested for possession of marijuana. It's real easy to go back because by then he's starting to get a full-blown addiction and never having the problem addressed and, even worse, having it addressed in the wrong way so that he learned to survive in the prison system but he wasn't getting to his core issues. He's just one of so many. 1 in 4 families are dealing with this in the United States and certainly you see this destruction in Mexico as well.

DB: Talking about the caravan…there's 80-90 people friends, relatives of those killed, disappeared, kidnapped in Mexico and that's a life lost, if you will, for these parents and friends. But the fact of the matter is here in the US we've had 40 million arrests for drug charges. That doesn't necessarily kill the person. What it does is fracture their future, their life's potential, right?

GRETCHEN BURNS BERGMAN: Tremendously so. Just having a drug arrest on your record can exclude you from so many things like housing, employment and in some states even voting. The list goes on. The roadblocks to actual recovery and re-integration with society are tremendous because of the punitive policies.

We need to develop compassionate, restorative policies in the United States because the problem is getting worse and the drug war has made it worse. It's really insane that it's gone on this long. But mostly because people like you and me have not spoken up enough to say, "This is enough. This is happening to my family. It's my job to protect the future of my family."

DB: How can people get involved with your efforts?

GRETCHEN BURNS BERGMAN: The easiest way is to go to the campaign website, http://www.momsunited.net That will connect you to the PATH website and is easier to remember. Please get involved. Speak out as much as you can even if it's just to your neighbor, even if it's just to bring up a conversation in a quiet room when you know the "elephant" is in the room. Certainly, if you're willing, talk to the press, talk to your legislators. Write OPEDS. Do anything. Any level of commitment that you can give is welcome and necessary.

RYAN GRIMM

Ryan Grimm is author of *This is Your Country on Drugs: The Secret History of Getting High in America*.

DB: I want to do a quick read from your Chapter 7: Dealing with Border Violence: "We were prohibited from discussing the effects of NAFTA as it related to narcotics trafficking," said Phil Jordon who had been one of the DEA leading authorities. "For the godfathers of the drug trade in Colombia and Mexico, this was a deal made in narco heaven," ...and it has been, has it not?

RYAN GRIM: It certainly has been. The early '90's were a perfect time to be at the top ranks of the Mexican drug trade, 'cause we had just smashed the Caribbean trade routes which pushed all the cocaine trafficking over towards Mexico. We had decapitated a lot of the Columbian cartel's, which then increased the strength of the Mexican's in relation to the Columbians, and we'd been going after the American meth industry, which also pushed it down into Mexico.

So in the early '90's, the Mexicans were really on the rise, so when they saw NAFTA coming around, it was a deal made in narco heaven, as the DEA knew at the time and Clinton specifically instructed all of his drug warriors to, 'Take a break from the drug war for the next few months, while I lobby Congress to push NAFTA through.' Because he knew he was only going to get it through with one or two votes and if people were talking about what it's impact was going to be on the drug trade, obviously to increase it, then he might lose just the few votes that he needed to get it through.

It wasn't until the late '90's that people finally started talking out about that, which was several years too late. Not that they would have not done NAFTA, but it may genuinely have imperiled it. Now it just shows how drug policy always takes a backseat in substance. It's great political theatre and it's something that politicians love to trot out, but when it's incontinent to them, they just ignore it.

DB: Also from the chapter, Border Justice, 'In 2007, Phoenix, Arizona's special task force to address the flood of violence coming across the border from cartel related murders, home invasions and kidnappings' and; a quote here from Lieutenant Lori Burgett, "It wasn't uncommon to have a new kidnapping case come into our offices on a daily basis." Folks talk about 'This is going to sneak across the border.' It's been here for years. Right?

RYAN GRIM: Right. Like I said, I originally filed this thing in September 2008 and for people that were paying attention to it, especially people like yourself who are down in Houston, we've seen this Mexican war coming and we saw it spilling across the border. It's only been in recent months that CBS and the mainstream media started to pick up on it. But once they, the mainstream media are reporting on violence in a place as distant in America's mind as Mexico, you know that it must be extremely severe. The blood must be running pretty thick down there.

DB: Over the years, they've used the violence, the death, the disease, the destruction, as justification to do more of the same.

RYAN GRIM: Yes. Actually Students for Sensible Drug Policy is just now starting a campaign to try to target reporters and persuade them to stop using the phrase, 'drug related violence' and use something closer to 'a prohibition related violence.' Making the prohibition case that, when alcohol was banned, it wouldn't have made sense to say that it was, 'alcohol related violence'. Alcohol and drugs are not violent things, they're just static objects that sat around. People use them. It's people who are fighting each other over these substances who are violent.

"LUCY," BLOG DEL NARCO

"Lucy" is not her real name. "Lucy" works for Blog del Narco, a heavily visited website that reveals the horrible savagery of the drug cartels, as well as the corruption and violence from the government itself. The following interview coincided with the release of Blog del Narco's new book *Dying for the Truth: Undercover Inside the Mexican Drug War* by the Fugitive Reporters of Blog del Narc. To protect the innocent, this interview was conducted using an anonymous interpreter to translate the words of the anonymous reporter. Century of Lies / April 14, 2013.

DB: There are reports that the levels of violence is coming down. Is that true?

"LUCY" [via translator]: You are correct. In some areas of Mexico, the levels have gone down, but there are still executions. There are still shootings. Also there are parts in Mexico where it used to be very calm that have higher violence now. It's kind of like an adjustment.

DB: I can understand that in any war the battlefield changes, the casualties move around. How widespread is the corruption? How widespread are these cartels and their members?

"LUCY": You can't really calculate how many members a certain cartel has. There is a big presence in Mexico. Within the years they have mixed with the civilians. It's really affecting the lives of normal people because they extort the people and charge them a certain amount of fees to let them work. The people have learned to identify who is a real civilian and who is part of the cartel.

DB: We have situations in Mexico where some of the cities, the populace of the city are starting to take back control, wanting to arm themselves, wanting to keep these cartels from remaining or taking over their city. Speak to that please.

"LUCY": People who have fear become tired of living in fear and eventually they lose their fear. There is some examples in the city of Naucalpan and the city of Guerrero where these people started to defend themselves. There are other cases also where people have just grabbed whatever they have within reach and defended themselves. This is a reflection of what is happening in society. People get abandoned by their own government and so they feel they have to do something. They have to take matters into their own hands.

DB: I hear stories that they busted Carlos Beltran; they killed other cartel leaders. Does this make any difference?

"LUCY": The War on Drugs has been going on for years. It's been a long time since the government declared the war against the drugs. This has been a problem because the innocent people are stuck in the middle of this. This is the difference that it has made—the innocent people are left in the middle.

DB: We talked about the populace rising up in certain areas. They raid birthday parties. They kill innocents just for the sake of showing that they are violent, to let people know they are real, a means to create fear, that even if it has nothing to do with drugs they want people to be afraid of them, right?

"LUCY": Fear is a very convenient way not only for the cartels but also for the government. It's almost like a game. Everything since Calderon started as President. It started with the authorities killing some cartel members. They would kill them very theatrically so it became a game. The cartels would start killing also very theatrically to create fear.

DB: You're talking about instilling fear into people. The book shows people beheaded. It shows people chopped up into tiny pieces stuffed into garbage bags and left on police station front steps. I want to ask you this. There's a chapter in the book that talks about a busload of people, 70-something people, being pulled over by the cartel, taken out into the desert and then killed. Let's talk about that situation. They wanted these people to either join the cartel or to die. Is that true? How often does that kind of situation play out?

"LUCY": That was a bus in Tamaulipas and there have been a lot of similar situations. There have been a lot of kidnappings especially in that part. There were instances where people would come from Central America to come to the United States so they would cross through Mexico and they would intercept whatever bus they were riding in and they would want them to work for the cartels. That happened a lot. That's because the military had a crisis. They wanted to grow the military so they were trying to get people to join them. In fact they had a lot of people from Central America doing that kind of thing. A lot of times they would have them join the cartels and then they would kill them.

DB: Here in the US the drug gangs (those gangs that sell drugs on American streets) love to recruit kids 15 and even younger to sell these drugs. You have a similar situation in Mexico where kids 15, 14, 13 and even 12 are being used by these cartels. Speak to that please.

"LUCY": That happened a lot in Mexico, too. We even had babies that got killed because of the cartels. For example there is this one little boy named El Ponche who got recruited very, very young to join one of the cartels. This little boy became a serial killer. A lot of people got affected. The government did not help, did not do anything about it. They were all victims and nobody could get saved. Not only kids were recruited but also elderly people from 60 to 70-years-old.

DB: In the book it talks about the violence, the influence of the cartel became so extreme in certain towns that people left. There are now some ghost towns because of the influence of the cartels. Will you speak to that?

"LUCY": There have been a lot of places especially that are very sensitive to the violence especially in Tamaulipas where the government, military, the navy, nobody could get to, so the cartels would come in and use this place as a base, their headquarters. They would take everything from the people. They would take their money, their ranch—everything that they could. The government was not helping them. A lot of these people left. They said, "What are we doing here? The government is never going to come and help us." A lot of people left. A lot of people who couldn't leave would commit suicide—not because they were hungry. They were hungry but they committed suicide because they didn't have any help. They would throw themselves from bridges.

DB: I hear so many stories that members of the government—police, federal, military—are involved, are part of the cartels, part of the problem.

"LUCY": We are in Mexico and Mexico is very corrupt. That answer will tell you everything.

PEPE RIVERA

In July and August of 2012 I traveled with the Caravan for Peace, Justice and Dignity across the United States, two busloads of family members who had lost a loved one to the surge of violence that is sweeping across Mexico. Led by Mexican poet Javier Secilia we traveled for 31 days, visited 29 major cities and traveled more than 7,000 miles to educate Americans to the horrors unfolding each day in Mexico's drug war. Century of Lies / December 23, 2012.

PEPE RIVERA: I'm a photographer right now who right now, as a coordinator for the documentation for the Caravan for Peace, Justice and Dignity, what I do is I document the stories of the War on Drugs in Mexico. Currently I'm also the coordinator for the communications commission for the caravan along with Daniel Robelo from DPA.

DB: The thing that strikes me most is the upbeat nature of all those involved in this Caravan for Peace despite the horrors they might have witnessed or that may have been inflicted on their family. They want to awaken other people don't they?

PEPE RIVERA: Yes, I think the victims when I talk to them they state that just being with other victims and being with members of the movement is something that is uplifting for them, something that gives them energy and gives them power and that's why they seem upbeat. But, also, some of them also say behind their faces there is sadness.

DB: Take us back to the other caravans and how it played out in Mexico.

PEPE RIVERA: Before the caravans there were the marches, the peace marches. Specifically there was a march that was very significant that went from Cuernavaca to Mexico City which is over 80 kilometers. That was a march that was made completely in silence because there wasn't much to say.

After that, when they arrived in Mexico City, Javier announced that we were going to march to Juarez—the heart of darkness, the heart of pain—because that was a place where maybe we could find some answers to understand what was going on. During the route we traveled to several states. It started out with about 12 busses and by the end we didn't really know how many busses were with us. That was the first caravan. We call that the Caravan Norte or Caravan Juarez.

Then we had a second caravan which went down Guatemala. The first one crossed El Paso. The second one crossed Guatemala. We wanted to see the dynamics of the southern part of the country. There we crossed a bridge. Javier asked for forgiveness for immigrants and migrants because of the way they were being treated in Mexico. We know that it isn't just a problem at the U.S./Mexican border but also when migrants are crossing Mexico. They're under threats basically because the migrants routes which are traditional which will never end just like the demand for drugs those are...the people get mixed with violence and the cartels and the drug routes and this makes it much more dangerous for them to travel and it's something that has to be dealt with. That's the responsibility of the Mexican government as well.

DB: We seem to have a prejudice of Mexicans coming north, and within Mexico there is a similar prejudice. Am I right?

PEPE RIVERA: Definitely. People who know about the issue we can say that sometimes we treat Central Americans worse than the Americans do because we act as a buffer and sometimes that is a...we know that they're traveling. We know that they have problems with our police, with our institutions who tend to be corrupt. They tend to extort the migrants. They tend to be aggressive towards them and to prevent their passage in order to make a profit from their hardship.

DB: We in the United States have a mindset, if you will, that doesn't recognize what's going on in Mexico. The 60,000 or more dead, the 10,000 missing—it doesn't seem to enter the conscience as of yet, and that's what this caravan is designed to do, to wake us up, to make us realize the situation, right?

PEPE RIVERA: Yes. We said from the start that there are two main objectives to the caravan. The first one is to end the violence, to end the drug war. The second one is to give visibility to the victims. What we say is...and this is not something that happens only in the US. A lot of the crimes, a lot of the violence is happening outside Mexico City, for example…people from the outside tend to criticize people from Mexico City because they say we don't understand what's going on outside. We feel that's exactly what the purpose of the other caravans were—to give visibility, to let people know what was happening.

I think eventually it's a greater challenge here in the US because people outside Mexico City aren't aware or are so insensitive to what is happening. We feel it's harder for people in the US to understand that. But we also understand that there are victims in the US. …to understand that it is a low intensity conflict. We know there's people especially in vulnerable communities—traditionally African-American communities and the Latin communities that tend to be the victims of the war as well but they're not seen or recognized as such. This is something that has to change. We need unity and solidarity between everybody because we're all hurting from this and what we say or what we are thinking when we arrived here in New York is that the only ones that are benefiting are the one-percents.

We're all being hurt. We're all at risk. We're all in danger. People missing their children and losing their families and disappearances besides all the mutilations and the beheadings and all these things that you hear about on the radio. Some-times…talking to one of the victims, for example, she was saying that what hap-pens is…the sad part is some of the communities who are under siege tend to become desensitized. There was another beheading, and they don't really react to it. Sometimes the consolation for them is, "Well, at least you got a head back or you got a hand back." That's sad. That's terrible.

DB: Well, we're in New York. We're going to Baltimore—another major drug chaos town here in these United States—and in a couple days we're going to Washington, D.C. to hopefully awaken some of these politicians. Closing thoughts?

PEPE RIVERA: I think this has been a learning experience for a lot of people. I think the people are much more aware of what is happening and motivated to do something about it. When we reach Baltimore, we hope to learn about a very specific case of the drug war which is the crack wars. We know that Baltimore has been affected by this and it's, again, the African-American community that's affected there. We're looking for solidarity. We've said from the beginning that if this caravan remains only something about Mexicans that we're not going to get anywhere. It's got to be something that included all races, all people, all com-munities.

By the time we reach Washington we hope we've made enough noise so peo-ple will put the spotlight on us and not forget that this is important. This is an issue that has to be dealt with. Recently it was mentioned that the Democratic and Republican conventions have not talked about the drug war and I think it's fundamental. We thank, for example, Shadow Conventions, who talked about it. They posted a report saying that about 14 billion dollars could be saved every year if the drug war ended. We know that the drug war can't be justified economically, morally, nor socially in any way or form and what we ask for is a dialogue. We've heard the drug issue is always taboo.

On the busses with the victims we've had discussions. We've tried to open up their understanding to how this all came to be. One of the things that we say there is that it's something that there is no logic to it and a lot of them think that when we start talking about something about the history and prohibition and talk about human rights their hope is that this will help them make sense of the violence and why things happen to them.

We have to explain to them that it is not their fault. There is nothing rational about war. Nothing makes sense. The sad thing is that it is a policy that nobody seems to take seriously or think that it's an actual war because it's being fought by police officers—the people who, in our case in Mexico—by the military. We can't have another 70,000 people dead during the next presidency. We need to change this.

JAVIER SICILIA

The leader of the Caravan for Peace both here in the United States and for numerous Caravans in Mexico is their equivalent of a Poet Laureate, Javier Sicilia. The interview was translated by John Lindsey Polland. Century of Lies / August 26, 2012.

DB: We are in Laredo, Texas. Señor, what are your thoughts at the reaction here in America?

JAVIER SICILIA: [via interpreter] This is a group or gathering that is self-referential. We haven't been in US media. There are very few people from the US in the plazas and the places that we are gathering, and that worries us. The people in the US are very generous but they don't know what's happening outside and we want them to see us because we have to work together in order to achieve peace for Mexico which is suffering so much.

DB: What is happening in Mexico?

JAVIER SICILIA: They have to recognize that Mexico is a very corrupt state and those who govern it are very corrupt—98% impunity rate. Drug trafficking has historically been in Mexico, but it's been controlled. Nevertheless, the war that Calderon has declared on drug trafficking has generated this huge problem. We don't have exact statistics but there are approximately 70,000 people who have been killed, about 20,000 people who have been disappeared and about 150,000 people who have been displaced from their homes.

But we have to recognize that the other side of the war, the dark side, is here in the US This is where the drug war was born and the weapons that are feeding the drug traffickers and organized crime are coming from here.

It's a bilateral issue. It's an international issue, and the drug war has to be at the center of discussion and the control of the unlimited, uncontrolled traffic in weapons and a final attack on money laundering and a humane immigration policy because this policy is criminalizing them just like it's criminalized African-Americans.

DB: Week after week we learn of more banks laundering billions, hundreds of billions and yet no one is arrested, no one goes to jail and yet drug users are penalized by tens of years.

JAVIER SICILIA: That's exactly the seriousness of the problem. This is designed to benefit those who are controlling or the capitalists who are benefiting from the violence of the war. It's as if the governments have advocated their functions to serve people but instead have decided to serve capital and the worst of capital, the worst of the money for violence and for war.

DB: Last week we were in Albuquerque. We went to a gun show. What were your perceptions of that show?

JAVIER SICILIA: It was terrible. I don't come from a culture of weapons. I've never owned a weapon or a gun. It seems like an instrument that just humiliates. And it was really disagreeable to see these high-powered weapons, assault weapons that are being sold like candy. To see families bring their children to see these guns as if were like a jewelry shop.

It's not a problem with the 2nd amendment. It seems to me that the gun dealers are spitting on and abusing the 2nd amendment in order to destroy it. The 2nd amendment is very clear. It deals with the right to weapons for defense and not weapons to exterminate. You saw this very clearly recently in Colorado. That young guy would not have been able to kill all those people if he had not been able to buy these weapons of extermination. If he had bought a pistol or a rifle or something to defend himself he would not have been able to kill so many people. That should worry us and lead us to attempt to regulate what is in the 2nd amendment. I think there's something like 75 million guns in the United States. Just imagine what would happen if those guns were turned on you all, or if they were turned on the government. That's what's happening to us because of the illegal smuggling of guns into Mexico.

DB: You mentioned corruption in Mexico and the fact of the matter is there is grand corruption in these United States as well. With the Bush administration into the Obama administration there has been an agreement that the Sinaloa cartel has been given preference, has been allowed to smuggle their drugs easier if they will only be snitches on the other cartels.

JAVIER SICILIA: I imagine that behind the political parties both in the US and in Mexico there are individuals that are colluding with narco-traffickers. I don't know if there is a preference for one or the other but the issue is that if it weren't for collusion between people within the government and the cartels then it would be more controlled.

DB: The drug war is based in fear. Without the fear the population could not be frightened into believing it necessary.

JAVIER SICILIA: Yes, there is propaganda that has been constructed and built generating fear—a fear that leads to violence and ultimately feeds into this war. It's terrible. Fear is the worst of vices.

DB: Your closing thoughts, please.

JAVIER SICILIA: I'm honored to accompanied by Law Enforcement Against Prohibition. To see the accompaniment and support you've given to help make this caravan possible is an example of citizen diplomacy between the United States and Mexico to build peace. A citizen diplomacy that is constructing an agenda that takes us beyond where we are and is really based on love which is how we should be constructing our relations.

FEAR IS WHAT THEY PREACH

"Government exists to protect us from each other. Where government has gone beyond its limits is in deciding to protect us from ourselves." —Ronald Reagan

My earliest memory is from when I was 4 or 5 years old, laying my head down on a hard wooden pew in a small rural church in Southern Illinois. I remember trying to sleep but the words of the pastor have stayed with me to this day. He spoke of God's intention that man should have free will. Sadly today, many preachers have decided that we must forgo our God given free will to follow the dictates of man. Preaching hatred and abomination for drug users, too many preachers have now lost sight of real compassion and of God's will for mankind.

Fear makes the drug war possible. Fear could make this drug war last forever! Fear is relative. It's based on our experience, our training, our upbringing, and just plain old propaganda. During WWII, in Germany, Jews and Gypsies were considered by the Third Reich as "unconditionally exterminable." Propaganda like this swayed the German population to support the Reich and unified the people in their hatred of Jews and other groups. They were led to believe that Jews were to blame for the war and for the German peoples other sufferings and grievances. Let's think about that idea: led to believe. We have also been led to believe that drug users are "unconditionally exterminable." We have been taught that users are damned, literally damned, and if we can't break them from their habits, then death would be the best we can hope for them. And why would we come to believe this? Why are users exterminable?

Fear—derived from endless propaganda, preached from the pulpit, spread by the media, flowing from the supposed bastion of truth, the US government, and the multinational corporations that love the drug war and the billions of dollars that flow their way because of drug prohibition. Would fear overwhelm you if you learned your child had been doing drugs? I'm sure that all of us would prefer that our loved ones, our children, never do heroin or cocaine, and yet, the truth of the matter tells us there are much more serious things to worry about.

Each year in the US, 400,000 people die of lung cancer, emphysema, heart disease and other complications, caused by smoking tobacco. Each year 300,000 die of obesity. Another 100,000 Americans die from alcohol, and that doesn't include car accidents; I'm talking about cirrhosis, kidney failure and so forth. 100,000 die from taking legal prescription medicines that were prescribed incorrectly, labeled incorrectly by the pharmacist, or dispensed incorrectly at hospitals by nurses in too big a hurry.

Each year here in America, we spend between 50 to 70 billion US tax dollars in fighting the drug war. Our ever-optimistic goal is the prevention of at least one death, from the use of illegal drugs. The result? More drugs than ever before, more purity than ever before, and prices that are falling through the floor.

So despite the fact that millions of us use drugs, what's the horrible death toll, where are they stacking all the bodies? For all illegal drugs, cocaine, heroin, LSD, cactus, mushrooms, designer drugs—how many deaths? The government does not keep very good records in this area of the war. Since the Viet Nam war, the government's accountants and any "body count" has been suspect to say the least. But best we can pin them down, the total "drug war overdose deaths" hovers between one thousand and 16,000 per year. That means somewhere between 3 and 40 Americans die from illegal drug use every day, in a nation that just passed 330 million people. Suicides claim about 85 people every day; slipping and falling at home claims more than 30 lives every day.

The stated purpose of this drug war is to save lives, or is it? A few years back, 14 young people died in just one weekend in Houston. Seems the cocaine they thought they were injecting was really high-grade heroin. They never stood a chance. What you may be unaware of is the ones and twos who die every day from using the wrong product, too much product, or from the impurities contained in this black market concoction. With education, treatment, and an open door for reporting overdose situations to the authorities without worry of spending a decade in prison for alerting the cops, we could prevent more than 90% of the overdose deaths, leaving basically those choosing suicide in the tally.

Fear then must not take the place of rational thought; nor must we allow reflex and panic to take the place of deliberation, analysis and progress. The place to start, is by legalizing cannabis. In the known 8,000 year history of cannabis, nobody has ever died from its use. Fact is, it had been in the pharmacopoeia of every nation up until the year 1942. For use as a medicine, a fabric, a fuel or otherwise, the cannabis plant has more than 25,000 uses to benefit mankind.

Why then all the fear, what's the purpose of all the fear? Let's start by looking at the big picture:

Control. Control of the people. When you are afraid, you are more willing to look to big brother for help and in return, you are willing to pay more taxes for a good plan and more of your liberty if you are assured it is for the good of the nation. Well we've gotten our money's worth out of 20 years of Miami Vice reruns and movies like Scarface, Traffic and Training Day. We've been inundated with now highly discredited stories, of PCP users stronger than Godzilla, crack babies with no possible future, and pot smokers who support terrorism.

The government is certainly involved in everything the press will let them get away with, in demonizing drug reformers, discrediting valid scientific studies that disprove government hype and in making up new lies to cover the holes in their previous lies.

Reality is what's really at stake here. It starts with marijuana and it goes right up to the newest part of the drug war, the war of terror. Obama likes to call it the war on terror, but it's a two-sided war, and both sides inflict terror. We have taken the mechanisms of the drug war and turned them loose on the whole world. This planet now belongs to America's warriors. They control the future of every nation, every person on earth. You're either with us or against us. If you are against us, you are evil and will be taken out, sooner or later. We'll entrap terrorists with money and lies, we'll hold snitches in jail forever if need be and we'll refuse to be held accountable to international law in accomplishing our goals.

Since 9/11, the US public has been held in hypnotic limbo by our government's secrecy, requests for hundreds of billions of dollars, unfounded threats of further attack and the further vilification of drug users, as collaborating with our terrorist enemies.

You may ask then, how do they manage to continue with such lies in their bag of tricks. Fact is, these hypocrites work very hard, to defend their lies. With so much valid, scientific data now available, how can they still have the upper hand? Again, the answer is fear. Fear of being labeled, searched, arrested, your whole life destroyed by the mechanisms of a state, much like the inquisition of old. Here in Houston, the cops used to take us in a side room and kick the dog crap out of us when we got arrested. It wasn't to make us snitch; it was to make us think. Well, I've thought about it a long time. I'm sure those supposed law enforcement officers were not true Americans at all, but rather fear mongers, purveyors of political statement, simple goons, for the state.

I am no longer afraid of this drug war, I know the positive results we will reap with regulated distribution to adults and I welcome any opportunity to discuss the possibilities with law enforcement, the ministry, politicians and school principals. Yet, for the most part, there can be no discussion, for the same reason I stated before: fear.

Embracing eternal fear empowers our enemies and becomes a voracious parasite and a blight on our nations soul. We need to use common sense, clear logic and value proportion. We need to embrace reality. Before prohibition, we had better focus, to catch the real criminals amongst us the murderers, rapists and molesters. Before prohibition we were not deceived. These compassionate, conservative Christians display an optimism for their stated goals, that defies all logic but which does serve to fully counterbalance their ineffective and draconian methods. Until such time that pastors, Rabbis and priests realize the utter failure of drug prohibition, we are certain to reap a continual harvest of ignorance, death, and disease while being robbed of our God-given free will.

RABBI JEFFREY KAHN

Reform Rabbi Jeffrey Kahn and his wife, nurse Stephanie Reifkind Kahn, operate
Takoma Wellness Center, a licensed dispensary in Washington, D.C. They became interested in medical cannabis after doctors recommended it for each of
her parents to manage the symptoms of terminal illnesses. Her father died of
multiple sclerosis in 2005 and her mother of cancer in 2009. Cultural Baggage /
July 8, 2012.

DB: In Washington, D.C there are going to be a limited number of growers
and a limited number of dispensaries, correct?

JEFFREY KAHN: Absolutely. That's correct. Initially the legislation allowed
for a maximum of 10 cultivators and 5 dispensaries. There were about 175 applicants all together. In the end they only awarded licenses to 6 cultivators and 4
dispensaries, so that's what we're working towards opening in the next few
months.

DB: Rabbi, you know in the past we've talked about the religious implications, God created it and who should be damning it, I suppose. And the fact of
the matter is there are less people damning it. How do you see this unfolding in
our nation's capital?

JEFFREY KAHN: This is really just a very small step but it's an important
one. Being able to provide medical cannabis to patients with five conditions here
in the nation's capital. It's not going to be a large program. It's not going to make
a giant dent in the black market or illegal sales or make any great changes. But
it is, I think, significant because it will be taking place here in Washington.

DB: Rabbi, I know that in many states, particularly in California and Colorado, there are the labs. They do a scientific analysis. They determine THC and
cannabinoid content. They look for purity. Will you have that available to you
there?

JEFFREY KAHN: We'll definitely have it available and it's required by our
regulations. We're not exactly sure how the Department of Health (which is our
regulating agency) is going to make the testing work. Initially the law requires
that the cultivators and the dispensaries all test but there is nothing in the law to
tell us what to do if our tests disagree with each other or are not compatible. There
are also problems with transporting the cannabis and who can and who can't. I
think once those things are worked out, there'll be an independent lab here that
we'll all be able to use.

We've gone through a two year process here in Washington with dealing with
the rules and regulations and eventually we wrote a 350-page proposal. One of
the important things that we had to do was to work closely with businesses and
residents in the neighborhood.

We did meet some resistance and we overcame it but there is a lot of fear and a lot of paranoia and a great deal of misunderstanding. We know why because it's all been pointed in that direction. People are terribly misinformed. But, it's interesting. Here in Washington the people in a referendum in 1998 voted in medical marijuana by 69% and congress prevented us from implementing that law. It's now 14 years and we're finally getting a chance to implement it.

One of the things we were able to show our neighbors by looking at the results of that election was that they, in fact, voted for it. They voted for it in even larger numbers. It passed with 75% of the vote in our neighborhood. We were giving our neighbors an opportunity to put their money where their mouth is and support a dispensary in the neighborhood. I think we've got a lot of support.

PETER LAARMAN

Peter Laarman is executive director of Progressive Christians Uniting, a network of activist individuals and congregations headquartered in Los Angeles. He served as the senior minister of New York's Judson Memorial Church from 1994 to 2004. Ordained in the United Church of Christ, Peter spent 15 years as a labor movement strategist and communications specialist prior to training for the ministry. The following is excerpted from the Drug Policy Alliance's Panel, "Can You Hear Me Now? Speaking the Language of Reform to Faith Leaders." Century of Lies / November 3, 2013.

PETER LAARMAN: I want to talk a little bit about good religion and bad religion. I use those terms freely, but I think the spirit of condemnation and punishment hangs over this whole discussion of criminalization. In my sense of things, we wouldn't criminalize users. We wouldn't have the capacity to criminalize users were it not for our predisposition to judge others and to reach conclusions about others, and bad religion has obviously played a huge role in building up the capacity for harsh judgment. I think Jesus warned people about this, but the capacity to come to church and say in their prayer, "I thank you father that I am not like those other people."

Our faith communities are bastions of respectability and they are bastions of denial in regard to our own participation in systems of oppression. So, yes, I think language is profoundly important. I think in respect to the resources that good religion brings to this conversation, we have the capacity theologically to raise up that different voice and raise it up powerfully in the pulpit and also in the life of the community.

In the pulpit the message is that we absolutely need to hear that addictions and use of substances are here to stay—not going away—and people use differently but just about everybody uses in some fashion or another. Not everyone who uses becomes an addict. Obviously criminalizing use or criminalizing users solves nothing and wreaks horrendous damage and suffering.

Theologically our God is a god of second chances and in as much as God still speaks to us God is saying, "Your addiction is your addiction to judgment and condemnation." That's the addiction that needs to be treated and it can only be treated in the spirit—I'll speak a moment as a Christian only—in the spirit of the Jesus who said, "Judge not lest you be judged. Why are you fussing over the speck in your neighbor's eye when you have this big beam in your own eye?"

The Jesus who went out in search for the lost sheep and embraced the lost sheep. The Jesus who taught us about the prodigal son. The Jesus who was the great physician not the great corrections officer.

This stuff is so deep and so embedded that you need to create an opportunity for people to meet and talk and expose themselves, reveal their own heart about how they judge, how they struggle with their own stuff and those conversations, of course, should be informed by the presence of formerly incarcerated people. It should be a safe place for formerly incarcerated people to be present and be welcomed and the families of the formerly incarcerated. That keeps it real. It grounds it.

As people in your faith community become aware, it doesn't stop there. It's not good enough to become aware and then say, "I'm done." With knowledge comes responsibility. We are building a movement here. I think it's possible in any church or any house of worship in this country to say honestly to people, "If you want to be part of the freedom movement of this era, this is the freedom movement. This is the struggle that you cannot be absent from." I'd like to say in my own tradition (I'm a Church of Christ minister) we have a bumper sticker that says, "The day of non-judgment is at hand."

May it come quickly. Amen.

WILLIAM MARTIN

William Martin, Ph.D., is the Harry and Hazel Chavanne Senior Fellow in Religion and Public Policy at the Baker Institute and the Chavanne Emeritus Professor of Sociology at Rice University. He also directs the institute's Drug Policy Program. His areas of research and writing focus on two major sets of issues: 1) the political implications of religion, particularly fundamentalist religions and the importance of the separation of religion and government, or "church and state"; and 2) ways to reduce the harms associated with both drug abuse and drug policy. His book "A Prophet with Honor: The Billy Graham Story" is regarded as the authoritative biography of Billy Graham. The following is a speech Bill gave at the 2013 DPA Conference. Century of Lies / November 10, 2013.

WILLIAM MARTIN: Opposition to reform is often rooted in the conviction that drug use is a sin and that not to oppose it is to condone or to encourage sin.

If we can't convince religious people to look at drug use (both benign and problematic) from different angles and to see the great harms caused by the War on Drugs then we are ceding a powerful force to the opposition.

With that in mind when I speak at a church whether it's from the pulpit or sometimes to a class or interdenominational gathering or testifying before the Texas legislature committee or writing an article or an OPED I try to keep that audience in mind knowing that even in a secular setting—particularly in Texas and the south but elsewhere as well—a biblical reference or allusion can strike a responsive chord, as George Bush understood. It can have wonder-working power.

Let me stipulate that I don't do that cynically, but I consciously hope that it works. I'll give you a few examples of different aspects of what we're talking about. I almost always start pointing out that alcohol causes far more problems than any other drug. When I'm in a church setting I notice the wide range of views about alcohol in the Bible from stern warnings of the perils of drink to the story of Jesus at the wedding feast in Cana. We know he wasn't making Blue Nun—that it was good wine. Whatever you think happened to give rise to that story it's clear that the early church saw it in a positive light and it was not something they felt they needed to explain away, "Well, surely it must have been grape juice." Overall the picture of alcohol in the Bible is you might be better off drinking but it's not forbidden and sometimes it's a really good idea. Use your head depending on your status and situation.

I urge people to remember that when you were talking about other drugs and I find that's a good way to lead into harm reduction. I'll give you a few examples. Take the environment. Liberal churches tend to take the environmentalism seriously and many evangelicals belong to a movement called Creation Care. So I talk about the harms caused by crop eradication by aerial spraying and the hundreds of tons of chemicals that clandestine cocaine laboratories dump into the water ways of the Amazon and other Latin American rivers.

Regulating marijuana, cocaine and heroin would eliminate much of that or certainly would reduce those harms. Jesus said, "Blessed are the peace makers." More than 100,000 people have been killed in Mexico in the last 7 years as a consequence of a war between the drug cartels and between the cartels and the Mexican government. This is often called drug violence but they're not killing each other because they wanted to smoke or for cocaine to snort or because they are high on meth. They are fighting over the billions of dollars that they can make by selling drugs whose prices have been driven to outrageous heights by prohibition. To oppose prohibition is to reduce violence and to further the cause of peace making.

I work on needle exchange a good bit. Religious people as well as many others view needle exchange as condoning, even abetting, harmful drug use. After seeing the fiscal and public health benefits of providing clean needles to injecting drug users many of them still say it sends the wrong message. I ask them to think about the message we currently send. "We know a way to dramatically cut your chances of contracting a deadly disease and spreading it to others including your unborn children but because we believe that what you are doing is illegal, immoral and sinful we are not going to do what we know works. As upright, moral, sincerely religious people we prefer that you and others in your social orbit die." Jesus had nothing to say about needles, but we know how he treated social outcasts and sinners, and he had a great deal to say about people who let prim concern with their own righteousness keep them from aiding those who were in peril.

Coming back to Matthew 25, as Brother Glaskow led us. After citing the sad data about incarceration and its effects I note that ought to particularly offend Christians. Jesus said he came to set captives free, and he died in custody, as did Peter, Paul, and John the Baptist. Christianity was founded by people in deep trouble with the law who knew what it was like to be in prison. Jesus said, "I was hungry and you fed me, thirsty and you brought me drink. I was in prison and you came to visit." That's what you should have done, but if you're a friend of Jesus or just think highly of him, suppose you try to imagine you hear his voice saying, "I was in prison and you didn't visit. I was in prison and you didn't care." Or if we do not do all we can to change the laws that imprison people at an unconscionable rate. "I was in prison because you let it happen."

Prof. Martin has been a guest on our shows numerous times. One of Bill's first appearances on DTN dealt with his idea that Texas should lead the US and the world in drug reform. Century of Lies, September 20, 2009

WILLIAM MARTIN: I have just written an article for *Texas Monthly* called Texas High Ways, really about why Texas should be the leader in legalizing marijuana.

DB: And Bill, this is not the first time you have delved into this subject certainly. Over the years you have been one of those responsible for bringing major drug conferences to the James A. Baker Institute, right?

WILLIAM MARTIN: That is correct and we plan to have some more programs this fall, at least, and perhaps beyond that but on November 19th Ethan Nadelmann is coming along with Mark Kleiman and perhaps one or two other people.

DB: Now, Professor, over the years, Texas has been kind of the fore runner. According to your column in *Texas Monthly*, Texas was perhaps the first, certainly El Paso, the first to put forward an anti-marijuana law. Talk about the beginning.

WILLIAM MARTIN: So it appears. In 1914, well, in the early parts of the twentieth century, there were partly because of the pressures of the Mexican revolution, the turmoil in Mexico and also because of the lure of jobs in the US, was a real flood of Mexican immigrants to this country. And they brought with them not only their desire to work but they brought with them their low cost drugs, cannabis, which they call marijuana.

And there was, as there is now, there was resentment of the Mexican immigrants and any opportunity that stirred that, they would seize on that. And there was argument that or feeling that when they came to town on the weekends and other times they were a little too rowdy and my suspicion is that it was probably cerveza rather than cannabis. But in any case, they began to initiate laws against the drug and along with that I think against the people themselves.

But it appears that El Paso was the first, passed the first ordinance prohibiting marijuana in the United States. And if I found that rather ironic or an interesting circle that this past January the city council of El Paso—councilman Beto O'Rourke, who is a native El Pasoan, made a motion, amended a motion, and, the upshot of it was the city council voted unanimously to urge a discussion of US drug policy with everything on the table, including legalization.

There California is considering it, legalizing marijuana. The attorney general of Arizona, Terry Goddard, has said we have got to consider what we can do to cut the profits—sixty to seventy percent of profits was the figure he used and others have used the same figure—of the profits going to the drug cartels, comes from marijuana and we have got to figure out what to do about that. Senator Jim Webb of Virginia is calling for a re-look, a new look at the criminal justice system and he says everything has got to be on the table.

Quite importantly I think that UN Latin American Commission on Drugs and Democracy earlier this year issued a little booklet in which the... and it was lead by the former presidents of Mexico, Colombia and Brazil and a really blue ribbon commission and they urged the United States to not just to tweak our drug policy but to really look at it seriously and see if our prohibition rules, our laws, are not contributing mightily to the problems that not just Mexico but Latin America in general is having.

So it is really bubbling to the surface, the problems that prohibition causes. And I haven't seen them yet but I am told that the current *Fortune* magazine and *New York* magazine and at least one other magazine all have cover stories this month about the possibility of legalizing marijuana. So I started on this a long time ago but it looks like I am not the only one.

DB: No, you are not, sir. And even major newspapers such as the *Washington Post*, the *New York Times*, the *Houston Chronicle*. The *New York Times* certainly has put forward some ideas. The war on marijuana was really instigated or escalated by a gentleman name of Harry J. Anslinger. Can you want to talk about how his involvement escalated this?

WILLIAM MARTIN: Harry Anslinger was the commissioner of the Federal Bureau of Narcotics which was the predecessor of the DEA, the Drug Enforcement Administration from 1930 to 1962. And he ruled that in a way the J. Edgar Hoover ruled the FBI for several decades. And he really belived that, he genuinely hated drugs.

He didn't think marijuana was as serious as the other drugs but he did throw himself into the efforts to demonize it and he called it an assassin of youth. He claimed it would lead to insanity and made a number of other charges against it.

In a hearing in the US house when they were discussing in 1937 whether to illegalize or to prohibit marijuana, Anslinger testified that one marijuana cigarette in some cases might trigger a homicidal mania. He said probably some people could smoke five before it would take that effect, but all the experts agreed that the continued use leads to insanity.

Interestingly, a doctor William Woodward, representing the American Medical Association, opposed the bill on a number of grounds. One of his grounds was its enforcement would be extraordinarily difficult, and he said he didn't think it was a good thing to have statutes on the books that could not be enforced.

The amount of time that was given in the US Congress to discussing this bill about marijuana took about two hours in the hearing before the House Ways and Means Committee, and then the vote on the House floor took less than five minutes. Some, one senator, one representative asked what was this about, and Speaker Sam Rayburn said, "It has something to do with a thing called marijuana, I think it's a narcotic of some kind." Another member asked if the AMA supported it, and a representative rose to say, falsely, "Their doctor came down here, they support this bill one hundred percent," which was not true, and he knew that, there is no question about that.

It passed without a recorded vote. The senate approved it with no debate, and Franklin Roosevelt signed into law a measure that would criminalize the behavior of millions of Americans. And it took—it was given very little attention—it took less than two and a half hours.

DB: Now this has had grievous ramifications over the decades since. Let's talk about the number of people who have been arrested and as I recall I think it was a gentleman named Caldwell up in Colorado who was the first person busted for marijuana. I think it was for two joints and he got I believe five years.

WILLIAM MARTIN:That sounds right. But the law, the laws ranged tremendously. The—in some states for example in… you could go to prison for ninety-nine years in Georgia selling marijuana to a minor could bring the death penalty. But states varied very much on that.

And you probably remember that here in Houston is the 1960s, Lee Otis Johnson was sentenced to thirty years in prison for passing a joint to an undercover narcotics investigator. And he was, I think the thing there was that he was thought to be a radical. He certainly was an active rights worker, agitator or advocate, is a better word for it.

And it reminds me of when Al Capone was put into prison for evading income tax. It wasn't really the marijuana that they were so afraid of but they didn't like Leotus Johnson. So it was used as a weapon against him. But in any case we had very strict laws at that time. They have been lessened considerably but are still, I think they are stricter than they should be.

DB: You have an article in *Texas Monthly* on why Texas should legalize marijuana. Let's talk again about why we should lead the way here.

WILLIAM MARTIN: The states vary greatly in their laws against marijuana still. In Alaska it is legal to possess four ounces of marijuana, which is enough to make close to a hundred joints, and to grow up to twenty five plants. That is completely legal but who knew? Who knew about that? Sarah Palin admitted that she had smoked it, but she says it was legal, so it couldn't have hurt her.

But my point is that I think the legalization of marijuana is going to come. One of the people I quote in the article who didn't want to be named said, every day somebody turns twenty-one and the same day somebody eighty years old dies, and it's just a demographic thing. That is, as a demographic change happens, more and more people are going to want to legalize marijuana. In fact, about fifty percent of the people in the United States now say they believe it should be legal.

But in any case, it is going to happen, so I think we should go ahead and press forward and have it happen as quickly as possible to cut down on the harm that is being done. The harm to the individuals who are arrested and certainly the harm that involves the enormous profits that go to the Mexican drug cartels who are fomenting tremendous violence in Mexico.

If a state like California or Texas or New York were to do this, then I think it is quite likely that certainly would get a great deal of attention, and I believe it would be difficult for the federal government to say well you can't do that.

California is certainly considering it. Texas currently isn't. If California does it, a lot of people will just say well that's just left coast loony-ness, and then gradually they will fall into line and follow California, as we usually do. But if Texas were to do it, it would be so unexpected given our conservatism, but also because of our independent streak and not wanting the government to tell us what to do, it would be appropriate. If Texas were to do it, it would garner attention all over the world, and I think it would lead in bringing about very important necessary changes to our national drug policy.

REV. EDWIN SANDERS

Rev. Edwin C. Sanders, II is the Senior Servant in the Metropolitan Interdenominational Church in Nashville, Tennessee. He serves on the Drug Policy Alliance board and leads an organization called Religious Leaders for a More Just and Compassionate Drug Policy. This. interview was recorded in Denver at the 2013 Drug Policy Alliance conference. Cultural Baggage / November 10, 2013.

DB: You just had a panel here at the Drug Policy Alliance conference. At the heart of this issue is moralistic posturing that entraps this whole situation, yes?

EDWIN SANDERS: I think one of the things that is a gift to us in terms of the primary faith tradition that we find represented here with just the Judeo-Christian tradition is that it's a tradition of the intellect. It's not a tradition that is exclusive to intellectuals, but it is a tradition of intellect, which means that we're called to think, and we're called to wrestle with the issues we frame usually as moral and ethical and that kind of thing.

This issue fits into that framework because, indeed, it is one where people are challenged to get beyond some of the stereotypes that have served to stigmatize the ways in which people are thought about and looked at as relates to the whole question of drugs in our society. What we're bent on doing is normalizing the way in which people look at drugs and appreciate the fact that, indeed, we're very much a society that is filled with drugs in every direction that you look—the mere fact that we have drug stores on every corner, the mere fact that when we go to the doctor it always includes a prescription.

We think that dealing with sickness is a matter of getting the right pill to take and that suggests that if you take the right pill it reestablishes the chemical balances which then allow you to feel better and the like. I would venture to say that people who use drugs that are not the drugs that are commercially sold in the mainstream are looking for the same things. Usually it's people who are trying to feel better, for people who are trying to address pain. It's to heighten pleasure and it's also to decrease pain but I think the issue is to feel good. I think we live in a society where there are so many pressures and so many anxieties that there are all kinds of ways in which people find themselves stressed out and not feeling good so I think that opens the door for the likelihood that you will try to find some chemical whether it be prescription or otherwise that will allow you to have the result you are looking for in terms of alleviating the pain or to elevate pleasure.

DB: I can't ignore the fact that it started out as racially motivated in so many ways and it continues to this day to operate in that fashion. Your thoughts, sir?

EDWIN SANDERS: I don't think you can forthrightly talk about this whole issue especially when you bring into the equation the whole reality of the War on Drugs and not see that the way in which the laws have been advanced are primarily the byproduct of the ways in which racist attitudes tend to be pervasive and tend to be a part of just about everything that goes on in our society.

When my kids were growing up sometimes at the dinner table, we'd talk about issues of the day, what was on the news, what was in the paper. I remember when they were young they said to me at the dinner table, "Daddy, is everything about race?" My response was, "Just about."

I think there's a way in which we need to appreciate that. It's not just drugs. I think it's true in terms of economic opportunity. It's true in terms of educational opportunity. It's true in terms of most of the things that we think of even as being basic necessities of life.

There are ways in which the dynamic of race are into it, and very often it translates into there being tremendous disparity which continues to grow between people on the basis of their ethnicity and their race.

WHAT IS THE BENEFIT?

"I couldn't have gotten so stinking rich without George Bush, George Bush Jr., Ronald Reagan, even El Presidente Obama, none of them have the cojones to stand up to all the big money that wants to keep this stuff illegal. From the bottom of my heart, I want to say, Gracias amigos, I owe my whole empire to you." —Joaquin "El Chapo" Guzman Loera, head of the Sinaloa cartel in Mexico

What is the benefit of drug war? What offsets all this horrible blow back? I challenge the intellect, the rationale for waging this drug war on a daily basis via my radio and TV shows. For more than a decade I have requested interviews with the ongoing series of directors of the Drug Enforcement Administration and the Office of National Drug Control Policy, to absolutely no avail. They have proven themselves unwilling to set a date and time to simply pick up the phone for an interview. I can come to no other conclusion but that they are riding a dead horse, for as long as doing so will pay the bills.

So what have the drug warriors wrought? Who benefits? What positives have we derived from maintaining this policy? What are we likely to derive if we continue this forever? After forty years, fifty years, more than a hundred years of Drug War, it's time to face facts. The Drug War is a pipe dream of men who died long ago. It has become a quasi-religion, a belief system that attracted many adherents within law enforcement and the criminal justice system to speak from ignorance and bigotry in steadfast support of primitive screeds, platitudes, and irrational tradition.

Those who make their bones from this policy—and by God the cemetery is overflowing from their efforts—cannot now back down from their prior pronouncements. They dare not jeopardize their reputations, their legacies, by now embracing the truth that the Drug War is vacuous, hollow, and a horrendous mistake. Until we face this truth, these cheerleaders for Drug War, these Drug War addicts, will continue their eternal chant, their everlasting rain dance in the eye of this Drug War hurricane.

If forced to respond to the words written here, drug war proponents will likely say I am a delusional doper, perhaps in league with the terrorists, cartels, and gangs that I constantly seek to eliminate. The truth remains, however, that there is not one high echelon proponent of drug war willing to discuss this subject on my radio or TV shows or in any open, public venue where I am present. Drug war proponents much prefer the bully pulpit, unsavory snitches, long-term incarcerations, thwarting new science, and always standing forth with a high-powered weapon at the ready.

In 2009 I attended a major drug conference in New Orleans, a gathering of approximately 1,500 people to examine the policy of drug prohibition. Our goal was to determine how to make best use of our fiscal and physical resources to protect our communities and to find ways to curtail our children's easy access to drugs. The luncheon speaker on the first day of the conference was Dr. Antonio Maria Costa, the director of the UN Office on Drugs and Crime. I asked him why we allow the Afghan traffickers to make billions of dollars each year turning opium flowers into weapons with which they continue their war against the US? Dr. Costa stated: "Drug cultivation in Afghanistan this year is out of control, about 200,000 hectares. A significant amount of money is being made in Afghanistan, about $4 billion, three accruing to traffickers in Afghanistan and one to farmers. Obviously we have to solve the problem of the war by dealing with demand, so that the Afghan farmers will then spend their life cultivating licit crops."

Rather than change our failed policy and end the funding of our enemies, Dr. Costa seeks to redirect the lives of millions of farmers and a hundred million drug users. I stated that after decades of failure of the UN and US polices, that the black market in drugs had become the world's largest multi-level-marketing organization. I asked Dr. Costa if his efforts were not akin to "shoveling sand." He replied: "Humanity has spent centuries, millennia, fighting crime, fighting homicides, fighting slavery. We still have crime, and homicides and slavery and rape. Should we legalize this?" None of these "Drug Czars" are obliged to address the fact that these non-violent crimes of drug usage were created from thin air by their predecessors a hundred years ago.

I reminded Dr. Costa that the US has spent approximately one trillion dollars trying to repeal the law of supply and demand, and that despite the UN and US efforts, the violent gangs that plague our neighborhoods continue to derive most of their funds by selling contaminated drugs to our children. He responded: "The strongest argument of the UN is to deal with demand prevention. To treat drug addiction as an illness and therefore offer to drug addicts the same assistance which is offered to those that suffer from diabetes or cancer or heart attack." Would that Dr. Costa had the courage of his "strongest argument," to mandate such a policy change in the United States.

The US runs the drug war in much the same way the drug cartels run theirs. Its "plata or plomo," silver or lead—take the money or be punished. Each year the US gives $500 million dollars to Mexico in exchange for their pledge to continue joining forces in our jihad on certain plants. We give Colombia a hundred million, Bolivia ten. Hundreds of millions disbursed like candy to nations round the world. If our "allies" in this first eternal war fail to show insufficient enthusiasm for the effort, we punish them; we refuse to trade with them; we have them removed from the UN list of favored nations until they repent their ways.

Is it possible to ignore the 100,000 dead and the tens of thousands of disappeared Mexican citizens? How about the more than 45 million US citizens, whose futures are forever constrained, saddled with a criminal record for doing no more than their current President did in his youth, enjoying a few moments with forbidden flowers and other plant products?

Forty-plus years of drug war? A century at heart. Hundreds of billions of dollars laundered, and no one is arrested. We are coerced into continuing this policy by corrupt politicians, judges, and cops. Prejudice abounds. The number of ways the drug war infects society is growing still.

Fear gives the drug war life. Without the murder, madness, and mayhem of this modern day witch hunt, we could, once again, judge adults by their actions, not the contents of their pockets. We will always have those who have problems with drugs, just as we do with alcohol. But we need not destroy the futures of our citizens with problems or deny them their place as full citizens if they do no harm to others. We have plenty of laws to judge people's actions; should not that be sufficient, as it was before this prohibition?

After investing more than 30,000 hours into this subject and interviewing a thousand experts, I know without any doubt whatsoever that there is absolutely no basis for this drug war to exist. There is no truth involved, no justice to be found, no scientific fact sufficient to justify this jihad, no medical data existent to excuse this inquisition. That to me is what this drug war is—an inquisition, a means to frighten the people with propaganda, moral posturing, and justifiable fear of the inquisitors.

The US Supreme Court claims a drug war exception to the US Constitution. Science has been corrupted for the last hundred years in the name of drug war. Medical practitioners have been corrupted as well and are now suffering for their cowardice as more pain doctors are locked up and their careers destroyed. Law enforcement has been corrupted, our legal system become a hell hole. Customs and border agents are bribed on a daily basis; prisons are filled to overflowing. The US is now the world's leading jailer. Children are enticed to join violent gangs or to use the tainted products circulated by the black market in drugs. Rebels and paramilitary in Colombia and Mexico are making billions and are escalating their wars, killing tens of thousands each year. Al Qaeda and the Taliban make billions from the opium trade in order to buy more weapons with which to kill our fine soldiers who are now assigned the duty of protecting these same Afghan opium fields.

Increased deaths, disease, crime, and addiction are necessary components of this drug war, so that the "moral" leaders in government, science, medicine, the media, and the legal system can point to the symptoms of drug prohibition and distort it through the lens of propaganda as a reason to call for more drug war.

This is akin to treason. Those who support this drug war, whether by outright complicity, superstition or ignorance are the best friends the drug lords could ever hope for, the wind beneath the wings of the terrorists, home-boys to the gangs, purveyors of deceit, enablers of crime, reapers of the harvest of non-violent offenders.

Bigoted and unconstitutional, drug prohibition is a betrayal of morality, science, medicine and common sense. Those who stand for drug war must be brought to justice. Once we remove these charlatans from positions of power, other social changes will become much easier.

This change can only be done by you, by your words, and by your courage. Our shaman, the keepers of public faith and morals are the President, Attorney General, the drug czar, the head of the DEA as well as state and federal politicians. Without the superstition, demonization, and the public's blind acceptance of our venerable "witch doctors'" constant, yet erroneous pronouncements, drug prohibition would easily be seen as an epic and utter failure worthy of condemnation.

What we have been doing in the US and mandating to the rest of the world for the last 100 years is vilifying certain of our brethren, because they use "drugs." Somewhat like the Civil War, which pitted brother against brother, father against son, so too does the drug war pit us against one another over ideologies. All of us would prefer that our loved ones, our children, never do heroin or cocaine, and yet there are more serious things to worry about. Each year in the US about 400,000 people will die of lung cancer, emphysema, heart disease and other complications caused by smoking tobacco. Hundreds of thousands will die of obesity. A hundred thousand will die from the use of alcohol. Another 100,000 will die from taking legal prescription medicines that were prescribed incorrectly, labeled incorrectly by the pharmacist, or dispensed incorrectly at hospitals. No longer can we afford the "luxury" of drug war. We can no longer allow the "morals" and ignorance of drug war loving elected officials to stand as credible, useful or appropriate in any fashion for this nation or any nation on Planet Earth.

A few politicians at the state and federal level have begun talking rationally about our drug war policy, mostly as it applies to the use of medical cannabis. An even smaller contingent of elected officials are addressing our policy towards all "recreational" drugs. This is happening because the futility of drug prohibition grows more obvious with each passing day. Any President or scrum of Senators and Representatives that eventually face down this toothless lion will ultimately be seen as goddamned heroes.

Nearly all the harms ascribed to drugs are the result of drug prohibition. Recognizing this fact/fallacy is only too easy for those who would spend a few hours examining the data, the beginnings, the outright bigotry that crafted and expanded this control mechanism world wide. All too often, newspapers and broadcasters speak of "drug-related" crimes, never stating and perhaps never realizing that if these forbidden drugs were made contaminant-free by Merck or Pfizer and sold to adults at Walgreen's for one cent on the black market dollar, their phrase would be seen more glaringly as the propaganda it is. When ignorance and disdain are allowed to stand as reasonable and informed, reality starts getting pissed off. The days of prohibition are numbered.

These ignorant, immoral, and selfish addicts must be brought to heel, to feel the pain they cause with their addiction. The addicts I speak of are legislators, prosecutors, police chiefs, and every true believer who thinks an eternal war on the people of Earth, over the use of plant products, will bring us peace. The prohibitionist belief that through spending well over a trillion of our tax dollars, while at the same time allowing terrorists, cartels and gangs to reap well over ten trillion in profits, will eventually work out in their favor is another of the invisible planks which support their policy. Their logic and this flow of trillions of dollars away from helping to hurting is vacuous and evil. Most broadcasters, politicians, and law enforcement will continue to feign ignorance and turn a blind eye to the misery that this policy inflicts until such time that we the people force them to face reality.

We are on the cusp of change, here and now. Politicians are frightened to repeat the propaganda that worked for them just a few years ago. The end of prohibition is near, but it lacks a few more adventurous souls, a few more willing to write or call their elected officials. But mostly we need voters to visit their state or federal senators and reps, their mayors and governors, to shake their hands, to hug them, to let them know that we all know the drug war is a failure, and we want them to get on the right side of this issue. Let them know it's okay to stop waging war on justice and logic. Trust that these officials will be glad to see you, thrilled to hear you calling for the end of drug war. They know the day is fast approaching when this madness will end, but they dare not act till you let them know "the coast is clear." Be bold. Share the truth with your elected officials so that someday soon we end this century of lies.

ACKNOWLEDGEMENTS

To the millions of listeners who have been fans of our radio and TV shows over the years, I thank you so much! For 15 years I have depended on the trust of strangers, many of them fearful of sharing with my radio audience what they know to be true. I have leaned heavily each week on reform groups and individual reformers for analysis of situations unfolding around the globe. I thank each of them for their courage and commitment to ending this seemingly eternal war.

I thank my mentors Dr. Al Robison and Jerry Epstein of the Drug Policy Forum of Texas. I deeply appreciate the advice and continuing support of Ray Hill, the patriarch of Pacifica's KPFT radio station who gave me my first segments on the airwaves and who taught me to not be afraid of lying cops or bastard prosecutors. I have great respect for former KPFT program director Otis Maclay, who offered me an hour of broadcast time each week. To KPFT and the more than 100 radio stations around the globe who have shared my radio shows, most of them without even asking permission, I say God bless you. I have deep appreciation for the reporters who voluntarily produced quality segments to share on the DTN, including Glenn Greenway, Loretta Nall, Winston Francis, Doug McVay, Mary Jane Borden, Phil Smith, Terry Nelson, and a host of others so willing to give of their time and talent. To the broadcast engineers who devoted years of their lives in support of DTN, including Steve Nolin, Lance Findley, Philip Guffy, and Laura Slavin—I bow to your commitment to the unvarnished truth.

For standing proudly with me, thus enabling me to better appreciate the dignity of reporting on the drug war, I must thank Superior Court Judge James Gray, along with Professor William Martin of the James A. Baker III Institute at Rice University. Turns out, I'm not a demented hippie after all.

In house, I must thank Pam Graham for her efforts and support over the decade-plus we've been together and for putting up with my 24/7 compulsion to end the madness of drug war.

On January 1, 2014, the same day Colorado pot went legal, I lost my best friend, Clay Jones, who, thanks to his extensive use of cannabis, died decades after the doctors had given up on him. He was the toughest man in Texas and my strongest ally and "co-conspirator" in changing the laws. This book is a result of "our" work, buddy.

I could not have written this book nor produced such quality programming over the years without the support and involvement of dozens of speakers from Law Enforcement Against Prohibition, my "band of brothers... and sisters."

Lastly and importantly, I want to thank William Dolphin, editor of this book, for his help and guidance in turning 40,000 pages of radio transcripts into a public-enlightening, politician-awakening, game-changing and drug-war-ending tour de force.

INDEX OF INTERVIEWS

ADDITIONAL RESOURCES TO HELP END THE DRUG WAR

Toll Free Number, ask for Your US Congressman or Senator: 1-800-985-8762

Law Enforcement Against Prohibition: www.LEAP.cc

Drug Policy Alliance (US): www.DrugPolicy.org

Canadian Drug Policy Coalition: www.DrugPolicy.ca

Drug War Facts: www.DrugWarFacts.org

Baker Institute Drug Policy: www.BakerInstitute.org/drug-policy-program/

Veterans For Medical Cannabis Access: www.VeteransForMedicalMarijuana.org

Marijuana Policy Project: www.MPP.org

National Organization for Reform of Marijuana Laws: www.NORML.org

November Coalition: www.November.org

Patients Out of Time: www.MedicalCannabis.com

Drug Policy Forum of Texas: www.DPFT.org

Students for Sensible Drug Policy: www.SSDP.org

MAPINC Resource/Letter Writing Center: www.MAPINC.org/resource

Americans for Safe Access: www.SafeAccessNow.org

Canadians for Safe Access: www.SafeAccess.ca

Mothers Against Teen Violence: www.MATVINC.org

Cliff Schaffer's Drug Library: www.DrugLibrary.org

Criminal Justice Policy Foundation: www.CJPF.org

Common Sense for Drug Policy: www.CSDP.org

Wo/Mens Alliance For Medical Marijuana: www.WAMM.org

To contact the author of this book, Dean Becker: Dean@EndTheDrugWar.US

We Can Do It Again!

In 1929, the leading prohibitionist in Congress confidently said, "There is as much chance of repealing the Eighteenth Amendment as there is for a hummingbird to fly to the planet Mars with the Washington Monument tied to its tail."

Three years later, alcohol prohibition was repealed.

CPSIA information can be obtained at www.ICGtesting.com
Printed in the USA
LVOW11s1818130614

389977LV00002B/440/P

[8]